LIFECYCLES

LIFECYCLES

*Jewish Women on
Biblical Themes in Contemporary Life*

VOLUME 2

EDITED AND
WITH INTRODUCTIONS BY
*Rabbi Debra Orenstein
& Rabbi Jane Rachel Litman*
OF THE WILSTEIN INSTITUTE

JEWISH LIGHTS PUBLISHING
WOODSTOCK, VERMONT

Lifecycles, V. 2: Jewish Women on Biblical Themes in Contemporary Life

© 1997 by Debra Orenstein and Jane Rachel Litman

Grateful acknowledgment is given for permission to reprint lines from "For Memory", from *The Fact of a Doorframe: Poems Selected and New, 1950–1984* by Adrienne Rich. Copyright © 1984 by Adrienne Rich. Copyright (c) 1975, 1978 by W.W. Norton & Company, Inc. Copyright (c) 1981 by Adrienne Rich. Reprinted by permission of the author and W.W. Norton & Company, Inc.

Library of Congress Cataloging-in-Publication Data

Lifecycles / edited by Debra Orenstein & Jane Rachel Litman.
p.   cm.
Includes bibliographical references and indexes.
Contents: v. 2. Jewish women on biblical themes in contemporary life.
ISBN 1-879045-15-X (v.2) : $24.95
1. Jewish women—Religious life. 2. Women in Judaism. 3. Judaism—Customs and practices. 4. Jewish way of life. 5 Lifecycle, Human—Religious aspects—Judaism. 6. Life change events—Religious aspects—Judaism. 7. Fasts and feasts—Judaism. I. Orenstein, Debra, 1962–   .
BM726.L5   1994 94-14799   296.7'4'082—dc20

First edition

ISBN 1-879045-15-X (Hardcover)

10 9 8 7 6 5 4 3 2 1

Manufactured in the United States of America

Jacket art: "Be Ye Holy"—Torah mantle by Ina Golub
(courtesy of Congregation Beth Am, Los Altos Hills, CA)
Front Jacket Photo: Erik Landsberg
Book and jacket design: Karen Savary
Page Composition: Doug Porter

Published by Jewish Lights Publishing
A Division of LongHill Partners, Inc.
P.O. Box 237
Sunset Farm Offices—Route 4
Woodstock, Vermont 05091
Tel: (802) 457-4000   Fax: (802) 457-4004

To our grandmothers

———◦《◦》◦———

Goldie London Litman z"l
*who provided countless intellectual discussions
and home-baked chocolate chip cookies*

&

Libby Polachek Mowshowitz
who continues to teach, inspire, and love.

כִּי עוֹד אַאֲמִין גַּם בָּאָדָם, גַּם בְּרוּחוֹ, רוּחַ עָז.

Contents

——◦◉◦——

i

4. *Themes of Numbers/*Bemidbar Rabbah:
Creating Community in Times of Transition 207

What is my place in the world?
How can I pass through the wilderness of my own life?
How shall I be part of a community,
and what sort of community do I hold as the ideal?

———◄◍►———

Editors' Notes

———◆———

The Wilstein Institute

Essays in this volume were generated as part of a research project of the Susan and David Wilstein Institute of Jewish Policy Studies. The Wilstein Institute is an international research center established to conduct Jewish policy analysis and to disseminate its findings throughout the community. The aim of the Institute is not merely to gather information and analyze it, but also to stimulate creative thinking and strategies and to become an instrument for change and growth in Jewish life.

Translation, Transliteration, and Abbreviations

Translations in *Lifecycles* are those of the authors unless otherwise indicated. Where translations are more than creative, and actually adapt the original, this is indicated by the word "after," (e.g., after Psalms 150:1). In order to remain accessible to readers of all backgrounds, it is the policy of Jewish Lights to translate a foreign term the first time it appears in any essay. A glossary of frequently used terms is also provided.

The transliteration system is intended to meet the needs of scholars, while serving as a pronunciation guide for those who do not read Hebrew. Details of the system are described in volume one of the *Lifecycles* series. Exceptions are made for words and names that have common English spellings.

Rabbis (capitalized) refers to the Talmudic sages, while rabbis (lower case) refers to religious leaders from subsequent generations. BT indicates the Babylonian Talmud, and JT the Jerusalem Talmud. Gen. is the abbreviation for Genesis; Ex. for Exodus; Lev. for Leviticus; Num. for Numbers; Deut. for Deuteronomy.

Using This Book as a Resource for Study

A particular life theme can be explored by reading essays, biblical passages, and Rabbinic texts that relate to it. Traditional sources are usually cited in the essays themselves, and more can easily be found—e.g., by searching for key "theme" words in biblical and Talmudic encyclopedias and concordances. The index of themes in the back of the book and the Suggested Readings may also be helpful. In addition, individual essays can be read side-by-side with the biblical passages on which they comment. It is especially illuminating to compare the texts at the start of each chapter to the biblical and Rabbinic sources that inspired them. Readers are also invited to write their own *midrashim* (legends in the Rabbinic style), and a guide for doing so is included in the afterword. That same afterword presents a variety of approaches to Torah text. Finally, a study guide with discussion questions to help the reader apply and expand on the authors' insights is available through Jewish Lights Publishing (P.O. Box 237, Woodstock, VT 05091; send a large SASE with request).

Acknowledgments

We wish to thank a number of people who aided us immeasurably in the crafting and completion of this book. Yoav Ben-Horin, associate director of the Wilstein Institute, for his time and thoughtful effort as sounding board and editor; Sara Beck for her dedication as both reader and friend; Sandee Brawarsky for her exceptional editorial skills and her friendship; Barbara Briggs, Maria O'Donnell, and Theresa Jones Vyhnal of Jewish Lights Publishing for many gracious efforts on our behalf; the office staff of Congregation Beth-El, South Orange, for kindhearted assistance and encouragement; Kathy P. Chiron and Lynn Golub-Rofrano for commenting on the manuscript with such care and enthusiasm; John Crites and Rose Levinson for their moral and practical support; the Dorot Foundation, Lucinda B. Ewing, and Diane Troderman for much-appreciated financial backing; Rabbi Emily Feigenson and Dennis Perluss for the generous loan of a computer; Jeni Friedman for reliable and cheerful assistance in preparing the manuscript; Drs. Joel Gereboff, Shoshanna Gershenzon, Edward L. Greenstein, Ora Horn Prouser, Blossom Primer, Maeera Schreiber, and Elieser Slomovic for their insightful comments on the book while in preparation; Laura Giacomini, Aundrea Katz, and Rina Natkin for their help in the Wilstein Institute office; Rabbi Neil Gillman for repeating the extraordinary generosity he showed with Volume 1 by reading and providing feedback on the entire manuscript; Rabbi Daniel Gordis for the gift of Hebrew software; Rabbi David Gordis for his sponsorship and support; David, Michael, and Benjamin Greenberg for assistance with computers; Jennifer Handy and Rachel Perse for special help at the University of Judaism library; Rabbis Robert Jacobs and Joseph Lukinsky for their valued feedback; Sandra Korinchak of Jewish Lights Publishing for the loving spirit and professionalism with which she performs her work; Jay Knopf for his bibliographic suggestions; Stuart Matlins, Jewish Lights' Publisher, for his vision of *Lifecycles* and of the Bible's place in the lives of women and men; Rachel Miller for her enthusiastic and indispensable service as editorial assistant; the Orenstein clan (especially Jehiel, Sylvia, Aviva, Rafy, and Sue) for help not only with *Lifecycles*, but in life—for love that is sustained and sustaining; Dr. Solomon Mowshowitz for reminding us that we are humbled by the task of learning and teaching Torah—and that everyone is called to do it; Catherine Nelson for her friendship and invaluable service to *Lifecycles 1* and *2*; Daniel Rosenberg for review of citations; Dr. Yona Sabar for his kindness and his expertise in Hebrew texts, vocalization, and transliteration; Stewart Schwartz and Sophie and Asher Litschwartz for the endless patience, personal forbearance, and loving support necessary to allow a family member to produce a book.

We wish to acknowledge the important role that the following Jewish women's communities have played in our lives: Bat Kol, B'not Esh, (Conservative) Women's Rabbinical Group, Dyke Shabbes, Isha l'Isha, and Mikveh Ladies.

We are grateful to the Satinover family and especially Terry Satinover Fagen. It was your faith in this project, together with your generosity, that made this book possible.

Finally, each of us wishes publicly to thank the other. We have influenced each other's writing and thinking, worked separately and together on most every page, and enjoyed the collaborative process. We believe that the book is stronger for it.

—J.R.L. AND D.O.
OCTOBER 3, 1996/20 *TISHREI, ḤOL HAMO'ED SUKKOT, 5757*

Stories Intersect: Jewish Women Read the Bible

DEBRA ORENSTEIN

"A new learning is about to be born—rather it has been born. It is a learning in reverse order. A learning that no longer starts from the Torah and leads into life, but the other way round: From life, from a world that knows nothing of the Law, or pretends to know nothing, back to the Torah.... [I]n being Jews we must not give up anything, not renounce anything, but lead everything back to Judaism. From the periphery back to the center; from the outside, in."
— PHILOSOPHER FRANZ ROSENZWEIG, "UPON
OPENING THE *JUDISCHES LEHRHAUS*," 1920

Lifecycle classifications have the unfortunate tendency of leaving out most of life. This is so not only because women are often overlooked or excluded, but also because the overwhelming focus is on milestones and changes of status, rather than the everyday. But how does one access and create

---

Rabbi Debra Orenstein, creator of the *Lifecycles* series, co-editor of this volume, and senior fellow of the Wilstein Institute, regularly writes and speaks on Jewish spirituality and gender studies.

xi

Jewish meaning when *not* experiencing childbirth, Bar Mitzvah, the High Holidays, or another major event? What exists in life's major passages, that doesn't cease to exist between them? Where is the holiness in daily life? How is the story of Jewish living from day to day connected with the rest of our heritage? What is Jewish—and what is gendered—about the way we understand our world? This book addresses those questions, even as it connects the themes of women's lives to the themes of the Torah.

Connections Between Life and Torah

In the epigraph above, Rosenzweig points to a modern, and now postmodern, phenomenon: Jews no longer necessarily discover Judaism through rituals, texts, and traditions. Often, Jews discover Judaism through personal quests and journeys—finding, as a seemingly belated surprise, that Judaism has something to say about their lives and circumstances after all. Life leads them, us, (back) to Torah.

Creating a more meaningful Jewish existence means strengthening the link, deepening the dialogue, between life and Torah. It means healing any rifts between what you consider important and what you address through Jewish ritual, text, and tradition.

While today's trend of returning to Judaism is remarkable, the phenomenon of (re)integrating Torah into life is not at all new. The day-to-day experience of being Jewish and even the very process of divine revelation have always been understood as a "two-way street." Torah informs our lives, and our lives inform our understanding of Torah. Lived experience prompts changes in Jewish law, custom, and symbolism, even as law, custom, and symbolism structure Jewish lives. A Torah-centered life and an enlivened Torah flow into one another. The lines of demarcation may even become blurred, as one strives to embody Torah.[1]

Self and Tradition Rosenzweig's statement confirms two radical ideas endorsed by Jewish tradition, both of which emerged for me with particular clarity from working on *Lifecycles 1* and *2*. The first principle is that each individual life matters profoundly. This may seem facile or obvious rather than radical, since we often pay lip service to the notion. But tradition takes us more seriously than we, for the most part, take ourselves. How many of us *really* believe that our passages deserve honoring (Volume 1), or that the ongoing issues in our lives merit discussion in relation to holy scriptures (Volume 2)? Imagine the respect we would have for ourselves and each other, if we fully absorbed the principle that every person is created in God's image. In the Jewish understanding, your life matters—not only to you and your family, but on a cosmic scale. The Mishnah instructs every person to say: "The world was created for me" (*Sanhedrin* 4:5). Likewise, according to one teaching, each of us must suppose that humanity's sins and *mitzvot* (sacred obligations, commandments) are in fateful balance, with our next act, at every juncture, tipping the scales of judgment for the world (BT *Kiddushin* 40b).

The second idea is equally extreme and perhaps more improbable: Ancient religious texts that never contemplated a women's movement and could never have anticipated the sweeping changes we have seen in history, culture, and technology, somehow remain specifically relevant to Jewish women today. Put differently, there is an unseverable connection between Torah and life. Our heritage contains tools sufficient for honoring, and creating meaning in, each of our unique lives. I had wanted this to be true, and was even committed to making it so. Working with women to create and renew lifecycle rituals, reading and editing women's interpretations of biblical themes, I became convinced that it *is* true. More, I came to see our ancient tradition's availability to contemporary women as a mark of its divine origin and influence.

By bringing individual experience into discourse with the scriptures, this volume affirms both the value of every person and the inexhaustibility of the tradition. It also asserts the link between life and, in all senses of the word, Torah. In this context, the statement "Torah informs life" refers to ethical and spiritual instruction (Torah in its broadest sense) *and* to a specific Scripture (the five books of Moses or Pentateuch).

Life's Cycle, Life's Themes

It was no accident that the first volume of the *Lifecycles* series focused on passages, milestones, and rituals. The moments that mark transitions—be they joyful or mournful—are life's most prominent opportunities for (re)creating community, meaning, and our ancestral history. Passages dot the lifecycle; their attendant liturgies and rituals enact in grand or simple style what it is to be a celebrant, a mourner, an honoree, a Jew, a human, a part of a cultural and belief system larger than ourselves.

If life passages "dot the lifecycle," then, in the image of a childhood game, life themes connect the dots. Where passages are periodic and exceptional, themes are more fluid and continual. Defined sociologically, life themes are "areas of meaning" endowed with "symbolic force" in order to "unify and give substance to [people's] perceptions of who they are and how they see themselves participating in social life."[2] Thus, *Lifecycles 2* is not about crossing life's major thresholds, but about what we regularly bring with us as we go across. That "package" includes such themes as sexuality, spirituality, learning, and identity—"areas of meaning" that are always present, though they may change over time. One is always a sexual being, always a spiritual being, always a learning being, and nearly always a being who is wrestling with these issues. Particular themes come in or out of focus, but they last a lifetime. As Kafka wrote, "The decisive moment in human development is a continuous one."[3]

Telling Our Stories

The primary vehicle for expressing and expounding life themes is story—a focus for this volume. Most of the essays begin with personal stories—with "life," in Rosenzweig's term—and lead into Torah narratives. Some do just the reverse.

Stories are particularly important in both the feminist and Jewish communities. Feminists draw on and honor women's experience, often using storytelling as a tactic to "hear each other into" being.[4] Formats range from consciousness-raising groups to the literature of women "writing their lives."[5] One collection of women's short stories is aptly titled *We Are the Stories We Tell*.[6]

(Re)telling and identifying with stories is in line not only with feminism, but with religious and philosophical trends toward narrative theology—i.e., expression of religious ideas through story. Narrative can be a religious *method*, as well as a mode of expression. Stories are a fundamental way of relating to ourselves, community, and God.[7] In fact, one broad interpretation of religion is "the (conscious) telling of a story with one's life."[8]

Jewish tradition, in particular, thrives on retelling sacred stories: Interpreting ancient texts anew in each generation, reciting the story of Passover again and differently at *this* year's *seder* (ordered readings and meal), cycling through the five books of Moses each week and each year. Jews, too, are defined largely by the stories we tell, and, especially, by the book we brought to the world.

This volume is organized around *the* Jewish communal story— the Torah. It is remarkable that, without being asked to mention or relate to the Bible, the first contributors who were solicited to write on life themes spontaneously used biblical images, characters, laws, and narratives. Their Jewish erudition allowed for this, but certainly did not require it. (Authors in *Lifecycles 1* did not use the Bible, and especially the Torah, as a model so often.) This hardly constitutes "proof" of a profound, organic, and unrehearsed relationship between women's themes and the Torah text. Yet, editorial and teaching experience assure me that the continuing issues and overarching motifs of Jewish women's lives find expression in Torah and its interpretation.

People of *all* stripes have long been guided by biblical laws and values. The Bible is both a source of personal meaning and an expansive mythic context within which to understand experience. Most Jews view freedom, at least to some degree, in terms of Exodus. Those on the verge of leaving the familiar behind might *also* see themselves as slaves escaping Egypt, or as Abraham, Rebecca, or Jacob leaving home. Even struggles *with* Torah are modeled *in* Torah: Shall we argue with God (as Abraham did concerning Sodom and Gomorrah?—Gen. 18:22f); shall we appeal for equality in laws that overlook women (as did the daughters of Tzelofeḥad—Num. 27:1f)?

For Jewish women throughout history, this kind of relationship to Torah was relatively elusive. Though women identified with biblical characters and themes, they were excluded from study houses and from many biblical laws and stories. Today, for Jews generally, the cultural influence of the Bible remains, but a personal interchange with scripture is relatively rare. In a sense, Jewish women are "coming into our own" as interpreters of Torah just at a time when much of the community has forgotten its own lessons on how to read text. This might be considered an ironic coincidence—or a redemptive one. Contributors to this volume build on the (neglected) connections made with Torah in the past, even as they build new bridges between women's lives and patriarchal scriptures.

At a Jewish women's conference held in Los Angeles several years ago, Rabbi Laura Geller made the revolutionary statement that women's lives are forgotten Torah. Our own story is a kind of holy scripture, crying out, as the Rabbis would say, *"Dorsheini!"* (interpret me). But also, the sacred texts we have inherited *are* our own story. They, too, cry out *"Dorsheini,"* urging us to ask how we may find ourselves in them, how we may live them out, and how we may, perhaps on the basis of our own experience, discover or derive new interpretations. That kind of inquiry sanctifies individual lives, even as it endows scripture with new vitality.

This book explores the permeable boundary between autobiography and biblical text. It speaks women's own stories and perspectives, insisting that the tradition respect and incorporate them. It also speaks the tradition, retelling its stories, listening for their abiding and unfolding relevance. Contributors engage the Bible in a highly personal manner—not, for the most part, analyzing it historically or according to strands of authorship, but rather taking it on as a whole, living text and wrestling it for a blessing.

Stories Overlap and Illuminate One Another Our subject is neither Torah nor women's life themes alone, but the intersection of the two. Essays explore the nexus of issues and stories that absorbs both women and Jews, as groups. Life themes covered in this book—memory, home, family, partnership, spirituality, work, food and eating, health, sexuality, community, learning, leadership—play out according to the various prisms through which they are viewed. They appear in certain guises when seen through biblical text and Jewish experience; in other forms from the perspectives of contemporary women; and in particular configurations for women within Judaism who share a complex dual identity. Each contributor also views life themes through the prism of her personal experience. Thus, contributors offer insights, based on women's perspectives, into both biblical and life themes.

Some women's concerns are not addressed explicitly in the Torah, and some aspects of the Torah are not particularly related to contemporary women's issues. But the extensive commonality—and limited areas of divergence—illuminate both the Jewish and female conditions.

The ancient Rabbis never plumbed the connections between women's lives and Torah in quite this way. Yet, they prepared the way for such exploration by developing a method of ongoing dialogue with the biblical text: *Midrash*.

What Exactly Is *Midrash*?

The Rabbis related to, and relied on, Torah in a variety of endeavors and formats: Commentaries, legal argumentation, law codes, responsa. *Midrash* was and remains the quintessential Rabbinic tool for accessing the Torah text from a *personal* perspective. *Midrash* is also the essential tool and metaphor of this book. It could even be said that this book is a *midrash*—an elaborative and explanatory text, a story in response to a story—on Torah.

The word "*midrash*" comes from the Hebrew root *d.r.sh*, meaning to search out or ask—in this case, the meaning of a biblical text. In broadest terms, *midrash* is a genre and methodological approach that combines inquiry, interpretation, and invention. It connects Jews to our most sacred text by asking questions about the Bible, expounding its meaning, and even amplifying it. Over many centuries, *midrash* has been instrumental both in making scripture come alive and in adapting it to current needs and idioms.

Definitions of *midrash* abound; the word, like the art, has many applications.[9] "*Midrash*" can refer to a genre, to texts written in that genre, *and* to collections of such texts. There are also different kinds of *midrashim* (plural of *midrash*). Some relate stories from the lives of ancient Rabbis, but the focus here, and of *midrash* generally, is on texts that respond to the Bible. Of such *midrashim*, some explicate law, others narrative. Some take the form of a line-by-line annotation; others, a continuous story or a sermon. Contributors to this volume use various forms to engage both Torah itself and classic Rabbinic writings.

"Stor[ies] of real importance," it has been said, "...invite one to tell one's own personal and collective stories."[10] Thus, the Bible invites *midrash*. *Midrash*, in turn, engages Torah using everything from puns to parables to (re-)punctuation.[11] Creative and often playful, *midrash* explicates individual phrases and also "takes off" in more fanciful directions. *Midrash* imagines what Abraham did before God called him (Gen. *Rabbah* 38:13); explains why Aaron's sons were consumed by a "strange fire" (Numbers *Rabbah* 2:23–24); extrapolates the proper attitude in prayer based on the way Hannah asked God for a son (BT *Berakhot* 31a–b).

The biblical text is often ambiguous, elliptical, and/or laconic; *midrash* fills in the blanks. Modern biblical critics were not the first to notice gaps and "seams" in the Bible. In the world of *midrash*, however, apparent inconsistencies—be they linguistic, logical, or moral—are understood as *surface* problems, designed to spark some deeper lesson. The methodological assumption might be phrased this way: The Torah never repeats or contradicts itself, and when it does—or seems to—it always comes to teach you something. On this basis, *midrash* creates readings that resolve a variety of textual problems—usually adding new insights in the bargain.

The idea that the text is actually perfect and inerrant might be expected to result in a fundamentalist reading. For the midrashist, however, the effect is to validate new insights, to apply biblical texts in unforeseen ways, even to provide the background or epilogue for well-known stories. Thus, *midrash* derives new interpretations and revelations from our long-established core text.

Midrashic insights and stories are generally linked in some way to the content or wording of scripture; however, the text may be the cause of a *midrash* or just the happy excuse for it. Textual problems can become convenient—even sought-after—"pegs" on which to hang Rabbinic teachings. Agreement among various readings—or even between a *midrash* and the Torah—is not necessarily required. "Torah has seventy faces" (Num. *Rabbah* 13:15–16); it holds a multiplicity of truths (BT *Sanhedrin* 34a).[12]

Scholars have long since noted that the Bible itself includes proto-midrashic material—verses that expound on other biblical passages.[13] This is hardly surprising from the point of view of biblical criticism, which posits the development of biblical texts over time and understands interpretation as part and parcel of transmission. Some traditionalists and philosophers hold that the entire

Bible is a *midrash* on the original, ineffable revelation at Mt. Sinai.[14] From that perspective, too, "nothing is prior to *midrash*."[15]

Midrash, extending the biblical precedent, uses one part of scripture to comment on, clarify, or even supersede another, routinely reading texts out of their original context. Anachronisms are generally permitted, since "there is no chronology in the interpretation of Torah" (after BT *Pesaḥim* 6b).

All reading is marked by the interplay between text and context, but midrashic reading is especially so, since it presupposes that the Bible is relevant to every age. In fact, *midrash* is created by the interaction between a fixed scripture and the evolving considerations of its readers. The Rabbis used *midrash* to connect the Bible—or, from a traditional viewpoint, reveal its already embedded connections—to their immediate concerns. A prime example of this is their use of *midrash* in interpreting the destruction of the Temple—their equivalent, in loss and historical discontinuity, of the Holocaust. The Rabbis questioned the Bible, our ancestors, and even God, in light of their experiences and moral sensibilities.

For cultures no less than individuals, successful adaptation relates past experience to current circumstance.[16] *Midrash* infuses the values and concerns of later generations into the biblical text, even as it infuses biblical values and concerns into later generations.

The Binding of Sarah: A Case in Point A *midrash* on the familiar story of the binding of Isaac demonstrates several of these generalizations and conveys the flavor of *midrash* as a whole.

> At that same hour [when an angel stayed Abraham's hand from killing Isaac], Satan went to Sarah and appeared to her with the visage of Isaac. She said to him, "My son, what has your father done to you?" He said to her, "My father...took me up mountains and down valleys, and brought me up to the summit of [Mt. Moriah], and built an altar and...arranged the firewood and set me up on the altar and bound me and took the knife to slay me. And if the Holy One blessed be God had not said to him, 'Do not send your hand against the child,' I would already be slaughtered." Satan did not even finish speaking these words before her soul went out of her. Thus, scripture says [immediately following the story of the

binding of Isaac]: "And Abraham came to lament for Sarah and cry for her" [Gen. 23:2]. From whence did he come? From Mt. Moriah. (*Tanḥuma Vayera* 30 on Gen. 22, 23:2)

This *midrash* is especially elegant because it responds to so many issues at once. On the most superficial level, it addresses the curious, and therefore problematic, locution "and Abraham *came* to lament for Sarah." It also implicitly deals with the ambiguous time-lag between the end of the story of the binding of Isaac and the news of Sarah's death that follows. *Midrash*—which loves to discover hidden relationships among proximate texts—posits a causal connection.

The biblical text itself prompts readers to imagine what Abraham and Isaac are thinking. It is not a far cry from there to wondering what Sarah knew. In addition, the appearance of Satan fits with another traditional *midrash*. Satan is said to have proposed a challenge: Even a person of great faith would not continue to love and obey God when stripped of rewards and incentives. This raises a key moral question: How and why would God command a parent to kill his child? Answer: It all originated with Satan. Second, more subtle answer: The moral objection must stand. After all, *it originated with Satan*—and what Satan spawns must be evil. Regardless of who set this trial in motion, our *midrash* makes it clear that Sarah found it literally insupportable. Thus, another moral question: How could Abraham comply? Isaac's innocence, the father-son bond in this biblical episode, and the contrast with Abraham's earlier plea to God to save the people of Sodom and Gomorrah (18:23–33) all raise doubts about the "greatness" of this father's faith.

The *Tanḥuma's* single tale about Sarah and Satan simultaneously makes use of two important gaps in the biblical story. First, Isaac is never recorded as returning from Mt. Moriah (22:19). Satan can therefore impersonate him. Elsewhere in Rabbinic literature, Isaac's disappearance is resolved by imagining that he actually died.[17] Over the centuries, Jews who suffered persecution wrote *midrashim* comparing their martyrdom to that of Isaac.[18] *Our midrash* portrays *Sarah* as a kind of martyr. It thus fills in the second major gap: Her absence from the story. Abraham's obedience seems paltry in contrast to Sarah's heroic death.

What Does Feminism Have to Do with It?

Over the years, with greater and lesser feminist awareness, *midrash* has enabled us to find or write women's perspectives in the heart of the story. Recently, women have written *midrashim*, self-consciously appropriating an ancient practice that remained popular for centuries.[19] The question "Where was Sarah?", first addressed in classical *midrash*, has been probed in contemporary feminist *midrashim* as well.[20] Thus, Rabbinic methods help women to reconstruct our place in a tradition that is itself continually, sometimes radically, reconstructed.[21]

Biblical laws about women reflect the social structure of their day, prescribing women's status and behavior in terms of their effect on men and regulating women's protection under male authority. Likewise, in the *peshat* (simple, contextual meaning) of biblical *narrative*, women are often presented as little more than vehicles or obstructions in men's stories.[22] *Midrash* lends itself to feminist interpretation, exactly because it raises questions, bridges gaps, infers or introduces new elements, and helps readers find multiple stories—including their own—in the Bible. The Bible was canonized and closed, leaving Deborah the nursemaid unknown (Gen. 35:8); Leah and Rachel's rivalry unexplored (30:14–15); Pharaoh's daughter un-named (Ex. 2:5–10); the cause for Miriam's severe punishment unspoken (Num. 12); the vows of women unheeded (Num. 30)—in short, leaving too many women out of the story, or at its margins. *Midrash*, however, was never closed; by design, "there is no end and no completion to midrashic stories."[23] Thus, *midrash* can continue to answer questions that the Bible leaves unanswered.

Even when feminists are not writing *midrash*, they are using its *methods* to interpret text. "Feminist hermeneutics" are methods of interpretation that use gender as a category of analysis and feature women's roles, experiences, perspectives, (in)visibility, and empowerment. Such methods are practiced by Jews and non-Jews, women and men.[24] Feminist hermeneutics are revolutionary: They introduce a framework in which women are at the center. Yet they are also profoundly traditional: The basic methods of feminist Bible readings are little different from those of *midrash*.[25] Thus, the major distinction between midrashic and feminist hermeneutics is in their *focus*, not their basic approach to text. For Rabbinic and feminist commentators alike, ostensible problems in the text become "a way of resolving crisis and reaffirming continuity with the traditions of the past."[26] At the same time, both groups expand—and, on some level, transform—the inherited tradition. Both include a diversity of styles and methods, but, in the main, *midrash* and feminist criticism share an interpretive stance. This approach can be (somewhat artificially) divided into five elements—the five "e's" below—that serve as a useful construct for thinking about Rabbinic and feminist Bible interpretation.

Eliminating Gaps and Other Inconsistencies The textual anomalies and ambiguities that stimulate midrashic rewritings also provide opportunities for feminist interpretations. These, like *midrash*, focus on open-ended and problematic texts, creating new readings that take account of them.

If there are gaps in the Bible generally, there are major chasms around women. Accounting for who and what is missing is vital to both Rabbinic and feminist scholars. For example, *midrash* abhors a vacuum created by un-named or misplaced characters; women are widely un-named[27] and feminists have a particular interest in exploring their identities.

Explicating and Extracting Textual Meaning As with *midrash*, some feminist interpretations are freewheeling and tangentially related to the text, while others illuminate scriptural subtleties. Both midrashic and feminist commentaries make use of what might be considered marginal, trivial, or obscure material. They also pursue hints, partial messages, and divergent interests in the text, including women's often eclipsed perspectives. Using a variety of literary styles, they uncover layers of (latent) meaning, infer (as yet) unspoken possibilities, and extract textual messages.[28]

Of course, there are no firm boundaries between "simple" contextual meaning (*peshat*) and interpretation or elaboration (*derash*). Feminist readings, in particular, may seem obvious in retrospect, but have gone unnoticed because they depend on the neglected perspectives of biblical women or the consideration of gender as a category. For example, feminist interpretation of the creation stories in Genesis (Gen. 1:27–28; 2:7, 21–23) has made it untenable for informed readers to ignore the narrative's sexual politics.[29]

Expanding on the Text In line with *midrash*, feminist readers explore and (re)construct biblical dialogue and narrative, basing themselves on textual cues and clues, as well as their own interests and imaginations. Entirely new accounts are sometimes generated; as with *midrash*, these usually respond to textual wordings and problems, including perceived moral problems. For example, Alice Shalvi's *midrash* expands on the story of Sinai, addressing key ellipses in the text, including women's absence during revelation and from the ranks of Israelite leaders.[30]

Just as *midrash* can contradict the *peshat*, so feminist readings sometimes supplant the surface message. Feminist interpreters commonly look for, or even invent, counter-readings, -trends and -traditions.[31] Like the Rabbis, they provide varying renditions of biblical passages, as well as sequels and "prequels" to biblical stories and legal scenarios.

Evaluating and Expounding Scripture Using Scripture Itself Feminist scholars of the Bible regard "Scripture" and "Canon" as (literally) man-made constructs. It may therefore be surprising that, like midrashists, they generally rely on the Bible as their ultimate resource and guide for its interpretation. They, too, interrelate biblical passages from different books and sources—this time, specifically to investigate women's roles and experiences.[32] They, too, cite prooftexts (i.e., definitive biblical quotations) in and out of their original context. Most notably, feminists, again in line with the Rabbis, often use the Bible itself to evaluate the Bible. Some feminists judge biblical passages using the prophetic standard of justice.[33] In harmony with liberation theology, others measure a given text against the biblical values of freedom and advocacy for the oppressed.[34] Many Jewish feminists assess biblical and Rabbinic laws in light of the principle that men and women are alike created in God's image (Gen. 1:27).[35] Certain interpreters use women's experience and empowerment as arbiters of scripture.[36] Even this position derives at least in part from biblical ideas of social justice and equality under God.

The difficult question for midrashists, as for feminist interpreters, is: How do we know which text is definitive, and whether it should support, limit, or trump another?[37] By what authority and criteria do we separate biblical "essentials" from "inessentials"?

(How) is it possible for feminists and modern critics generally, to distinguish the Bible's sacred and timeless messages from its temporally-bound (male-authored) verses?[38] The danger is that a reader will subjectively label as divine Word or inspiration "the part I like" and as social context or overlay "the part I don't." Yet, virtually *every* biblical interpreter—ancient or modern—prioritizes certain passages. Any valuation is more credible when it is consciously made and its methodology and motivation are explained.[39]

Evoking Morality, Homiletical Messages, and Current Dilemmas Moral lessons for the current day are at the heart of both feminist and midrashic interpretation. Moreover, if *midrash*, among its many roles, responds to ethical and theological dilemmas, feminist interpretation is generated primarily from one such dilemma: How can an holy, ethical tradition so often violate our contemporary sense of justice? We look to the text for answers and often discover new readings. In Rosenzweig's language, the driving force behind feminist interpretation is a learning that starts from life and goes back to the Torah.

Feminist hermeneutics have been characterized as a "process of interrogation between text and experience" that "proceeds over time."[40] Those same words serve as a wonderful definition of the Rabbinic/midrashic method.

"What is new about feminist hermeneutics is not the category of experience as a context of interpretation."[41] *Midrash* has always reflected the experience of each generation. The innovation of feminist interpretation is the focus on *women's* experience. Now, *eleh toldot raḥel vele'ah*—this is the history of Leah and Rachel as well as Jacob (after Gen. 37:2).

Torah, Life Themes, and a New Set of Questions

Midrash and liturgy are both popular, accessible modes of religious expression. Both started orally, both found expression in the synagogue early on, and *both were meant to develop continuously, with new ideas and formats virtually unrestricted by Jewish law.*[42] It is not surprising, therefore, that Jewish feminists have begun reading themselves into tradition by writing new prayers, rituals, and *midrashim.* Nor is it a coincidence that liturgy and *midrash* are the focus for *Lifecycles 1* and *2*, respectively. The first volume sought to include women equally in the world of ritual; the second seeks to enfranchise women fully in the world of textuality.

The first volume of the *Lifecycles* series came after twenty-five years of engagement by feminist Jews with lifecycle ritual; the second is at the cusp of something relatively new. Jewish women are now beginning to practice and publish deeply personal, textually grounded, feminist interpretation of the Bible.[43] Twenty years after the Christian theologian Letty Russell published *The Liberating Word*, one can still say of the field, and particularly of the Jewish community's relationship to it, that "[a] guide to nonsexist interpretation of the Bible is both long overdue and premature."[44]

Certainly, there are important precedents. Christian feminist Bible scholarship paved the way for Jewish efforts in many respects. *Rosh Ḥodesh* (New Moon Festival) groups have related to the Bible and created *midrash* in light of their own experience.[45] Jewish women have been among the pioneers in reclaiming *midrash* as a living tool, but are hardly alone in pursuing this vision.[46] Within the Jewish interpretive tradition, there is nothing new about looking to Torah for insight and relevance to *any* topic. Notwithstanding this background and groundwork, when it comes to reading women's lives in(to) the Torah and the Torah into women's lives, when it comes to understanding our life themes in midrashic terms, we are still "In the beginning."

Women engaging in *midrash* and Torah study may feel moved to innovate, given that women have been largely excluded from the centuries-long process of redacting and interpreting the Torah. At the same time, most of us have been reared to respect Rabbinic Torah scholarship and to revere the Five Books of Moses as the most authoritative in the Bible. Historical and personal inexperience with "owning" so highly esteemed a tradition may leave women feeling unqualified, even unworthy, to comment. But the interpretive tradition *asks* students of Torah to comment![47] One not-so-hidden purpose of this book is to empower women to speak and respect their own words of Torah. Another goal is to encourage women and men to approach Torah more personally, with the expectation that it can offer parallels and insights into life today. With this approach, we can learn to read experience not only psychologically, sociologically, and anthropologically, but also midrashically, in terms of Torah played out in the interpretation(s) and setting(s) of the contemporary scene. Thus, my hope is that this book will inspire people to read *the* Book. (The afterword introduces several methods for studying and relating to Torah.)

Reading This Book

While there are many other ways of "slicing" life themes, this book is structured to reflect its central thesis: Our lives find guidance and expression in Torah and its expansions. Thus, the division into five sections: Themes of Genesis—roots and beginnings, family and tribe; Themes of Exodus—transformations to freedom, holiness, and Torah; Themes of Leviticus—the sacred body of Israel; Themes of Numbers—creating community in times of transition; and Themes of Deuteronomy—second law, new visions.

The contributions—essays, prayers, poems, visualizations, and, *midrashim*—all reflect encounters with scripture. Each of the five sections begins with a text written in the style of a traditional form of Torah interpretation. (These are taken up by Rabbi Jane Rachel Litman in "Claiming Textuality.") Some contributors read biblical passages closely; many engage Torah themes more broadly. Essays establish *theories* of such themes as body image (Glass), partnership (Akabas and Cardin), work (Bardack), and speech (Alpert). A variety of writings interpret the *history* of everything from community (Ackelsberg) to agitation for freedom (Ostriker) to the Jewish relationship with food (Myers) and sex (Litman). *Textual analysis* dominates contributions on family patterns (Zeitlin), managing change (Prouser), and, fittingly, learning (Fagen). All the pieces are personal, if not autobiographical.

Some life themes are covered in more than one section, since, clearly, several biblical books may address a particular theme. After all, themes in the five books, like themes of life, build, intersect, and comment on one another. For example, Dr. Martha Ackelsberg (Numbers) and Rabbi Dianne O. Esses (Deuteronomy) examine issues of authority from the perspectives, respectively, of community and transmission. Rabbis Amy Eilberg (Exodus) and Sheila Peltz Weinberg (Numbers) deal with prayer in ways fitting for their chosen biblical books. Still, each of the five Books of

Moses, and their corresponding sections in *this* book, has its own distinctive and dominant themes. These are explored in the introductions to each section.

In harmony with traditional *midrash*, contributors represent diverse viewpoints and genres. At the same time, there are shared concerns. Authors seek to imagine future stories—to envision and invent a fully Jewish and feminist life—as much as to recount and recapture forgotten "her-story." They acknowledge the problems, but focus on solutions, or at least on getting us to the next stage. For example, Ruth Fagen (Exodus) and Rabbi Emily Feigenson (Deuteronomy) lay out problems faced by women studying Judaica—problems that will not be solved overnight. Yet each offers constructive models for setting us on the path toward transforming Jewish learning.

Essays use and also transcend gender as a category, thereby developing insights into biblical and life themes that apply to all. Rabbi Susan Schnur brings Jewish women's double minority status to bear on Deuteronomic and contemporary assessments of justice. Barbara Eve Breitman (Numbers) examines Jewish communal values in light of feminist theories of moral development, ultimately joining what have been called "male" and "female" relational styles. Contributors agree that gender analyses and women-only groups can bring out women's voices and contributions. At the same time, transforming society often means transcending gender. "Women's issues" with the Bible are everyone's issues. Exclusion, alienation, bridging the gap between ourselves and Torah, contending with the Bible's morality, are general, human concerns, brought into high relief by women's experience.

In *Composing a Life*, Mary Catherine Bateson points to the organic growth and the role of improvisation in our life journeys, concluding that we will all "need to reinvent [our]selves over and over in response to a changing environment." Once that "is seen as a pattern rather than an aberration, it takes no more than a second look to discover the models for that reinvention on every side...."[48] The Torah—our holy, canonized, fixed text—is itself continually reinvented. And because of that, Torah and its interpretations contain many wonderful models for composing a Jewish life.

Contributors to this book present a variety of models for understanding life themes and "living off scripture." Embodying

Sabbath and weekday (Levinson and LeVee), remembering what is most forgotten (Orenstein), becoming new and improved incarnations of the spies who saw the promised land (Prouser), following the example of the daughters of Tzelofeḥad (Prouser, Shalvi), practicing creative betrayal of the tradition (Esses), regarding ourselves as holy vessels (Ochs), are just some of the models explored in these pages. Many paradigms for and by women have only been glimpsed, or perhaps not yet seen at all. I hope those presented here, along with the overall structure of the book, will invite the reader, in the spirit of *midrash*, to identify and infer still more models of discovery and invention, to capture the holy sparks,[49] on every side. If that is accomplished, then Rosenzweig is right that we need not renounce anything. We can bring Jewish women "from the periphery back to the center; from the outside in."

Claiming Textuality: Jewish Women and the Written Tradition

JANE RACHEL LITMAN

Jews are commonly referred to as the "people of the book." For two thousand years, Jewish culture has been oriented around sacred writing, producing a complex system of literary institutions and textual forms. However, this extensive written tradition is not the creation of the entire Jewish people; it is primarily the product of Jewish men. What is the relationship, then, between Jewish women and text?

Jewish women today often approach Torah, Talmud, and other Jewish writings with trepidation. The voices and concerns of these works are overwhelmingly male, and women wonder how to insert our voices into this centuries-old conversation. This volume engages that task on a multitude of levels. *Lifecycles 2* explores the relationship between the mythic narrative of Torah and the deep substructures of human existence. It examines this connection through the perspective of women.

Rabbi Jane Rachel Litman, co-editor of this volume, is on the faculty of California State University, Northridge, and serves Congregation Kol Simcha of Orange County, California.

Women of the Book: Gender and the Rabbinic Tradition

The challenge to women to find meaning in the Jewish textual tradition is more nuanced than it initially appears, for even if women
did not write the sacred books, they certainly constituted half of
the society that produced and consumed them. Women's lives
were undoubtedly shaped by religious writings, although at a distance. What did women contribute to this tradition, and how were
they affected by it? What does this mean for contemporary
women? To explore these questions fully, it is important to
remember that some texts were read by women as members of the
larger community; much material was written by men about
women; other works were specifically directed to women; and
some Jewish literature was written by women. Each of these categories provides a different perspective on women's roles, status,
thoughts, and real lives.

There is substantial evidence that Jewish women through the
ages engaged with the Pentateuch in several ways: Reading it,
hearing it read, listening to homilies about it, or learning it infor-
mally. The Bible itself is an early witness to women's involvement
in interpreting Torah. During the reign of King Josiah, a mysterious scroll is found in the less-traveled regions of the Temple
(2 Kings 22:14ff). The scroll, which modern scholars identify as the
Book of Deuteronomy, is brought to a woman, Huldah the
prophet,[1] to explain. Subsequently, the prophet Jeremiah directs
women to receive the word of God, and to teach lamentations to
their daughters (Jer. 9:19). Proverbs (1:8) commends its readers not
to forsake the "teaching of your mother." After the return from
exile in Babylonia (sixth century BCE), when Ezra the scribe proclaims the Torah to the Jewish people, women are clearly included
in the congregation (Neh. 8:1–8). The apocryphal story of Susanna,
set in Babylonia, comments that "her parents instructed her in the
Law of Moses" (Susanna 1:3).

Scholars debate the extent to which women participated in the
public religious institutions created by the Sages in the post-biblical period. As that Jewish society became increasingly urban and
Hellenized rather than agricultural and homogeneous, life
resolved itself into separate spheres: Home and forum. Women
were more associated with the private domestic realm, and men

operated in the public arena. Much of ritual, such as holiday celebration, dietary laws, and purity concerns, was shifted from Temple to home, giving Jewish women greater access to ritual observance and a high level of autonomy. However, as Rabbi Emily Feigenson points out in her essay on education, the Rabbis changed the venue of formal Torah study from the home to the school. Although women had been part of the informal, organic, domestically based educational program, they were excluded from the newly created public study houses, where the Jewish textual tradition was formed. Before the modern era, even women's formal education was most often based in the home, primarily in families or cultures that could afford private tutors.[2] However, the public/private religious split was not universal in late antiquity, for women continued to exert leadership in synagogues.[3] Some mystical and monastic Jewish societies also provided religious equality to women.[4]

The male Rabbis generated considerable material about women. Numerous women, named and unnamed, appear in texts such as the Mishnah (early Rabbinic code compiled c. 200 CE), *midrash* (Rabbinic genre of lore often based on biblical texts), and *Gemara* (commentaries on the Mishnah completed by the sixth century CE) that were produced in the study houses. It is extremely difficult to determine if these female characters are literary devices personifying male expectations of women's behavior, or if the representations present information about the lives of real women of the time. Of course, although male cultural expectations of women and the actual social world of women are not identical, neither are they wholly unrelated.

Women as presented in Rabbinic literature are generally involved in domestic concerns such as cooking, weaving, healing, and tending children. However, there are a few women scholars and a number of wealthy matrons who appear to study with the Sages.[5] Individuals such as scholarly Beruriah and folk-wise Abaye's mother can serve as exemplars or points of entry for contemporary (and perhaps contemporaneous) women who look to these texts for meaning.[6]

The issue of women and study is itself engaged in Rabbinic literature through one such female character, the matron who poses a study question to Rabbi Eliezer. Eliezer dismisses his questioner, asserting that women's wisdom is in spinning rather than Torah study. He comments, "Let the teachings of Torah be burned rather than handed over to women." It is unclear whether the story as a whole supports Eliezer or presents his viewpoint in an ironic, unsympathetic light (JT *Sotah* 3:4; BT *Yoma* 66b).

Beyond anecdotes of individual women, Rabbinic considerations of women as a collectivity do not appear to reflect the full reality of ordinary women's lives. The Rabbis are most interested in women when they come into contact with men, that is, in terms of marriage, divorce, sexuality, and transfer of property.[7] Women's lives, including intellectual and spiritual concerns, beyond these rather narrow categories, meet with a resounding silence. Only brief snippets of Rabbinic text give us some clues. For example, women's educational activities can be inferred from a passage stating that a women who is ritually impure due to menstruation or other factors may study Mishnah, *Midrash, Halakhot* (Jewish laws), and *Aggadot* (Jewish lore) (*Tosefta Berakhot* 2:12). The Sages are concerned with the issue of sexual purity and contamination; women's study only becomes relevant to them in that context.

Women were increasingly marginalized and legislatively restricted from Jewish sacred writings. Although initial Rabbinic literature (*Tosefta Megillah* 3:5) affirmed women's fitness to read Torah publicly, the Talmud subsequently revoked that right (BT *Megillah* 23a). Except for small numbers of exceptional women, usually from Rabbinical families with no sons[8], later Jewish culture assigned women the duty of familial and communal activity, and allocated intellectual and legislative enterprises to men. The medieval Rabbinic textual tradition including liturgy, codes, mystical texts, and commentaries was produced by men.

The "Books" of Women: Female Literary Form and Genres

The fact that women were in essence excluded from Rabbinic institutions and texts from the time of the codification of the Talmud to the modern era does not mean that they had no literary tradition at all. Women appear with frequency in legal documents; personal letters are also an important women's literary genre. In addition, poetry and diaries are sources of women's writing in the premodern Jewish world.

Marriage, divorce, and property documents reveal a great deal about real women's lives. The *ketubbah* (marriage contract) of Mibtabiah,[9] an Egyptian Jew, demonstrates that women owned property and had the right of divorce. The legal archives of Babata,[10] uncovered in excavations of the caves of Bar Kokhba (a second-century Jewish revolutionary leader) reveal a woman who owned substantial property and had a complex family life involving several marriages. Various records of lawsuits, wills, and manumission bills paint a picture of women's role rather different from that of the Rabbinic texts. Non-Rabbinic documents portray Jewish women involved in street fights, serving as wet-nurses, appearing as witnesses in court, practicing magic, buying houses, even sponsoring synagogues.[11] It is noteworthy that in these texts many women appear alone or in relation to other women, not merely as derivative beings attached to men or passing through men's lives.

The Cairo *genizah*, a medieval storehouse of sacred and secular Jewish documents covering a period of several hundred years, contains a number of letters by women. These messages are in both Arabic and Hebrew. Other examples of Jewish women's correspondence are extant from civic archives of European cities.[12] Various letters deal with economic concerns such as business deals, women's textile collectives, dowries for prospective brides, and ransom money for captives taken during the Crusader wars. They also cover familial issues such as the welfare of relatives, births, deaths, and the education of children, including daughters.

The relationship between women and Torah is illuminated by a particularly interesting letter, in excellent Hebrew, from a woman named Maliha. She discusses the practice of bibliomancy—consulting the Torah at random for an oracular sign—in regard to a journey she is about to undertake. This indicates that even if women did not study the Torah according to mainstream Rabbinic methods, the text played an important part in their religious belief system.

The mystical and symbolic function of Torah in the lives of women is also shown in the medieval Hebrew crusade chronicles. The chronicles provide extensive discussion of the behavior of women. Viewing the desecration of a Torah scroll by crusaders, "the women cried out in unison, 'the holy Torah, perfect in beauty.... We used to bow before it in the synagogue; we used to kiss it; we used to honor it.'" In response to the dishonor to the Torah, the women inspire the entire community to attack the crusaders.[13]

Other women maintained a tactile relationship to the Torah, as copyists or sewers. A Pentateuch from medieval Yemen contains the following inscription, "Please do not fault me if you find a mistake, as I am a nursing woman, Miriam bat Benayah, the scribe."[14] The eulogy written by Rabbi Eleazar ben Judah of Worms for his wife Dulcia, killed by crusaders, states, "She spun gut for stitching Torah scrolls...she girded her loins with strength and sewed forty Torah scrolls."[15] In Italy, Jewish women made Torah binders with elaborate embroidery in Hebrew.[16] An opinion by the scholar Maimonides and passages from the travel diaries of Petaḥiah of Regensburg indicate that several medieval women actually ran schools and taught Torah.[17]

Poetry, in both Hebrew and the vernacular, was a literary form open to Jewish women. The "Golden Age" of Spanish Jewish life, which witnessed the flowering of Jewish verse, produced a number of women poets including Kasmuna bint Ismaila who dealt with the romantic concerns of single women.[18] The wife of Dunash ibn Labrat (famous tenth-century Spanish grammarian) wrote him in elegant metered Hebrew stanzas.[19] Huldah bat Judah Halevi wrote a poetic acrostic using her own name, a common medieval literary device, that is included among the works of her well-known father.[20]

Women's poetry was not limited to Spain. Sham'ah bat Shalom Shabazi wrote Hebrew couplets in Yemen.[21] In Renaissance Italy, a number of female poets gained prominence: Giustina Levi-Perotti wrote sonnets; Deborah Ascarelli produced rhymed Italian translations of Hebrew liturgy; and Sarah Copia Sullam wrote not only poetry, but also philosophy and theological polemic.[22]

An extremely revealing piece of Jewish women's literature is the diary of Gluckel of Hameln (1646–1724).[23] This intimate journal combines historical observation, including Gluckel's dealings with survivors of the brutal Chmielnicki massacres and her in-laws' obsession with the Messianic leader, Shabbatai Zevi; details about social, communal and economic life in the ghettos of Germany; ethical instruction for her children; spiritual meditation; and numerous folktales and parables. The work is in Yiddish, the language of most European Jews of the time, and contains numerous

Hebrew quotations from Bible, Talmud, and the prayerbook. Gluckel mentions her education in *ḥeder*, evidently an early co-educational public elementary school. Gluckel's memoirs, created in manuscript but popularized in printed form, mark the transition to a more fully developed Jewish women's literature that emerged in Europe with the advent of the printing press.

Books for Women: Gender and Technology

The invention of the printing press and its enthusiastic adoption by Jews created a revolution in literary production. Prior to mass production of books, manuscripts were hand-copied. Scribes devoted their lives to making religious texts for sacred purposes. Works by or for women rarely fell into that category, thus even those that existed were consigned to the exigencies of time and deterioration. If not for archaeological discoveries such as the Bar Kokhba Caves and the Cairo *genizah*, we would have almost no Jewish texts authored by women prior to the printing press. Although much of early Jewish printing was devoted to the Bible and Rabbinic literature, eventually the press created a market economy for the transmission and dissemination of information. Subsequent to its invention, Jews who were not of the Rabbinical elite could assert their literary desires through the pocketbook. Printing was profitable because it created many copies of a single work. Thus, even if some volumes were destroyed, it was likely that others might survive.

In sixteenth-century Northern Italy, an early center of Jewish printing, numerous Yiddish and Judeo-Italian editions of the Bible and prayerbooks were published. Since Hebrew was the language of the educated male elite, it may be assumed that these books were intended to reach a largely female audience.[24] Many of the early printers were women. One historian of Hebrew printing cites approximately sixty women who worked at typesetting or owned early Jewish print shops.[25] These printers occasionally presented information about themselves and their families in the books they produced. Several dedications and printer's notes refer to the spiritual fulfillment such women found in their profession.[26]

As the printing industry became more sophisticated, books were directed to specific audiences, including women. "How to" guides for women, such as Benjamin ben Aaron's *Frauen Buechlein* (1577) appeared. A quasi-secular literature emerged, largely in Yiddish and designed for a female readership, of bible renderings, religious folklore, contemporary prayers, and ethical manuals. The preeminent work of this sort was the *Tze'enah U're'enah* ("Go Out and See," oldest extant is the fourth edition, Basel, 1622), a rendering of the Torah, Prophetic writings, and festival scrolls intermingled with midrashic stories and romantic folklore. It became known as the "women's Torah," and achieved virtually universal acceptance among Ashkenazi women.

Although most of the authors of this new genre of Yiddish literature were men, some were women. Rebecca Tiktiner's *Maneket Rivkah* ("Rebecca's Nurse," Prague, 1609) was an extremely popular compilation of its author's poems, responses to women's questions on Jewish law, moral advice, and interpretations of Bible and *midrash*. Sarah Bas-Tovim (late seventeenth century) was a highly regarded and well-known composer of *tkhines*, women's personal devotional texts.

People of the Book: Mixed-Gendered Jewish Literature

Initially, bilingual Jewish publishing in Europe reflected its bi-gendered audience. In theory, at least, the sacred Hebrew books were for men; the popular Yiddish works for women. In practice, men also read the emergent Yiddish literature—and not only unlearned men but also those who were literate in Hebrew.[27] The Hasidic movement produced a number of religious narrative texts in Yiddish that further blurred the distinction between men's written tradition and women's literature.

During the nineteenth century, a fully secular, mixed-gendered Jewish writing was popularized. In Western Europe and the United States, it was written in the vernacular and promoted social acculturation. In Eastern Europe, it was in Yiddish and featured non-religious stories, novels, and political tracts. The Ashkenazi Jewish community also produced a large number of journals, monthlies, and newspapers in the languages of the countries where Jews resided, as well as in Yiddish and Hebrew. Though not the dominant voice, hundreds of women writers and poets were part of the Yiddish and secular literary movements.[28]

With the maturation of Yiddish literature and the social emancipation of Jews in the United States and Western Europe, Jewish women and men shared a large territory of the word. Indeed, the shift toward secularism that marked twentieth-century Jewish life ensured that this shared literary domain claimed a population and influence far greater than the male landscape of Rabbinic writing. Poetry, fiction, social and political theory, history, even theology, resided squarely in the mixed-gendered territory of inscription increasingly available to women and reflective of women's concerns. Much of the poetry and prose in this volume grows out of this fairly recent secular realm of Jewish writing. Some, however—such as Francine Klagsbrun's letter to her daughter; Zilla Jane Goodman's rendering of the Garden of Eden story; and the prayer texts of Rabbi Sheila Weinberg, Arlene Agus, and Esther Cameron—deliberately draw on the pre-modern women's literature of personal letters, the *Tze'enah U're'enah*, and *tkhines*.

A Book for Women and Men: Back to the Future

The essays that begin each chapter, and to some extent, the book as a whole, set a different, yet related, literary agenda. These pieces intentionally engage with Rabbinic text, the male word. In them, the female authors consciously retroject themselves into the androcentric Jewish written heritage.

That rich body of material consists of a wide variety of content and forms. Using the Torah as a foundation, generations of male scholars built an extensive and multifaceted literary edifice. The Mishnah gathered laws based on the Bible, along with aphorisms and brief stories; the *Gemara* elaborated on these, bringing together edited "transcripts" of several hundred years of commentary. Other textual forms include collections of *midrash*, including the *Haggadah* (text of the Passover *seder*); the *siddur* (prayerbook); codes, distillations of Jewish law in brief apodictic form; responsa, Rabbinic answers to Jewish legal questions; mystical testimonies and meditations; and expository philosophy and polemic. Many of these works are highly stylized, in that a piece of text will appear in the middle of a manuscript page, and different commentaries will surround it. Sometimes, the primary text will alternate with commentary text.

Lifecycles 2 reads itself into that tradition as a series of inter-reflections between the themes of Torah and contemporary Jewish women's lives. However, five essays in this volume consciously seek to enter the realm of masculine inscription and bring women's voice to it. This is a daring task in that women are often delegitimated as participants in that tradition—discounted in terms of knowledge, scholarship, Jewish legal status, and training. Women are not part of the lifelong *yeshivah* (traditional academy of Jewish learning) study environment.

However, contemporary women writers, scholars, and rabbis are unwilling to be locked out and consigned to insignificance. The five pieces that introduce the Torah interpretation in each chapter of *Lifecycles* 2 assert co-ownership by women of the Rabbinic textual heritage. In the Genesis chapter, Zilla Jane Goodman blends women's genre with Rabbinic forms. She renders a biblical story in the style of *Tze'enah U're'enah*, and a commentary after the method of Rashi (Rabbi Solomon ben Isaac of Troyes, 1040–1105), the foremost Jewish biblical interpreter, and his disciples. Drorah O'Donnell Setel creates a fragment of a radically new *Haggadah*, recounting Miriam's role in the Exodus. Shirley Idelson, in the opening piece for Leviticus, produces several pages of a complex feminist Talmud, complete with commentary. For Numbers, Vicki Hollander writes her own midrashic interpretation, incorporating both the text from Torah and traditional Rabbinic *midrash*. Finally, Alice Shalvi presents two *girsa'ot* (variant readings) of the revelation at Sinai, the foundational story of all this literary product. The authors use traditional Rabbinic methods to explicate new and radical contemporary women's ideas. In doing so, they claim the right to study, to critique, to create, and to restructure.

People of the Books: A Fully Inclusive Written Tradition

Although *Lifecycles* 2 is written by women, its intended audience consists of both genders. Just as women must enter the previously male territory of Rabbinic literature, Jewish men must read and engage the work of women. It might seem ironic that a book espousing egalitarian values, restricts the voices it presents to those of women. Such volumes can be only an interim step—a form of literary "affirmative action" designed to bring previously unregarded insights into communal discourse.

Ultimately, Jewish creativity rests on the integration of formerly disparate elements. Jewish secular literature increasingly deals with spiritual themes. Religious writings grapple with social and cultural issues. Mysticism and rationalism are experiencing a rapprochement. The modern era has proved that jettisoning large segments of the rich and varied Jewish heritage is pointless and self-destructive. This is true in terms of gender as well. The days of separate gender spheres have passed. It is time to integrate fully the voices and concerns of women into the Jewish communal conversation, in every venue, including text. Then Jews will truly be the *people* of the book.

1

Themes of Genesis/Bereshit Rabbah:
Roots and Beginnings,
Family and Tribe

＝━●━＝

Who am I? How did I get here? What is my story?
Where is my home? Who are my people?

I grew up listening to my grandmother's stories: How as a girl
she came to America on a steamship (second class) and, for the
first time in her life, ate all the food she wanted; how she was
the first girl from Hope, North Dakota, ever to attend university; how she was thrown out of her sorority for being a commu-
nist; how she and my physician grandfather made bootleg liquor
out of medicinal alcohol; how she worked for the federal government during the Depression and sent her four sons to integrated
schools; how she loved playing cards and baking cookies, and

most of all, how she cared for her family. When I think of Jewish women, I picture my grandmother telling these stories, or her friends chatting on the porches of apartment buildings, or my mother leaning over the backyard fence to speak to her neighbor.

Jewish women are talkers. Across generations, as friends, at organizational meetings and support groups, we exchange opinions and share stories.[1] It is as if, like God, we call the world into being with the word. Traditionally, women have lived much of our lives at home, out of the public eye. Those of us who spend substantial time in public often must keep our authentic selves private in order to be accepted in a "man's" world.[2] It is in telling our stories that we emerge from isolation to become fully present. For women, this everyday activity can take on a revolutionary quality. In the words of poet Muriel Rukeyser, "What would happen if one woman told the truth about her life? The world would split open."[3]

Storytellers capture a level of honesty that often eludes those giving speeches or analytical lectures. Narrative holds the power to sift experience, to shape its meaning. In its early days, the women's movement adopted the slogan, "The personal is political"; through reviewing her life experience, a woman could gain insight into the larger social forces of our culture.

This ability is neither new nor necessarily limited to the present. Our foremothers almost certainly told stories over campfires in the Judean deserts. Many of their legends, and the social meanings of those tales, are recorded in Genesis. Unlike the other books of the Torah, Genesis contains very little legal material; it is not concerned with rules of social behavior. Rather, the book is a literary anthology, reflective of a long oral tradition that imparts its message through the medium of storytelling. Its focus is often individual and personal, and it explores morality through the complex dynamics of human relationship and interaction with the divine.

The Sacred Story: Narrative Theology

This method of conveying religious truth is known as narrative theology. Each separate tale of Genesis proclaims a sacred message. For example: The epic of the great destructive Flood culminating in the rebirth of life symbolized by the rainbow, underscores the human propensity for evil, the divine power of retribution, and—eventually—the promise of future salvation. The various Genesis tales include a number of literary styles: Narration, poetry, flashbacks, conversations, proclamations, word repetitions, oracles, anticipatory visions. These transform a linear exposition into a richly textured cyclical flow.

In addition, groups of stories are woven together to develop larger themes, such as parental favoritism or leaving home. Leora R. Zeitlin's essay in this chapter explores the relationship between the tale of fratricide in the opening chapters of Genesis and the reconciliation among brothers in the closing chapters.

Narrative theology presumes an involved audience. It expects to elicit emotional as well as intellectual responses. There is a dynamic interplay between the reader and the text. The sacred story is subtly refracted through the cultural and personal lenses of its viewers' life experience. This form of theology invites the reader to enter into a dialogue with the narrative, to interweave ancient text with contemporary context.

Lifecycles 2 is itself a narrative theology, reflecting and refracting the most ancient and fundamental text of our people, the Torah, with contemporary women's lives and thoughts. Many of the essays in this book cast modern Jewish women in the role of the Hebrew tribes in the wilderness, a generation in transition, fleeing slavery and seeking redemption. Genesis is the important substructure on which this story rests. Its concerns of sacred memory, family, and home set the stage for the further development in the spiritual narrative.

The Table of Contents

Genesis is the "introduction" to an even larger sacred narrative, the grand epic of Torah. As such, it is concerned with beginnings; its opening lines relate the creation of the universe. Genesis describes the birth of humankind and recounts the origin of the Jewish people. It presents the "history" of Israel prior to its becoming a nation. Tales of origin repeat and recur throughout the narrative. The world is created, and then destroyed by the Flood. The human race builds a mighty tower to the heavens and is then dispersed. God chooses the family of Noah, then chooses the family of Sarah and Abraham. Genesis is about starting, but also about starting over, about Creation and Redemption.

The legends that comprise Genesis may be organized according to several different models. They are easily divided into two distinct sections: The universal past of all humanity, including Creation, Eden, Cain and Abel, the Flood, the Tower of Babel, and extensive genealogies; and the dramatic highlights of Judaism's "first family": Sarah, Abraham, and their progeny, including the stories of Hagar and Ishmael; Isaac and Rebecca; Jacob, Esau, Rachel and Leah; Dinah; Judah and Tamar; and Joseph and his brothers.

The first eleven chapters of Genesis take place in Mesopotamia. The final eleven chapters transpire mostly in Egypt. The intermediate chapters recount the nomadic wanderings and sacred understandings of the earliest generations of the people Israel. Similarly, the essays in this chapter move from more universal thoughts on sacred history, to a particularistic focus on clan, territory, and God's presence in our lives.

God, the Protagonist

Interpreters of Genesis must deal with a number of theological considerations. God is the central character in all the stories of the Genesis anthology. "He" is presented in strongly anthropomorphic language, e.g. "walking through the garden" (Gen. 3:8). God is on close personal terms with many of the human protagonists, particularly Abraham. Some of the women of Genesis, such as Sarah, Hagar, and Rebecca (Gen. 18:15; 21:17; 25:23) experience direct communication with God.

Genesis calls God by many names including *YHVH* (commonly pronounced *Adonai*), *Elohim* (God), *El Elyon* (God on high), *El Shaddai* (God of mountains), *El Beth El* (God of Beth El), *El Roi* (God of Roi), and on occasion names that specifically speak of relationships to people, such as *Elohei Shem* (the God of Shem) or *Paḥad Yitzḥak* (Fear of Isaac), and at times combinations of the above.[4] These appellations are all male. Rabbinic tradition interprets the variant names as attributes or qualities of God. It is likely that at some time in Israel's history various mythic traditions about different names of God were woven together. The various "gods" represented by these different names were demythologized and merged into a single tribal God, the God of Abraham, Isaac, and Jacob.[5] The tribes also had various "goddess" names and traditions. However, gender proved an insurmountable barrier to monotheistic[6] merger. The early Hebrews could not contemplate female language for their almighty deity. They did not demythologize the earlier goddess traditions and blend those into a gender neutral God.

Consequently, God as represented in Genesis is unmistakably male in gender. "He" is an image consistent with patriarchal culture, in which ultimate power and authority rest with the male populace. However, male God-language should not be taken as an inalterable fact of Jewish existence. Later biblical authors (e.g. Psalms 131), the Sages, and Kabbalistic mystics all use female imagery in relation to the divine. Contemporary Jews need not feel overly constrained by the cultural limitations of ancient Hebrew society.

The Character of Woman

The story of Eve is often a difficult one for contemporary women. It is of interest that Genesis' initial account of human creation is bi-gendered: "God created the human; male and female, God created them" (Gen. 1:27). It is only in the second Eden narrative that Woman is birthed from the body of Man (Gen. 2:22).[7] This is a mythic reversal of the normal order of nature—in which everyone is born from the body of a woman—similar to Greek tales that describe Athena as "born" from the head of Zeus. Our culture is also powerfully influenced by Christological interpretations of this story that emphasize doctrines of "original sin"[8] and heavenly retribution. Although Jewish readings of Genesis cannot overlook the male-oriented features of the creation epic, they nonetheless do not blame women as a collectivity for the entrance of sin into the world. The Sages instead view Eve as the negative paradigm of stereotypical "women's weaknesses":

> He [God] considered well from what part to create her. He
> said, 'I will not create her from [Adam's] head lest she be

light-headed; nor from the eye, lest she be a flirt; nor from the
ear, lest she be an eavesdropper; nor from the mouth, lest she
be a gossip; not from the heart, lest she be jealous; nor from
the hand, lest she be a thief; nor from the foot, lest she stray;
rather from the inner part of a man, which is covered even
when he is naked. As He created her, He ordered, 'Be a modest woman; be a modest woman.' Yet in spite of this,...she is
lightheaded,...she is a flirt,...she is an eavesdropper,...she is
jealous,...she is a thief,...and she strays. (Gen. *Rabbah* 80:5)

Three essays in this chapter deal with the story of Woman's
creation. Zilla Jane Goodman retells the story of Eve and the fruit
with Eve as the heroine of the narrative; Meg Akabas and Rabbi
Nina Beth Cardin present Eve as an exemplar of human relationship; and Dr. Ellen M. Umansky discusses the tale in terms of later
Rabbinic *midrash*. Umansky notes that the Sages sought to reconcile the two different accounts of the creation of Woman. All these
essays explicitly reject common cultural perceptions of the Eve
story in which woman is an inferior derivative creature, or subservient to man due to divine ordination.

Gender and Plot Line

Genesis is the one book of the Torah in which many of the central
characters are women, nearly as many women as men. From Eve
to Potiphar's wife, women play active roles in the unfolding
drama. Sarah, Rebecca, and Tamar exercise significant influence
over such concerns as choosing an heir and ensuring the heritage
of the Davidic monarchy. Often this influence takes covert forms—
Rebecca tricking her husband Isaac in order to gain the birthright
for her favored son, or Tamar disguising herself as a prostitute to
become pregnant—since deception is one of the options available
to those with less social status.[9] However, on occasion, the influence is overt and explicit. Sarah determines the inheritance of her
son in accord with God's public intervention (Gen. 21:12).

Although the women generally appear in relation to men, as
wives, sisters, and mothers, they are presented as fully human
with complex personalities—variously intelligent, compassionate,

high-handed, fearful, brave, loving. Genesis also gives us rare glimpses into the private world of women. The reader is privy to intimate interchanges between Rachel and Leah around sexuality, Sarah's inner thoughts regarding childbirth, and descriptions of Rebecca's personal jewelry.

Anonymous Was a Woman:
The Un-named and Unbegotten

Despite the relative profusion of women in Genesis, the clan structure is completely male. Women are virtually absent from the exhaustive lists of tribal begetters and begotten. The core Hebrew family of Sarah and Abraham; Rebecca and Isaac; and Rachel, Leah, and Jacob is related both matrilineally and patrilineally, yet the text only takes note of the patrilineal line of descent. Even though Genesis declares that "a man shall leave his father and mother and join with his wife" (Gen. 2:24), it is the women of Genesis who inevitably leave their homes to join with the patriarchal household.

Significantly, women are defined in terms of their marital clan, and have no independent claim to lineage. The text at times even views women as entirely derivative, and does not reveal their names. Noah's wife, Lot's wife and daughters, Potiphar's wife must be supplied appellations by Rabbinic legend, since the biblical text itself is silent.

Since a number of women are nameless, it is ironic that naming often appears in Genesis as a mother's prerogative. Eve, Sarah, Hagar, Rebecca, Rachel, Leah, the daughter of Shu'a (Judah's wife), and Tamar are all involved in the naming of their children. In a number of cases, the child is named after a prophecy or utterance made by its mother.[10] Like the female characters in Genesis, real-life Jewish women have transmitted their sense of moral values and aesthetics through the act of naming, particularly of female children. Vernacular names such as "Gracia" (graceful), "Bella" (beautiful), and "Dalale" (precious) in addition to popular biblical names give modern readers clues to the cultural ideals of generations of women throughout Jewish history.[11]

The Motif of Sexuality and Procreation

It is not a coincidence that the procreative realm is the one in which women appear to have the greatest sovereignty. Women's presence is largely defined through the roles they play in the male society. The frequent connection of women to sex betrays the male orientation of the text. Women are a necessary part of men's lives in regard to sex and procreation. Other women's activities, which are not involved with men or viewed as necessary by men, are given far less attention. From Eve onward, sexuality and procreation are particular areas of focus for the women of the Genesis narrative. A case in point is Genesis 6:1–4, which describes "daughters of men" cohabiting with "divine beings." This appears to be a problem because it blurs the distinction between the mortal and heavenly spheres. The Eden story and the account of the Tower of Babel deal with the same theme. However, in these stories, Eve and Adam sin by eating, and the human race errs through building (the Tower); it is only when the wrongdoing specifically involves sexual activity that women, as opposed to humanity, are held responsible.

Three matriarchs of Genesis—Sarah, Rebecca, and Rachel—have difficulty conceiving children. Though not barren, other important women—Leah, Tamar, Dinah, and Potiphar's wife—have problems associated with sexuality. Scholars debate whether the barrenness motif is representative of actual ethnographic practice, in which high-status women employed lower-status women as "surrogate mothers." Women gained prestige by having children, particularly male heirs.[12] In the Genesis tales, the difficulties over barrenness are successfully resolved through divine intervention or annunciation, and heirs eventually appear. In addition to themes of barrenness, Genesis employs the ongoing motif of water, particularly wells, in relation to women's sexuality. Both Rebecca and Rachel are drawing water from wells when chosen as marital partners (Gen. 24:15–20; 29:1–14). Hagar receives a divine oracle about her pregnancy at a well (16:7–14). Images of the well as the birth canal, and water as amniotic fluid resonate to archetypal human symbols of fertility.

The Dramatic Finale

The closing chapters of Genesis move from the stories of individuals and families to those of a sizable tribal community. Women play comparatively minor roles in the Joseph narrative, the final tales of Genesis. The only woman of significance, Potiphar's wife, makes her appearance early in the story when it is still a household tale, prior to the introduction of governmental institutions and the economics of empire.

The shift from the domestic stage to the public one signals the end of women as central heroic characters in the stories. Woman's world—the tent and family—is supplanted in the narrative with "larger" concerns. Although later scripture occasionally returns to the more intimate view, most notably in the Book of Ruth and the story of the birth of Moses, from this point forward the Bible generally favors public institutional considerations—laws, wars, plagues, rebellions, struggles for political power among the mighty—over tales of human relation.

Themes of the Genesis Essays

The essays and poetry in this chapter are divided according to the central ideas of Genesis. These revolve around themes of history, myth, and memory; home and homeland; clan and kin. The works often engage the narrative theology of Genesis with contemporary theological sensibilities. Like Genesis, they vary in style—poetry, familial letters, personal stories, guided meditation, and contemporary *midrashim* alternate with more conventional expository essays.

The opening piece in this volume of women's writings on Torah quite naturally addresses the story of the first woman in Torah, Eve. Goodman transforms the scriptural tale into a vindication of Eve's activism and capacity to make choices.

The three poems that follow, "Hiding" by Florence Weinberger, "Matriarchs" by Leah Bat Luria, and "Weaning: An Archaeology" by Miriam Flock, form a unit. They explore the paradox of the traditionally private nature of women's lives against the need to be known to others. The poems suggest that it is possible for inchoate physical and emotional knowings to serve in the stead of cognitive communication.

Rabbi Debra Orenstein's essay, "'For Life, God Sent Me,'" also examines the nature of women's traditional invisibility and the need for women to experience a sense of historical rootedness. She uses the Joseph and Tamar stories to develop a theology of memory, in which hiddenness creates the possibility of recreated recollection.

The next group of articles, about home and homeland, opens with storyteller Penina Adelman's vision of the home as a sacred site and herself as its priestess. Adelman also ties her religious understanding to the matriarch Sarah and the sacred tabernacle.

In "Returning to Zion," Israeli-born Rabbi Einat Ramon moves from home to homeland, telling how she recreated in her own life the nomadic experience recounted in Genesis. She is a modern-day wandering Jew who longs for the time of her youth, when, as in the days of the matriarchs and patriarchs, the Israeli people lived in closer harmony to the land.

Orenstein's companion piece, "At Home with God," poignantly describes using Jewish observance to give her home an authenticity denied to young single people by social convention.

"Marking Our Doorposts" caps this section with a liturgical reminder about the spirit and purpose of home.

The final section engages the fundamental topic of much of the biblical book—the nature and structure of "clan" across generations. In "Eve: A Model for All Partners," Meg Akabas and Rabbi Nina Beth Cardin return to Eden to examine the original human family, indeed the first interpersonal relationship of any kind. They analyze Eve's creation for its religious message concerning human partnerships and connections.

In "Family as a Vehicle for the Transmission of Values," Zeitlin observes that family life in Genesis is often dysfunctional, filled with bitter rivalries and painful divisions. Yet, she champions the underlying redemptive message as a model for healthy family relations and personal growth. For all its portrayal of the difficulties of family life, Genesis ultimately—in the dramatic climax of the Joseph epic—depicts the family as a salvific institution and a force for unity.

Rose L. Levinson and Dr. Ellen LeVee bring this insight to contemporary life in "Family." In their personal account of a non-traditional family arrangement, these authors understand the Torah, particularly the story of Creation, as a set of paradigms for everyday Jewish living.

Levinson and LeVee indicate that women's "families" are not always biologically based. Often they include networks of close women friends who become spiritual "sisters." Jewish feminist scholar Ellen M. Umansky draws upon her life experience to investigate friendships among women in the biblical text. Umansky surveys classical *midrash* and finds some models for women's companionship. She believes, with Akabas and Cardin, that authentic relationship requires constancy in addition to fond feelings. She demonstrates, too, how contemporary women's *midrashim* employ this principle to create stories where none previously existed.

Poet Merle Feld furthers the theme of relationship in her touching work, "Moving ahead moving on moving along moving." Feld uses her numerous, tattered, out-of-date address books as metaphors for changes generated by the passage of time. She implicitly compares our restless highly mobile society to the tribes of Genesis, reminding us that today as ever we find meaning in being part of an interconnected web of human beings.

The last essay in this chapter is an ethical will from author Francine Klagsbrun to her daughter. Paralleling the blessings Jacob offers his children in the final chapters of Genesis, Klagsbrun bequeaths her daughter a touching rendition of spiritual and ethical wishes for her future. This is an intensely personal document, yet the particular nature of the writing is transcended by the universal concerns of family, religious faith, and cultural continuity.

—J.R.L.

History, Myth, and Memory

Eve Envy

ZILLA JANE GOODMAN

*"In the past, Adam was created from the ground, and Eve from
Adam; but henceforth it shall be, in Our image, after Our
likeness (Gen. 1:26): Neither man without woman nor woman
without man, nor both of them without the* Shekhinah *[close
dwelling presence of God, associated with the feminine]."*
—GEN. *RABBAH* 22:2

*The events in Genesis 3 that led to the exile from Eden are most often read
in a negative light. The snake is the tempter and initiator of the saga.
Ḥavvah (Eve) gives in to temptation and, in disobedience of God's command, eats the forbidden fruit, prompting Adam to do the same. From
this tale ensue many negative beliefs about Woman.*

    *The following text is an alternative reading, presented after the form
of* Tze'enah U're'enah *("Go Out and See"), the popular seventeenth-
century Yiddish paraphrase of bible and* midrash *(Rabbinic legends)
written for women. This version, "Eve Envy," sees Ḥavvah's action as
pivotal to the completion of God's creation of the world. It intentionally
rereads the biblical text from a perspective that sees Eve as the hero of the
tale. The chapter and verse numbers correspond to the verse numbers in
Genesis that convey parallel events in the traditional story of Adam
and Eve.*

    *The commentary is based upon the traditional Torah commentary by
Rashi (Rabbi Shlomo ben Isaac, the preeminent biblical exegete). It
responds to his interpretation, so that his perception of Ḥavvah and her
actions shifts in an extended prism. The commentary on* Tze'enah
U're'enah *is in the manner of Rashi's own disciples, the Tosafists, who*

Zilla Jane Goodman teaches Hebrew literature at the University of Texas at
Austin.

often argued with their teacher's interpretations. Verse numbers in the commentary refer back to those in the core Tze'enah U're'enah/biblical text. It should be noted that neither Rashi's commentary nor this "Tosafist" reading necessarily agree with the plain meaning of the biblical text, or with the Tze'enah U're'enah rendering. The textual layers of the Bible swell with multiplicities of meaning. These are but a few.

In reading "Eve Envy," it will be helpful to consult Genesis 1–3 with Rashi's commentary, which is available in English as well as Hebrew.

Tze'enah U're'enah

2 20-22God built the Woman from the Man's rib, because all the animals of the earth and all the birds of the sky had mates, and the Man was alone: 23-24Then the Man had a sense of belonging, of almost being doubled, for he felt a physical kinship with the Woman: He said: "This one now is a bone of my bones, and flesh of my flesh." He called her Woman, *Isha*, because she was taken from Man, *Ish*: But he also felt some resentment because his rib was gone, and he was no longer the only human. He named her *Isha* so that he could have dominion over her as he had over the animals: Calling her by a name based on his, he sought to be her master by defining her, and also to show her total dependence: 25The *Ish* and *Isha* were naked together in the Garden, and did not

CONTEMPORARY TOSAFIST COMMENTARY

2 23"He called her Woman [*Isha*] because she was taken from Man [*Ish*]." The Man decides that this is theft. And who is the implicit thief but the Divine? The *Ish* indicts God while pretending to accept the Woman willingly. He experiences a sense of loss and feels diminished by the Woman being taken from him. From *Ish* to *Isha* is an extension. The Man, through naming, seeks to ease his feeling of loss and to establish his dominion over the Woman. She is dependent because she is created from him and named by him; just as God named Creation and it came into being, so the man becomes a god to her. He thought that the addition of the final Hebrew letter *he* ה would vitiate her power and did not realize that the *he* ה would actually enhance it. The addition of that letter added abundance and holiness to her, for the *he* ה was a symbol of God's name, *Hashem*. With this letter, Avram אַבְרָם became Avraham אַבְרָהָם and Sarai שָׂרַי became Sarah שָׂרָה. The open syllable ending of the word *Isha* אִשָּׁה prophesied her ability to contain the Other, to unite and go beyond *Ish* אִישׁ with its closed ending. In the first Creation story, it is the Androgynous Human ("male and female created God

feel any sense of shame or self-consciousness: 3 ¹But in the Garden there was a sly (*arum*) animal, the most sly that *YHWH* God had made. And he said to her: Did God not tell you not to eat from all the fruits of the garden trees? ²She answered: From the fruit of the garden trees we may eat. ³And from the fruit of the tree that is in the center of the Garden, God said: "You shall not eat from the tree or touch it" else we might die: ⁴But the Snake said: You will not die: ⁵God knows that if you eat from the tree, you will be like God, for you will truly see, knowing the difference between good and bad: ⁶The *Isha* heard the Snake's words, and looked at the tree, and for the first time really perceived. She saw that the tree was attractive, that its fruit looked good for eating, and that it promised the acquisition of knowledge. She wanted to acquire knowledge and did not think that becoming like God would be bad because, even though the Snake had not shied away from using the pronoun "you" to distinguish her from God and had emphasized the difference between her and the Divine by using the comparative word "like," she could not yet understand the distinction. She was

them") who names the animals as a mark of dominion over them, following God's instruction. Here the Man, as the first human in the second creation story, names the Woman of his own accord. There is no mention of God's participation. Is this, rather than the eating of the fruit, the first act of rebellion? The first heresy?: 3 ¹**"But in the Garden there was a sly (*arum*) animal..."** Note there are two meanings of the Hebrew word *arum* (naked, sly). The use of this word introduces the element of lust and allies it with slyness. Rashi's explanation aligns the sly, lustful Snake with the Man, ascribing to the Snake the desire to copulate with Ḥavvah as the Man had done. But if the meaning "sly" is taken in context, it reflects not libido, but domination—the sly gesture by which the Man rebelled against the Divine, trying to become identical to It by autonomously naming Woman. ³**"You shall not eat from the tree or touch it."** She did not receive this particular commandment from God. It was given before she was made. Did she add the prohibition not to touch the tree then, or was it Man who added it? Another interpretation: She adds the words, "or touch it," because she intuits the Snake's desire to touch her. With these words, she brings herself into being. She was "built" (*b.n.h*) by God, not "created" (*b.r.'*) and given life from God's breath, as was the Man in Genesis 2:7. Thus the Maharal (Rabbi Judah Loew ben Bezalel, 1525-1609) and others say that Woman is form and not spirit. Because of this difference, she has to midwife herself into full being, blow the breath of life into her core. She does this through virtuous speech. Unlike Man's speech when he names taken from *Ish* and further incorporated into him by the name he had given her. Her being was all toward union, for that was all she knew. Not yet knowing the difference between good and bad, she also did not know that female obedience and ignorance were thought to be "good." So she took the fruit and ate it, and gave it to her *Ish* who was there with her, and he too ate it: ⁷When they ate it, their eyes opened, and they saw they were the possessors of bodies. They began to perceive themselves as objects and were no longer identified in an all-embracing consciousness. They saw themselves as images, separate "selves," and lost their sense of whole being. Becoming self-conscious, they developed boundaries. The *Isha* and the *Ish* felt split off and apart, unconnected to other entities. They were exposed, naked to a world that was separate from them. The *Isha*'s process of perception then came to full fruition. The *Ish*, whose name was Adam, had been created and named by God. He had expressed the power God assigned him by naming the animals of the land and the fowl of the sky as God had commanded him. The *Isha*, on the other hand, created her own

---

her (2:23), she does not speak in order to emulate God's power, but to enhance and protect it, out of fear of Heaven. This act eventually brings her creative power. But the purpose of these, her first words, is to be faithful to God's command. She feels at one with it: ⁶**"She saw that the tree was attractive..."** It seems that she can discern what is attractive and desirable, which suggests that she can also understand their opposite—the bad and despised. This is the paradox at the heart of the narrative. For the Man and the Woman to know it is good to hearken to God's voice, and believe it, they must already have an innate power of discrimination—to see good and bad, to disobey and obey. This contradiction allows us to view the text as a Creation story disguised, as we shall see later. **"...that its fruit looked good for eating."** The clause ends with "for eating." Having survived touching it, what was the harm in eating from it? The Woman was innocent of evil, as she had not yet eaten the fruit. Therefore, everything that was shown her, she believed true. **"So she took the fruit and ate it..."** This fact is not a mark of Havvah's temptation and failure, but of her, and the world, coming to life. It is the act by which all is vivified, moved out of discrete but undiscriminated matter and into the kinesis of individual consciousness. Havvah eats from the tree and creates. This tale of eating the forbidden is then the third, and final, Creation story. **"...and gave it to her *Ish*..."** So that he too might benefit. **"...who was there with her..."** And had expressed no objections. **"...and he too ate it."** Of his own accord. ⁷**"When they ate it, their eyes opened."** She gave him wisdom by

power. She midwifed herself into being through acts of perception and action. Fearful of this, the humans hid, hoping to conceal their spiritual power and nakedness. God saw them and knew what had happened. God said: "Here the Humans have become like One of Us for the *Ish* and the *Isha* have become knowers of distinctions. They are now self-conscious observers. Since the *Isha* has eaten of the forbidden fruit, now she and Adam are exiled from the Eden of unaffected and unaffecting consciousness." Eve's active choice created the moment of Exile from Eden and the entry into chronology and the world of separate consciousness. The divine words that created Heaven and earth and all the distinctions, merged and re-emerged into images of change and time, no longer bound in the splendor of eternal, static perfection. And God said: "Exile is the price of Creation, not the punishment for a sin. It is the fulfillment of My creative will": [20]After all these events, the *Ish* named the *Isha* a second time. Once more, he wanted to dominate and colonize *Isha* because of her power to create and make choices. Again his effort was counter-productive to his intent. The name he called her—Ḥavvah—was prophetic. He wanted to name her the "Mother of all humankind," the maker of babies who gives birth in pain. But she was much more. She was Ḥavvah in the fullest sense—Mother of all life and living, the Mover and Cause. It is she who completed the work of creation by setting it into motion. Creation was accomplished in thirds. In the beginning, God created the world and an androgynous humanity—"male and female created God them." When no plant of the field was yet in the earth, God created Adam and built Eve from his rib, furthering distinction and difference, and moving further away from the stasis of unity. In Eden, Eve brought forth a differentiated world, with the creation of consciousness and the beginning of a world-narrative.

presenting him with the fruit. It was precisely this disobedience that made possible the fulfillment of the very first positive commandment: "Be fruitful and multiply and fill the earth" (Gen. 1:28). For it was only after their acquisition of self-consciousness that "Adam knew Ḥavvah his Woman, and she became pregnant, and gave birth to Cain." And it was with her awareness of the creative force of her act in the Garden that she named her son Cain, for, in her words, she "acquired [or created] a Man with God" (Gen. 4:1). Indeed, she created worlds with God.

Hidden Memories: Three Poems

"...I will bless her, and she will become whole nations; rulers of peoples shall rise from her."

—GEN. 17:16

Hiding

FLORENCE WEINBERGER

In the Garden of Eden, there are no mirrors,
no locked doors. There is trust.
We call it ignorance.
The snake said I will show you
the other's back, the other's dirty mind.
Soon you will understand
how desire makes you devious,
how hunger makes you suspect.

It became necessary to hide;
this is the origin of engorgement,
of cabinets with locks the size of vaginas,
phallic keys, and all the accoutrements
of concealment, like blankets, clouds,
newspapers, and the smoke
of the everlasting pipe in my husband's hand.

In the Garden of Eden, I saw a man.
He was very beautiful. I was curious,
and curiosity turned to trouble,
and trouble turned to interesting times.

Florence Weinberger was born in the Bronx, educated at Hunter College; California State University, Northridge; UCLA; University of Judaism; and the feet of gurus, rabbis, and poets in whatever part of the world she could reach; and writes poetry because she has to.

I saw his back only when he turned from me.

It is I from whom Adam was hiding, I,
who knew the meaning
of inside before I was born,
when I still lay curled and waiting
under his anxious heart.

Matriarchs

LEAH BAT LURIA

I bless my daughter "May you be like Sarah, Rebecca, Rachel,
    and Leah,"
and I wonder:
"What were they like?"
It seems sadly fitting that so
much of who they were is
lost to me
and tradition.
I hardly know my own mother,
though I am tied to her
and wish my daughter could grow up
like her
and wish she, too,
could be proud and known.

Leah Bat Luria is a pseudonym.

Weaning: An Archaeology

MIRIAM FLOCK

An ancient city, my body bears the impress
of habitation: The permanently broadened
pelvic girdle, like a worn mortar;
a certain mottling along the forehead,
as when the blood of men and women fleeing
some disaster dries and stains the mud;
the brown of the areola rubbed pink
around the nipple like a trafficked path;
and the stretch marks, corrugations captured
for the life of me like waves in shale.
A woman you remember used to live here.
You have the photographs, like a map
to reconstruct the Temple's fallen walls.
Get out the soft brush, the delicate pick.
Traces of me must still exist.

Miriam Flock's poems have appeared in *Poetry, Georgia Review, Salmagundi,* and other journals.

"For Life, God Sent Me":
Jewish Memory, Jewish Women,
and the Joseph/Tamar Story

DEBRA ORENSTEIN

*"And Joseph said,'...Be not grieved nor angry with yourselves
because you sold me here; for it was for the preservation of life
that God sent me before you.'"*
                                                    —GEN. 45:4–5

*"Freedom is daily, prose-bound, routine
remembering. Putting together, inch by inch
the starry worlds. From all the lost collections."*
                    —ADRIENNE RICH, "FOR MEMORY"

On New Year's Eve a few years ago, I attended an inter-faith service that ushered in the secular new year with devotion and a
gospel choir. The preacher led a meditation: "I submit to you," she
began, "that the only reality of this past year was love; everything
else was an illusion. Remember the love." I accepted the suggestion, let go of a few petty grievances, and felt uplifted. "And
maybe," she extended the proposition, "throughout your life, the
only real thing, the only thing to remember, is love." Along with
the rest of the congregation, I meditated on that hopeful possibility. "And maybe," she said, "all through this century, the only
thing to remember is love."

I bolted out of my meditative state. The preacher continued in
the same vein; I could and would not. The argument is complex in
both directions, but at that moment, I simply said to myself: "I
must remember the Holocaust."

This encounter with memory brought to mind another inter-
faith event I attended: a lecture on Jewish spirituality by Ram

Rabbi Debra Orenstein, creator of the *Lifecycles* series, co-editor of this volume,
and senior fellow of the Wilstein Institute, regularly writes and speaks on Jewish
spirituality and gender studies.

Dass, the Jewish-born master of Eastern philosophy. Ram Dass described how he explored Judaism after years of being away from it:

> God is saying, "You'll come into Me as a result of remembering Me." The first thing I did was buy a *mezuzah* [box/scroll on doorpost containing the *Shema* prayer].... Pretty soon I was so busy going somewhere that I forgot it. The minute I realized that, I took a string and hung it over the door, so that it hit my forehead when I walked out, which reminded me the *mezuzah* was there, which led me to turn and kiss it."[1]

In reclaiming his faith of origin, Ram Dass created a reminder that would trigger him to kiss a box, which, in turn, is a reminder of the text inside, which itself is a reminder to have one's hand, one's third eye, and the very doorposts of one's home become signs—reminders—of the commandments. The pathway to Jewish meaning and observance is memory, and memory needs to be jogged.

Valuing memories, treasuring the capacity to remember, have been essential components of Jewish identity. Yet, for many contemporary Jews, Jewish memory goes back only as far as their grandparents. *Certain* memories can be readily reclaimed. But others are at risk of being lost to us, if they haven't been lost already—memories of relatives killed in the Holocaust, of a now-dying Yiddish culture, of Jewish women's lives through the ages.

A civilization that prides itself on remembering and reminding has too often forgotten its women. From biblical times to our own day, family trees commonly record the male line. Women's interests, contributions, and perspectives are poorly preserved. Today's Jewish women were born into a tradition and a century many of us have vowed never to forget, though they sometimes forgot us.

Memory may seem the most theoretical of life themes, but it is also highly personal. A filter universal to all human beings, memory is uniquely configured by each. To appreciate its personal importance, consider what Alzheimer's disease does to a human being. Without memory, the self is displaced. Relationships are not possible in the way they once were.

We explain who we are, to ourselves and to others, through memory. When first getting to know someone, we "catch each other up" on the last few decades. At a funeral, we sum up the meaning of a life through the memories left behind. Jews have traditionally presented themselves this way: "My forefather was a wandering Aramean, and he went down to Egypt..."(Deut. 26:5; Passover *Hagaddah*).

If we relate to the Holocaust, a *mezuzah*, and ourselves through memory, how can we relate to memory itself? How might we use biblical precedents to establish a theory of memory that reflects time-honored values *and* fully includes women?

"And You Shall Remember"

The Bible enjoins us to remember numerous ideals and happenings: The Sabbath, the day we left Egypt, the miracles God performed for us there, Miriam's affliction with the plague, God's role in our material successes, the evil of Amalek, the trials of desert wanderings.[2] Remembering our slavery in Egypt is associated with commandments to keep the Sabbath and leave crops behind for the underprivileged (Deut. 5:15, 24:22). It is also the basis of injunctions against oppressing slaves, strangers, orphans, and widows (15:15, 24:17–18). In biblical theology, remembering God, covenant, and commandment leads to observance and hence to harmony and reward. Forgetting them leads to sin, chaos, and oblivion (Deut. 11:13–28, Num. 15:39–40).

Memory as the Goal More than a mechanism or process that initiates Jewish observance, memory can be seen, in and of itself, as a supreme and sacred goal. Yes, remembering the commandments—whether through the written word, the spur of punishment, or the habits of ritual—leads people to observe them.[3] At the same time, one profound purpose of observing the commandments is that they cause us to remember. For example, it is not simply that we should remember the Sabbath in order to keep it. It is also that we keep the Sabbath in order to remember it and its values[4]: The sanctity of creation, relationship, work, rest, and freedom.[5] In the upward spiral where memory leads to observance and observance in turn to memory, memory is an essential, if sometimes unspoken, independent value.

"And So My Covenant with Abraham, Will I Remember" (Lev. 26:42)

Memory is also essential to God's side of the divine-human relationship. God, in whose image we are created, is distinguished by the capacity to remember and save, as well as by specific remembrances. God "remembered Noah and every living thing...," allowing life to continue (8:1). God vowed never again to destroy the world by flood—and always to *remember* that vow (9:15f). When we were enslaved in Egypt, others forgot or dismissed us, and we ourselves forgot who we were as a people. But God remembered and reminded us. Tradition holds that God continues to remember, and fondly recalls the merit of our ancestors to our favor. Even when it appears that the covenant between God and Israel has been broken by sin (on our part) or exile (on the part of God), God upholds the promise (Lev. 26:40–45). This unconditional remembrance assures our redemption, but does not grant us leave to forget the commandments, our relationship with God, or our purpose. In the biblical ideal, God and we remember each other mutually.

Remembrance—both our own and God's—is a divine gift. Jews curse someone by saying, *"yimmaḥ shemo"*—"May that name be erased."[6] Being forgotten is like being wiped out (Zechariah 13:2, Psalms 88:6, Nehemiah 13:14).

But What about Sarah?

That is precisely the problem for Jewish women, since so many women, in the Bible and throughout Jewish history, are forgotten. Of course, we can point to numerous biblical women who *are* remembered—and for significant, positive achievements. Other female figures, neglected in the biblical text, are fleshed out in Rabbinic lore and books like this one. Looking at the *peshat* (simple, contextual meaning), however, we can only conclude that, overall, women are underrepresented.[7] Many women characters go un-named, known only as the daughter, wife, or mother of a certain man.[8] Even women about whom we know a great deal seem to be easily forgotten. Rebecca's death is never reported, and Miriam's story—more than that of her brothers—is full of ellipses.

The Book of Genesis is particularly associated with memory—of primordial prehistory, tribal origins, encounters with God, and, in many cases, our own first classroom experiences. Happily, complex portrayals of the matriarchs are part of this larger history. Even so, brothers' rivalries, male lineage, and God's covenants with men remain the focus.

When God remembers Sarah, Rachel (and, later on, Hannah), it is for fertility, not covenant (Gen. 21:1, 30:22; 1 Samuel 1:19). The matriarchs' ability to have children secures the *brit* (covenant) for the *patriarchs* (Gen. 17:3f). Women gain prestige, security, and personal fulfillment by becoming mothers, and may form impressive connections with God along the way (Gen. 21:12, 25:22–23; 1 Samuel 1:15, 25f). However, it is the sons (and sometimes husbands) of formerly barren women who gain stature as covenental partners and divinely-chosen leaders.

As "secondary characters" in the Bible and the ancient world, women were cut off in some significant ways from the corporate process and practice of remembrance. In most biblical examples, the commandment to remember is given in the second person masculine. More importantly, women were excluded or exempted from many commandments, as well as the values those commandments recall. This hardly means that Jewish women were religious amnesiacs, cut off from ancestral narrative and law.[9] Still, men, not women, engaged in advanced Torah study. Men were considered the primary bearers of text and tradition.

There is an unfortunate linguistic irony in the fact that the Hebrew root for "remember"—*z.k.r*—is also the root for "male."[10] In contrast, forgetfulness is female-identified. The Israel who *forgets* God is commonly represented as an adulterous wife or harlot (Ezekiel 16:15f, Hosea 3:1f).

In a culture that values memory as a path to living rightly, connecting with God, and finding salvation, it is painful to embody the dominant symbol of forgetting and, at the same time, to be so frequently forgotten. It is not malicious, but it is also not accidental, that women have been "written out of history."[11] As philosopher Jean François Lyotard has noted, along with the history and theology of remembering, there is also a politics of forgetting.[12]

Memory: A Point of Entry

The saving grace is that Jews are more attached to memory than to history. In crudest definitional terms, history is our selective record and, necessarily, our *interpretation* of the past. Memory is even less fixed and more subjective; it is the way we know and recall the past.[13]

If history were our primary guide, then patriarchy might be considered sacrosanct precedent. According to biblical and Rabbinic theology, however, history is only a series of twists and turns controlled by God, leading to lessons along the way, and, eventually, to the time of messiah. If Israel is enslaved in Egypt, then the finger of God is at work, and if Israel is freed, the same holds. The details are purely instrumental and of no ultimate importance.

Memory is considered far more significant and sacred. An ever-lasting, renewable resource, it helps us locate ourselves—one of the central purposes of religion—because it relates the present and future with the past. According to traditional understanding, memory provides us access not just to history, but to *direct experience*. Through memory, the past—recalled in texts and re-enacted in rituals—can be made eternally present. Memory both transcends time and endows it with meaning. Thus, God renews creation each day; Jews of every generation experience the exodus from Egypt; we all receive the Torah at Sinai. Such timeless master stories—i.e., creation, exodus, and revelation—are sometimes called "Jewish collective memory."[14]

Memory, like *midrash* (Rabbinic genre of lore often based on biblical texts), is a medium through which we dialogue with the past. The conversation never ends and is never—or perhaps continually—canonized. Generations of experience and interpretation form the holy tradition. Thus, it is never too late for women, or anyone, to join in the conversation.

Memory in the Joseph Cycle

The Genesis stories of Joseph and Tamar are powerful sources and favorable points of entry for a discussion of memory. Both narratives deal extensively with the subject.[15] And while only the Tamar story focuses on women's status (or, for that matter, female characters), the two tales yield a useful model for finding and interpreting women's place in Jewish memory.

The reader will recall that Joseph's resentful brothers abandon him in a pit, see him sold into slavery, and fake his death. Though protected by God all along the way, Joseph suffers other hardships. He is falsely accused of rape, sent to jail, and forgotten by a servant of the king who promises to rescue him. Years after he is remembered and released, the brothers come to Joseph, now governor of Egypt, to obtain food in time of famine. He makes himself unrecognizable to them, but they oddly remember him, inappropriately announcing to the governor of Egypt that "We your servants are twelve brothers," though Benjamin has been left at home and Joseph "is not" (Gen. 42:13, 32).[16]

The brothers' suppressed guilt flies to the surface as the past is re-enacted. They, like Joseph, are placed in a *bor* (pit or dungeon). Joseph releases them, but forces them to leave one of their own (this time Simon) behind. The brothers also face the possibility of losing Benjamin, Joseph's only full brother—the *other* of Jacob's two favorites. At that point, they suddenly begin to speak of "our [unnamed] brother," Joseph, and of the sin committed so long ago against that boy (Gen. 42:21–22).

The brothers had planned that a Joseph out of sight would be a Joseph out of mind—or at least out from underfoot. But absence made their father's heart, already preferential toward Joseph, grow fonder. And it made their own hearts grow guilty. Joseph loomed large—maybe larger than when he was present (37:35). Despite the brothers' attempt to purge Joseph from the family, Benjamin is said to have named his ten children after Joseph (Gen. *Rabbah* 94:8). Joseph names his own son in memory, paradoxically, of forgetting his family, "for God has made me forget all my toil and all my father's household" (Gen. 41:51).

In the theology of the story, what is lost or forgotten is actually *most* remembered. The repressed is acknowledged, according to God's plan and for the ultimate good of all. It is God who unravels the denial, unmasks the brothers, uncovers the sins. Joseph's brothers meant him ill, but God meant only good (Gen. 45:5; 50:20). God, not they, sent Joseph to Egypt (45:8). God had them follow and encounter their brother, bringing old memories and new healing to the fore. Thus, the two main ingredients of redemption are human memory and divine plan.

Tamar: Most Forgotten and Most Remembered The prospect that what is lost or forgotten is secretly remembered, sometimes *most* remembered, is particularly exciting for women. It implies the potential to restore forgotten women to a position of honor. This potential is evident in the story of Tamar, which is itself embedded in the Joseph story (Gen. 38:6–30), but often forgotten in the re-telling.

After Joseph is sold into slavery, we learn of Tamar, Judah's daughter-in-law. A tragic figure, she is repeatedly left behind and forgotten. Her first two husbands, both sons of Judah, die because of their sins. The second cheats her, as well as his own brother (38:9). Judah is required to give Tamar in marriage to his third son, so that she can produce progeny for the line. But he considers her a "black widow," sends her to her father's house, and never summons her back for the promised wedding. When Tamar finds out that Judah is coming to town, she poses as a prostitute and is impregnated by him. Thus, she secures what are rightfully hers: Children, membership in the clan, and protection by its men. When Judah learns of her pregnancy, he orders her killed for "whorishness." But Tamar produces the collateral she had demanded of Judah while impersonating a prostitute, and he realizes both his paternity and his unfairness: "*Tzadkah mimenni.* She is more righteous than I" (Gen. 38:26). The forgotten Tamar; the brothers' neglected obligation to father her children; Judah's lapsed sense of duty are, in the end, most remembered. It is from the line of Judah and Tamar that the messiah will be born (Gen. 38:29, Ruth 4:18–22).

According to midrashic readings, Judah's realization can be rendered, "She is right (*tzadkah*). It is from me/Me (*mimenni*)." That is, the child is from me, Judah, but also from Me, God. "A heavenly voice said [concerning Tamar], 'From Me have these things happened, and through me can the hidden be witnessed.'"[17] As in the story of Joseph, it was God's will and plan that the forgotten be remembered. The difference is that Tamar takes greater initiative in actualizing God's plan.[18] Even if oppressed, she is also a clever agent on her own—and God's—behalf. In contrast, Joseph does not become God's "co-conspirator" until the very end, when he replays history for his brothers. For years, God's will for Joseph is carried out by divinely orchestrated twists of fate that he must simply learn from and endure.

The stories of Joseph and Tamar implicitly advocate a complex and hopeful relationship to difficult memories: Remember the forgotten and oppressed; recall history from their point of view; acknowledge their Joseph-like endurance and their Tamar-like attempts to intervene; recognize their love and triumph, along with their pain and victimization.

Despite human suffering, these stories assert a divine intention for our ultimate good. Yet, it is only Joseph who says that *all* is to the good. Perhaps this is a mark of unconditional faith. Perhaps, as the favorite son who gets everything he wants in the end, he can afford to have that view. Tamar never declares that all is well. She wins the argument—and her life, and she even becomes the messiah's foremother through her son Peretz. Yet, "many days" (38:12) of loneliness and abandonment do not end with Judah's admission of paternity. Judah never again has sex with her; she, thrice partnered, never (to our knowledge) has a real marriage. The belief that God has a benign plan does not explain human suffering; nor does it necessarily recast human experience as wholly benign.

Oppression and Repression of Jewish Women

Like Tamar and Joseph, Jewish women have suffered not only oppression, but also repression—exclusion from the collective, conscious memory of our people. Perhaps the nature of repression—and the need to expend energy in maintaining it—explains why some of the most misogynist biblical stories yield some of the most exciting and radical feminist interpretations. By definition, repression leaves a trail, which points to buried problems—and treasures. Thus, in biblical tales of women's victimization, the woman's point of view is often recoverable. Moreover, dignity and insights are (re)gained by telling the familiar story from her perspective.[19] Forgotten women have power and a point of view within themselves, whether or not, like Tamar, they find a way to express these. Some of the most maligned and mistreated women of the Bible—Tamar among them—are also, when one scratches the surface, some of the bravest, most independent, and most spiritually evolved.[20] There are many possible explanations for this: That the cauldron of suffering tempered their characters; that God "hands us only what we can handle"; that these women are holy, and the sacred, like the repressed, "remains what is unperceived, hidden, protected, ineffaceable";[21] that men may sometimes have dominated women—in the ancient world and in the editing of the Bible—precisely because they feared their strength.

The notion that women and women's issues were present all along, though often repressed or forgotten, fits the paradigm not only of the Genesis stories and of memory itself, but also of the way Jewish history evolves. As historian Yosef Yerushalmi writes:

> Every "renaissance," every "reformation," reaches back into an often distant past to recover forgotten or neglected elements with which there is a sudden sympathetic vibration, a sense of empathy, of recognition…. [I]nexorably, it denigrates the intermediate past as something that deserves to be forgotten…. If the achievement is not to be ephemeral, it must itself become a tradition, with all that this entails.[22]

Jewish feminists have built on a forgotten, but procurable past. We have criticized—even denigrated—the past treatment of women and sex-role division. Now, Jewish feminism is well on its way to becoming feminist Judaism—a tradition of its own, fully integrated with the Jewish past and offering new rituals, texts, and interpretations.

Integration is not helped by pretending that everything which has been hidden is recoverable. Some facts, names, and stories are irretrievable; Jewish women, and Judaism itself, have suffered permanent and tragic losses. "What is most forgotten is most remembered" applies in some instances, for some texts, and not for others. But the *principle* that "what is most forgotten is most remembered" always applies for contemporary feminists reading the Bible. *We* remember women. Then, we can be consistently alert to the possibility of using fragments and suppressed elements to reconstruct a "usable past."[23] Weaving memories of women into the stories we tell, the main focus is on women's forgotten contributions and hidden perspectives. Tools for the venture include archival research, archaeology, rhetorical criticism, attention to women's absence and presence, and a midrashic imagination. The process of retrieving memories about women is not only an academic pursuit of historians and biblicists. It can be applied to the stories of our immediate families, as well as distant ancestors. Either way, it is empowering to women.

For women in Judaism, as for Joseph and his brothers, whatever the overlay of fraternal animosity and forgetfulness, the core, the wholeness of the family, can be recovered; equality can be reclaimed. "You"—an individual oppressor, patriarchy as a whole, misogynist texts—"did harm, but God intended the good" (after Gen. 50:20). After many long years, we have come to an age of reunion among brothers and sisters. The result is *"lehaḥayot am-rav,"* to revive and revitalize a great nation through the contributions of women and feminists.[24]

This is not to say that a redemptive ending erases past suffering, or that oppressive influences within patriarchy will now suddenly disappear. It would be naive to consider patriarchy played out, and arrogant to declare it "forgiven." Judaically, patterns are broken and forgiveness is earned through a process of *teshuvah* (repentance or return): Regret and explicit acknowledgment of past wrongs, amends to whatever degree possible, commitment to do things differently, and evidence of change. *Teshuvah* is crowned by having the opportunity, as Joseph's brothers did, to repeat a misdeed—but, this time, choosing a new path.

The Finger of God and the Problem of Evil

I close this essay with a cautious return to the topic with which I began: The Holocaust. "Cautious"—for all the obvious and serious reasons: Enormity of the subject, departure from my main focus, limited space. "Cautious" also because I arrive at these remarks having mentioned, in relation to other topics, God's benign plan. "Return"—despite all that—since a discussion of Jewish memory that ignores the Holocaust seems to me cowardly, in denial, or irrelevant. The Holocaust dominates contemporary Jewish thought on memory.[25]

Not every theory of Jewish memory is Holocaust-centered— the one presented in this essay certainly isn't. But no theory can afford to ignore this ultimate test case. Nor can any theory pass the test; the best it can do is not be invalidated by it.

There is no correlation or equation between deliberate geno-cide and the historical trend of patriarchy. Still, a theory of memo-ry developed in relation to women's place in patriarchal Judaism can be applied to the Holocaust. For post-Holocaust Jewry, as for Tamar, no promise of redemption—whether through a newly founded State or one's own blood line—can balance the scales. Yet, without in any way curtailing our moral outrage or undermining a survivor's right *not* to forgive, without necessarily conceding to Joseph that *all* is to the good, it is possible to find and empower tiny sparks of good in the evil abyss of the Holocaust: The moral courage under tyranny, the will to live, the will to die in dignity, the example of righteous gentiles. In Holocaust studies, as in Jewish women's studies, the focus today is as much on the human-ity of the (forgotten) oppressed, as it is on the oppression of humanity. Moreover, what was repressed and forgotten during the Holocaust—the ethical monotheism of the Hebrew Bible—turned out, in the end, to survive domination.

How could the world forget us? Where was the *zokher habrit* (One who remembers the covenant)? *Any* theology of memory is painful in relation to the Holocaust. The basic hermeneutic of this one—the prism through which texts and experiences are read—is *ḥesed* (lovingkindess, grace).[26] Reviewing the narratives of Genesis, the emerging story of Jewish women, and even the history of the Holocaust, I neither excuse nor repress the harm done. It is not that I *remember* only the love. It is that I *empower* only the love.

Home and Homeland

A Light Returns to Sarah's Tent:
My Home Is the Sacred Tabernacle

PENINA V. ADELMAN

*"And Isaac brought [Rebecca] into his mother Sarah's tent and
she became his wife, and he loved her; and Isaac was comforted
after his mother's death."*
                                                   —GEN. 24:67

Before I knew a word of Hebrew, I learned about the *Shekhinah*
(close-dwelling presence of God, associated with the feminine)
from an Israeli college professor. I learned that *Shekhinah* was the
part of God that is manifest in the world, God's consort.[1] The
Shekhinah became the symbol of all I was searching for because it
represented what had been missing in my own life: A feminine
Guide to the sacred; a Wise Woman; a Keeper of the Knowledge of
Life and Death; a Homemaker. It seemed somehow more natural
for me to focus on *Shekhinah* than on the Changing Woman of
Navaho religion, one of my previous models of the divine
Feminine, but I could not have articulated the reason.

   Twenty years have passed since I prayed to the *Shekhinah* to be
my Guide in the wilderness, twenty years during which I married,
became a mother, and made my own home; twenty years during
which the women's movement has grown and become more
diverse and more factionalized, more sophisticated and more corporate, more effective in the secular world and more cognizant of
the lack of a spiritual core. I speak Hebrew now, and when I have
a difficult question, I am able to look into Jewish sources myself to

---

Penina V. Adelman is a writer and social worker who makes her home in
Newton, Massachusetts.

find an answer. In a sense, I have come home to Judaism. I have found the particular spot in the world where I will pitch my tent. For now.

Sacred Tents

In the ancient Hebrew society recounted in Genesis, our ancestors were also nomads. They dwelled in tents, homes that could be moved or shifted as the need arose. "*Ohel*," the Hebrew word for tent, comes from an Arabic word meaning "to be inhabited" that is similar to the Assyrian, *alu*, settlement or city, and *ma'alu*, *ma'altu*, bed.[2] The Bible tells us of *ohel sarah* (the matriarch Sarah's tent) and the *ohel mo'ed* (Tent of Meeting), where the Holy of Holies was housed during the period of desert wandering before the Children of Israel entered the Promised Land.

The *midrash* states that while Sarah was alive, a light burned in her tent from one *Shabbat* (Sabbath) to the next; dough for the loaves of bread was blessed; and a cloud (signifying the divine Presence) always hovered over her tent (Gen. *Rabbah* 60:16 and Rashi on Gen. 24:67). When she died, these things ceased. However, when Isaac's new wife, Rebecca, came into Sarah's tent, the light, the dough, and the cloud all returned. According to *midrash*, Sarah's tent foreshadowed the *ohel mo'ed* (Tent of Meeting) with its accompanying fire, sacrifices, and cloud of the *Shekhinah*. Sarah and Rebecca were precursors of the priesthood; they were the holy women of their sacred tents.

The *ohel mo'ed* was the designated place where human beings went to receive oracles from God. Its structure conveyed the message of a gradually intensifying meeting with the sacred. A worshipper first entered the outer court of the *ohel mo'ed*. Then the devotee reached the altar; finally, only the High Priest himself was able to enter the Holy of Holies where the Torah was kept inside the Ark. Even the materials used to make the *ohel mo'ed* correlated with the relative degree of holiness of each item. The Ark was made of pure gold and the altar in the outer court, of bronze.

Only the woman destined to be Sarah's successor, Rebecca, could come into Sarah's tent and make the light, the dough, and the cloud reappear. So too in the *ohel mo'ed*, only the high priest, the properly designated descendent of Aaron, could enter the innermost sacred sanctuary (Holy of Holies). The *ner tamid* (eternal light) of the *ohel mo'ed* was like the light that burned from one *Shabbat* to the next in Sarah's tent. The sacrifices of livestock, grains, and produce offered to God can be likened to Sarah's blessed dough. Finally, the cloud signifying the *Shekhinah* hovered above both the *ohel mo'ed* and Sarah's tent.

The *Shabbat*: A Contemporary *Ohel Mo'ed*

In our day, the *Shabbat* table is an analog to the table in the *ohel mo'ed*, where twelve *ḥallot* (loaves) were placed. The candles are lit, analogous to the seven-branched lampstand in the *ohel mo'ed* that always remained lit. In short, the everyday life of the house in which we dwell is elevated to the very highest level of *kedushah* (holiness) simply by carrying out preparations for *Shabbat*. It is no surprise to realize that many Jews define making a Jewish home in terms of making *Shabbat*. One way to look at homemaking, in all senses of the word, is as the elevation of the mundane into the sacred, as one cooks, cleans, celebrates, repairs, rests, studies, converses, and makes blessings.

Contemporary *Shabbat* preparations parallel the physical approach to the inner Holy of Holies in the *ohel mo'ed*. Even as the holiness gradually increased in intensity as one drew nearer to the Holy of Holies, so Sabbath preparations gradually intensify as the time draws closer to the moment of candle lighting, the opening ritual of *Shabbat*. The Day of Rest informs my entire week. Like a priestess, like a keeper of the Holy Temple, I prepare my home— with errands and intentionality, tasks and Torah—to be a suitable vessel for receiving *Shabbat*.[3]

I enjoy bringing guests into my home on *Shabbat*. In so doing, I connect with the traditions of my grandparents that fell into disuse. In so doing, I follow the tradition of my ancestors, Abraham and Sarah (Gen. 18:2f). One of the greatest *mitzvot* (commandments, sacred obligations) is *hakhnasat orḥim* (welcoming guests). Among the Jews of Ethiopia, there is a saying for bringing guests into the home: "Please come in! My house is the house of Abraham." Ethiopian Jews consider guests to be sacred messengers from God like the angels who came to visit Abraham and

Sarah (Gen. 18:1–16). According to the *midrash*, Abraham and Sarah were model hosts in their desert *ohel* (Gen. *Rabbah* 48:9). Abraham would not just wait for people to come to his tent. If he saw strangers in the distance, he would run to greet them and welcome them into his home (Gen. 18:2).

Home Can Be a Holy Place

The unique sacred qualities that the *midrash* attributes to the original Jewish dwelling demonstrate how the tent/home is the archetype of a holy place. The first holy space that accompanied the Jews on their desert wanderings recalls Sarah's tent. Because the *ohel mo'ed* had to travel along with the Jewish people, the manifestations of the sacred had to be portable. Perhaps that is why it is so difficult to define the Jewish home in terms of palpable objects. Rather, what one does in the home is what makes it holy. For those, like myself, who did not grow up in a Jewishly observant home, the way to make one must be discovered anew.

Through the prayer technique of meditation,[4] I have learned to slow down and relish homemaking for the connection it creates to place and to all my ancestors—male and female—who prized the homes they made. I have learned to focus my attention on the task at hand—cutting vegetables, sweeping the kitchen floor, changing diapers, helping with homework—in order to participate fully, with my entire being. I used to notice my Granma Bela doing this as she cleaned her stove. She treated the scouring and polishing as an act of ritual purification. *Kavvanah* (spiritual intentionality) is this very quality of giving full attention to the activity of the moment and dedicating it to a force beyond oneself. I find that it is possible to employ this spiritual practice in my domestic tasks.

We must contend with the current devaluing of housework and women who work in the home. We must challenge the historical dissociation and sex-role division between work in the home and work outside it, between women's blessings in the home, and men's prayer in public. Yet creating a home and, specifically, doing housework—making food, preparing for *Shabbat*, cleaning the house—*can* feel like an honored sacred role, an opportunity to bask in the light from Sarah's tent.

A Visualization for Home

Home stems from visualization. To make a home, one has to imagine it first and then fill it with objects, atmosphere, and *kavannah* (spiritual intentionality) to realize the vision. "Home" is known by elements one has conceived: A certain light filtering through the place, special aromas, tastes, rhythms. I felt a powerful sense of "home" when I first arrived in Israel. I felt I had at last arrived in the place where I belonged. This was a marked contrast to my earlier attempt camping out in the mountains of Tucson, Arizona, reading stories of the indigenous tribes that lived there, trying to be "home" and definitely not succeeding. The following visualization explores elements that make up home for you:

> Imagine the places you have felt home as a human being, as a Jew, and as a woman or man. These may be apartments, a retreat, or a community center, a kibbutz, a friend's house, a library, a synagogue, or the local YMCA.
>
> Picture the place where you first felt "home" in your life, where someone else made a home for you. Where was this place?... Now, walk up to the entrance. What do you notice outside? As you first go in?... Is it quiet, or are there lots of activities? Go into a room where you are particularly comfortable. What do you see?... What can you hear?... How does this place smell?... What is the temperature?... What do you touch when you let your fingers wander?... Let yourself be in this place for a while until you have a sense of that familiar feeling of being home again.
>
> Before you leave, look around the area and bring back one memento. It can be whatever you wish, even something you can't pick up and carry. Take your time. What will it be? What do you always want to remember about this place?
>
> Now see yourself and the souvenir at the entrance to the building where you currently live. Walk in. Your home is at its best; things are in just the order you would like them to be.... What do you notice first?... (How) does the place look different to you in its ideal state? Walk around. Where exactly are you drawn to? Find something about this place that makes you *feel* at home.... Be here with all your senses: See the place in your mind's eye; listen to it with your inner ear;

smell it; experience it with your entire being. What does this place mean to you as a human being? As a Jew? As a woman or man? Notice what this home has in common with your childhood place.... Find a spot here for the souvenir from your childhood home. Where does it fit best? Put it where it belongs. Be fully home.

When you are done with this meditation, reflect on any "places," objects, images, or values that you might want to bring into your life, your residence, and your other "homes."

Returning to Zion

EINAT RAMON

"And Adonai *said to Jacob, 'Return to the land of your ancestors and to your homeland, and I shall be with you....*
Get up and leave this land....'"
—GEN. 31:3, 13

Sometimes, we must leave the people and places we love, only so that we may return to them after a long journey. This complicated relationship between the People of Israel and their Land has been a central theme of our national story for generations.

In 1988, I left Israel to pursue my rabbinic ordination in New York City. Like Sarah and Abraham, I left my home. Like Jacob, I eventually returned to the Land, after a practical education. I spent approximately seven years between Broadway, Berkeley, and the forests of Montana. Some Israelis I knew were quite suspicious of my intentions and considered me a *yoredet* (someone who "descends" from the Motherland of Israel), perhaps even a "traitor" who betrayed the holy cause of rebuilding the Land. This has

Rabbi Einat Ramon, a third-generation Israeli, was the first Israeli-born woman to be ordained. A Ph.D. candidate at Stanford University, she now lives and teaches in Jerusalem.

long been the typical attitude toward Israelis who have left the country permanently or for a long period of time. After seven years of exile in places where the lightness of being was both emancipating and unbearable, I returned with my husband, Arik. Arik became a new *oleh* (immigrant; literally, "ascender") to the Land of the Jewish people's dreams. Israel has always been not only our dream as a couple, but *The* Dream: The Promised Land, the embodiment of the *Shekhinah* (close-dwelling presence of God, associated with the feminine), the fantasy of heaven on earth.

Ironically, this place of ancient dreams is one of the places where it is most difficult to fulfill a new dream. In the process of returning to Israel, we are learning that the only way to live out our dreams is to find creative ways to update them. Wars take a high toll, as do limited resources, the lower standard of living, and people's roughness and cynicism. This small country takes in many people. This young state fails to learn from the mistakes of older states and, seemingly, must imitate them all. Is Israel a Land of Milk and Honey (Num. 13:27) or a Land that eats her inhabitants, as observed by the Israelite spies (Num. 13:32)? Natives, immigrants, and visitors, and even many who have only read about the land, perceive Israel at its best and worst, as reality, as dream, and as home.

In my Labor Zionist family, the concept of *ahavat ha'aretz* (love of the Land) represented all the good things that a person could do. A person who loved the Land treated people respectfully and lovingly, spoke politely, helped immigrants and tourists, and took good care of the landscape. This was what we learned in Israeli kindergartens in the 1960s, before we realized that the term *ahavat ha'aretz* could also be manipulated by nationalist and religious extremists to justify all kinds of cruelties. In my childhood memories, nostalgic images of rocky, rural landscapes blend with seasonal smells of the Land of Milk and Honey and with the sounds of melancholy Israeli folk music. Once upon a time, in the 1960s, Israeli cities looked more like extended villages. Neighborhoods in Jerusalem were set apart, and in between there was much space for us to play our games, to hide and seek and dream our dreams.

For two thousand years, the Jewish people had a dream to return to Mother Zion and to renew our days there. In Jewish tradition, the Land of Israel and particularly the city of Zion have been imagined as a Mother of the People and God's wife (Isaiah 50:1, Ezekiel 19, BT *Ketubbot* 75a). The Land of Israel was a beloved, elevated woman; we always "went up" to Her (*alinu*) and "descended" (*yaradnu*) when we left Her. Perhaps the dreams prevented us from staying with Her for more than a few generations at a time. We always expected Israel to be more than She could be. Perhaps we were capable of loving Her only from afar.

Early Zionists like my grandparents tried to educate the Jewish people to be more realistic about what they could expect from this Land and thus to avoid the Jews' disappointments with their Motherland when they returned to Her. Ironically, the *halutzim* (pioneers) of my grandparents' generation also created new ideals and institutions that were produced and marketed as packaged Zionist dreams to many, many "consumers" around the world. Unlike Zionist propaganda, the Hebrew Bible taught us that the Land and even the God of Israel (the Land's male consort) had their dark sides. The Land often demanded from Her children more than they could give. Her supernatural powers were demonstrated by the fact that She would vomit them out when they transgressed and when they shed blood (Lev. 18:24–28). The Bible, the source of Western society's vision of a just world, never offered packaged dreams to anyone.

Visions, I was taught by our tradition, must be revised and implemented gradually, through sober encounter with life's mundane and trivial routines and ambivalences. I therefore try not to forsake my Zionist dreams. I cannot renounce the pioneers' aspirations for gender equality in Israel, and their hope that the Zionist striving for a just and egalitarian society would inspire the rest of the world.[1] I look forward to the day when Judaism will inspire Israeli Jews and become the source of our faith and our sense of justice and care. I look forward to the emergence of greater responsibility for ourselves, our neighbors, our land, and our world. And lastly, I work for the day when the constant external threat will no longer consume our energies. I search for these dreams or the spark of them in this Holy Land that is so immersed in bitter and profane struggles. The country has changed and so has the nation. Yet, the core of the Israeli soul longs to explore and to fulfill old and new hopes.

Arik and I try to remember the earth that is underneath the traffic jams, to inhale the intoxicating scents of this Land's seasons, and to awaken the dreams that people buried under the weight of bank overdrafts, burnt buses, military reserve duty, and an assassinated prime minister. In the days when many developers and politicians want to make Israel the "Singapore of the Middle East," we try to remind ourselves and others that the best product that ever came out of this Land was prophecy. This is the not-so-modest goal of two non-Orthodox rabbis, *ivrim*, Hebrews and crossers-over, who have seen the Land from both sides of the ocean.

At Home with God

DEBRA ORENSTEIN

"God was in this place, and I, I did not know."
                                               —GEN. 28:16

A number of years ago, I moved to California. The nearest member of my immediate family lived over 2,500 miles away. The nearest members of the extended clan, beloved cousins whom I had not visited in fifteen years, were an eight-hour drive from my new home.

Like many Jewish families in North America, mine considered the true home of a single daughter in her twenties to be that of her parents. At twenty-six, I had been out of the house for ten years—in dorms, shared rentals, and my much-loved and -awaited New York solo apartment. Yet when relatives, friends, or professors asked if I would be "home" for the holidays, they were not referring to my studio in Manhattan. In countless small ways, people

Rabbi Debra Orenstein, creator of the *Lifecycles* series, co-editor of this volume, and senior fellow of the Wilstein Institute, regularly writes and speaks on Jewish spirituality and gender studies.

around me sent the message that the place I lived was not only impermanent—it might not be a real home at all.

As for me, I internalized and ambivalently assented to that message. I loved my parents' home and wasn't quite prepared to give up resident alien status for a visitor's visa. I never consented, however, to the patriarchal condescension behind the message that having a home was impossible for a woman so young, still a student, and, of course, unmarried. The truth is that, had I been married, I would have had a fancier set of dishes; my parents would have come to my residence, rather than I, always, to theirs; the Jewish community would have considered me a full-fledged adult with a "real" home.

Until I moved to California, I had spent every Passover of my life "at home," with family. It was a wonderful time of reunion, which I had always appreciated, and that year, for the first time, sorely missed. On my first Passover at my own home, as I laid out the bread crumbs for the ritual of *bedikat ḥametz* (search for leaven that is deliberately hidden following the cleaning for Passover), I felt very sorry for myself. I recalled nostalgically the year my younger brother divided the two slices of white bread my mother gave him into about fifty morsels, hiding them all over the first floor of the house. When my parents went looking for the bread by candlelight, ritual feather and wooden spoon in hand to scoop up the leaven, they were dismayed by the number of pieces to be found. We all laughed and sweated a little when my brother couldn't quite remember where he put the last several.

It was great fun hiding the *ḥametz* and watching my parents find it. We never got a prize, as we did for hiding[1] the *ufikomen* (*matzah* eaten for dessert at a Passover *seder*), but this game of hide-and-go-seek was always more precious to me than the one that ended the festival meal. Intimacy, awe, and mystery prevailed in the quiet of the night before all the Passover guests arrived, as my parents, brother, sister, and I first pretended to restore, then hunted and eliminated, the leaven we had cleaned out of our lives.

The night before the Passover of my first spring in Los Angeles, I "hid" some stale crackers in several places around the apartment. As I reached for my ritual feather and spoon, I tried to meditate on the spiritual meaning of *ḥametz*: That there are things, perfectly allowable and appropriate in our lives at a certain point, which, at another time, are no longer fitting. They need to be cleaned out and perhaps ritually or metaphorically burned.[2] I contemplated what I needed to let go—including certain attachments to my parents' home—and imagined this release as a form of Passover liberation.

But these enlightened thoughts did not cure my homesickness nor my sense that I was, in the current ritual, quite ridiculous. How pathetic to hide leaven and then pretend to find it yourself! I was lonely.

Suddenly, some strange, disconcerting words came into my head: "This must be how God feels." The experience of hiding bread and then going through the ironic exercise of "discovering" it, is a metaphor for God's position in the universe. God sows away light for the righteous, only to recover it and bestow it as a gift (Psalms 97:11; Ex. *Rabbah* 35:1); God disseminates broken vessels through the process of creation, that they and the world might be repaired.[3] God plants the seeds of redemption, knowing the end already at the beginning and yet playing the game. In a profound and mysterious twist, God hides God, and relies on humanity to do the looking.

Depositing and then elaborately collecting breadcrumbs is, by itself, merely absurd. But collecting breadcrumbs on one's own as part of *bedikat hametz* is absurd in the existential sense; it points to the logical pointlessness of God's creating a universe that can offer no surprises. In that framework, the place where one distributes and gathers leaven becomes holy—a home where God is recalled and imitated and, in some limited way, understood. That Passover in California, I thought of Jacob's realization when he was away from his parents' household for the first time: "God was in this place, and I, I did not know" (Gen. 28:16).

In Genesis, lone individuals—Abraham, Sarah, Rebecca, Jacob, Joseph—leave the homes of their parents suddenly and with relatively few assurances, in order to create new homes and, sometimes, families. In Exodus, Moses, relying on God's miraculous intervention, rushes an entire people out of a land not theirs and toward an unknown holy mountain. I had always conceived of *bedikat hametz* in terms of Exodus, a Liberator God, and my parents' household. Now, I saw it in terms of Genesis, a Creator God, and my own ability to fashion a Jewish home.

There is no reason in doing *bedikat ḥametz* by oneself, and there is no reason in God creating the world or interacting with an utterly predictable humanity. There is only a kind of loving game—like the game of "here I am" one plays with a baby, first hiding behind one's hands, then popping out. Or perhaps the game is hide-and-seek, after all.

> Rabbi Barukh [of Mezbizh's] grandson Yehiel was once playing hide-and-seek with another boy. He hid himself well and waited for his playmate to find him. When he had waited for a long time, he came out of his hiding-place, but the other was nowhere to be seen. Now Yehiel realized that [his friend] had not looked for him from the very beginning. Crying, he ran to his grandfather and complained of his faithless friend. Then tears brimmed in Rabbi Barukh's eyes and he said: "God says the same thing: 'I hide, but no one wants to seek me.'"[4]

Sometimes God needs to be found—and sometimes we do, too. Sometimes God turns the corner to find only the divine plan and Self—no partner at all. Sometimes, especially for single people, it is the same. And all through the hiding and the seeking, God dwells on high and in our hearts, and we live in our ancestral and our private homes. And God and home are wherever we let them in.[5]

Marking Our Doorposts:
A Reading for Dedicating a Home

EDITED FROM EXCERPTS BY RABBIS VICKI HOLLANDER,
GAIL LABOVITZ, AND ELANA ZAIMAN

"And behold, [Sarah was] in the tent. And Sarah laughed..."
                                        —GEN. 18:9, 12

The following reading can be recited at a Ḥanukat Habayit *(ceremony when affixing a* mezuzah).

We mark our doors,
physically attaching God's name to the posts,
so that as we enter, and as we go out and walk in the world,
as we lie down, and as we rise up,
as we grow and age, and dance and sing,
and safely return
we do so invoking God's presence.

"Yossi of Jerusalem said: Let your house be open wide; let the
    poor be members of your household..." (Mishnah *Avot* 1:5).
The *mezuzah* reminds us that life is wider than our doorways.

"By wisdom a house is built, and by understanding it is
    moored.
By knowledge the rooms are filled with all precious and
    pleasant treasure" (Proverbs 24:3–4).
May wisdom enter with her companions of love, joy, and
    blessing.

Rabbi Vicki Hollander resides in Vancouver, B.C., where she weaves together ritual, poetry, spiritual counseling, and retreats.
Rabbi Gail Labovitz, ordained in 1992, is currently pursuing a Ph.D. in Talmud and Rabbinics at The Jewish Theological Seminary, where she serves as a visiting instructor.
Rabbi Elana Zaiman serves the Park Avenue Synagogue in New York City.

May all who cross this threshold find here a place of refuge
and renewal.
"Blessed are you in your coming in, and blessed are you in
your going out" (Deut. 28:6).

Clan and Kin

Eve: A Model for All Partners

MEG AKABAS AND NINA BETH CARDIN

"And Adonai *our God said: 'It is not good that Adam should be alone; I will make him an* ezer kenegdo, *a helpmeet opposite him.'"*
—GEN. 2:18

Love and partnership are timeless. Yet, being a partner isn't what it used to be. For good and ill, the rules of intimate relationships are in flux—as attested to by rising rates of divorce and intermarriage, the increasing numbers of egalitarian marriages, and a greater openness about homosexuality. Partnerships in other areas of life—business, education, philanthropy—are no less important and also require religious response. We, like so many others, have wondered how to understand ourselves as partners, how to become better partners, what to expect from our various partners, how, in fact, to define partnership and its ideals. Wrestling with these challenges, we confront not just our own lives and relationships, not just the wider contemporary situation, but also a complex heritage. The model provided by the first, prototypical partners, Adam and Eve, has not generally been interpreted to women's favor. Nevertheless, this couple—and particularly Eve—can help us understand the holy face of partnership.

Eve was created specifically for the purpose of being a partner. Unlike Adam, she was not born into aloneness; she did not know

---

Meg Lowenthal Akabas is a pianist, management consultant for non-profit organizations, mother, and partner to her husband Seth.
Rabbi Nina Beth Cardin is editor of *Sh'ma: A Journal of Jewish Responsibility* and associate director of the National Center for Jewish Healing. She is in constant partnership with her husband, children, co-workers, and other human creatures.

self without another. She was created in response to the need of another human being.

This story has often been read through gendered and even sexist eyes: The woman, Eve, representing all women; the man, Adam, representing all men; the woman to serve, the man to be served. But, in some sense, Eve's story is everyone's story. Created second, Eve is truly the "mother of all life" (Gen. 3:20), for hers is the prototypical experience of all humans after her. No one, man or woman, has ever experienced the singleness of creation as did the first man. Everyone since has been born into relationship. We are children, spouses, lovers, parents, friends, group members, co-workers—and here, in the case of this article, co-authors. Eve can therefore be viewed as the exemplar of relationship for all people—women *and* men.

A prime form of relationship, indeed the first model of relationship, is partnership. With no history of human partnership, it was up to the first woman and man to establish its contours and rules. Was it to be one of hierarchy, perhaps of servitude? Was it to be one of equity and reciprocity? Or, despite their proximity, was it to be one of parallel aloneness? The example of the world's first partnership can teach women and men today a healthy paradigm.

What Is a Helpmeet? *Ezer* in Divine and Human Incarnations

It is clear why Eve is created: "It is not good that the human should be alone" (Gen. 2:18). However, Eve's function as a partner is less clear. What does it mean that Eve is to be "…a helpmeet opposite" Adam—*ezer kenegdo*?[1] Despite the flat and singularly subservient implication traditionally ascribed to the translation "helpmeet," the meaning of *ezer* is richly textured.

The Hebrew *ezer* probably comes from either the root '.z.r or g.z.r—thus implying either "rescuing" and "saving" (in the first case), or "power" (in the second)—more positive meanings than the English "helpmeet."[2] Indeed, rather than being subservient, an *ezer* often wields more power than the person being helped. Dozens of times in the Bible, God is referred to as an *ezer*. In these instances, God is imagined as fighter, protector, comforter, avenger, refuge.[3] Sometimes, God's help takes the form of power in action, sometimes the quiet strength of an embrace or the protective presence of a shield. Still other help requires the simple promise of readiness: "God is our refuge and our strength; an *ezer* in trouble, very present" (Psalm 46:2).

Be it from superior or peer, God or human, help is always responsive to the one being helped. Being helpful means being attentive to another's needs. Help—like the first woman—is quintessentially a partner, born of relationship, but not necessarily subservient.

In her role as *ezer*, Eve assists not only Adam but God as well. Looking at creation, God recognized: "It is not good that the man should be alone." Although God was complete as "one," the human was not. Adam's loneliness was an incompleteness. God did not bridge the distance between human and divine by saying *"hineni"* (here I am), by becoming Adam's partner. Rather, God responded by creating a surrogate, a partner in Eve. God needed a helper to bring the presence of God to Adam.

As children of both Adam and Eve, every human being plays both roles. Now, Adam-like, we look for someone to quell our loneliness, help us with our existential and practical dilemmas, meet our needs. Now, Eve-like, we act as true partners, emissaries of God, sent to heal loneliness and provide help.

Opposite, but Not Opposing

But Eve is more than *ezer*; she is *ezer kenegdo*. No one else in the Bible merits this juxtaposition of terms. Together, the two words spell out a complex and profound recipe for partnership. *Keneged* literally means "present," "in front of," "right there." Readers of the translation "opposite" miss the spatial aspect of that word and generally infer opposition or conflict. *Kenegdo* rarely bears that meaning.[4]

In true partnership, the role of *ezer* needs the complement of *keneged*, that is, constancy and reliability. One cannot be a reliable helper and decide, on a fancy, to be present one day and absent the next. Relationship implies covenant, readiness to be there for another, whatever one's momentary desires. To be an *ezer* means one *can* be a helper; to be an *ezer kenegdo* means one *must* be a helper.

Combining *Ezer* and *Kenegdo*

The relationship between Eve and Adam is built on this mixture of *ezer* and *kenegdo,* of support and complement. To be complementary to a person requires that one is fully present for her/him *and* that the other person is present for oneself. One's identity is determined in part through the give and take of the relationship. True, trusting relationships entail such a degree of mutual helpfulness (*ezer*) and consistency of presence (*kenegdo*) that ego boundaries are expanded to include the other. We have each learned and grown from acknowledging and experiencing the differences between ourselves and our life partners.

Meg's Vision of Complementarity On occasion, *keneged* can mean "opposite" in a non-spatial sense. Eve's role "opposite" Adam suggests that partners complement each other by contributing opposing qualities—for example, patience countering impulsiveness, wittiness countering seriousness, toughness countering sensitivity. One of many biblical instances of such a complementary arrangement is found in the relationship between Isaac and Rebecca. Rebecca is often active, and Isaac, passive. Rebecca volunteers to leave her family with little or no notice and travel with a servant she doesn't know in order to marry a man she has never met. Isaac is waiting at home, quietly meditating in a field when she arrives (Gen. 24:63). At the end of their lives, Rebecca, having received a divine revelation that the older will serve the younger (Gen. 25:23), conspires with Jacob to realize God's intention that Jacob receive the blessing of the firstborn. The plan works both because of Isaac's quiet acceptance—knowing or unknowing, according to different interpretations—and because of Rebecca's activity.

A mix of personal characteristics brings complexity and balance to a relationship. Yet, one partner's strength does not imply any inadequacy in the other, or any obligation to render one's partner "complete."

To apply this in concrete, contemporary terms, Meg, for example, finds that her emotional, intense, artistic side tends to balance her husband Seth's unflappable, pragmatic, and "lawyerly" nature. One way this manifests itself is in their different styles of handling conflict. Meg and Seth admire each other's opposing personality traits, in part because they provide a contrast and lesson for one another.

In addition to complementing and helping one another, partners must share certain basic tenets, ideals, and goals. It is a dynamic tension. Most successful partnerships are those in which people mirror each other in some ways and also let "opposite" qualities shine.

Eve—A Model for Humankind

Look at humanity as a family: Adam is like the firstborn child, and Eve and all the generations following are like children who are not firstborns. We are born into a world where we *must* be cooperative social beings. Eve's creation as the first partner provides a paradigm of balance for *every* partner in *every* relationship. As stand-ins for God, we should play the role of *ezer kenegdo* in all our partnerships. Likewise, we are also all, as Adam was, in need of an *ezer kenegdo*.

Much has been written about the dilemma of approaching the story of Adam and Eve from a feminist viewpoint, and many solutions have been proposed. Our reading of this creation story suggests that the feminist dilemma may arise partly from limited, culture-bound interpretations. Eve, the original *ezer kenegdo*, was not, as some commentators have imagined, created merely to "help out," for women have been, from the beginning, dynamic partners in successful relationships—unions that are greater than the sum of their parts. Genesis offers a message of personal dignity and power, and a deeper understanding of the balance between mates, through this reading of Eve's role in relationship to Adam.

Re-Reading Genesis and Our Lives[1]

LEORA R. ZEITLIN

"'Go forth [lekh lekha] from your land, from your community
of birth, from your ancestral home...' (Gen. 12:1). One teacher
explains the verse means 'Go to yourself.' Go back to your
essence to find out what you are really made of."
                    —LAWRENCE KUSHNER AND KERRY OLITZKY,
                                SPARKS BENEATH THE SURFACE

Two years ago, seven months pregnant and feeling the fetus
squirm inside me, I re-read the Book of Genesis. That month, my
eldest niece, whose family lives around the corner, prepared to
enter university. For our family, one child would soon burst from
the womb; another would step out of her home and into her adult
life. As the world beckoned to each of them, I found myself mus-
ing about childhood and families, and wondering what our tradition might say at this dramatic juncture in our lives.

Recently, the notion of family has become a lightning rod for
all sorts of public clamor. Some perpetuate the one-dimensional
myth of the Happy Household headed by two heterosexual adults
with 2.2 kids, the foundation of oft-trumpeted, but never defined
"family values." Others point to teenage pregnancy, sexual abuse,
child criminals, deadbeat dads, killer parents. We hear facile references to organizations as disparate as religious communities, ther-
apy support groups, political parties, youth organizations—even
countries—as "like a big family." Whose family? And what drives
people to turn every group into one? Of course, there are some
who demonize the family as much as others romanticize it, blam-
ing it for all manner of individual and societal pathology.

Jewish tradition offers a more complex picture. Genesis, the
prototypical text on the subject, turns every idealized image of
family life on its head. Our ancestors' narratives depict violent
familial jealousies, terror, incest, revenge, deception, betrayal, and
murder. Cain slays Abel, Sarah cruelly casts out Hagar and

Leora R. Zeitlin is an editorial co-director of Zephyr Press, a writer, and a mother of two living in southern New Mexico.

Ishmael, Abraham nearly kills Isaac, Lot's daughters inebriate him and have sexual relations with him, and younger brothers repeatedly usurp older ones: Think of Isaac and Ishmael, Jacob and Esau, Joseph and his brothers. Yet, from these dramas emerge moments of great love, yearning, loss, reconciliation, and profound human connection. That Genesis sets forth the family as a venue for violence *and* nurturing is a credit to its realism.

But since Genesis is not overly—or overtly—concerned with the transmission of values and commandments, why is it included in the Torah at all? The other books make numerous references to how the religion should be practiced, and what we should teach our children to ensure the continuity of faith. Genesis offers stories of families. What does it teach us?

The Lessons of Genesis for Families

Each of us begins our own life-narrative with stories from our family. Those tales of childhood, with their inevitable hurts, delights, and confusion, shape the beginning of our identity. Even as we widen our identities as adults—as we take on professions, choose partners, create households, and add other facets to ourselves—we continue to revisit these earlier episodes and scrutinize their impact.

Similarly, Genesis shapes the early identities of its two main "characters." The lead protagonist is God, whose identity in the book runs the gamut of attributes: Compassionate, jealous, impulsive, remorseful, loving, omnipotent; sometimes accessible, and, other times, beyond comprehension. The other "character" is a multi-generational family that originates at creation and develops until in Exodus it matures into the people of Israel. The tales of Genesis can be seen as the "childhood" stories of our people. Just as we cannot fully understand ourselves as adults until we have grappled with our childhoods, so we cannot fully understand what it means to stand at Sinai and be transformed into a people, until we have looked closely at the stories of our progenitors in Genesis. Those tales, in turn, can guide us through the immense transformations in our own lives.

Reading Genesis on the verge of giving birth, I was struck by the character of its clan: Profoundly divided, repeatedly and tragically rent apart. Cain is banished to wander the earth, torn from his parents and brother Seth. Abraham and Sarah leave their ancestral home for a new land as well as a new faith. Isaac and Ishmael are separated by the hostilities between their mothers. Jacob and Esau begin their enmity even in the womb. Leah and Rachel strive against each other in their marriage to Jacob. Joseph lives for years estranged from his family.

Yet, the narrative of this *divided* family—and in particular its relationship with God—also provides us with the model of the deepest kind of connection: The notion of *brit* (covenant). By its very nature, a covenant binds two or more parties together. Even as it relates stories of family schisms and catastrophes, Genesis posits that we are equally capable of entering covenants—relationships that can withstand the fractures of our lives.

This idea alone explains the inclusion of Genesis in our tradition, for its concept of covenant is central to all that follows. The most famous covenants in the book transpire between God and various individuals. God promises Noah never to destroy the earth again. God promises to multiply the seed of Abraham and to give him a fertile land in which to dwell. God reiterates that covenant in different words to Isaac and to Jacob. And while the word *brit* is not used, God makes a similar promise to Hagar, consoling her in exile that her son, too, will be father of multitudes. These promises, which do not require much in return, echo those of a parent to a child: I will do this for you because I am responsible for you and I love you.

But Genesis also asks questions about our covenants and responsibilities to one another. The entire book can even be read as a treatise on the very first question that a human asks, Cain's query, "Am I my brother's keeper?" (Gen. 4:9). Many of the stories that follow continue to examine this familial issue: What are our obligations to each other, and what are the limits of those obligations? The specific problems posed in the Cain and Abel story—that primordial tale of sibling rivalry and the first "family drama" of Genesis—are not, in fact, fully answered until the last such drama of the book, another story of brotherly struggle, that of Joseph and his kin. The two stories parallel and speak to one another in striking ways, from opposite ends of the narrative.

Redemption and Brotherly Love

In the first tale, the elder brother murders the younger in a jealous rage (Gen. 4:8). In the last story, the equally jealous brothers threaten to kill the young Joseph but do not; a voice of conscience stays their impulsive hands and, instead, they throw him into a pit and sell him as a slave (Gen. 37:20–28). Cain becomes a wandering vagabond who cannot successfully till the ground. Joseph's brothers also must wander far from home, when famine drives them into Egypt. Cain fears that strangers will kill him to avenge his brother. Joseph's brothers fear the same about the Egyptian leader, who, unbeknownst to them, is Joseph himself, and who accuses them of spying (Gen. 42:14).

But while Abel can never reconcile with Cain, Joseph does reunite with his family. Cain's question reverberates unanswered throughout his story. Joseph, finally, calls back across the generations with an answer. Yes, we are our brothers'—and our sisters'—keepers. When Joseph sees that his brothers have sincerely repented for their cruelty, he offers them life-giving aid: "Now, therefore, do not fear. I will nourish you and your little ones" (Gen. 50:21). Even the most profound betrayal can be transformed into an embrace. The curse of Cain can be transmuted into the blessings bestowed upon Joseph and his brothers. Genesis' progression of brothers serves as a paradigm for salvation and redemption.

One might say that the Joseph story not only brings peace to his own kin, but acts as a kind of cosmic reconciliation for the entire history of the Genesis family. It prepares us for the greater responsibility we take on in Exodus. Only after we learn to make responsible covenants with each other can we enter into the relationship of *reciprocity* at Sinai. There the covenant is no longer one between Parent and child, but one of partnership, with mutual obligations and responsibilities: I will be your God, and you will be My people.

I know that my state of mind during my pregnancy colored my reading of this family saga. I have not always been so sanguine about this most basic of human social units, and I have never lacked for examples or sources to support my perspective. Genesis provides ample proof-texts to suggest that family is but a well-spring of anguish and torment. The book rivets our attention precisely because it mirrors the many dimensions of our lives, never settling for a one-sided portrait. It "reads" differently, at different life moments. Just as we read and re-read our own family stories to better comprehend ourselves, so Jewish tradition bids us to re-read Genesis and the rest of the Torah, each time offering a new "spin" on the text.

Finding Personal Meaning in Our People's Story

Watching my niece in the weeks before her departure, I felt again how separating from one's family can at times be exhilarating, at times wrenching. In the past year, she began to wrestle with a world more alarming than she had previously perceived. Her struggle was amplified by the fact that like other educated children of 20th-century America, she has inherited multiple legacies, not just Jewish ones. She is heir to all of Western civilization and, increasingly, the works of other cultures as well. These may enlighten her, but confrontation with the wider world may also trigger crises of faith and identity.

I suffered my first such crisis after I graduated from high school. One dramatic summer night, after years of believing strongly in a personal God, a curtain dropped before me, and I could no longer conjure up an image of God that made sense. Remembering that incident last summer, I pulled out some old journals and found this entry, written three days before I left home for college:

> I used to speak and talk to God. I would ask questions and when I thought of answers, I would "try them." If they didn't work, I would try again. If they did, I would thank God. Is my journal any different? I speak and write and answers come, and I feel such joy and love. Then this is God! It is internal.

The entry ends in a state of peaceful calm, much as I felt earlier when I would pray. But the calm did not last. A number of years later, sometime in my early twenties, my journal carries these undated, scribbled, and truncated thoughts:

We are exiled into the future, away from our present lives and the past. We flee into it…. All of life summed up as tension between times of holding on, times of leaving go; between resting secure and breaking loose…. Gather your belongings and leave this land. Sweep the floors before you go…. All our lives in the Diaspora, fleeing *ourselves*. When do we come home into our body and heart?

We know the sound of women wailing and keening. What would happen if all the men of the world were keeners, if *all* could cry and, then, cry together?

How difficult those years were! And how many of us trod slippery ground at that age, often only to find ourselves peering into a dark abyss. I shared these entries with my niece to point out that she is not alone, and that one's transitions and struggles can take many shapes during a lifetime.

Women's Stories

The Book of Genesis comments on transition and struggle through another story: That of Lot's wife, who turns around to see the fire and brimstone hailing down on Sodom and Gomorrah (Gen. 19: 24–26). Much has been written about whether her action bespeaks inner strength or weakness, or for what she might have been looking.[2] For me, the salient message is that in looking back she becomes paralyzed, unable to go forward. She becomes a pillar of salt—the very image of tears petrified, ossified. That is her tragedy.

Many people become paralyzed by "looking back"—and for a variety of reasons. For some, childhood proves too bitter, hurt and anger too great. Others find Jewish or global history too fraught with pain to want to engage with it. Still others observe our tradition only in its most superficial forms and, rather than probing deeper, abandon it for something else. Or people can become paralyzed if they have lost all sense of meaning.

As my niece embarks on her own journey, she will find that the challenge throughout one's adult life is to be able to look back *and* to move ahead. One look is rarely enough; and there is no "final" analysis. As I discovered again last summer, we have to keep *re*-reading—our lives and our texts. By stepping into the fray—questioning and answering, turning and returning, wrestling and resting—we engage with our past and become a part of its formidable transmission.

Each time, new paths are illuminated. This time, as my niece left home and as I brought another child into this world, the family, with a mixture of apprehension and pride, said to each: "Go forth" (Gen. 12:1). Out of these wrenching schisms and separations, the most enduring covenants can emerge.

Family

ROSE L. LEVINSON AND ELLEN LEVEE

"What is given at the beginning challenges man to the self-transformations that will allow him, in spite of everything, to stand in the Presence of God."
                    —AVIVAH GOTTLIEB ZORNBERG,
                    GENESIS: THE BEGINNINGS OF DESIRE

The table is set with a white cloth. Smells of fried onions, baked *hallah* (braided egg bread), vegetable stew fill the house. The candles are lit, and *Shabbat* (Sabbath) has begun. At the table sit three adults, two small children, and a baby. The baby is crying, the two children are fighting. The husband-father is tired from a long, hard week at work. The wife-mother is tired from struggling to get everything and everyone ready for *Shabbat*. The third adult, a widow, is angry because she feels like an outsider in her own home. The wife picks up the baby; the father claims the attention of the little boy; the widow calms the girl. Each makes the effort to

Rose L. Levinson writes, manages a public broadcasting station, and continues to be an aunt, friend, and companion.
Dr. Ellen Lasser LeVee lives in Berkeley, California, with her husband and three children. Her hobbies include writing and teaching.

let in *Shabbat* peace. They are not totally successful, but neither do they completely fail.

A Different Kind of Jewish Family: Context

Until a few months ago, we were two of three Jewish adults who lived, for eleven years, in one house. In the beginning, we were a newly married husband and wife and a not-so-recently widowed, childless woman. Each of us had our own reason for making this arrangement. About the husband, we shall only say that he saw himself as protecting the widow, an old friend, along with struggling to build a business and starting a family. Our tale focuses on the women in the house; another time, another story, may tell the husband's tale.

Much happened in our eleven years together. Three children were born. A Ph.D. was earned, a retail business begun and established, a career in media forged. Plays and articles were written; serious study undertaken. A parent was buried. Holidays were celebrated. And every day, the children were washed and fed and clothed and entertained and loved by all three grown-ups. There was much joy. Eventually, the wife-mother and the husband-father left to establish their own household. The financial incentive for shared living was lessened, and they wanted more room and independence.

On the surface, ours was a highly unconventional, even radical arrangement—on the edge (geographically) of Berkeley, California, and on the margins (sociologically) of the territory known as "Jewish family." In other ways, we were quite conventional. We were Jewishly observant, and our focus and love centered around the children we raised. We women divided our roles along conventional lines: Stay-at-Home Wife/Mom and Unmarried, Career-Woman/Aunt. In the end, the uniqueness of our arrangement would help us transcend those roles and the polarization they reflect.

The process of living with others involves an ongoing attempt both to recreate the past and to free oneself of it. We women wished—not always on a conscious level—to find a way to integrate our pasts, absorbing and continuing what was good and re-forming the rest. The psychological term for this is "working through"; the everyday term is "living sanely."

The widow sought to heal deep wounds, to honor parents whose difficulties left a lonely and frightened child under the adult veneer, to contend with the panic and unresolved grief of a spouse's early death.

The wife, highly trained and educated, struggled with the confines of being Mother and Wife—home and its quotidian activities defining the shape of her years to the exclusion of much else. Her desire for self-assertion continually battled her temperamental introversion.

Creating a family structure, we contended with shared issues as well: Stresses of a triangulated relationship, jealousy over the children, resentment as roles shifted, and confusion as boundaries were redefined. As we altered familiar patterns, we provided a mirror for one another. And we two women were for each other what most people never have—a household member, other than mate and children, to whom each could turn and find new resources.

A Different Kind of Jewish Family: Subtext

Our distinctive family both confirmed traditional Jewish structures and expanded them. Over the centuries, the Jewish family—defined biologically as mother/wife and father/husband with their children—has been the locus for working through personal issues. Family, together with community, has been the chief means for living one's life authentically and fully as a Jew. One's place in community is itself traditionally defined by one's position within a family structure. Equally fundamental to Jewish life is the continual exhortation: "*Zakhor*" (remember). Judaism insists that we not only move forward in time, but also re-experience historical time through rituals and structures.

Rituals, particularly Sabbath rituals, helped us to remember (re-member) continually, individually and as Jews. No matter how upset, tired, or overwhelmed any of us were, *Shabbat* was a time to put it all aside. Friday night dinner was a ritual not to be foregone. *Zakhor\shamor et yom hashabbat*—remember and observe *Shabbat* resonated with our personal *zikhronot*, our rememberings. And while coming together at the dinner table on a Friday often highlighted our tensions, it also made everything possible. The Friday night table was the altar upon which new realities were forged.

Our ritual enabled the wife-mother to extend the nuclear family. Learning to be a wife, adjusting to the arrival and growth of each child, burdened by the physical stress of pregnancy and nursing, she pushed beyond her naturally retiring temperament to reach out to one more person.

As the habits and practices of the nuclear family evolved, the widow learned to deal with the cry of her internal voices: "You can't handle intimacy; anger is your only strength; no one is to be trusted." She, too, pushed beyond herself and reached out to others.

Living Out the Model of Creation

The very first story in the Bible is that of the creation of the world—and of the first Sabbath. The Rabbis ask why it is necessary to begin here, rather than with the journey of the Jewish people. One answer is that there is an important and universal model in the process of creation.

We lived out that model. Initially, the creativity of work—the six days of creation—and the creativity of rest—the Sabbath— were near-opposites for us. The wife was a "Sabbath specialist." She undertook the physical preparations for *Shabbat*—shopping, cooking, cleaning. She was also spiritually allied with the Sabbath. Tranquil and calm, she made the home into a peaceful, Sabbath-like haven, even during the week. This renewed her own and the other family members' energy and creative thinking. At the same time, especially when the children were small, she needed and appreciated the window onto the adult world provided by the widow.

The widow was a specialist in the "six days of creation." Out in the work world, she fostered not just one but several successful careers. She saw herself as a role model of a productive and working woman for the children, especially the girls. She was spiritually aligned with the creativity of work—always on the go, often juggling many public responsibilities at once. Perhaps for that very reason, she especially needed and appreciated the Sabbath spirit that the wife brought to their home.

Over the course of time, the polarization between private and public, and between productivity and restfulness, was healed. Each of us saw in the other new ways of being. The wife learned to be more extroverted and took on public roles. The widow developed internal resources for tranquillity and rest, and discovered the satisfactions of creative Jewish domesticity. These means of transcending personal limitations also signified that we had heard and appreciated each other, and, on a profound level, had accepted one another—even as we accepted the suppressed aspects of our own creativity and allowed them to emerge.

We realized, finally, that three forms of creativity presented in the biblical creation story are needed to raise children: Biological (pro)creativity, the creativity of work, and the creativity of rest. A good home, a whole person, needs all three elements. We provided these for the children, first by exemplifying primarily one or another, and later by modeling the ways in which individuals, as well as families, can develop a balanced repertoire of creative expressions. The mother now writes and teaches. The widow has a partner with whom she shares her life.[1]

Our Lives as Torah

In Torah it is writ large; in our own lives it is written small. We are two individuals who became more than what we were when we started out together. Judaism guided us throughout, defining and enriching our journey. We worked hard, learned to love one another, dared to be vulnerable, honored and gave life to expanding ideas of family and friendship. When the time came to part, we were more whole than when we started.

Within the ordinariness and domesticity of the lives of women, Torah is revealed. We offer the account of two Jewish women's lives in the latter part of the twentieth century as a testament to hearing women's voices in the Bible's words, to telling a new/old story about and to Jews.

Seeking Women's Friendship

ELLEN M. UMANSKY

"...And [Leah and Rachel] and the two handmaids and their
eleven sons crossed together at Ma'avar Yabbok."
                                           —AFTER GEN. 32:23

"Honor thy friends, for thou art the accumulation of them."
                            —E.M. BRONER, *A WEAVE OF WOMEN*

Throughout my early childhood, I had close male and female friendships. Many of these same friendships continue to thrive to this day. My male friends and I had great difficulty openly expressing our affection for one another, lest we be taunted and (erroneously) labeled "boyfriend and girlfriend." Yet my girlfriends and I found that our feelings of mutual affection were accepted and even encouraged.

It is painful and ironic, then, that the Torah provides us with so little validation of women's friendships. Biblical and classical Rabbinic references to female friendship are relatively few and generally laconic, leaving us to conjecture about the kinds of friendships that women actually formed with one another. They leave us wondering, also, how to recognize and celebrate friendships among women in a Jewish context.

Because of the importance of friendship in the lives of contemporary women, we have added to the classical *midrash* (Rabbinic genre of lore often based on biblical texts), envisioning models of friendship. In fact, many women experience their network of friends as a chosen family, even as many of us consider family members among our closest friends. In addition, many women feel a particular kinship and sympathy with female biblical characters.

In current women's *midrash* on Genesis—and, to a degree, in classical Rabbinic *midrash*, as well—the theme of sisterhood dominates. The women of Genesis share certain perspectives and

---

Ellen M. Umansky, professor of Judaic studies at Fairfield University, co-edited *Four Centuries of Jewish Spirituality: A Sourcebook* (Beacon, 1992).

experiences. They recognize a basic likeness among themselves, mirroring and resonating with each other.

How the Rabbis Viewed Women's Friendships in Genesis

Based either upon implicit biblical references or conjecture, the Rabbis speculated about lives to which, from the biblical text alone, there is little access. Thus, in numerous *midrashim* they moved beyond the overriding biblical image of Rachel and Leah as rivals and imagine the two sisters as friends. In one *midrash*, for example, Rachel's envy of Leah is reframed as admiration. It is not that Rachel begrudges her sister the good fortune of marrying Jacob. Rather, she envies Leah her piety, saying that Leah must have been able to bear children because she was so righteous (Gen. *Rabbah* 71:6). Another story tells that Rachel entered Jacob and Leah's bridal chamber on the evening of their wedding and answered Jacob every time he spoke to Leah, so that her sister would not be cast off. In still another version, Rachel gave her sister the identifying tokens given her by Jacob so that Leah would not be humiliated on the evening of her wedding (BT *Megillah* 13b). Indeed, the *midrash* holds that Rachel's kindness to Leah sets a proper example for no less a figure than God (Lamentations *Rabbah* 24).

The Rabbis used the birth of Dinah to point to the closeness between Rachel and Leah. Apparently, Leah was to bear seven instead of six sons. However, she realized that Jacob was to have twelve sons and calculated that, if she had a seventh and their handmaids had two sons each, Rachel would only have one son and, therefore, be unequal to the servants. Thus, Leah prayed to God to change the male embryo in her womb to that of a female (BT *Berakhot* 60a). In yet another story, all of Jacob's wives prayed to God to remove Rachel's barrenness (Gen. *Rabbah* 72:6). In short, the Rabbis created that which seems to be absent in the biblical text: A friendship among wives and sisters.

This model of friendship is not rooted in spontaneous feelings of affection as much as it is in mutual concern, compassion, and a sense of connection. The wives of Jacob do not—in the biblical text, at least—claim undying love for one another. What brings them together, biblically and midrashically, is a recognition of some commonality in their lives: Their love of Jacob or their response to Rachel's barrenness, rooted in their own experiences as women living in a culture that valued women largely for their fertility.

Expanding on Rabbinic Insights

Contemporary women have applied the Rabbis' approach to Leah and Rachel in cases where the Rabbis themselves did not. The Rabbinic story of Lilith, for example, has been extended by modern writers to include a friendship with Eve. The Sages sought to reconcile the two different biblical accounts of the creation of woman (Gen. 1:27 and Gen. 2:22). In the first, humanity is created with the world's other species—male and female. In the second, Adam is the initial human, and Eve is created from his rib. The Rabbis wonder what happened to the woman of the first creation story. Building on an ancient Middle Eastern cultural tradition of female demonic spirits identified as *Lilitu*, they explain that the first woman, Lilith, was created at the same time as Adam. According to midrashic account, she was insistent on equal rights and disputed taking a submissive posture during sexual relations. An argument ensued; Lilith invoked the ineffable name of God and flew off to the demonic habitation of the Red Sea. At Adam's request, God sent angels after her, threatening to kill one hundred children each day if she did not return. Lilith rejected the threat, and so became the demonic murderer of newborns (*Alphabet of Ben Sira*).

The Jewish feminist theologian Judith Plaskow has rewritten this *midrash* so that Eve and Lilith become friends and join forces against Adam and God.[1] By the end of Plaskow's *midrash*, Eve and Lilith like each other tremendously and undertake to transform the Garden together. However, their initial attraction to one another is based simply on a perceived similarity: As the two women in the Garden, they have a great deal in common. What's more, their initial conversation involves a certain amount of risk, particularly in light of Adam's certain disapproval and the negative comments that they have previously heard about one another. They do not know where their conversation will lead (and indeed, when several conversations later they decide to join forces, they are more than a little anxious about where *this* decision will lead them). Yet the sense of connection that they immediately feel for one another gives Lilith and Eve the desire and the courage to develop what becomes a fast-growing friendship.

Rabbinic *midrashim* on the story of Dinah attribute Dinah's "go[ing] out to see the daughters of the land" (Gen. 34:1) as the cause of her rape. Even as they criticize and blame the victim for being in the wrong place, they also imagine that she enjoyed going out *as a woman* (Gen. *Rabbah* 80:1; *Tanḥumah Vayishlaḥ* 7 on Gen. 34:1).

In a *midrash* that I have written on the biblical Dinah, I also focus on Dinah's interest in "seeing the women of the land."[2] However, I do not ascribe to her an unseemly desire to show off her beauty or to go out in public, to spite cultural prohibitions against her doing so. Rather, I attribute her motivation to a simple desire to see her friends. While the biblical text gives us no clue as to why Dinah went out among the Canaanites, neither does it indicate that there is anything wrong in her actions. Perhaps, then, despite their different religious beliefs, Dinah and the Canaanite women developed a friendship based on the fact that they lived in close proximity to one another and, as women within patriarchal cultures, faced similar problems, concerns, and challenges.

A similar model of friendship is reflected in several Rabbinic and feminist *midrashim* about Lot's wife (Gen. 19).[3] While some ancient sources interpret her looking back at Sodom and Gomorrah as a sign of compassion, others vilify her for turning longingly toward sinners and sin. In the biblical text, she is never actually instructed *not* to look behind her at Sodom and Gomorrah, and her motivations are not noted. Contemporary *midrashim* suggest that Lot's unnamed wife looked back (and hence became a pillar of salt) out of the positive connection she felt to so many of those left behind. She turned back to catch one last glimpse of the friends and neighbors with whom she had shared so much. Whatever the consequences, she simply could not bear to leave them without saying goodbye in some way.

Friendship Beyond Genesis

The story of women's friendship does not end in Genesis. It continues most notably in the Book of Ruth, in the relationship between Ruth and Naomi. While neither Ruth nor Naomi literally refers to the other as "friend," their concern for one another, the sense of intimacy between them, and the respect that they have for one another's beliefs transform their relationship from that of daughter-in-law and mother-in-law to that of friends. Like another major biblical friendship, that of David and Jonathan, Ruth and Naomi's relationship is, above all else and with all they share, rooted in strong and mutual feelings of affection.

The theme of women's companionship—noted in the *midrash* on Lot's wife and in biblical and midrashic texts on Dinah—is taken up again in Judges 11 with the unnamed daughter of Yiftaḥ (Jephthah) and her *rei'ot* (female companions).[4] Yiftaḥ unwittingly condemns his daughter to death by rashly vowing to offer in sacrifice that which he first sees upon his return home, if God will assure him victory over the Ammonites. His daughter, sadly, is first to greet him. She asks only that her father give her a two-month reprieve in which to mourn the loss of her virginity (and/or her youth) with her companions. Though the biblical text does not reveal either the identity of these women or the nature of their relationship with Yiftaḥ's daughter, one can easily imagine them (in contrast to Ruth and Naomi) as peers—young women of the same age, living in close proximity to one another. It is not only concern over the fate of Yiftaḥ's daughter that leads them to form a bond. Rather, Yiftaḥ's daughter requests to be with them because of their pre-existing friendship.

Over the years, I have become increasingly conscious of the ways in which biblical models inform my understanding of what it means to be a friend. Some of my friendships draw primarily on the model of spontaneous affection, as exemplified by Ruth. Other friendships—with women whose children play with mine or women who share some of my academic interests—represent a connection borne of similarity or likeness. My closest friendships are with the women in my own family and from my early childhood—connections with a profound, shared history, like that between Rachel and Leah or Ruth and Naomi.

In our days as in Rabbinic times, the search and (re)construction of models of women's friendship in Genesis and beyond reflect a perceived connection among women. By virtue of being women, because we see each other as like, women are gender-identified and, in turn, re-enforce gender identification. This does not mean that every woman feels a bond with other women. Not every woman interprets the reality of likeness to mean that she and other women are sisters under the skin. Nor does it mean that men are excluded. Men may identify socially and politically with the constellation of perspectives and experiences that women share. Contemporary feminist *midrashim* do, though, implicitly demand that we listen to and learn from women's friendships. That same demand is made of the Bible itself.

Moving ahead moving on
moving along moving

MERLE FELD

*"And Lemekh took to him two wives; the name of one was Adah,
and the name of the other Tzillah. And Adah bore Yaval; he was
the father of such as dwell in tents and have cattle. And his
brother's name was Yuval; he was the father of all such
who handle the lyre and pipe. And Tzillah, she also bore
Tuval-kayin, forger of every sharp instrument in brass and iron;
and the sister of Tuval-kayin was Nu'amah..."*

—GEN. 4:19-22

Merle Feld is an award-winning playwright, a poet, a political activist, and a long-time Jewish feminist.

The cover of my old address book
fell off, the pages are tearing.
I bought the new book this morning—
small, brown, fake leather cover,
Woolworth's.

I think that's the problem:
If I bought a really good one
it would last forever
and I wouldn't have to redo it
every couple of years
but since it's something only for me
something no one else sees
(sort of like my underwear)
I'm cheap about it.

People move so often nowadays
I really should do the whole thing
in pencil, just keep erasing.
That's not the real problem though,
the problem is, what to do with the people.

Sometimes there are dead people
in my old worn-out address book.
I can't write them into the new one of course,
but it hurts to leave them behind
yet another time.

There are distant relatives,
people I haven't seen in years,
and I transfer them
from book to book to book.
I have no intention of contacting them,
but my mother would be disappointed
if she knew I had left them behind
on purpose.

Here's a family that settled in Israel
more than a year ago
they never sent me their new address.
In my old book
they still live in Los Angeles
and we're still friends.

There's a man I liked a lot,
met him in a T-group.
I just have the phone number, no address.
It's hard to let go of people
who've seen you without a mask.
If I recopy the number
maybe sometime I will call.

Here's a boy I thought I loved
in 1967. We lost touch
and when he turned up again
he was "religious"
with a wife and three kids.
We kept promising to get together
but I couldn't bear to see him
with a wife in a wig and three toddlers
in a dingy Bronx apartment.
They left the country years ago
but I keep recopying his name
(and hers—the wife I never met)
with an address in the Bronx.
Really, in my mind's eye,
he's still a Harvard undergraduate.

There are the requisite number
of divorces with arrows to show
they've gone their separate ways.
Once I recopy them it will look as if
they were never
together.

Sometimes I remember to pencil in
a new baby
otherwise I tend to forget
the name
the sex
the fact of existence.

You probably think I'm crazy
but I save
all my tattered
fake leather
Woolworth
address books.
They're in the top center drawer
of my dresser.

An Ethical Will

FRANCINE KLAGSBRUN

*"And Jacob called his children and said, 'Gather yourselves
together, that I may tell you that which will befall you in the
last days. Gather yourselves together, and hear, children of
Jacob.'"*

—GEN. 49:1–2

*The practice of bequeathing moral advice to one's children has its origins
in the Bible. Jacob offers his children words of admonition and love shortly before he dies, and other sages follow that practice. But written testimonies designed to convey parents' spiritual and ethical wishes for their*

Francine Klagsbrun is the author of more than a dozen books on social, family,
and religious issues, among them *Mixed Feelings: Love, Hate, Rivalry, and
Reconciliation Among Brothers and Sisters* (Bantam, 1992) and *Jewish Days* (Farrar,
Straus and Giroux, 1996).

children first became popular during the Middle Ages. Some of these took the form of letters given to children during the parents' lifetimes; others were to be opened after a parent's death. Some were written at the end of one's life; others over a period of years or on a special occasion. Many were written during times of crisis and persecution, including the Holocaust. All types are known as ethical wills. Moral, and not financial, documents, they leave a lasting record of a parent's advice, hopes, and ideals.[1]

To my daughter Sarah Devora, written on her twenty-fourth birthday:

My darling Sarah,

At your Bat Mitzvah[2] celebration, when you were twelve years old, I toasted you with a story from the Talmud. It was the story of Rabbi Naḥman who asked Rabbi Isaac to bless him as they were saying goodbye. Rabbi Isaac responded:

> [A] man rested in [a] tree's shade, ate of its fruits, and drank its water. When he was about to leave, he turned to the tree and said: "O tree, beautiful tree, with what shall I bless you? Shall I say that your fruits should be sweet? They are sweet. Shall I wish that your shade be pleasant? It is already pleasant. Shall I ask that a brook flow by you? A brook does flow by you. Therefore I will bless you by saying: May it be God's will that all the shoots taken from you be like you." So it is with you [Rabbi Isaac said to Rabbi Nahman]. What can I wish you? Learning? You have learning. Wealth? You have wealth. Children? You have children. Therefore I say: May it be God's will that all your offspring be like you." (BT *Ta'anit* 5b–6a)

Now, twelve years later, I know more deeply and with even greater joy that wishing you offspring who will be like you is, indeed, the finest dream I can have for you. For, to paraphrase Rabbi Isaac, you have beauty and generosity and sensitivity that come from the depth of your being. These, transmitted to your children, will surely make them a blessing to you, as you have been a blessing to Dad and me.

Why do I think of children at a time when you have not even launched into marriage yet? Because I know, and you have said many times, that as determined as you are to become a physician, you are equally determined to have a family of your own one day. What I do not know, of course, is how you will be able to juggle all the determinations.

My generation of women has bequeathed to yours opened doors and great new worlds to conquer. What we have failed to pass on to you, because we have not devised them ourselves, are formulas for organizing the myriad demands those many worlds will make on you. I simply trust that in your wisdom you will find your way.

But I write of children also because, as Jews, when we look to the future, we do so in concrete terms, in images of people and generations to come. Before Abraham had even one child, God spoke of offspring who would be as numerous as "the dust of the earth" and inherit the "length and breadth" of the land of Canaan (Gen. 13:16–17). So I do not feel altogether uncomfortable speaking to you of children not yet born and of nonexistent scenes that nevertheless exist full-blown in my mind.

Dearest Sarah, will you laugh if I tell you that the mind-picture of the future I most cherish is of you studying Torah with those children to be? It sounds so corny, and we both remember the hours we spent together during your day school years poring over Hebrew texts, your homework assignments. I would get impatient (Can you ever forgive the impatience?), and you, frustrated with the amount of study time your demanding classes required. Grandpa had studied with me the same way when I was young. Dare you repeat such family patterns with your own children?

I think you will. I think you must. From those hours and years of study grew your love of Torah and your delight in chanting from the Torah scroll. There grew also, I believe, even with the impatience and frustrations, a bond between us, linked inseparably in some mysterious way to the tradition and the texts we studied together. That, too, is sacred.

These days many women—you and I among them—increasingly question the texts and traditions to which we have devoted so much energy. You know the problems well: The relentless maleness in our religion; the silences that surround the birth, thoughts, and feelings of women in sacred texts; the sense of exclusion we so often experience even today. It is terribly important for you to hold those issues in your mind, so that you can apply your own skills toward working with other caring women and men committed to bringing about change.

But I hope you will never fall into the trap of thinking that because some things are wrong, everything is wrong. I hope the process of questioning and creating change will lead not to rejection, but to a deeper love and more profound understanding of our tradition, to a greater desire than ever to be fully included within it. As for the Scriptures, even if they sometimes pain us, they are the heartblood of all that we hold dear as Jews. They form the core of our history and values, our myths and love stories, our sociology, our legal doctrines, our soul as a people. Know them, Sarah. Teach them to your children—yes, one on one, as Grandpa taught me and I taught you. Without knowledge of our texts, whatever else they know of Judaism will be insufficient. With that knowledge, they will know how to learn everything else.

On *Yom Kippur*[3] this year, just two weeks before your birthday, I listened with pride, as I always do, while you chanted the Book of Jonah, the annual reading you have taken on since your Bat Mitzvah. But this year, I swallowed tears as I watched you, wrapped in your prayer shawl, standing tall and confident, singing out the familiar Hebrew words in your lovely, strong voice. I thought about the birthday to come and the twelve years that had slipped by, and I decided to write you this letter, the way Jewish parents of the past often wrote to their children. I pray that I will be able to share the years ahead with you (and I count, under my breath, on the longevity that runs in our family). But what I have written today are things I want to say to you no matter how many years I may have.

Dear Sarah, I live in gratitude for the sweet sunshine of your presence in our lives and in hope that all your offspring will be like you, guided by you.

————◦《◉》◦————

2

Themes of Exodus/Shemot Rabbah: Transformations to Freedom, Holiness and Torah

———◆———

What does it mean to be free?
What is my relationship with God? Where am I headed?
What is my purpose? What are the means to achieving it?

The distinctions between Genesis and Exodus are vivid and dramatic.[1] If Genesis is about origins, ancestors, and family, Exodus is about the demographic and spiritual growth that transformed an extended family into a nation. God makes a covenant with the patriarchs in Genesis, and with an entire people (at Sinai) in Exodus. The experiences of the ancestors in Genesis inculcate the values of faith and progeny, which are reinforced, for the men, by circumcision—the imprinting of personal covenant on their bodies. The experiences of the former slaves in Exodus inculcate the values of freedom, peoplehood, and responsibility, imprinting a lesson of compassion on their souls: "[For] you know the soul of a stranger, [having been] strangers in the land of Egypt" (Ex. 23:9).

Both Genesis and Exodus reflect two essential coming-of-age themes: Breaking away and returning home. Breaking away is the minor theme in Genesis. While Abraham goes permanently forth from his father's house (Gen. 12:1), most figures in Genesis require only a temporary separation before returning, wiser and more mature, to people and places of their past. Reunion is the ultimate goal and value among Abraham's sons, grandsons, and great-grandsons. It is also the larger story of human history as seen through traditional interpretations of Genesis: We leave Eden to embark on a journey of consciousness and growth. When fully cognizant and deserving of the many blessings bestowed by God, we will (re)gain Paradise.

The relative emphasis on breaking away and returning is exactly reversed in Exodus. Exodus can certainly be seen as a tale of return—return to the land of Canaan after a sojourn in Egypt, return to a vision of peoplehood and covenant that went unrealized during 400 years of slavery, return to a life in which Israel's exploding population represents a fulfillment of God's promise rather than a provocation to the Pharaoh. Mostly, however, Exodus is about a definitive break with the past, an ending to the only life that generations of Israelites ever knew—the life of a slave. As the title of the book suggests, Exodus hinges on an uncompromised leave-taking: Not just for a journey of a few days (8:23), not just on the part of the men (10:9–11) or within the kingdom (8:21), but permanently, for *everyone*, and to a holy land.

Exodus is about the transformation from slavery to freedom, from abject hopelessness to miraculous salvation. It is concerned with those moments in life by which "before" and "after" are measured. Sometimes, you do not and cannot and should not go home again. In many ways, this is the story of the women's movement. A liberated Nora can neither live in nor return to *A Doll's House*.[2]

Both the paradigm of reunion and that of exodus are characteristic of women's relationship to Judaism. As women increasingly take on new roles and tasks—serving as lay and religious leaders, studying Talmud, entering infant daughters and sons into the covenant—there is a serene and rightful sense of coming home. And yet, there are also aspects of women's status and experience that require nothing less than the full and sudden power of liberation. Under current Orthodox law, for example, a woman who is abandoned or civilly divorced by her husband may remain chained to him via a Jewish marriage that only *he* can dissolve. Women's liberation—whether by Rabbinic edict or by laywomen's own assumption of power—can bring a transformation as dramatic as the freeing of the Israelites. The authors in this chapter portray the feminist revolution as a return to Jewish values, even as they redeem Jewish choices and approaches from patriarchal strains within the tradition.

Exodus: Structure and Themes

The Book of Exodus can be divided into three main sections. The first (Ex. 1:1–18:27) deals principally with events leading up to and including the exodus from Egypt. The second (19:1–35:3) covers the Sinai experience, the Ten Commandments, various further commandments, and the episode of the Golden Calf. The final section (35:4–40:38) describes the building of the tabernacle and, in the last chapter, the dwelling of God's presence there. Scholars have felicitously named these divisions care, covenant, and communion.[3]

The themes of Exodus are better known than those of any other biblical book. Jews may have been reared on the stories of Genesis, but it is the theme of freedom, complete with its attendant risks, transformations, costs, and obligations, that we discuss at the Passover *seder* (ordered readings and meal). It is the revelation and commandments received at Sinai that occupy Jews in daily prayer and practice. It is the synagogue, our modern-day tabernacle, that houses communal activities, offerings, and services. In line with the example set out in Exodus, our sanctuaries are also meant to shelter the *Shekhinah* (close-dwelling presence of God, associated with the feminine).

Much of what happens in Exodus serves as a model. God's early revelation to Moses at the burning bush presents, in microcosm, the divine message to an entire nation. It also anticipates the revelation of the Torah in form, locale, and content.[4] Liberation from slavery isn't a one-time event, but an ever-present reminder of God's love, relived in the daily liturgy and on Passover. That God intervenes and miraculously ends our misery is a foundational and recurring tale of the Jewish people. The exodus is an image and a promise that Jews have turned to in the best of times—as a spur to deal kindly with the stranger (Ex. 22:20), and in the worst of times—as an assurance that God hears even wordless cries (2:24). Beyond its influence on Jewish theology and political theory, Exodus has also become a model for liberation in the larger Western world.[5]

Immediately upon their deliverance from slavery, the Israelites faced a series of issues that would return throughout history (Ex. 15:22–18:27): Provided with food in the wilderness, they began the process of trusting God; battling local enemies, they prepared for conquering the Land; establishing a court system that would both assist and outlast their generation's charismatic leader, they confronted the problem of government. Their subsequent experience of revelation at Mt. Sinai did not happen just once; ideally, Jews of every generation "stand at Sinai" (*Tanḥuma Yitro* 12). Moreover, the event that gave the Torah to the Israelites also gave it, for all time, to the rest of humanity. Finally, the building of the tabernacle at the end of the Book of Exodus continues to serve as a model for work, holiness, and generosity, as well as the contemporary synagogue. From beginning to end, therefore, Exodus invites us to see ourselves in the text.

The Problem of Being Other: Slavery/Exclusion

A problem arises for women, however, in that many times, we are *un*invited. Throughout Exodus, women are absent or excluded—implicitly and explicitly—from a wide variety of essential activities and positions: The census, service in the sacrificial system, tribal leadership, judgeships, and building administration.[6] Women who exercise authority seem to operate in a separate sphere (Ex. 1:17, 2:2, 15:20–21). Several commandments devalue and ignore women, reflecting their subjugation (Ex. 21:22, 22:15–16).[7] The Ten Commandments are issued in second person masculine singular—not only omitting women from the congregation being addressed, but also including them in a list of properties that might be coveted (20:14).[8] Even apparently positive attitudes toward women in Exodus may actually render them helpless or invisible (e.g., 22:21–23).

Probably the most famous example of women's exclusion in all the Torah is found in Ex. 19:15, which states, concerning preparations for Mt. Sinai: "And [Moses] said to the people, 'Be ready by the third day; come not near a woman.'"[9] In traditional Jewish understanding, the revelation at Sinai bridges the gap between creation and redemption. Yet this miraculous turning point at which Jews of every generation imagine themselves present, seems to have excluded women in the first place. Women are not of the people, and women have the potential to render men, and perhaps revelation itself, impure.

None of this is surprising if we believe that the biblical Israelites and/or redactors of the Bible, careful as they were in transmitting sacred words, were also socialized and disposed to marginalize women. Paying attention to possible cultural influences, we can suppose that exclusion is descriptive of past generations and not necessarily prescriptive for future ones. In fact, a close reading of the text preceding Moses' instructions to "the people" bears this out: God said only, "Go to the people and sanctify them today and tomorrow and let them wash their clothes and be ready by the third day, for on the third day *Adonai* will come down in the sight of all the people…" (19:10–11). Arguably, it is Moses' cultural assumption about what it means to be sanctified (or, worse, a full member of the people Israel) that causes him to add: "Come not near a woman."

So, our most extreme example of women's exclusion may also be our most extreme example of human mishearing, of the confusion between *mitzvah* (sacred obligation) and *ḥumrah* (additional stringency), or simple fact and social overlay. Preservation of the discrepancy between the words of Moses and those of God can be read as the Torah's own lesson on fallibility and cultural subjectivity in human transmission of divine messages. While it is undeniable that the Book of Exodus presents significant barriers to women's full and equal participation, a close reading of chapter 19 suggests that the source of those barriers is not necessarily divine. The *midrash* (Rabbinic genre of lore often based on biblical texts) largely agrees with this conclusion, since several sources assume or argue for women's presence at Sinai.[10]

Overcoming Barriers Along with chapter 19, other key Exodus texts can be interpreted as models for women's inclusion. The construction of the desert sanctuary, for example, conveys important messages about gender, diversity, and sanctity. Men and women alike contribute generously to the communal effort; some items are brought by all, and other items by one gender or one class (35:23–28). There is some sense of difference here, but not of hierarchy. The statement that all gave with a willing heart and spirit (Ex. 35:21, 29) frames the listing of details and differences, as if to say that everyone performed a unique service toward the common goal. Men and women bring gifts—shared and particular—to the building of holiness.

The instructions God provides for constructing the *mishkan* (tabernacle) are a blueprint not just for the edifice itself, but also, as Amy Bardack points out in her essay, for the all-embracing and generous community we must create if God's presence is to dwell among us. In Exodus, creating a holy place requires the collaboration and participation of all tribes, social and economic classes, and genders.

Also essential to a holy environment is *Shekhinah*, the manifestation of God associated with immanence and the feminine. The *Shekhinah* makes her home in the *mishkan*—and both words come from the root *sh.k.n*, to dwell. Today, the Jewish renewal and feminist movements seek specifically to include female images of God. With Rabbi Amy Eilberg in "Where Is God for You?", they search for an immanent Presence to balance the well-entrenched metaphors of God as powerful king or all-knowing, distant (male) judge. The tradition itself teaches that the one God is variously revealed over the course of our lives and the course of the centuries (Ex. *Rabbah* 34:1, Mekhilta *Beshalah* 4). The God of Exodus is not only the God of history and miracles, who lifts us up on eagles' wings (Ex. 19:4), but also the One who dwells with us, where we are (Ex. 40:34–35; Ex. *Rabbah* 2:5). These insights mitigate against idolatry; a male warrior is no more the correct and fixed image of God than a golden calf.[11]

Women as Role Models

Powerful, independent heroines and positive birth imagery are the clearest examples of women's inclusion and validation in Exodus. Women of different classes, religions, professions, and cultures "choose life" in Exodus—birthing Moses and the entire Jewish people. The standard they set in the context of a struggle against oppression is an inspiration for those who believe that Judaism has often ignored both the subjugation and the contributions of women. This book brings women's point of view to bear precisely because—(past) restrictions notwithstanding—women *have* made abundant contributions to the tradition, and have still more to make. In this regard, both Drorah O'Donnell Setel and Ruth S. Fagen look to the women of Exodus as role models.

Women engage in heroic, creative rebellion that makes the exodus possible.[12] Israelite males are saved by the midwives, Shifra and Pu'ah, who dare lie to Pharaoh, out of reverence for a higher Authority. Moses in particular is saved by the sacrifice and generosity of his mother (who sends him in a basket down the Nile to hide him), the cleverness of his sister (who keeps guard at the water and delivers him back to his mother), and the compassion and independence of Pharaoh's daughter (who draws him out of the water and adopts him despite her father's edict). Moses is pictured as the gallant rescuer of Tzipporah in the episode at the well (Ex. 2:17), but their marriage rescues *him* from trouble. Her father's home becomes his place of refuge from Pharaoh. In one of the Bible's most cryptic episodes, Tzipporah saves and symbolically "births" her husband by circumcising their son (4:24–25).

Childbirth in Exodus cannot be seen as a disgrace or punishment, as some have read it to be in Genesis (Gen. 3:16). As Fagen points out, Exodus and its Rabbinic interpreters view childbirth as a heroic act. The exodus story is framed by positive fertility and birth images—from Pharaoh's concern about the increasing Israelite population, to the birth of a nation that leaves constriction (the literal meaning of *mitzrayim*, Egypt), surrounded by water, through a dry canal, to the wide, free world.[13] Note that each woman of Exodus mentioned above is associated with water—and specifically with waters of fertility and life.

The women of Exodus give life not only to Jewish infants and Jewish freedom, but also to an alternative model for the use of power. On a certain level, Exodus operates from the paradigm of "them or us." As in many stories of national origins, there is a terrible and sometimes deadly connection between an elder nation's trials and a younger one's miracles. In the structure of this story, *someone's* first born had to die. Yet, worldly power, in the way it is used in Egypt's patriarchal, despotic culture, is to be neither envied nor imitated.[14] It fails. The seemingly all-powerful Pharaoh appears to have a lock on the freedom of the seemingly powerless Israelites. However, freedom is won by (among others): The midwives, through their disobedience and stratagem; the daughter of Pharaoh, due to her mercy and generosity; and Moses, by his protection and leadership of the defenseless. The power they use is different from the power of Pharaoh, not only politically, because of their inferior position, but in the very definition of the word, because of their values. They seek power or empowerment for the purpose of liberation, rather than domination. Their quest fits a definition offered by Carolyn Heilbrun: "Power is the ability to take one's place in whatever discourse is essential to action and the right to have one's part matter."[15]

This feminist understanding is essential to the critique of sexism, exclusion, and slavery and to the achievement of equality, inclusivity, and liberation. It also suggests multiple alternatives to destroying an oppressor, many of which are used by the women of Exodus: Civil disobedience, negotiation, subversion, deception, purely technical obedience, rehabilitation of the enemy, quiet refusal to cooperate, transforming the situation. The tendency of this approach is to distribute power, rather than to hoard it.

"For the Oppression of the Poor and the Sighing of the Needy, Now Will I Arise" (Psalms 12:6)

Because of its theme of liberation, Exodus is the basis and primary text for a school of thought called liberation theology. The basic tenet of that school is that our Liberator God continues to hear the groaning of those who suffer (Ex. 2:23–25), and to enjoin human responsiveness through the biblical text. Oppressed groups and their advocates—from abolitionists to North American seminarians to Latin and South American activists—have drawn on the Book of Exodus (and, often, the life of Jesus) in the creation of liberation theologies. Among Jews, our generation has understood the unfolding of Soviet Jewish destiny as a modern exodus story. Soviet Jews crossed the seas to Israel and the West, as their supporters chanted "let my people go." World Jewry played the role of Moses, privileged sibling, appealing and applying pressure to an angry, ineffective Pharaoh, who would keep our sisters and brothers inside the empire and forbid them to worship. God wrought a miracle, and Jews who had been almost entirely cut off from their history now rejoined it.

While these applications are new, the principle is not. Each time Jews were under the thumb of an oppressor, they read their experience in light of the exodus story, and renewed their hope. *Midrashim* addressed Jewish suffering under Babylon, Persia, Greece, and especially Rome (Ex. *Rabbah* 15:17, 26:1). The *Haggadah* (text of the Passover *seder*) can be read as a *midrash* on God's nearness to physical suffering, the downtrodden, and political rebellion.

Feminist Bible scholarship reflects and promotes liberation theology, particularly as it applies to women. Feminist and egalitarian *Haggadot* view the exodus story as a paradigm for women's liberation. Feminists as a group, like Jews as a group, value choice and freedom: The choice to control one's own body and one's own calendar; the freedom to be responsible ultimately for oneself and to God alone—not to a Pharaoh, husband, or father.

Theologian Letty Russell applies liberation theology to gender issues and to the Bible itself: "[I]t has become abundantly clear that the scriptures need liberation, not only from existing interpretations but also from the patriarchal bias of the texts themselves."[16] Thus, the lessons of Exodus may be used in extension of the book, against traditional readings of its restrictions on women, and toward the fulfillment of its larger vision.

The Nobility of Suffering?

If God hears the cries, and acts as Liberator, and even goes into exile with those who suffer, is there a holy spark in suffering? Jews and women have both been accused of wearing their oppression proudly. Yet in ideology and especially in practice, suffering is hardly noble. In traditional Jewish understanding and in Setel's "Fragments of an Old/New *Haggadah*," pain is not necessarily virtuous, though growth is not usually painless (Ex. *Rabbah* 1:1). Suffering is ultimately transformed in Exodus. The lowly thornbush becomes the burning bush, and a despised slave people are redeemed as purveyors of Torah. God's connection to suffering heightens our awareness of it, and, more importantly, of the need for human, as well as divine, remedies. This point is brought home by Eilberg's "Where Is God for You?" and Bardack's "In God's Shadow."

Jews and women, as groups, have a long history of being Other, and of being oppressed for their distinctiveness. One of the "benefits" of marginalization and even oppression is that they offer wonderful lessons in how *not* to run things. Of course, sometimes people with a history of abuse, especially those without a voice, continually relive the horror in their minds or do what they know—harm others or subject themselves to harm. Thus, the need for recording and re-telling the story of oppression *and* liberation. Thus, the commandment is repeated 36 times: "Love the stranger, for you were strangers in the land of Egypt."

Judaism and feminism both have an ethic of communal responsibility that extends beyond the immediate close(d) circle. They share the aspiration not to abuse another, even as and even though we may have been abused. The experience of having been in narrow places (i.e., *mitzrayim*) can—and, according to the commandment, *shall*—endow us with expansiveness toward people different and less privileged than ourselves. Likewise, feminist ideology is concerned with discrimination on the basis of race, class, and differing abilities, as well as gender. The principle is that differences should be neither ignored nor condemned.

Freedom from Slavery, Freedom for Torah

Escape from oppression is a first, indispensable condition for freedom, but freedom is not complete with escape. The real question is "exodus to where and for what?" Already at the burning bush, God tells Moses that, following the exodus, the Israelites will "serve God upon this mountain" (Ex. 3:12). The purpose of the

exodus is to receive the Torah at Sinai, to serve God as free people,[17] to take on and expand a sacred ancestral covenant. Through
brit (covenant), God and Israel express mutual obligations, declare
their love for one another, and even share a destiny (6:4f, 32:12–14).

In Exodus, the divine-human relationship takes on a greater
mutuality than it had in Genesis. Moses receives revelation
through a dialogue (Ex. 19:19). The Israelites become partners with
God, putting blood on doorposts to participate in their own salvation, fashioning a *mishkan* designed by God. More than anything
else, it is the voluntary affirmation of the commandments that pro-
pels the Israelites into a new level of religious responsibility and
maturity (19:8, 24:3). They participate in the process of revelation,
accepting a promise and contract, a kind of marriage to God, that
will define them *and* their descendants. As a consequence of this
covenant and their new-found freedom, the people face new and
complex problems, responsibilities, and opportunities.

Contributors to this chapter generally see a link between the
sudden transformation of the exodus (liberation) and the ongoing
journey of interpreting Sinai (traditionally, law). In harmony with
both Judaism and feminism, Eilberg, Fagen, and Bardack explore
the relationship between "transformation" and "journey"—
between momentary inspiration (*kavvanah*) and the day-to-day re-
enforcement of it (*keva*), between a gift of sudden insight and a
self-conscious calling to mind—and action. *Kavannah* sustains you
to do the work of *keva*, while *keva* prepares you, in many cases, for
the "spontaneous" gift of *kavannah*. In line with this notion, feminist "click stories"[18] both inspire and support a sometimes arduous
revolution.

According to the *midrash*, commandments graven (*harut*) in
stone are the key to freedom (*herut*) (Ex. *Rabbah* 32:1, 41:7, 51:8).
Liberation ultimately involves embracing a commitment—in the
case of the Bible, covenant. In fact, Rabbi Nehemiah teaches that
exodus frees you materially (from Pharaoh), but Sinai frees you
spiritually (from the angel of death).

Even so, there is significant debate in the feminist community
as to the value of law. As noted, many individual laws in Exodus
are problematic for women. The existing *halakhah* (Jewish law) is
slow to change and, in certain areas, painfully at odds with contemporary needs and social structures.[19]

Some feminists—along with many liberal Jews—go so far as to question the centrality of law as a category. If women were the main crafters of our heritage, is it possible that law would be of lesser importance? Jewish women from Emma Goldman to Judith Plaskow have speculated on that question.[20] In "Talmud Torah" Ruth S. Fagen demonstrates the confluence between women's relational styles and the dialogical nature of Rabbinic law and lore, even as she calls attention to some contradictions between them. In the end, much depends on one's definition of "law." Legal scholar Robert Cover's understanding—law as a bridge between current reality and our ideals—should be of supreme interest and sympathy for Jews and feminists.[21]

While we may re-interpret, overturn, or even reject individual commandments, the essays in this chapter attest to our continuing desire for commandedness—a sense of being called and obligated to something greater than ourselves. Eilberg demonstrates and discusses this in relation to God and prayer; Fagen, in relation to study; Bardack, in relation to work. *Commandments* may seem like nothing more than a mountain looming over your head, ready to crush and kill you for non-compliance, as one *midrash* maintains (BT *Shabbat* 88a).[22] Covenantal *commandedness*, however, means that there is a Partner who calls you, a mission to which you are called, and a community with whom you carry out that mission.

Themes of the Exodus Essays

The essays in this chapter fit, more and less squarely, into the three major sections and themes of Exodus: Exodus/freedom, Sinai/revelation, and Tabernacle/holy work and holy spaces. Like the other pieces that begin a chapter, Setel's is in the style of a traditional Jewish text—in this case, the Passover *Hagaddah*. Thus, even in its format, her essay makes the statement that women's voices must be heard in our tradition. Basing herself on some of the same biblical verses as the Rabbinic *Haggadah*, Setel provides new interpretations, focusing on the women and female imagery in the story.

Poet Alicia Ostriker also celebrates both women and liberation. She sings out about the theme of freedom, as it originates in the

Jewish imagination and as it applies to contemporary women and girls of different backgrounds.

Dr. Judith Plaskow reviews the problems of constriction and exclusion and transcends them, providing the map of a Jewish woman's journey to intellectual and spiritual freedom. Drawing on her autobiography, she traces the progress Jewish women have made in the last twenty years. One measure of liberation, in her view, is an unfragmented Jewish feminist identity.

Eilberg bridges Exodus and Sinai—liberating herself from ingrained, restrictive views of the God, conveying the freedom that comes from being open to God's Presence, and inviting all to connect with the divine in personal prayer and relationship. Eilberg has learned to find theophany not only in the dramatic miracle at the Sea or in the climactic revelation at Sinai, but in small, daily revelations and miracles.

Like the prayers explored by Eilberg, Torah learning is a method of worship and of opening oneself to revelation. Fagen employs Rabbinic writings on the exodus to unpack the complex relationship between Jewish women and our holy texts, said to have been revealed at Sinai. Teaching a lesson on Exodus symbols, she explores four alternative methods for studying the written Torah (the text of the Bible), as well as the oral Torah (the Rabbinic interpretation of same), in relation to women.

Bardack examines our relationship to work through the theme and laws of the *mishkan* that occupy the last section of Exodus. She focuses on particular issues that women face and illuminates our need to expand the definition of "work." Using as paradigms both God's creation of a world for us and our creation of a home for an omnipresent God, she provides a broad, sanctified vision of how we might find meaning and make contributions through work.

Finally, Rosie Rosenzweig offers a poem that deals with the connections among work, creativity, holiness, and community.

Exodus from Egypt, revelation at Sinai, and building the tabernacle would mean nothing if the people emerged from those experiences unchanged. Each of the Exodus essays deals in its own way with transformation. For example, Plaskow transforms her own relationship to being a woman and a Jew; Fagen transforms her relationship to a particular Passover symbol and to Jewish texts.

The reader, it is hoped, will also be transformed—by the inspiring example of others, as well as by specific suggestions and guidelines (e.g., Eilberg's meditation and interpretation of prayers, Bardack's exercises).

Interestingly, Eilberg and Bardack both emphasize the principle introduced in Genesis that each of us is created in the image of God. They seem to imply that if you didn't, in some sense, already have "it"—a spark of God, freedom, Torah, holiness, generosity— you could not receive it anew. Our worthiness to receive—even our ability to understand—redemption, revelation, and divine immanence, emerge from having the divine around us, within us, and in support of us. They are a blessing from the God who took us out of the land of Egypt to be our God.

—D.O.

Liberation

Fragments of an Old/New *Haggadah*: The Song of Miriam

DRORAH O'DONNELL SETEL

"Each one of us, of every generation, must look within ourselves to understand our own liberation from slavery."
  —ADAPTED FROM THE PASSOVER *HAGGADAH*
          AND BT *PESAHIM* 116B

The Haggadah *(text of the Passover* seder*) is an interpretive meditation and* midrash *(Rabbinic legend) on the exodus. What follows is a meditation/*midrash *that relates to the biblical text in a similar manner and focuses on the women in the story. Moses' sister, initially unnamed and later assigned the name of Miriam, is a central figure. In reading this "Old/New* Haggadah," *it will be helpful to consult the traditional one. Also, see Exodus 1:1–15:21, Deuteronomy 6:20–25, and the sources that are expounded in the text that follows. —Eds.*

※※※

Know surely that your descendants will be strangers in a land not theirs; and they shall afflict them four hundred years.

(GEN. 15:13)

Drorah O'Donnell Setel is a Jewish feminist scholar and activist living in Seattle, Washington.

Four hundred years she labored
Her groans rising in the dispirited souls
of children beaten to submission
of parents worn out by fear
hearts closed by exhaustion and despair.

Four hundred years she labored
and brought forth only
the bitter cruel constriction
born of enduring misery.

Do not be misled:
Although freedom may require suffering,
Suffering does not bring freedom.

———

And there went a man of the House of Levi, who took
[for a wife] a daughter of Levi. And the woman conceived....

(Ex. 2:1–2)

It is said: When Yokheved the Levite delivered her firstborn,
her agony was so great that she dedicated the child, her only
daughter, to the priesthood. But others say, when Yokheved the
Levite delivered her firstborn, her agony was so great that she
dedicated the child so her daughter would never conceive. Why
would that be? Her brothers, Aaron and Moses, were also priests
and yet fathered children. But, others object, only the male priests
performed the blood sacrifice and only they were permitted children. The women laughed: We are the keepers of the blood of life,
of New Moon blood and the blood of birth. You take the blood of
cattle or goats or sheep or birds or foreskins only to imitate that
power. They said, you can never forget that power. But they were
wrong.

———◦(◉)◦———

And his sister stood far off to know what would be
done to him.

(Ex. 2:4)

The girl's name is forgotten
but we know of her skill.
Assisting the midwives,
she carried water from the river
in preparation for the birth.
It was she who circled the bed and sang,
her voice a liturgy
of guidance for the woman in labor,
of celebration for a safe delivery,
of delight in a healthy baby,
of mourning for those who died in the process.

The woman's name is known
but its meaning was forgotten.
Some said "bitter"—
bitter with jealousy
bitter with sorrow
bitter with barrenness
bitter with shame
Because her power was forgotten.

———◦(◉)◦———

And all the water that was in the river turned to
blood...And all the cattle of *Mitzrayim* [Egypt]
died...And there was a black darkness in all the land
of *Mitzrayim*...And it came to pass that at midnight
the Source of Being smote every firstborn of the land
of *Mitzrayim*....

(Ex. 7:20, 9:6, 10:22, 12:29)

All creation gives birth in pain
Each new life forcing the breach of transformation
Pushing, pulling, wrestling a way into being.

It is said:
When the hour of birth came
the earth convulsed
in pestilence, darkness,
and even death.
Blood running like a river,
Torment tearing through the cities,
through the fields,
Bearing down on the cycle of
destruction and creation
death and new life
Until time stopped in anticipation.

Then Miriam and the Israelites sang this song to the
Source of Being.

(Ex. 15:1, RECONSTRUCTED)[1]

At that moment the woman sang
Encouragement to She Who Brings Forth
Deliverance to those who come forth.
Through the body split apart
the opening to life,
Through the waters of birth
the tears which are ocean
the ocean which is blood,
is the sign of the covenant of life
made with all who pass through.

She sang the ancient songs of victory
She sang the song of Anat,
She Who Conquered Sea,

She sang the song of Asherah,
She Who Tread on Sea,
She sang the song that would be handed down
to Deborah and to Hannah,
She sang the song of the Source of Being,
And her voice opened the sea.[2]

Her voice opened the sea,
As she sang the song of Miriam, *Mar-yam*,
the one who orders the sea.

Oh Freedom

ALICIA OSTRIKER

"It says: 'In all their affliction He was afflicted' (Isaiah 63:9).
God said to Moses: 'Don't you feel that I live in trouble, just as
[the people] Israel live in trouble? Know from the place whence I
speak to you—from a thorn bush—that I am, as it were, a part-
ner in their trouble.'"

—EX. *RABBAH* 2:5

What was Fannie Lou Hamer singing in 1945, I wonder, down
there on the plantation in Mississippi picking her three
hundred pounds of cotton a day, what did she hum to herself
while the sweat poured down? Angela Davis, girl my age,
where was she while I was going to Pioneer Youth Camp, what
songs was she learning at the same time as I was learning *No*

Alicia Ostriker is a poet and critic; her most recent book is *The Nakedness of the Fathers: Biblical Visions and Revisions* (Rutgers University Press, 1994).

More Auction Block for Me, and *Solidarity Forever,* and *Allons
Enfants de la Patrie,* and *Hatikvah?* I was learning those
songs at the same time because it was the same struggle. *Oh
Freedom.* When the war was over and those other camps were
opened, pouring the bones and hair, the tattered shoes and
teeth, the eyes of the dead into my shaking cup, what was
Audre Lorde—girl my age—studying? Was she studying hope?
Was she learning *Many Thousand Gone?* Did her grandma teach
her *Let My People Go?*

Critique and Transformation:
A Jewish Feminist Journey

JUDITH PLASKOW

*"It was not only our ancestors whom the Holy Blessed One
redeemed, but us also did God redeem along with them."*
                              —PASSOVER *HAGGADAH*
                              BASED ON BT *PESAHIM* 116B

To many feminists as well as many Jews, the concept of an integrated Jewish feminist identity seems thoroughly contradictory.
For me, however, the development of a feminist consciousness has
brought with it a deepened and transformed understanding of my
relationship to Judaism. I have learned to see Judaism not as a
fixed reality "out there" that I must accept or reject, but as a complex and malleable set of traditions that I and others can shape
toward a feminist future.

Dr. Judith Plaskow, professor of religious studies at Manhattan College, is co-
editor of *Womanspirit Rising* and *Weaving the Visions*, co-founder and former co-
editor of the *Journal of Feminist Studies in Religion*, and author of *Standing Again at
Sinai* (Harper and Row, 1990).

My belief in the possibility of a whole Jewish feminist identity is not something I arrived at quickly or easily. When, toward the beginning of my feminist journey, I spoke at the first National Jewish Women's Conference in 1973, I depicted Judaism and feminism as profoundly at odds with each other. I not only rebelled against the androcentrism of the Jewish tradition that continually turns women into strangers and outsiders, but I felt pulled between Judaism and feminism as competing communities.[1] It was only through a long intellectual, emotional, and spiritual process that I came to see my positing of a split between Judaism and feminism as evidence of my own internalization of Jewish androcentricism.

Beginnings

Not surprisingly, my position at the 1973 conference grew out of and reflected my situation at the time. In the early 1970s, I was an advanced graduate student at Yale, beginning to carve out a feminist scholarly agenda and identity. But in the same period I was coming to feminist consciousness, my Jewish life was moving in a different direction. Having grown up in a Reform home, I began as an adult to explore traditional Jewish observance. At Yale in 1968, I began attending the traditional Hillel *minyan* (prayer quorum) on *Shabbat* (Sabbath). Thus, at precisely the time I became a feminist, I was spending my Saturday mornings as one of very few women sitting segregated at the back of a chapel filled with young men. While I wanted the knowledge and experience that attending the *minyan* gave me, I came to resent deeply my marginality and irrelevance to the purpose for which we were gathered. Women's lack of access to public Jewish religious life was not theoretical for me, but affected me very concretely.

As a graduate student in the back of the Yale chapel, I felt like I was sitting in the back of the bus. Indeed, throughout the 1970s, except for a two-year period when I lived in New York and was a member of the New York Havurah (Jewish worship / study fellowship), I lacked a religious home in the Jewish community.

I had glimpses during this same period of the possibility and reality of women's full participation in Jewish life, but they tended to be fleeting. At the women's conference in 1973, I attended the

Shabbat morning service, where five hundred women prayed together, led entirely by women. A year later, I went to the New York Ḥavurah on *Rosh Hashanah* (New Year) and had my first *aliyah* (honor of reciting the blessings before and after the Torah is read). These moments simultaneously moved and enraged me. At the Jewish Feminist Conference, I was deeply touched to see women carrying and reading from the Torah, to watch middle-aged women who had been traditional Jews their whole lives holding and looking into a Torah for the first time. I was overwhelmed at my own first *aliyah*, hardly believing that there was a place where women could be called to the Torah on the same basis as men. At the same time, however, I was furious that I should have to feel moved and grateful that adult women were now doing what boys and men had always taken for granted.

By the mid-1970s, there was a definite tension between my academic perspective on women and religion and my own relationship to Judaism. As a feminist scholar of religion, I was, in the course of the 1970s, developing a nuanced understanding of the role of women in Western religions. On the one hand, I was deepening my analysis of the ways traditional religions had excluded women both from public leadership roles and on much more fundamental levels of theology and symbolism. On the other hand, I was starting to see that this exclusion was not the whole truth, that women had always found ways to express themselves religiously within and against traditional religious frameworks. On an intellectual level, I began to apply this insight to Judaism, to consider how women had participated in Jewish religiosity—whether as charismatic leaders in the biblical period or as guardians of home observance throughout Jewish history. But even setting aside the fact that virtually no serious historical work had yet been done on women's religious lives in traditional Judaism, the reality of women's subordination and exclusion was far more immediate to me on an emotional level than were the ways women had managed to carve out a niche for themselves in a patriarchal tradition. I recognized that critique was only part of the feminist scholar's task, but emotionally, I was stuck there.

Turning Points

It was only in the course of the 1980s that several turning points led me to a new place as a Jew and a scholar. The first of these was a class I taught in Jewish feminist theology in the summer of 1980, at the first National Havurah Summer Institute. While I had been teaching on women and religion for many years, I had never had the opportunity to focus on Jewish feminist issues in a Jewish context. I offered the class on Jewish feminist theology, unsure whether more than a handful of women and men would be interested in the theological questions that excited me. When I saw my students' hunger for serious theological conversation, however—a number of them had come to the Institute specifically to take my course—I realized that there was a way for me to bring together my Jewish, feminist, and theological concerns. That class was my first experience of Jewish feminist community, and it gave me a sense of personal integration and wholeness that made me hopeful about finding a home within Judaism.

The class and my students' responses to it pushed me to articulate a thorough theological critique of Judaism as a patriarchal tradition. While I had previously developed a theological analysis of Christian patriarchy and had long sensed that the specific manifestations of women's subordination in Judaism were only symptoms of a far-reaching patriarchal worldview, I had never before had a context for working out the connections between women's marginalization and the central categories of Jewish thought. In the aftermath of the Havurah Institute, I wrote "The Right Question is Theological," in which I criticized the concepts of Torah, Israel, and God from a feminist perspective. I argued that halakhic (Jewish legal) change of itself cannot rectify women's situation because *halakhah* is part of the system that women had no hand in creating. Feminists must therefore reach beyond *halakhah* to transform the bases of Jewish life. We must redefine Torah from a starting point that acknowledges the injustice of Torah; we must redefine the community of Israel in such a way as to include the whole of Israel; and we must create new images of God that reflect a holistic understanding of Jewish humanity.[2]

A second development came out of my class and the other feminist classes at the Institute: The decision of several women to create a Jewish feminist space where we could pursue feminist issues in a focused and ongoing way. The next May, sixteen women met at a retreat center in Cornwall-on-Hudson with the modest goal of reconfiguring Judaism in four days! It was the beginning of B'not Esh (Daughters of Fire), a Jewish feminist spirituality collective that has been meeting annually ever since and has been the central context in which I have come to a new understanding of Judaism and of myself as Jew.

This new understanding did not happen all at once. In fact, at this point, two years after my class at the Havurah Institute, I felt as if I had come up against a very solid wall. I had set out a theological critique of Judaism that I could teach, develop, and refine, but it only made me all the more aware of women's marginalization and exclusion. I had called for the reconceptualization of Torah, Israel, and God, but had no idea *how* to reconceptualize them, how to move beyond critique to transformation. I felt that Judaism was what it was, that in many ways it had been destructive to women. It was not clear to me whether it could change or how I could affect it.

I experienced this impasse, moreover, as a communal rather than simply a personal problem. It was mirrored, for example, in our first arguments about liturgy at B'not Esh. The first time we met, we celebrated a traditional *Kabbalat Shabbat* (Friday night service). Part of the group felt empowered and exhilarated at welcoming *Shabbat* in a community of women, and part of the group was furious that we had used traditional male God-language and wasted the opportunity to create something new. But even those of us who were angry had no idea what we wanted to do; we just felt that the purpose of our gathering was to do *something* different, to begin somehow to reshape tradition as women.

Breaking through this impasse was, for me, the result of a confluence of many factors. What symbolized and precipitated it on the academic side was my reading of Elisabeth Schüssler Fiorenza's *In Memory of Her*. This book, which first appeared in 1983, is a feminist theological reconstruction of Christian origins. While fully acknowledging the patriarchal character of Christianity, Schüssler Fiorenza begins from the premise that "the

Christian past [is] women's own past, not just a male past in which women participated only on the fringes or were not active at all." To assume that androcentric texts offer an accurate depiction of reality, she argued, is to collude in women's oppression, for it "does not allow us to restore history to women or to reconceptualize history as *human* history."[3]

I read this book both excited and resisting every word. I made furious notes in the margins asking, "How do you know women participated? Isn't this a large assumption, indeed an *a priori* commitment?" Forced to sort out my feelings for an American Academy of Religion symposium on *In Memory of Her*, I realized that I found the book deeply disturbing because it thrust women into an unaccustomed position of power. To take seriously the notion that religious history is the history of women and men imposes an enormous responsibility on women: It forces us to take on the intellectual task of rewriting all of history; it compels us to take on the communal responsibility of demanding that Judaism transform itself by integrating women's experience. It does these things, moreover, without allowing us the luxury of nursing our anger and waiting for the patriarchs to create change, for it reminds us that we are part of a long line of women who were simultaneously victims of the tradition and historical agents struggling within and against it.

Formulating and analyzing my resistance to Schüssler Fiorenza's book allowed me to see clearly where I was in my relationship to Judaism, and it precipitated an intellectual and emotional shift. I had been angry at "them" for excluding women from Jewish history and Jewish religious participation, and I was waiting for "them" to open the doors. But as Susannah Heschel points out in the introduction to *On Being a Jewish Feminist* (Schocken, 1983), there are no doors or guards that keep women from taking control of our own Jewish lives. In pleading for entry into Judaism, in offering arguments and counter-arguments to attack or mitigate our exclusion, we hold onto the status of outsiders, beholden to others for an active relationship to Jewish tradition. We become like the wicked child of the *Haggadah* (text of the Passover *seder*) who hands over Jewish history to "them," rather than like the wise child who reads herself into the Jewish saga. I realized that, just as I/we were present at the Exodus, so too could I/we take the power to define Judaism and shape what it will become. True, everything in Jewish women's education militated against such activism. I knew few Jewish women who had not internalized a sense of our own ignorance and inadequacy. We Jewish feminists, said the voices in our heads, were not steeped enough in traditional Judaism to dare to change it. Virtually none of us had the advantages of a *yeshivah* (traditional academy of Jewish learning) education. We were not experts in Talmudic argumentation; we did not know midrashic sources like the backs of our hands. And yet given the diversity, fragmentation, and openness of American Judaism, we could begin to create religious communities that filled our needs as women and took our experiences, as well as the tradition, seriously. We could seize the power to create change and see what would happen.

Toward a Feminist Transformation of Judaism

From this point on, my intellectual and Jewish lives began to come together on a new basis. In the winter of 1984, I gave two lectures on Jewish feminist theology to the Women's Rabbinic Network. I had thought I would simply reiterate and expand a theological critique of Judaism, but in fact found myself laying out a fairly detailed program for theological reconstruction. These lectures formed the outline for my book, *Standing Again at Sinai* (Harper and Row, 1990), the writing of which was not only an intellectual project for me but also an important religious one. I experienced writing as an act of reclaiming tradition in light of women's experience. And as I tried to bring together twenty years of Jewish feminist experimentation and writing, repeatedly grounding myself both in other feminists' works and in my own experience of feminist community, I hoped to empower others to find their own voices, construct their own theologies, and reshape tradition from their various perspectives.

Throughout the 1980s, I found my theological commitment to women's empowerment changing my Jewish practice, and my practice feeding and grounding my theology. Indeed, the two have been so closely connected, it is difficult for me to discern the actual direction of influence. I trace my first important experiences of liturgical transformation to a crucial decision made by B'not Esh.

Toward the end of our second meeting, at which we had again struggled with the question of how to worship together, we agreed that, in lieu of seeking consensus on questions of prayer, we would authorize different members of the group to create the kind of religious services that they themselves most wanted. We would all try to be open to a variety of experiences with the understanding that we could discuss and analyze them after the fact. If one of us felt she could not participate in a particular service, that individual would quietly absent herself from the proceedings.

This was one of the most important decisions we ever made. Freed from the futile task of finding a non-existent common denominator, we gave ourselves and each other permission to try out forms of prayer and celebration that opened our imaginations and challenged our religious boundaries. After the second year, we never again read from *the* Torah. Instead, we experimented with different ways of creating and connecting ourselves to Torah. The oldest members shared some piece of their wisdom with the group; we wrote the stories of our mothers and pieced them into a scroll; we told the story of Sinai round-robin in a circle. We left the prayerbook behind and sought to capture its deep structure. We shared poems, food, stories, sacred objects. We sang and danced, and joined in healing circles and group meditations. We had a four-hour *havdalah* (distinction-making ritual that separates Sabbath or holiday from weekday), as well as a brief one in which we were the light and the spices. The result has been that, while different women feel most comfortable with different modes of worship, everyone has had a turn at liturgical invention. Everyone has felt the power of women taking charge of our spiritual lives and speaking out of our own experiences. Everyone has seen how radically a service can depart from traditional form and content, and still feel deeply Jewish and deeply connected to tradition.

During the first years of B'not Esh, I was ideologically committed to bringing this kind of spiritual exploration back to the Jewish community at large, but in fact I experienced such openness to experimentation only in communities of women. There was a large gap between the kind of freedom and spiritual depth I experienced at B'not Esh and the basically sterile traditional egalitarian *davenen* (praying) in which I participated during the rest of the year. I felt—and still feel—that while the non-Orthodox community has been willing to accept egalitarianism, it has, for the most part, not been willing to confront the deeper issues of liturgical change that emerge from a commitment to exploring women's experiences and perspectives. Many *minyanim*—and, indeed, many liberal Jewish institutions—are happy to have women participate in the tradition on male terms, but not at all interested in the kind of transformation that would result from taking women's questions and viewpoints seriously.

Then, several years ago, I found a *havurah* of women and men that has enabled me to experience throughout the year the kind of openness and connection that once I found only at B'not Esh. Meeting one *Shabbat* a month in members' homes, we have made the same agreement with each other that I learned to value at B'not Esh: We take turns at leadership, sharing with the group the kind of davening we most want for ourselves. Using the Sudbury *Siddur* (Beth El, 1980) and *Kol Haneshamah* (Reconstructionist Press, 1994) as our primary sources, we have had services ranging from the fairly straightforward and traditional to those that rely on the underlying structure of the service but fill it with new content. Moreover, in the last couple of years, another *havurah* to which I belong, which for a long time was wary of experimentation, decided to try out new forms of prayer. As we began to spend more time with song, meditation, poetry, and personal reflection, everyone felt amazed at the sudden depth and spiritual liveliness of our services, and our successes have made us more willing to experiment further and differently.

These experiences have strengthened my conviction that feminist concerns are translatable to the larger Jewish community and that feminist experimentation need not be limited to women-only groups. Many of the issues feminists have addressed—the longing for real community, the need for meaningful God-language, the quest for a history that responds to contemporary questions of meaning and identity—are really problems posed by modernity but felt with special keenness by women, who have always been marginalized in the Jewish community. Those of us who, out of desperation, have found ways to address these problems for ourselves have mastered important lessons about process and content from which the larger community can benefit.

If I had to characterize the shift that has occurred in my Jewish life as a result of my feminist commitments, I would say that I have come to a sense of my own power and responsibility to shape my Jewish identity. When I began twenty years ago documenting the grievances of women against Judaism as a patriarchal tradition, it never occurred to me that women could do anything but knock hard on the doors of our traditions, demanding to be let in. I was prepared to argue, to demonstrate, to make a fuss, but I did not believe I had the right or the power to make change in the absence of communal consensus.

To be sure, there are disabilities of women—the continued suffering of *agunot* (women chained to dead marriages) is one example—that can be changed only through broad-based communal action. But, in many areas, women do not have to wait for the entire Jewish community or its leadership to undergo a feminist conversion; we can begin to create spaces in which we practice today what we hope will be the Jewish future.

People sometimes ask me how I keep writing and speaking hopefully about Jewish feminism when often the problems seem overwhelming and there is so much resistance to change. The answer is very simple: I belong to several small communities that nourish and sustain me on a day-to-day basis by honoring women's differences and trying, within their fields of influence, to turn the feminist vision of Judaism into a reality. I feel I have been on a profound intellectual and Jewish spiritual adventure, one I could never have anticipated so long as I envisioned my Judaism and feminism as separate and in conflict.

Revelation

Where Is God for You?
A Jewish Feminist Faith

AMY EILBERG

*"Remove your shoes from your feet, for the place on which you
stand is holy ground."*

—EX. 3:5

*"God says to [us], as...to Moses: 'Put off thy shoes from thy
feet'—put off the habitual which encloses your foot, and you
will know that the place on which you are now standing is holy
ground. For there is no rung of human life on which we cannot
find the holiness of God everywhere and at all times."*
        —THE RABBI OF KOBRYN, ḤASIDIC TALE

Less than two weeks after I was hired as the Jewish chaplain for a
large Christian hospital in the Midwest, I was called on what I still
remember as one of the most difficult pastoral encounters of my
career. I was asked to visit two young parents who had just
learned that their newborn baby had died after several days of
neonatal intensive care. I knew what I was "supposed" to do—
offer the couple a chance to grieve and say goodbye, help them to
plan the difficult days ahead. Yet, when I entered the parents'
room, I was overwhelmed—by the sadness and the sense of
responsibility. How could I possibly be of help to these people?

I did the best I could. Later, I needed some help myself. I
turned to a friend, one of the Christian chaplains at the hospital. I
cried and expressed my feelings about the encounter—my sorrow,

---

Rabbi Amy Eilberg, the first woman ordained by The Jewish Theological
Seminary, serves as the director of Kol Haneshama, the Jewish Hospice Program
of Ruach Ami, the Bay Area Jewish Healing Center.

my helplessness, my sense of inadequacy. She listened, hearing what I needed to say, and then asked, "Amy, where was God for you in that moment?"

I was stunned by the question. After all, Jews do not tend to think about God that way. We do not think about God as an immediate, caring, comforting presence to be called on at moments of personal need. We do not think of God as a resource at moments of deep feeling. Most of us do not think about God at all. Until, that is, we are really in trouble, really in need, when we are hurting too much to play by the old rules. Then we often find ourselves looking for something more.

I was raised by the old rules. When I was growing up, I never heard a sermon that helped me in any way to think of a God who might work in my life or be of any use to me at all. The austere rabbi of my childhood pronounced "God" as if it were spelled "G-a-w-d." It was clear to me that this was not a God who was likely to have anything to do with my life.

Raised in a nominally Conservative Jewish family, I absorbed a form of Jewish spirituality based on social action, ethics, and justice for the oppressed and the underprivileged. This kind of spirituality-in-motion bred in me a commitment to *tikkun olam*, to seeing myself as a partner in the work of healing the world. Along with this spirituality, I was raised with a model of Jewish life rooted in ethnicity and acts of identification with the Jewish people. Through this sense of belonging, I learned that I was never alone in the world.

Later, as a teenager, I discovered the world of traditional Jewish ritual, a life of Torah and *mitzvot* (commandments; sacred obligations). I began to connect deeply with Jewish ritual, experiencing the quiet sustaining moment of *Shabbat* (Sabbath) candle lighting, the exuberant joy of *Shabbat* meals shared with family and friends, the deep connectedness of wishing friends in synagogue "*Shabbat Shalom*" (good Sabbath; literally, a Sabbath of peace). I was moved and nourished by eternal Jewish experiences like the profound, wordless comfort of the *Yartzeit* candle (candle burned after a Jew dies, annually on the anniversary of a family member's death, and for the Day of Atonement), or the cleansing "high" of *Ne'ilah* (closing service at the end of *Yom Kippur*).

Adult Spirituality

But when, as an adult, I experienced private pain and struggle, the spirituality I had known failed me. I needed something that would be available to me between rallies, between legislative campaigns. For all the richness of Jewish ritual, I still lacked a way to relate to God between Jewish holidays, between Sunday and Friday, when there was no major life passage at hand, when it wasn't time to *daven Minḥah* (pray the daily afternoon service), nor *Ma'ariv* (daily evening service). I needed a spiritual discipline that could speak to the private places of pain and joy within me. I needed a God who could envelop me when I suffered shame or grief or loneliness, a God who could celebrate with me when life was full of beauty and blessing.

I spent about ten years of my life at The Jewish Theological Seminary. Despite the name of the institution, I was never asked who or what God was in my life, never supported in the difficult and wonderful process of working out a personal theology that could be a resource to me.

Then I landed at a place called Methodist Hospital, and, in a moment of pain, a Christian pastor-friend asked me, "Where is God for you?" The question gave rise to many other fruitful questions that have guided my spiritual journey ever since: Why have we as Jews moved so far away from heartfelt experiences of God/the Creator/the Source of Being/A Higher Power? How do we go about retrieving this essential part of who we are? Where do we turn in times of crisis? What soothes our pain when we hurt, gives us hope when life is cruel, fills in the gaps when we feel wounded and empty? How do we connect our own spiritual lives with our people's collective journey? How can we continue to experience divine revelation and guidance? I thank God for the people sent into my path who asked, "Amy, where is God for you?" Teachers began to show up in many unlikely places.

Male and Female Images of God

For years before that turning point at Methodist Hospital I had been deeply engaged in exploring the meaning of the fact that Jewish liturgy predominantly imagines God in male terms, as father, king, warrior, judge, and lawgiver. Now, in feminist spiritual communities, I began to experience the different texture of women's spirituality, the sense of feminist religious community as a source of nurturance rather than judgment, of comfort more than command, as midwife to growth, connection, and spiritual immediacy. I wondered how we might expand our images of God to embrace women's experience as well as men's. More and more often, I asked myself, "What kind of God do you believe in?" Answers began to appear everywhere—everywhere, that is, that I brought my full attention, every time I could become conscious of the gifts of life.

Then, I gave birth to my daughter. Exhausted for some days afterwards, I let ten days go by without davening (praying), despite my years-long practice of praying every morning. On the second *Shabbat* of Penina's life, I was again physically and emotionally able to open the *siddur* (prayerbook). For an exquisitely clear moment, I realized that, before giving birth, I had a very specific image of God in my head. It was a male God, a punitive God, a judge, who would be critical of my allowing days to pass without praying to Him, even as I healed from surgery and cared for a newborn baby. This was the old-man-with-the-long-white-beard-God of my childhood, reinforced, I must admit, by my internalized image of some of my teachers at the Seminary. This, I now painfully realized, was the God to whom I had always prayed.

God of the Everyday

In my prayer that extraordinary evening, I encountered a new (read: ancient) image of God—feminine, loving, embracing, joyful. Far from wanting to judge me for the lapse in performing my normal religious obligations, this Mother God rejoiced in just how sacred these last days had been. I had not prayed from the *siddur*, but I had been filled with silent prayers as I anticipated Penina's birth. I was overwhelmed with gratitude when she emerged healthy. I was struck by the utter holiness of the tasks of caring for her, nursing her, rocking her, marveling at her. The God I encountered for the first time that night understood all this very well. The Mother God rejoiced in my birth as a mother.

This experience helped me shift the site of my theological journeying from my head down toward my heart. I learned that I did *not* believe in that Sunday School version of God, the God who is the answer to the question, "Is there Someone sitting up there in heaven?" God was becoming for me an answer to a different set of questions: What is it that makes life worth living? What is it that allows people to find meaning in the midst of unspeakable suffering, to find strength in times of pain and loss? How do I cultivate a sense that life is good, that I am cared for, that I am not alone, even in difficult times? What can I do to nourish sanctity in my life?

I began to experience God in unpredictable times and places. Gradually, I found myself no longer needing to wait only for the grand peak moments of life—the birth of a child or a visit to Grand Canyon—or the great Jewish peak moments like the *Kol Nidrei* (*Yom Kippur* eve service) or the arrival of a planeload of Soviet Jews in Israel. I would find myself stopping in the midst of everyday activities and noticing, with wonder and satisfaction, that I felt myself standing on holy ground. There was sanctity, there was an awareness of a Higher Power, there was a sense of divine revelation for me when: One bereaved family turned to comfort another in the waiting room of an intensive care unit, after the death of their own loved one; a woman dying of anorexia told me of her hope that she might learn to experience the small miracles in life—like the presence of someone who cared on a day when she felt very low; a woman struggling with profound depression spontaneously opened her well-worn Bible to Psalm 126 and joyfully read to me, "Those who sow in tears will reap in joy"; a friend spoke to me from a place of deep genuineness and caring, and, listening, it suddenly clicked for me—this is the voice of God.

I have been finding God at absolutely ordinary moments: When a stranger admires the natural streak of white in my hair, when the clouds hang in a particularly beautiful way over the hills where I live, when my daughter reaches for my hand, when a friend calls to say "I was thinking about you." I have begun to find God in the everyday events of my life, in the awesomely abundant gifts of friendship in my life, in the twists and turns of events that so often bring me exactly what I need, in the opportunities I am given to touch and care for others.

I am beginning really to know that I can find God within me as well; for me, the teaching of the first chapter of Genesis—that we are all created in the image of God—means that God is present within me. When I am really present to myself, when I say "no" to the noise and distractions that keep me from my innermost sense of what is true, when I slow and quiet down and listen to the still, small voice within, the voice of God can speak to me and through me.

Finding God in Prayer

I have learned that God is in every breath I breathe. This is precisely the biblical teaching: That humanity was created as the union of the dust of the earth and the breath of God. If I am quiet enough, attuned enough, ready enough, I can find the presence of God moving through me with each breath. This is implied, too, in the teaching of the last verse of the Book of Psalms: "*Kol haneshamah tehallel yah* (with every breath I praise God)." Every moment can be an opportunity for gratitude, for awareness of everyday blessings, for a sense of the miraculous. My very breath, my every breath, can be a vehicle for awareness of God in my life at any moment.

The work of gaining awareness of God's presence began for me with learning to take notice of the real events of my life, learning to cultivate everyday consciousness of the beauty and blessedness and sanctity in life, moment by moment. Having devoted years to this goal, I found the *siddur*—formerly a beloved collection of familiar, required prayers—suddenly opening itself to me anew as a source of sometimes-overwhelming riches.

Some days it is the *Birkhot Hashaḥar* (morning blessings based on BT *Berakhot* 60b) that speak most deeply to me. These blessings are a spiritual exercise walking me through the gifts of morning: The gift of being created just as I am; the capacity to see again, to dress again, to move my limbs, to touch the earth beneath my feet, to know that my every need will be attended to. This is an exercise in mindfulness, teaching us to slow down and fully awaken, preparing us to take grateful notice of the unique gifts of each moment of each day.

Some days it is the *Modim* (thankfulness) prayer of the *Amidah* (series of blessings that is the centerpiece of every prayer service), that most powerfully claims my attention. *Modim anaḥnu lakh...* "Thank You, God, for our lives that are placed in Your hands, for our souls that are entrusted in Your care, for the miracles that are with us every day, the wonders and the goodness that are in each moment, morning, noon, and night. God of goodness, Your mercy is unbounded. God of Compassion, Your lovingkindness is everlasting. We turn always to You." This is a powerful lesson in gratitude and surrender.

At other times, when I am fearful or agitated, out of balance or confused, I am helped to place my life in God's hands with the powerful words of the *Adon Olam* prayer: "In Your hand I place my soul, when I wake and when I sleep. My spirit and my body are in Your care. God is with me, I have no fear."

The question "Where is God for you?" is no longer so hard to pose or to answer. The language of this search may have grown foreign to us as Jews, but, thank God, we are beginning to reclaim it. The territory is not far from us. It is extremely close—embedded in our own lives and in our sacred texts. As with Moses, so with us, holy ground is right under our feet. We need only open our eyes and see.

Noticing the Flame: A Meditation

The following meditation explores how we may become aware of God's presence in our lives, how we can notice the sacred and extraordinary in the apparently ordinary twists and turns of life. It is inspired by the story of Moses at the burning bush (Ex. 3:1–5), particularly as interpreted by Rabbi Lawrence Kushner in *God Was in This Place and I, i Did Not Know* (Jewish Lights Publishing, 1991). Through Kushner's eyes, I came to understand that the story of the burning bush is not that of an external miracle, but of an ordinary person in the midst of ordinary life, suddenly waking up to the wonders around him and within him, suddenly hearing the voice of God. It could be the story of every one of us, every day. Personal revelation continues after the communal revelation at Mt. Sinai, even as it happened to Moses and others before Sinai.

Let your eyes close. Allow your body to find a comfortable position in your chair. Give yourself a leisurely moment to make yourself perfectly comfortable. Notice the air moving through you as you breathe. Feel the air entering your nostrils, moving through you, filling your lungs, and then flowing out again. Be aware of the peaceful rhythm of your breath—in and out, in and out.

See yourself at an important time in you life—a time of transition and change. You have seen conflict, you have known fear, you have had to travel far from home. You sense that more changes may be coming.

Imagine a grassy hillside and, in it, a large herd of white and spotted sheep, grazing. You are the shepherd caring for that herd: Many creatures are dependent on you. You are busy with the countless daily tasks of caring for them, moving them along, through the wilderness, feeding them, keeping them on course. There are many demands at every turn. Think of all your daily cares and responsibilities. You are much too busy to pay attention to the scenery or to your own inner life.

Pause for a moment. As you hurry along a path, notice a bush that is on fire. Your first instinct is to move on. A small brushfire in the wilderness—it will take care of itself; you must hurry on to your tasks. You have so much to do.

But something captures your attention. You pause to take notice. Watch the bush quietly for a few moments, see that the bush is burning, but not being consumed. There is something wondrous here. Take some time to peer into the fire. Quietly watch the flicker of the flames, the play of light and shadow. You are bathed in the soft light of the crackling fire. Still, the bush maintains its size and shape.

Then, you hear it: It is the voice of God, calling to you. "Yes," you answer, "*Hinneni*, I am here." "Stay where you are," says the Voice. "This is holy ground." "I have a job for you," says the Voice. "I am listening," you answer silently.

Look closely, and savor the sight of this extraordinary place. What does it look like? Sound like? Smell like? Notice how you feel being here, in this place, in this dialogue with God. Listen to the Voice.

Allow yourself to linger for a while. Ask yourself and discover: What have you been sent here to learn today? Peer into the flames for a few moments, and honor this holy place you have encountered. Know that you can come back any time you choose.

Very gently, prepare to return to the room where you are sitting. Draw slowly away from the lovely sight of the burning bush. Ask the Voice to speak once more. Pause and listen. Now let the Voice fade into silence. Watch the bush grow smaller and smaller in the distance. Remember the room you are returning to. Notice again the breath moving through you, the breath of life, the breath of God. Stay with your breath for as long you like, then slowly open your eyes.

As you return to full consciousness, remember the image of the burning bush that captured your attention. What are the small flames in your life that can bring you to an awareness of God's presence, the vehicles that bring you close to a sense of the holy in you and around you? Who or what jolts you out of busy-ness and routine and into aliveness to the beauty and wonder of life? Is it a partner? a child? a friend? the memory of someone you have lost? Is it a conflict, a source of pain, a loss that may actually invite you into God's presence? Is it solitude? Is it being in nature? Is it an experience of joy? Of gratitude? Is it the lights of *Shabbat* (Sabbath)? Of *havdalah* (distinction-making ritual that separates Sabbath or holiday from weekday)? Is there a single "flame" that regularly gets your attention? Do you shift from one to another? Have your "flames" changed over the years?

You may wish to do this exercise periodically, to check in on the ways you are growing in connecting with the sacred in your life. You really can find that holy place again. The place can be right here, right now.

Talmud Torah

RUTH S. FAGEN

"Those who study Torah give light wherever they are."
                               —EX. *RABBAH* 36:3

"Why was the Torah given first to women?...So they would
lead their children to Torah."
                               —EX. *RABBAH* 28:2

A memory of a first beginning, Jerusalem: My first taste of Talmud. Oh
the sweetness of it—I feel swept away, drifting on the sea of the Talmud.
My soul yearns for the words on pages I did not even know existed a few
months earlier. Time stands still—2 a.m., 4 a.m., and I am still in the
beit midrash *(study hall), swaying my new sway, thinking, probing,*
exploring the same words over and over. I love as I have never loved
before; I think in a way I never knew I could. My mind expands, and I
feel that I can now find the answers to all the questions I have been ask-
ing. I sense the Shekhinah *(close-dwelling presence of God, associated*
with the feminine), and I know that if every Jew engaged in talmud
torah *(Jewish learning; study of Jewish texts) for at least part of every*
day, olam haba *(the world to come) would be established here on earth.*

A memory of a new beginning, New Haven. I have just finished pre-
senting our Shabbat *(Sabbath) study group with an overview of femi-*
nine/feminist symbols in Exodus and the Haggadah *(text of the*
Passover *seder). Pregnant with my first child, I have found images of*
birth, renewal, women's stories, women's dreams everywhere I looked
this year. Old symbols have taken on new meanings; recently discovered
interpretations have enriched my appreciation of ancient events. I feel
transformed, infused with a new understanding of the Festival of
Freedom, of myself, and of my relationship to Exodus. I feel as if I have
been reborn, as if I have passed through the narrow walls of water lead-
ing me from Mitzrayim *(the confining place; Egypt), to the promised*
land of Torah. I start the afternoon gingerly, almost apologetically, afraid

---

Ruth S. Fagen teaches Talmud and Rabbinics in a variety of forums, including
The Jewish Theological Seminary, the Drisha Institute for Jewish Education, and
the Department of Jewish Education in New Haven, Connecticut.

of appearing too radical, too much a "feminist," at the same time wary of failure, knowing that in different circles I am accused of not being "feminist" enough. As the afternoon wears on and we move toward the dawn of a new week, I feel strengthened, confident. I know that by adding my insights, asking my questions, I am helping to complete the picture that the Rabbis began drawing 2000 years ago.

The Nature of Study

To approach a text is to discover new meanings and fresh insights, even when the questions and answers seem old. It is an experience at once communal and personal. We are in dialogue with the words on the page, with the Sages of the past, with future generations who will study these same texts, reflected through *our* interpretations and explications. A product of the divine-human interaction through the ages, these are the writings of that which cannot be written, the attempts of mere humans to understand what God wants from us. We turn the words over and over, discovering what they offer, listening for revelation. Losing ourselves in the text, we let the spaces as well as the letters speak to us. In the act of *talmud torah*, we are partners with God, helping to bring the *Shekhinah* back to her rightful dwelling place on earth. "When two people are engaged in Torah study, the *Shekhinah* dwells with them" (BT *Berakhot* 6a). Thus, study is for me a religious act.

And yet, and yet. Slowly a note of dissent creeps in. How can I ignore the marginality of women in Rabbinic society? How often do I have to grapple with a source that demeans, or perhaps (just) ignores, women? Will the knowledge that women's voices and experiences have for the most part been left out of the sacred discussions I am studying ultimately drive me away from the texts that have come to be such an integral part of my life? In 1990, a female rabbinical student asked me how I could teach Talmud, since the Talmud is such a misogynist document. At that moment, I am afraid, I did not have much of an answer for her. Can books that we might call sexist also be called holy? What shall we do with the negative messages of our past? How is it that I, as a woman, not only teach these texts, but love them, too?

Women Readers and Male-Authored Texts

Over the past years, these questions have come to occupy me more
and more. It is both necessary and easy to acknowledge that *talmud
torah* appeals to me specifically as a woman. The emphasis on
study with *ḥavruta* (study partner), the notion that collaboration
and cooperation yield the best results, resonate with my own
thoughts and needs. The fluidity of interpretation, the dialecti-
cal/dialogical nature of Talmudic rhetoric remind me of
approaches women generally take to problem solving. The tendency of the Talmud to investigate all aspects of an issue, to consider all possibilities, no matter how remote and seemingly
divorced from reality, lets me feel that nothing, *no one* is beyond
the scope of inquiry and discussion. The fact that many Talmudic
passages do not resolve the legal question at hand reminds me that
getting an answer is not always important, that sometimes we *cannot* get an answer. The Talmudic concept that there is no one truth,
but rather that the very act of inquiry is the essence of what God
wants from us, reflects the way in which I as a woman try to conduct my life. In all these areas, I feel drawn to, not alienated from,
traditional modes of study.[1]

Yet none of this explicitly addresses the concerns raised above.
For women to be fully included in Rabbinic sources written by, for,
and about men, requires four separate endeavors, none of which
have been a part of traditional study until recently.

- **First**, it is vital to acknowledge the misogynist elements
  within a text, whether they ignore women or are overtly
  negative toward them. Since these sources comprise a significant portion of traditional texts, it would be dishonest if
  not destructive simply to bury them, striking them from
  our collective consciousness. Yet they need to be taught in
  an aware fashion that allows us to express our discomfort.

- **Second**, we need to seek those traditional texts, sometimes
  well known, more often hidden and esoteric, which speak
  to us in positive terms of women and women's experiences.[2]

- **Third**, in those places where women's voices are overtly silent, we need to uncover the echoes and whispers that have been left us.[3] Where no voice is heard at all, we need to add our own voices, creating stories that speak from and to our experience, as well as from the experiences of the women in our past.[4]

- **And finally**, after infusing questions of gender into our study, we must strive to reveal that *talmud torah*, like all forms of worship, in its purest sense transcends easy classification by gender and ultimately reveals itself as a *human* endeavor. Thus, what might begin as a woman-centered reading should ultimately provide us with a reading that enriches the understanding and identity of all.

Obviously, these approaches are not strictly sequential. And one cannot always apply all four principles to the same text. The methodology emerges *from* the text and is not *imposed* on it. In fact, my formulation of these principles of Torah study emerged from study sessions. I would like to invite you to join me in a text study that will, I hope, illuminate how I approach *talmud torah* and how these four methods and endeavors can be applied.

Haroset: Oppression and Redemption

That positive views of women can remain hidden, forgotten, or ignored was vividly illuminated for me a number of years ago when I encountered a statement in the Talmud: "It was as a reward for the righteous women at that time, that the children of Israel were redeemed from Egypt" (BT *Sotah* 11b). Why had I not found this statement and the accompanying *midrash* in any liberal *Haggadot*? The second endeavor noted above points to the need for exploring traditional texts that reflect and value women's experiences. Further investigation revealed that this *midrash* is linked to the *haroset* (sweet apple mixture) found on the *seder* plate (ritual object displaying six Passover symbols).

In BT *Pesahim* 116a, two explanations are given for the requirement to eat *haroset* on Passover. The more famous, offered by Rabbi Yohanan, is *zekher letit* (in memory of the clay). *Haroset*, a sign of our oppression, reminds us of the mortar used by the slaves to build bricks in Egypt. Rabbi Levi, however, suggests that *haroset* is *zekher letappua'h* (in memory of the apple tree). While this response explains the common Ashkenazic custom of using apples for *haroset*, its meaning is not at all clear. In his commentary on this passage, Rashi explains that the Israelite women gave birth to their children outside, under apple trees, to prevent the Egyptians from realizing that they were in labor and killing their male infants. Rashi supports this story by quoting from the Song of Songs 8:5: "Under the apple tree I roused you—it was there your mother conceived you, there she who bore you conceived you." The Hebrew word *orartikha* (I roused you) is understood by Rashi to mean under the apple tree *I brought you forth, I gave birth to you*. Thus, the *haroset* is a sign of the bravery of Israelite women, who left their homes to give birth in the open fields, where, miraculously, they experienced no struggle or pain.

Other Versions of the *Haroset* Story

Our understanding of the role of the Israelite women and the symbolism of *haroset* is enhanced by still other texts, including Rashi's commentary on the laver and its stand in the ancient tabernacle (Ex. 38:8); these ritual objects were made from "*mar'ot tzov'ot*." The meaning of the Hebrew word *tzov'ot* is uncertain, but the phrase is generally understood to mean "the mirrors of the women crowding." To explain this difficult phrase Rashi draws on a *midrash* found in *Tanhuma Pekudei* 9. According to this source, the mirrors were cosmetic compacts that the women would use when beautifying themselves. Moses rejected the women's donation of these mirrors to the tabernacle because he felt that their purpose was to further the *yetzer hara* (evil inclination, the common Rabbinic term for human passion and sexuality). God, however, exclaimed, "Accept them, for they are more precious to me than all other contributions, for it was through these mirrors that the women gave birth to *tzeva'ot* [huge armies] while in Egypt." When their husbands were exhausted from the labor Pharaoh had imposed upon them, the women would bring them food and drink and induce them to eat. Then they would take their mirrors and gaze at themselves together with their husbands, all the while teasing and flirting. After thus arousing the men, they conceived and gave birth out in the open, as it says in Song of Songs 8:5—"I roused you under the apple tree" (referring to the fields where the men worked).

This story is obviously connected to Rashi's Talmud commentary, but it differs in a number of key points. In his commentary on Exodus, Rashi connects the apple trees (which are not mentioned in *Tanḥuma*) to the place of seduction and conception, as well as birth. (Notice that the verse from Song of Songs speaks of both birth and conception.) As a result, the daring and brave nature of the women's action is related to their sexuality. Here, as a woman, I begin to feel uncomfortable with what Rashi says. I must face the first, painful endeavor laid out above: Encountering misogynist elements within a text. When women exercise their capacity for seduction, Rashi, in keeping with much of Rabbinic literature, focuses on what he perceives as the negative and potentially dangerous side of women's sexuality. Women's sexuality is apparently antithetical to sacred structures. Thus, it is possible to read this text as one among many that marginalize women, prevent them from partaking fully in religious life, and emphasize the fundamental otherness of female sexuality. Yet the continuation of the story is vital. For here, in contradistinction to Moses, *God* lovingly and completely embraces the women's gift. Indeed, God vindicates female sexuality by explaining to Moses that the purpose of the women's overt sexuality *is* sacred, i.e., to raise an army of hosts that will ultimately leave Egypt to serve God at Sinai. Inasmuch as both Moses and Rashi, by virtue of their humanity, are bound by the attitudes of their historical periods, their negative attitude toward women and female sexuality can been seen as ephemeral. This stands in contrast to the unimpeachable divine affirmation of women's centrality and connection to the sacred. By focusing on the end of the story, on God's reaction, we can (re)claim this *midrash* as a celebration of female sexuality.

It is vital to acknowledge that, even according to this reading, women's sexuality is valued only within the "safe" confines of marriage and sex for the purpose of procreation. Therefore, we cannot pretend that this *midrash* unhesitatingly embraces women as powerful sexual beings. Nevertheless, we must not minimize the importance of what is being said. The very act of seducing their husbands brings the Israelite women closer to God by helping to fulfill God's covenantal promise: "I shall surely make your descendants as numerous as the stars in the heaven...." (Gen. 22:17)

We ought to marvel as God did at their actions. It is incumbent upon us to investigate and celebrate their behavior, to uncover that which is only hinted at in the text (the third endeavor), to let the voices of these women ring out loud and strong from the pages of the ancient text. We must assume that the women, like the men, found themselves utterly depleted physically. Yet for the men, exhaustion seems to have spread from the body to the soul. Surely we are to infer from the "forward" actions of the women that the men had stopped sleeping with them. In the version of the story presented in *Tanḥuma*, it is Pharaoh himself who forbids the men to return home from the fields at night, in order to prevent cohabitation. Thus, the seduction of the men is also an act of defiance against Pharaoh. Gone unchecked, the nation-wide celibacy, whatever its initial cause, would have meant success for Pharaoh and decimation, perhaps disappearance, for the Israelites.

In the midst of this darkness, through the depths of despair, the Israelite women clung to life, present and future. What did it mean at that time to seduce one's husband and harbor hopes of conceiving? Where did they find the courage, the vision, the *faith* to understand that reaffirming life was the only appropriate response to the inevitable death that seemed to await them and their children? Can we imagine a more powerfully religious response to Pharaoh's actions than the one provided by the Israelite women—to trust in God sufficiently to act for the continuity of God's people?

Women and God's Deliverance

It is this trust that Rabbi Avira refers to in BT *Sotah* 11b. He tells a story quite similar to the one provided by Rashi in Exodus, but its implications are more affirming of women, and thus it better serves the (second) endeavor of seeking out texts that relate women's experiences in positive terms. When the Israelites were in Egypt and the women went to draw water, God arranged for small fish to enter their pitchers. Armed with these aphrodisiacs, the women cooked the fish, washed and anointed themselves, and fed their husbands in the fields. They seduced their husbands and conceived there, returning to deliver their children in the fields under the apple tree, as it says in Song of Songs 8:5: "Under the apple tree I caused you to come forth [from thy mother's womb]." Playing on the word "I" in the verse, Rabbi Avira enlarges on God's role in helping not only to conceive but to birth these children. Since there were no midwives present in the fields, God sent down from the heavens One who washed and straightened the limbs of the babies. The prooftext is Ezekiel 16:4–5: "As for your birth, when you were born your navel cord was not cut, and you were not bathed in water...nor were you swaddled.... [O]n the day you were born, you were left lying...in the open field."

Thus, it is God who washes, straightens, and beautifies these children, God who performs the human (female) function of midwife, God who miraculously saves the children. When the Egyptians come to the fields to kill them, the women and their babies are swallowed by the earth, and the Egyptians plow over their backs. After the Egyptians depart, the women and their children burst forth like the grass of the fields, in fulfillment of the words of Ezekiel (16:8). These very children, whose conception, birth, and young lives were overseen by God, are the first to recognize the Holy One when God is revealed by the Red Sea. It is they who shout with recognition, "*This* is my God whom I will exult; this is my Lord whom I will revere" (Ex. 15:2).[5]

Here again we see the power and potency of the Israelite women. Even more clearly than in the story drawn from the *Tanḥuma*, women fulfill the divine plan through their actions. They usurp the traditional male role by initiating sexual contacts with their husbands, but here there is no suggestion that women's sexuality is dangerous or negative. Rather, by virtue of exercising their sexuality, the women actually become partners with God, as much as with their husbands. As the women step out of their traditional role, God steps into theirs. God assumes the role of midwife and ultimately protects the newborn children when their mothers, who surely wish to do so, cannot. The awesome nature of what the Israelite women take upon themselves when they go down to the river to find their husbands becomes clear from Rabbi Avira's introductory comment to this entire story: "It was as a reward for the righteous women who lived in that generation, that the Israelites were delivered from Egypt."

The Transformation of Symbols, Text, and Self

How is it that we do not all know this story? We women, who all too often find ourselves in the kitchen tending to the meal while the *Haggadah* is being recited by our men in the dining room, we women were the impetus for God redeeming the people of Israel from Egypt! In telling (us) this story, Rabbi Avira clearly draws on the role that the Bible assigns to women in the story of the Exodus. Long before Moses is ready to confront Pharaoh, the first chapter of Exodus tells us of two courageous midwives, Shifra and Pu'ah, who defied Pharaoh and refused to kill the newly born Israelite males. Long before the community of Israel stood at the Red Sea, the unnamed sister of Moses stood by the water, waiting to see what would happen to her baby brother, assisting at his (re)birth when he was lifted out of that slimy, pitch-encrusted vessel that had been floating on the water, arranging for her mother to nurse the boy, reuniting her family, and insuring that her brother's initial upbringing would be in an Israelite environment. It is surely this biblical background that Rabbi Avira brings to his story. Shifra and Pu'ah, Moses' sister, and even Pharaoh's daughter all defy Pharaoh in their refusal to oppress the Israelites. The Bible and Talmud point to a variety of vital roles played by women. It is our responsibility to uncover them, make them explicit, and share them with all those who are interested in understanding the role the Israelites, as well as God, in bringing about the redemption from Egypt.

This last point is crucial. For ultimately, a fuller understanding of the meaning of *ḥaroset* enriches not only those concerned with women and their role in the Exodus, but all Jews, male and female. Taking the stories in their totality, we can now see that *ḥaroset* is at once *zekher letit*, a sign of our oppression, and *zekher letappua'ḥ*, a sign of the courage shown by the Israelite women in the face of that oppression—the courage that leads to our redemption. These interpretations not only illuminate our view of women's roles in the exodus, but provide a deeper insight into the fundamental message of the *Haggadah* itself, engaging the fourth endeavor by transcending gender issues. Exodus celebrates the movement from oppression/slavery/distance from God to redemption/freedom/closeness to God. The dual meaning of *ḥaroset* reminds us that oppression and redemption are linked as surely as the physical and spiritual are connected in our own lives. It is up to us to take the symbol of our oppression and transform it into something redemptive, whether that "symbol" is *haroset* or a particular page of Talmud. *Matzah* (unleavened bread), the paradigmatic Passover symbol, represents both poverty or affliction on the one hand and God's covenantal relationship with Israel on the other (Deut. 16:3, Joshua 5:9–12, BT *Pesahim* 115b–116a).[6] It is our task to transform every symbol into something not only palatable, but somehow nourishing. Linking the spiritual to the physical, we must call God into our lives and our sexuality. Linking Exodus to the lives of women, we also link ourselves to one another, women to men, generation to generation, united in the ongoing process of fulfilling God's covenant with the people of Israel.

Constructing Holiness

In God's Shadow: The Holiness of Human Labor

AMY BARDACK

"Six days a week you must labor and do all your work."
—EX. 20.9

"They shall not toil to no purpose."
—ISAIAH 65:23

Most of our waking hours are spent working. In homes and offices, for money and for free, we lend our time, talents, and resources to various activities and projects throughout our adult lives. For most of us, work and spirituality are two separate entities, complementary perhaps, but not integrated. Judaism is a religion that concerns itself explicitly with the exigencies of daily life. In the Ten Commandments and several other places in the Torah, we are commanded to work.[1] Yet we lack a theological perspective on work. We look for God on *Shabbat* (Sabbath) and holidays, at weddings, funerals, and baby namings. Work is not the site of our search for the sacred.

Nevertheless, connections between "holy" and "profane" endeavors abound. Working with people with disabilities has shaped my critique of Jewish law on disability; working in theater has affected my experience of ritual. Hearing a surgeon comment on biblical sacrifice, an artist discuss the aesthetics of the *mishkan* (tabernacle), a psychotherapist analyze family dynamics in Genesis, I am convinced that our communities and our Torah can be enriched by the interplay of Judaism and work.

Amy Bardack is a rabbinical student at The Jewish Theological Seminary in New York.

What Do Working People Want?

Our working lives are replete with yearnings. We struggle for recognition from others and pride in ourselves, for fair treatment and just compensation. We want to contribute something unique, to be indispensable, to make a lasting impact. Above all, there is a desire for meaning and purpose in what we do. As Nora Watson, an editor interviewed in Studs Terkel's book *Working*, stated: "Most of us...have jobs that are too small for our spirit. Jobs are not big enough for people."[2] We want our work to propel us to new heights of achievement, to reflect all our creativity, strength, and idiosyncracies. The role of religion is to help people frame their lives with meaning. The agonies and aspirations we face in our daily work merit a religious response.

Women face particular frustrations in the workplace. Our advancement is impeded by glass ceilings and mommy tracks. Our pride and recognition are compromised by sexual harassment and sexist double standards. Those of us who enter male-dominated fields struggle to assert our female distinctiveness while proving that we are as competent as men. There is inadequate child care, and "pink collar" jobs, as well as housework, are devalued. We are still not getting equal pay for the same or comparable work. A Jewish theology of work encompasses our struggle against gender discrimination as part of a larger religious mandate.

A Jewish Definition of Work

Judaism defines work as *melakhah*. This term is used not only in the command to work six days and rest on the Sabbath, but in two central and extensive biblical accounts of work: God's creation of the world in Genesis and Israel's building of the tabernacle in Exodus. The Rabbis explored the meaning of *melakhah* in order to specify which kinds of activities were to be forbidden on the Sabbath.

Melakhah, as expounded by the Sages, is a relatively broad concept. An activity may be considered *melakhah* whether or not it is done for pay. In this regard, the Rabbis did not distinguish between vocation and avocation. *Melakhah* includes traditional "women's work" such as cooking, cleaning, and sewing, and things we might do purely for fun, such as painting or skating. The command to work six days a week, then, includes certain kinds of housework, leisure activities, and volunteer work, in addition to paid employment.

Melakhah can be a helpful concept in the self-perceptions of working women. Women today continue to suffer from the industrial revolution's restriction of "real work" to the public realm. Our working lives are complicated by parenting, elder care, and household responsibilities, which we shoulder in significant disproportion to men. We receive no compensation and little recognition for all the work we do in the home. Viewing our activities as *melakhah* can help us integrate the tasks we perform at home into our identity as workers.

Most of us do not find perfect correspondence between our sense of mission or calling and our job description. "Rabbi" does not encompass all the skills that I consider part of my identity. When we expand our concept of work into *melakhah*, we do not define a person's work in terms of her job title. She is not a "banker," but someone who works with money, plays the piano, cooks meals, and repairs the leaky faucet—all forms of *melakhah*. From this perspective, a person without a salaried job is not "unemployed," as one certainly "employs" skills and talents in *melakhah*, paid or unpaid. The productive undertakings of retired people and children are also recognized. At the same time, the concept of *melakhah* is helpful on the job. Every paid worker uses a variety of skills—only some of which are part of an official job description. Seeing all our daily activities as *melakhah* helps to elevate and sanctify what we do.

Basing a spirituality of work on the Rabbinic concept of *melakhah* introduces the problem that the holiness of *Shabbat* and holidays derives from the avoidance of *melakhah*. Since holy time is characterized by not working, it might seem inconsistent to claim that *melakhah* has intrinsic spiritual value. However, in examining the biblical and Rabbinic understandings of *melakhah*, particularly in relation to the stories of creating the world and building the tabernacle, the sanctity ascribed to human work becomes apparent. In relation to work as well as rest, *Shabbat* is attached to the creation stories and to the story cycle of the Book of Exodus. We rest in memory of the creation and in imitation of God; we rest, too, in memory of the exodus, as a demonstration of the freedom gained to set our own communal calendar and by refraining from the activities used to build the tabernacle.[3] We work in memory of the creation and in imitation of God; we work in our capacity as free agents and by performing and sanctifying the activities used to build the *mishkan*.

Creating the World

The Torah opens with the beginning of work and the beginning of the world. In six days God imposed order, shape, and definition upon an unformed mass. God differentiated categories (light and dark, land and sea, male and female) and invented new forms of life (plants, animals, humans). At each stage, God evaluated the products of divine labor. Once having created humanity and pronounced the totality of creation "very good" (Gen. 1:31), God took a day to refrain from creative work.

The observance of the Sabbath is understood as an imitation of God's abstinence from work on the seventh day.

> "Six days you shall labor and do all your work (*melakhah*), but the seventh day is a Sabbath of the Lord your God.... For in six days the Lord made heaven and earth and sea and all that is in them, and He rested on the seventh day" (Ex. 20:9–11).[4]

Implicit in these verses is the message that our work is also meant to be done in imitation of God. God's activities through the first six days serve as a paradigm of human labor.

Human metaphors are used to describe God's work throughout the Bible and Rabbinic literature. The verbs used for the creation of the world—'a.s.h (make) and y.tz.r (form, create)—are used in relation to human creative acts as well. In a *midrash* (Rabbinic legend) on the creation story, God is likened to an architect who consults blueprints (i.e., the Torah) in building the world (Gen. *Rabbah* 1:1). The Book of Jeremiah compares God to a potter and Israel to clay (Jeremiah 18:3–10), a metaphor that is expanded in the *Yom Kippur* (Day of Atonement) liturgy, where God is alternatively potter, mason, craftsman, seaman, blower, tailor, and smelter, and we are the clay, iron, wheel, glass, cloth, and silver.

God shapes, molds, and forms us. We, in turn, were given the ability to shape, mold, and form. In granting humans the ability to work creatively, God made us "in Our image, after Our likeness" (Gen. 1:26). Working is both a fundamental part of being human and the aspect of our humanity that is godlike. Human beings are to "fill the earth and master it" (Gen. 1:28), i.e., according to Ramban, to use the earth's resources in the production of new things.[5] We fill the earth by engaging in creative labor, just as God did, and thereby become partners with God in creation.

The obligation to teach one's child a trade (BT *Kiddushin* 29a) is seen by the Rabbis as central: "Rabbi Ishmael taught 'Choose life' (Deut. 30:19)—this refers to [learning and practicing] a trade" (JT *Peah* 1:1). Work also binds us to God, as a *midrash* implies: "Just as the Torah was given as a covenant, so was work (*melakhah*) given as a covenant" (*Avot Derabbi Natan* 11:1). Through human labor, the innovative productivity of the first six days is re-enacted and becomes an *ot* (a sign, especially of covenant). Together, God and human beings create the world anew each day.

Building the *Mishkan* (Tabernacle)

The value and sanctity of human work is made most evident in the account of the construction of the *mishkan*. The Rabbis associated their understanding of *melakhah* with this very account, prohibiting on *Shabbat* the actions deemed necessary to build the tabernacle.[6] But these same activities, when performed during the other six days, brought God closer to Israel than ever before. God said: "Let them make me a sanctuary, that I may dwell among them" (Ex. 25:8). Doing *melakhah* is what enables God's presence to reside within a community. Through our work, we can make space in the world for God.

On the individual level, work helps us cultivate ourselves. By developing and perfecting our special skills and talents, we come to a fuller sense of our own uniqueness. At the same time, people also find work valuable on the communal level. It is rewarding to feel that we are contributing something to society. Even when we cannot map the effects of our work on others, just knowing that we are part of a chain of transmission brings its own satisfaction.

Working takes us beyond individual concerns and needs; it connects us to other people and to the world at large.

Both self-cultivation and contribution to community were integral aspects of the building of the *mishkan*. The Torah, normally
quite terse in its descriptions of human activity, recounts every element of this project in detail. The scrupulous attention given to
each task bespeaks the honor and value attributed to individual
skills. Each person in the community is invited to contribute his or
her own particular expertise to the job (Ex. 35:10). Talents and
skills are seen as gifts from God. God says of Betzalel, the head of
the project: "I have endowed him with a divine spirit (*ru'ah elohim*)
of skill, ability, and knowledge in every kind of craft" (Ex. 31:3).
Ru'ah elohim was also present during the creation of the world
(Gen. 1:2). Betzalel, expert craftsman of the tabernacle, is a reflection of God, who is master artisan of the world. Hence Betzalel's
name, parsed *betzel el*, means "in the shadow of God," recalling
Genesis 1:26. The craftspeople who made the priestly garments
were also filled with God's spirit (Ex. 28:3). All those who contributed their skills to the *mishkan* derived their proficiency—literally their "wisdom of heart"—from God (Ex. 36:1–2). We are all
like Betzalel, because all human beings were created *betzel(em) elohim* (in the image/shadow of God). Thus, *ru'ah elohim* can be present in *all* forms of *melakhah*. When people work to perfect their
special skills, God's spirit is inside them.

The story of the *mishkan* also highlights the communal dimension of work. *All* the members of the community of Israel were
involved in the building of the sanctuary. In several instances, the
Torah specifies that women contributed labor and resources to the
project.[7] Such explicit reference to the public contributions of
women in communal activities is quite unusual in the Bible. In this
ideal work situation, women and men participated together without discrimination or competition. Every person had an equal
stake in the goal of their labor: To enable God's presence to dwell
among them. Moreover, the *midrash* stresses that each person's
work was valued equally: "God's command [to build the ark]
applied to each Israelite alike, so that no one should say to his fellow 'I contributed more to the ark than you'" (*Tanhuma Vayakel* on
Ex. 25:10).[8]

The community itself was transformed by the work. The construction of the *mishkan* united the Israelites in common purpose, and had a therapeutic effect on the group. Following immediately after the incident of the golden calf, the building of the *mishkan* functioned, according to a traditional interpretation, as *teshuvah* (repentance) for their sin.[9] The people of Israel progressed from worshipping the product of their labor, the golden calf, to worshipping the source of their creativity, God. Labor was central both to their spiritual failings and to their spiritual development, and that, I think, is why Moses blessed them after they finished the work (Ex. 39:43). Through that work project, the people of Israel liberated themselves from the labor of the past—slave labor. The exalted, non-oppressive work of the *mishkan* was the antithesis of slavery. In contrast to slaves who are forced to work, they contributed voluntarily (Ex. 25:2) and could use their special skills and talents. *Melakhah* was the vehicle by which Israel completed its evolution from an enslaved, oppressed people to a productive, free society. The account of the tabernacle teaches us that the work of a community and its spiritual welfare are interdependent: The Israelites were both united and transformed by working together.

Work and Redemption

The construction of the *mishkan* is a model of sacred work. When we develop our best skills and talents, when we contribute toward the good of a community, when we work with others in a non-competitive, non-discriminatory manner, *melakhah* can be a vehicle for spiritual growth. Unfortunately, for many people there is a great disparity between this ideal vision and their real work experiences.

The Torah acknowledges this disparity. Adam's curse describes the unfulfilling, unexalted drudgery with which many workers today can identify: "Cursed be the ground because of you; by toil shall you eat of it all the days of your life.... By the sweat of your brow shall you get bread to eat" (Gen. 3:17–19).

The curse may be descriptive of human work, but it is not prescriptive.[10] Rather, it is our responsibility to transform work from a curse to a blessing. This may seem utopian. How can we find meaning as workers in the face of an unfulfilling job, a difficult boss, or working conditions that are otherwise intolerable? We can try to improve a job situation by joining unions, asking for a promotion or transfer, filing harassment charges. We can think about ways in which goods or services we help produce are ultimately beneficial to people, recognizing that our own job, however seemingly minor, is indispensable toward that end.[11] We can remember that our best *melakhah* might be found outside of our job, in other activities in which we engage, that our job is not the sole reflection of our abilities as workers. It is helpful to understand, too, that job alienation and dissatisfaction are widespread social problems and not just our own private concern. In general, they reflect the inadequacies of our society, rather than its individual workers.

The redemption of Israel from Egyptian bondage is a paradigm of the ultimate redemption of all humanity. Some people still toil under oppressive conditions not unlike those of slavery in Egypt. Yet, as the *Haggadah* (text of the Passover *seder*) teaches: "In every generation, each person should feel as though s/he were redeemed from Egypt." Transforming work from a form of bondage or a matter of indifference into a holy activity is central to the process of redemption. That discrimination, dehumanizing conditions, and insufficient training deprive many people of sacred work experiences is unacceptable from a Jewish perspective. It is a religious obligation to help all people discover the holiness of human labor.

There is a Ḥasidic tale about a man who knitted hosiery all day long, reciting psalms by heart as he worked. He derived satisfaction from doing his work well. The Baal Shem Tov called him "the cornerstone which will uphold the Temple until the Messiah comes."[12] When we give people the opportunity to do purposeful, non-oppressive *melakhah*, we bring the world nearer to redemption. Toward that end, we should strive to redeem human labor itself.

Taking Personal Inventory: Exercises and Meditations

The Rabbis detailed the thirty-nine categories of *melakhah* to specify what we should *not* do on Shabbat. It is also possible to use the six days of creation to explore what we *should* do on weekdays.

1. Write down all the activities you engage in on a regular basis, not just in your salaried jobs but in chores, volunteer work, and leisure time. Then read through the first chapter of Genesis and try to find parallels between your labor and God's. For example:

   God: Ordering, classifying, and systematizing matter.
     Us: Sorting, computing, and analyzing data; advancing scientific theories; cleaning and organizing homes and offices; repairing and perfecting machinery; helping people make order of their lives as counselors or therapists.

   God: Creating through speech (e.g., "and God said, let there be light, and there was light" [Gen. 1:3]).
     Us: Writing, public speaking, teaching, and performing.

   God: Evaluating products of labor (1:4, 10, 12, 18, 21, 25, 31).
     Us: Marketing, critiquing, consulting, editing.

   God: Giving food and nourishment (1:29–30).
     Us: Cooking, farming, nutrition counseling, waiting tables.

   God: Designing and building a world.
     Us: Architecture, engineering, construction work, carpentry.

When we try to find meaning in what we do, it can helpful to see how some seemingly mundane activities had cosmic significance in bringing the world to being.

2. Jewish liturgy presents other images of God's labor. In *Birkhot Hashaḥar* (morning blessings based on BT *Berakhot* 60b), we speak of God working for people in various capacities:

God: Clothing the naked.
　Us: Social service for the poor and homeless, clothing sales or manufacturing.

God: Opening the eyes of the blind.
　Us: Optics, ophthalmology, or anything that helps people "see" things in new ways.

God: Freeing the imprisoned.
　Us: Lawyers, judges, jurors; teaching language to new immigrants; helping homebound people; breaking through to autistic or mentally ill people, who are "imprisoned" or isolated from others.

Look through the prayerbook for other examples of divine activities that match your own working life. Choose a favorite passage and read, sing, or meditate on it at the start of your work day.

3. Imagine a favorite skill and envision God doing it. Write a *midrash*, draw a picture, or compose a song to describe your skill on a divine scale.

The image of a working God can help generate a sense of pride and purpose in human labor. Seeing your work as a reflection of God's can help you recognize how you maintain and fortify the world.

Meditations

1. A meditation before work: God filled Betzalel with the divine spirit—literally "the breath of God"—before he worked (Ex. 35:31). Recite: וַיְמַלֵּא אוֹתָהּ/אוֹתוֹ רוּחַ אֱלֹהִים. *"Vayemalleh otah/oto ru'aḥ elohim"* ("And He filled her/him with the divine spirit" [Ex. 35:31]), breathing in the first two words and out the last two. God's gender may be changed to the feminine: וַתְּמַלֵּא אוֹתָהּ/אוֹתוֹ רוּחַ אֱלֹהִים. *"Vatemalleh otah/oto ru'aḥ elohim"* ("And She filled her/him with the divine spirit").

2. A blessing after work: According to Rashi (on Ex. 39:43), Moses blessed the people with the following words upon completion of *mishkan*: "May it be (God's) will that the divine presence abide in the work of your hands."

I suggest reciting this verse or an adapted form:

יְהִי רָצוֹן מִלְּפָנֶיךָ אֲדוֹנָי אֱלֹהַי וֵאלֹהֵי אֲבוֹתַי וְאִמּוֹתַי, שֶׁתִּשְׁרֶה שְׁכִינָה בְּמַעֲשֵׂי יָדָי.

Yehi ratzon milfanekha adonai elohai ve'elohei avotai ve'imhotai shetishreh shekhinah bema'asei yadai.

May it be Your will, *Adonai* my God and the God of my fathers and mothers, that the divine presence abide in all my works.

Creativity

ROSIE ROSENZWEIG

"And every wisehearted woman spun with her hands, and [they] brought that which they had spun, in blue and purple and scarlet yarn, and in fine linen. And all the women whose heart stirred them up in wisdom spun goats' hair.... The children of Israel brought a willing offering to Adonai, *every man and woman, whose heart made them willing...."*
—EX. 35:25–26, 29

"Two cherubim of gold spread their wings out on high, shielding the cover of the ark with their wings, facing one another...."
—EX. 37: 7, 9

Rosie Rosenzweig, author of *The Jewish Guide to Boston and New England* (Jewish Advocate, 1995), has published liturgical poetry and is presently working on a book on the Jewish-Buddhist connection.

Amid the sweet smell of incense and acacia wood,
We work in community with our pictures and words:
As one colors the rams' hair red,
Another carves the jewels into the breast plate,
And, yes another, neck tough, muscles wet and bright,
Tans and smoothes the *taḥash* skins;[1]
Leather-lunged, he croons an unending song.

We sing in concert, all being one, we offer up our skills:
The silver, the gold, and the copper craftsmen
Orchestrate and mold the vessels according to the plan;
The women weave the twisted linen into cherubim,
Lacing the scarlet, purple, and turquoise wool
Into lions, eagles, and oxen.

One begins with timbrel, another a drum
Until we all, as one, are swinging arms and legs
Skirts and hands high in prayerful reach;
In gratitude after a long crossing,
We rest and hope to bring down blessings for our work.

Then out of the gold four wings rise up,
Feather by feather, precious and precise.
Two angels arch above our eyes—
Facing their other in the other;
A shining circle frames their mirrored gaze and glows—
A pulsing Spark—brought down to hold us in its throb;
It stretches towards us, entering and cleansing our hearts,
And makes them wise.

3

Themes of Leviticus/Vayikra Rabbah:
The Sacred Body of Israel

———◉———

What is the relationship between body and soul?
What is holiness and how can I be holy?

omen's lives are collections of little details. We spend our days focused as much on the small items as on the sweeping vistas of human endeavor. Cleaning, cooking, mending clothes, making beds, these have traditionally been the concerns of women. The writer Tillie Olsen perfectly captured this feature of female self-understanding in her story, "I Stand Here Ironing,"[1] in which the entire account of a woman's life is set against the backdrop of this simple repetitive task. Beyond the home as well, women are generally the social workers of culture, tending to the poor, the sick, the aged, and the young.

This "female" attention to minutia is most evident in the Torah in the Book of Leviticus. Biblical scholar Tamara Eshkenazi once remarked—in response to Harold Bloom's theory that a woman wrote much of Genesis[2]—that if any part of the Torah was written by a woman, it was Leviticus. Leviticus is the recipe book, the operating manual, for a complex and finely drawn system of communal holiness. After the intimate family narratives of Genesis and the sweeping theological epic of Exodus, it can be both surprising and disconcerting to encounter the Levitical concern, even obsession, with the detailed rituals of daily life.

In the ancient world of the Torah, the Levitical system was reserved for the priesthood, the descendants of Aaron. After the destruction of the Temple (70 CE), the Rabbis transformed the intricate rules of the priesthood into a set of equally elaborate practices for the common folk, whom they now viewed as an entire "nation of priests" (Ex. 19:6). The average home, particularly the ordinary woman's kitchen, became the site of sacred worship, as historian Dr. Jody Myers discusses in her essay, "The Altared Table: Women's Piety and Food in Judaism."

Jewish women through the ages saw themselves as "priests" in relation to household duties and laws of purity. A wide range of *tkhines* (petitionary prayers for and/or by women, traditionally written in Yiddish) explicitly compare women's sacred household duties—kindling the Sabbath lights, baking *ḥallah* (loaves for Sabbaths and holidays), and going to the *mikveh* (ritual bath)—with the rituals of the High Priest in the ancient Temple.[3] These women's prayers well serve as models for adapting ancient Jewish religious activity to make it relevant to contemporary life.

In addition to style, the basic themes of Leviticus set patterns for centuries of Jewish women's practice. Concerns about food, sex, body image, illness and healing, language, and moral behavior are as profound today as they were in the era of the Bible. What contemporary Jewish woman has not struggled with the shape of her body? Who hasn't welcomed healing in time of illness? Who doesn't have a complicated relationship with food? These are not passé topics.

The Sacred Structure and the Paradigm of Perfection

Leviticus' regulations on these subjects are extensive and minute. Anthropologists such as Mircea Eliade and Mary Douglas explain the underlying purpose of Leviticus as the creation of a social order that makes manageable a chaotic natural world.[4] The well-regulated system of human action in Leviticus symbolizes a sacred cosmic harmony of divine origin. Trespass of the rules threatens the whole community with anarchy, not only in terms of the societal structure, but throughout the entirety of God's universe. Through the divinely revealed social order, the disorderly natural world is to some extent tamed, domesticated, and endowed with blessing.

The religious structure detailed by Leviticus associates differentiation of roles with gradations of holiness. The most holy human being is the male High Priest, then other members of the priesthood, and other functionaries of the cult, and the Israelite male laity. Non-Israelites and women stand at the outer circles of holiness and power.

This sacred hierarchy was represented spatially in the architecture of the Temple and its environs. The innermost room of the Temple, known as the Holy of Holies, was reserved for the High Priest, and even then, only after he had performed numerous immersions and other purification rituals. Women were restricted to the very outer court of the Temple. The Temple modeled structural perfection, and women were peripheral to that model.

The High Priest's body was the equivalent to the Temple in human terms. The High Priest and the animals he offered for sacrifice were "unblemished" males. A physical anomaly or deformity symbolized disharmony and disqualified a man from the priesthood. The "unblemished male" was the paradigm of orderliness—physically "imperfect" men and *all* women did not qualify. In her essay, "Afterbirth," Dr. Judith Glass explores this stigmatization of the anomalous from both a personal and a theoretical perspective.

Although the ideological assumptions of Leviticus may seem remote, in our society as well, women and the disabled are given the message that our bodies are somehow inadequate or unholy because they are "imperfect." Our society has its own physical paradigms, which are especially stringent for women. Today, the ultimate woman is the very thin, trendy, chic fashion model. Like the ancient High Priest she must spend intensive periods of time devoted to maintaining her "perfection." Yet, even then she is not sacred—merely an emblem for our consumer culture.

The drawbacks of the "perfect paradigm" system were addressed in part by the process of democratization begun by the ancient Rabbis after the destruction of the Temple. Through study and observance of sacred ritual, *all* men were elevated to holiness. The full equality and participation of Jewish women would further this expanded understanding of what constitutes sanctity.

Women, Disorder, and Pollution

Since Leviticus views the system of the human community as parallel to the plan of the natural world, it devotes considerable attention to physical concerns that absorb both the social and the natural orders, and form the intersection between the two. Many of these concerns are of particular significance to contemporary women. Menstruation, childbirth, and female sexuality are seen by the Bible as physiological processes that serve the vital social process of procreation, yet are difficult to control (particularly by men). This gives them a quality of danger and, therefore, a need for exacting supervision.

A common misconception is that religious impurity or pollution associated with these disorderly states (translated in many Bibles as "uncleanliness") is the same as physical dirt, lack of hygiene. Rather, ritual impurity was symbolic of disturbances in the harmony of the universe. It was caused by a contact point between the forces of life and death. That is why leprous skin, menstrual blood, men's ejaculate, the blood of childbirth, and dead bodies are all considered to be sources of ritual impurity—disruptions in need of spiritual control. The pollution is symbolically rather than physically washed away through ritual immersion.

Menstruation—which signifies non-pregnancy, the absence of the possibility of life—was regarded as a form of pollution, parallel to other genital discharges that occurred in both men and women (Lev. 15). Genital pollution appears to have symbolized a lack of fecundity—a key value in a tribal society. Purification of pollution required immersion and offerings. However, a man who was "healed" from genital disorder appeared directly "before God," (Lev. 15:14) to make his offering, while a woman approached only to "the entrance of the tent" (Lev. 15:29). She never reached the innermost (highest) area of holiness, even when in an unpolluted state. Eventually the Rabbis nullified all the Levitical purity laws with the sole exception of those involving women and menstruation, thus establishing ritual purity as primarily a gender issue. Dr. Rachel Adler's piece, "'In Your Blood, Live': Re-Visions of a Theology of Purity" chronicles the author's thought over the past two decades on the significance of this Rabbinic categorization of gender.

Whether menstruating and post-childbirth women were actually separated from religious ritual in the post-biblical period is a matter of debate. The Mishnah speaks of "places of uncleanness" (Mishnah *Niddah* 7:4) in regard to menstruation, implying the existence of an isolated sector. However, the non-Talmudic prohibition against a menstruating woman praying, entering the synagogue, or having blessings recited in her presence, is quite late (*Baraita Demasekhta Niddah*). The Rabbinic legal anthology, *Tosefta*, states, "menstruants and women after childbirth are permitted to read from the Torah, and to study Mishnah, *Midrash, halakhot* and *aggadot*" (*Tosefta Berakhot* 2:12).

Sexuality and a Woman's Worth

The importance of fertility and the issues of purity symbolized by the rules on genital pollution generate a series of regulations about sexuality. These are not restricted to women; for example, male homosexuality is biblically prohibited (Lev. 18:22). However, in ancient Israel's male-dominated society, one "function" of women was sexual procreation, and the regulation of female sexuality was a significant social and religious goal. Specifically, relations during menstruation, between certain relatives, and with a married woman were all forbidden. The prohibitions were issued to, and from the viewpoint of, men. My essay, "When the Siren Stops

Singing," challenges this male monopoly and explores sexuality from the perspective of Jewish women.

Modern commentators, most notably lawyer and historian Judith Romney Wegner, assert that the sexual prohibitions are less about morality than property.[5] All the various specific forbidden women (mother, sister, granddaughter, niece, etc.) listed in Leviticus are the sexual "property" of other males, either their husbands or fathers, and are a sub-category of the general prohibition against married women. The list, rather than focusing on incest, is concerned with clarifying the legal status of ambiguous sexual "property"—that is, which male owns each particular female's sexual "function." It is interesting to note that in the extensive list of relatives who are prohibited to a man, a daughter is conspicuously absent, since her sexuality does belong to him, if not necessarily to use, then to sell. This entire view of sexuality raises difficult questions for modern people, since we generally view a woman's sexuality as her own.

Human property concepts in Leviticus are not limited to women's sexuality. The final chapter of the book discusses the monetary worth of each person according to age and gender. In general, women are valued at about sixty percent of the worth of men; young women (ages five to twenty) are worth only half the value of young men, and old women (over sixty) are deemed to be about two-thirds the value of their male counterparts. Feminist biblical scholar Carol Meyers suggests that these amounts accurately reflect the non-domestic economic productivity of women.[6] Since women were busy with childbearing and rearing, their agricultural or manufacturing output would be lower than a man's. It's certainly of interest that these biblical valuations mirror the wage differentials of our own society in which women earn less than men.

Holiness in Time and Table

Just as Leviticus emphasizes holiness in (the Temple) space and holiness in body, it describes a complex cycle of sacred times, days, and seasons (Lev. 23). Sabbath and the fundamental Jewish holy days including Passover, *Shavu'ot* (Festival of the giving of the Torah), *Rosh Hashanah* (New Year), *Yom Kippur* (Day of

Atonement), and *Sukkot* (Festival of Booths) are enumerated and described in terms of ritual requirements, primarily sacrificial offerings. The transformation of holiday observance over the course of Jewish history is evident. The evolution of food offerings into elaborate festival meals is of particular importance to women. In the ancient Temple, preparation of the sacred food was reserved for men; in our day it is almost entirely women's work!

Not only on special sacred occasions, but in general, food, eating, and diet composed yet another category of human process fundamental to life, and thus in need of regulation. Leviticus (chapter 11) catalogues and categorizes wildlife and domestic animals in terms of their place in the system. Life is classified according to the pattern of creation in Genesis 1. The divine order establishes plants in the ground, winged creatures in the air, swimming fish in the seas, grazing and creeping animals on land. All plants are explicitly fit (*kasher*) for human consumption. Within each category of animal exists a paradigm, similar to the High Priest as paradigm for humans. Animals that fit the paradigm (e.g. grazing animals that have cloven hooves and chew cud) are fit for human consumption. This complicated taxonomy forms the basis for Rabbinic *kashrut* (dietary laws). In the understanding of Leviticus and its later Rabbinic interpreters, the purpose of following these rules is to create distinctiveness, even holiness, by making physical distinctions. To be *kadosh* (set apart, separate, holy) is a major theme and aspiration in Leviticus, and remains a fundamental concern of Jewish life to the present.

Rabbinic Connections between Self and Society

The *midrash* (Rabbinic genre of lore often based on biblical texts) on Leviticus expands the Bible's theme of the physical body as the body politic. The Rabbis equate skin disease with evil talk:

> Rabbi Yohanan said in the name of Rabbi Yose ben Zimra, "Evil talk is a denial of God,…whoever engages in evil talk is visited by plagues." …Resh Lakish said, "The phrase, 'this is the law for a leper [*metzora*] (Lev. 14:1)' means this is the law for one who engages in evil talk [*motzi shem ra*]." (BT *Arakhin* 15b)

According to the *midrash*, each individual Jewish body is a miniature scale model of the community's structural body. Physical abnormality, in this case leprosy, signifies moral problems—evil talk—that have communal repercussions.[7] In the above passage, the author, Resh Lakish, employs the metaphor of leprosy—its corrosiveness, its contagiousness—to describe the impact of gossip on a community.

The *midrash* on Leviticus describes five particular abominations from "head to toe": Haughty eyes; an evil tongue; hands that shed innocent blood; a heart of wicked thoughts; feet that run to do evil (Lev. *Rabbah* 16:1). The body and soul are inextricably intertwined. Of these abominations, the Rabbis ascribe the first two moral deficiencies specifically to women: The "haughty daughters of Zion acted like harlots" and contributed to the fall of Jerusalem to the Romans; Miriam the prophet spoke against Moses and was made leprous (Num. 12:1–9). While feminists may reject the Rabbinic interpretation that blames women in particular for human moral faults, we endorse the notion that societal and individual deficiencies are linked. The personal, in both its positive and negative aspects, is political.

Body and Soul

Western thought asserts a dualistic separation of body and soul deriving from Platonist philosophy. Contemporary feminists, such as Sherry Ortner, maintain that this dualistic vision permeates the way we view gender roles.[8] In the Platonic division, the mind is male, the body female. Culture is male, nature is female. Male is superior, spiritual, the essence of creation. Female is inferior, physical, the receptacle of male essence.

Obviously, Leviticus knows of no division between body and soul. It understands the body as the fully integrated mirror of the inner self. Spiritual malaise inscribes itself on the body in the form of abnormality and illness. While this view has the disadvantage of perhaps stigmatizing those with physical ailments, it represents a more holistic way of perceiving dysfunction, one in keeping with current thought about the relation between psychological and physical disorders.

Debbie Friedman, in her essay, "Shattered and Whole," discusses how these concerns have impacted her personal life. She notes that the Bible and *midrash* raise important questions for contemporary Jewish women in relation to the integration of body and soul. How do we view our bodies? In our world, bodies are not considered sacred at all. They are for many women a source of anxiety as we compare them to an unreal societal ideal promoted by advertisements and the media. Physical pleasure, even sexual pleasure, is often packaged as a commodity. How then do we begin to reconnect our bodies to our spiritual selves?

The Individual, the Community, and the Environment

The *midrash* on Leviticus promotes the idea that individual sin, particularly women's sin, has powerful consequences for the community. Leviticus sees the individual not only as a member of a community, but as organically parallel to it. If an individual has a skin disease, the community is also not intact. If a woman has "haughty eyes," group destruction may well result. Modern thought dismisses such a notion as "magical thinking," an irrational human atavism. Jeffersonian Enlightenment ideology emphasizes the separate and unique quality of the individual and pursues an agenda of radical personal autonomy.

Recently, many feminist thinkers have reconsidered this premium placed on individualism. Are personal autonomy and fulfillment of self really of ultimate value? Leviticus sees each person, the community, and the natural world as key elements of a divinely integrated system of sanctity in which the well-being of each is profoundly related to the good of the others. Although its system might seem somewhat authoritarian by modern standards, it evidenced a concern for the underprivileged—the poor, the stranger, the disabled (Lev. 19)—that our world has yet to match. Laws concerning overharvesting, crop rotation, and fallow periods show that environmental concerns were accorded the status of religious law (Lev. 19:23, 25:2–7).

Ritual and Ethics as One

Classical nineteenth-century Reform Judaism incorporated both the Enlightenment notion of individual autonomy and the separation between body and spirit. Many Reform thinkers divided the *mitzvot* (sacred obligations, commandments) into separate categories of "ethical" imperatives and "ritual" customs. The former were eternal and universal, while the latter were considered specific to certain times and places and thus subject to revision or elimination. This viewpoint has had far-reaching consequences for modern liberal Judaism.

Recently, there is a renewed emphasis on ritual as a method of concretizing moral values. Women's rituals, in particular, have experienced a dramatic growth in popularity. Reform Judaism in our day increasingly embraces many of the physical religious activities described in Leviticus, such as building a *sukkah* (temporary dwelling for the Festival of Booths) or observing the dietary laws.

In the biblical world, there was no separation of ethical and ritual behaviors. Purity, in the physical sense, was inseparable from morality, for both the individual and the group. Holiness presumed a special state of being that included both symbolic purification through ritual and ethical behavior. In addition to its lengthy regulations about purification, Leviticus also presents moral instructions as intrinsic to holiness. Leviticus 19, known as the "holiness code," charges the community with its ethical responsibilities, including respect for parents, truthfulness, care for the needy, and regard for the disabled. It preaches: "Love your neighbor as yourself. I am God" (Lev. 19:17). Just as there is an order to food, sexuality, and sacrifice that must be preserved, so there is a God-given moral order to the world. In both ethics and rituals, order is created by making distinctions. Blessings follow from respecting the order and the commandments that uphold it. Curses follow from ignoring or violating the order (Lev. 26:3ff).

Themes of the Leviticus Essays

The essays in this chapter focus on the core issues of embodiment, community, ethics, and purity that are the themes of Leviticus.

They are divided into four sections, covering the Levitical topics of proper speech; food and sacrifice; bodily perfection and imperfection; and sexuality and ritual purification.

Rabbi Shirley Idelson opens the chapter with a disturbing *midrash* about the only named woman in Leviticus, Shelomit bat Divri. Idelson formats her piece as several pages of an imagined feminist Talmud, which continues beyond the small section available to the reader. She raises troubling questions about free speech and rebellion against authority. Rabbi Rebecca T. Alpert extends the discussion about speech in her essay, "The Power of Words." Alpert explores parallel Jewish and feminist beliefs about the import of language.

In the section on food, Myers contributes an overview of the evolution of attitudes about eating, ritual, and sacrifice in Jewish tradition, which also serves as the context of her personal commitment to vegetarianism.

Companion pieces include Michelle Nordon's lyrical story of how food was the symbol of creative survival for her mother who lived through the Holocaust, as well as the symbol of her own liberation as a second-generation daughter. Educator Beth Huppin recounts nostalgic memories of hospitality at her grandmother's table. She links the camaraderie and warmth of mealtimes in her ancestral home to Leviticus' ethical command to care for the stranger.

Rabbi Vicki Hollander draws on her own experience with illness and health to compose a prose poem that adapts the traditional Jewish blessings and prayers for bowel/bladder function, travelers, and thanksgiving into contemporary egalitarian language. She elaborates on the themes of the prayers to enrich traditional Jewish understandings of the body and wholeness.

Also engaging issues of physical wholeness, composer Debbie Friedman explores the idea of physical illness and impairment from *her* personal perspective. She shares her grief and anger resulting from her disability, yet focuses on the lessons in holiness that this illness has bestowed on her and those close to her.

Both Hollander and Friedman describe the difficulty women have in identifying and communicating needs. Friedman explores how our society idealizes women as selfless enablers, and stigmatizes assertive women as demanding and unreasonable. Hollander calls attention to the importance of self-care, of the need for commitment to personal health and well-being.

Glass deals more directly with the specific social issues raised by Leviticus and subsequent Jewish tradition in regard to birth anomalies. Glass recounts her journey from childlessness to becoming the mother of a beautiful baby with a physical anomaly. Feminist ideas of self-worth, diversity, and the importance of language gave her the tools and the strength to follow her own inner voice about what was best for her child. Glass concludes her article with a moving new Hebrew *berakhah* (blessing) celebrating the wholeness of each unique being set against the variety and universality of physical "imperfection."

My article explores sexuality in Judaism from the inner viewpoint of contemporary women. It critiques traditional Jewish understandings of sexuality as male-oriented, and reframes Jewish sexual ethics from a woman's perspective.

The chapter closes with a contemporary reevaluation of the relevance of *niddah* (menstrual impurity) and *mikveh* (ritual immersion). Adler renounces her former, widely disseminated, advocacy of *mikveh*. She now sees her previous view as an apologetic attempt to minimize gender differences in the hope of promoting an egalitarian perspective on the topic of purity. In Adler's current revisioning, women use the *mikveh* for purification from their own personal experience of pollution and woundedness such as sexual attack or grave illness, not from male definitions of impurity. Adler is passionate in both her anger at a past that subjugated women and her vision for a sacred future that honors them.

All of the articles deal in some way with the central theme of Leviticus: What constitutes holiness. They explore the timeless issues of speech, food, health, sexuality, and purity, to illumine the path of sanctity for ourselves and the Jewish people.

—J.R.L.

Powers of Speech

Shelomit bat Divri

SHIRLEY IDELSON

*The following piece might seem somewhat complex in format for those
unaccustomed to the study of Rabbinic literature. The initial quote,
which serves as the Mishnah, is an actual one from the Book of Leviticus.
The rest of the piece should be read in relation to it. The text is set out as
an imagined page of a women's Talmud that engages the story from
Leviticus. Like the Talmud, it blends biblical quotations and Rabbinic
lore in a associative "stream of consciousness" style and has limited
punctuation, including a lack of quotation marks. A reader should begin
with the "Gemara" in the larger type on the left-hand column of page
149, which continues in larger type on the following pages. The text in
smaller type is a commentary on the bolded words of the "Talmud." The
commentary ends in mid-sentence, inviting the reader to imagine what
will be on the next page. —Eds.*

Rabbi Shirley Idelson is the director of religious activities and chaplaincy services at Vassar College.

———◦◉◦———

מת' LEVITICUS 24:10–16, 23: There came out among the Israelites one whose mother was Israelite and whose father was Egyptian. And a fight broke out in the camp between that half-Israelite and a certain Israelite. The son of the Israelite woman pronounced the Name in blasphemy, and he was brought to Moses—now his mother's name was Shelomit daughter of Divri of the tribe of Dan—and he was placed in custody, until the decision of the Lord should be made clear to them. And the Lord spoke to Moses, saying: Take the blasphemer outside the camp, and let all who were within hearing lay their hands upon his head, and let the whole community stone him…. Moses spoke thus to the Israelites. And they took the blasphemer outside the camp and pelted him with stones. The Israelites did as the Lord had commanded Moses.

If she was such a **chatterbox**, why is there no record of her speaking? **She could not any longer restrain them**, i.e., she refused to be controlled. Women must have full control over our own bodies, understand this in the broadest sense possible. Leviticus describes patriarchal control of the body through notions of purity, forbidden sexual relations, forbidden foods, the forbidden leper, etc. Patriarchal control of the body? Of my body, said Shelomit bat Divri. And she said: I think sometimes when women refuse to eat, or when we succumb to silence, or when we minimize our physicality and our bonds with other women, or when we travel (in the words of our teacher Adrienne

גמ' Who was Shelomit bat Divri? The reader will certainly know that Shelomit bat Divri was not born with this name but acquired it. The Rabbis explain that she had quite a reputation—she would say *shalom* to any man, and she was a notorious **chatterbox**. She would speak her mind to anyone. Even when she was a child she lived always with the imperative to speak (*dibri*) her thoughts. With menses she was taught such banter was unsavory for an Israelite woman, but she thought that through speaking she might emerge whole into the world. Anyway, when she tried to hold her tongue the words bottled up inside her until **she could not any longer restrain them**

Rich) as disembodied spirits, we are actually seeking control over our bodies but in ways that will not provoke male violence against us. We develop anti-skills. What are anti-skills? They are a form of having control (I won't eat; I won't speak) but they are self-destructive. No wonder they do not provoke violent male response; it is not called for. We sometimes destroy ourselves. **To stand**, as it is written: And he shall place lots upon the two goats, one marked for the Lord and the other marked for Azazel. Aaron shall bring forward the goat designated by lot for the Lord, which he is to offer as a sin offering; while the goat designated by lot for Azazel shall be left standing alive before the Lord, to and—despite herself? out they burst. And so, she named herself Shelomit bat Divri, for it was only through speaking out that she could be at peace (*shalom*). What did she have to say? She was a woman full of curses, who acted contrary to the will of God and derogatory to His power. On many occasions, in a public setting she spoke contemptuously of the Deity. She had no regard for the precepts that the Israelites were commanded by the Lord through Moses to do. She was a blasphemer if ever there was one. She fell in love with an Egyptian. They did

make expiation with it and to send it off to the wilderness for *Azazel* (Lev. 16:8–10). **Head**, as it is written: Aaron shall lay both his hands upon the head of the live goat and confess over it all the iniquities and transgressions of the Israelites, whatever their sins, putting them on the head of the goat (Lev. 16:21). **Goat**, as it is written: …And it shall be sent off to the wilderness… Thus the goat shall carry on it all their iniquities to an inaccessible region; and the goat shall be set free in the wilderness (Lev. 16:21–22). Our teacher Adrienne Rich says, She became a scapegoat, the one around whom the darkness of maternity is allowed

not marry but together they lived in the midst of the Israelite camp. They had a son, and as the boy grew Shelomit taught him everything she knew, and he learned the contentious ways of his mother. The Rabbis teach (Lev. *Rabbah* 32:3–4) that one day, when the son was a young man, he went out to pitch his own tent in the camp of the tribe of Dan, on the land possessed by his mother's father. It was then that he got into the fight recorded in the biblical text. He had barely pounded the first pegs of his tent into the ground when a crowd of men from the tribe of Dan gathered around him. They jeered at him and taunted him, and one Israelite took his hammer from him, saying he had no right to set his tent on that land. The son of Shelomit bat Divri who named herself, who insisted always on her autonomy even as she refused marriage and loved an Egyptian, who raised a son to challenge and question everything even the divinely ordained, refusing to leave, declared: I descend from the daughters of the tribe of Dan. The to swirl—the invisible violence of the institution of motherhood, the guilt, the powerless responsibility for human lives, the judgments and condemnations, the fear of her own power, the guilt, the guilt, the guilt... The scapegoat is also an escape-valve; through her the passions and the blind raging waters of a suppressed knowledge are permitted to churn their way so that they need not emerge in less extreme situations as lucid rebellion.... The scapegoat is different from the martyr; she cannot teach resistance or revolt. She represents a terrible temptation: To suffer uniquely, to assume that I, the individual woman, am

crowd scoffed at him and roared with laughter. Then they seized him and carried him to the court of Moses, where he was convicted of trespass. Said the judges, Has not the Lord said: The Israelites shall camp each with his standard, under the banners of the house of their *fathers...* (Num. 2:1). Before the court and a crowd of witnesses said the son of Shelomit: Cursed be this Lord. For uttering these words, he was led in shackles through the camp to its outskirts, where he was held in custody. When word of his imprisonment reached his

mother, she rent her garments for she knew her son would not be spared. Have I not brought this upon him? she cried. For by refusing to marry an Israelite she had dispossessed her son of property rights. By teaching her son to challenge things as they are, she had given him the tools that led to his own destruction. Now the blasphemer was to be taken outside the camp and in the eyes of the people and by the hands of the people he was to be stoned to death, for thus the Lord had commanded. Shelomit hastened **to stand** with her flesh and blood one last time, in this moment of his death. The whole community gathered in a crowd outside the camp. Above the people's murmur a shout went out. It was a summons: Those who had been within hearing of the blasphemous words were to come forward. Shelomit watched as the men surrounded her son, placing their hands upon his **head**. Shelomit watched as they pelted her son with stones until he was dead. What happened to Shelomit? She left the day they stoned her son, the "problem."[1] **Pigeon**, as it is written: ...And he shall take the live bird, along with the cedar wood, the crimson stuff, and the hyssop, and dip them together with the live bird in the blood of the bird that was slaughtered...and he shall set the live bird free in the open country (Lev. 14:6-7).

Azazel, the Levitical notion of hell, was in the wilderness; there, Shelomit would be free of order and purity. Or, another interpretation: Come and listen: This is what happens to the woman who blasphemes. For claiming wholeness, for speaking out, for challenging the fathers—she was dispossessed, her child was killed, she was exiled from her community, her place was with *Azazel*. And these are some of the women who came from Shelomit bat Divri: Eve, and Sarah, and Dinah, and

Miriam, and the midwives, and Deborah, and Jael, and Beruriah, and Sarah the Yemenite, and Dahiyah Kahinah, and Esther Kiera, and Sarah bat Tovim, and Cecilia Bobrowskaya, and Anna Kuliscioff, and Felicia Sheftel, and Sofya Ginsburg, and Fanny Kaplan, and Rosa Luxemburg, and Esther Frumkin, and Pessia Abramson, and Rosa Manus, and Emma Goldman, and the women deported and sent into exile whose names are not recorded, and Rokhl Brokhes, and Fradel Schtok, and Yente Serdatzky, and Kadia Molodowsky,[2] and Hannah Szenes, and Rachel Bluwstein, and Ethel Rosenberg, and Leah Goldberg, and the women who crossed the Sudan, and Women in Black and Lil Moed, and Women at the Wall, and women

setting out in the direction of the **goat** and the **pigeon**. She was looking for *Azazel*, the demonic being who resided in the desert, whose abode was the place of all the world's impurity. She said, I choose *Azazel* over this hell where a woman is punished for claiming personhood and a son is murdered for claiming his mother. She would rather live with the goat and the pigeon.

The Power of Words

REBECCA T. ALPERT

"You are not to traffic in slander among your kinspeople."
(LEV. 19:16)

About twenty-five years ago I made a decision to live and work as a feminist and as a Jew—to me, these are a pair of intertwined commitments. The conflicts between Jewish and feminist approaches to life are real: These worldviews don't easily coincide. To Jews with whom I came in contact, including other women in the rabbinate, feminism was often perceived as a threat to the very fabric of Jewish life; to feminists, religious commitment seemed at best quaint and at worst an absurd capitulation to patriarchy. Along with many other Jewish feminists, I have spent the last quarter century working to reconcile the conflicts between these two worlds. Our efforts have resulted in some inroads, but most Jewish practice today still bears the stamp of a male-centered and -dominated tradition.

In light of my desire to reconcile these differences, it is very exciting when I discover that there is at least one issue on which Judaism and feminism seem to speak with one voice and teach the same lesson: The power of words. Lest postmodernists despair, let me acknowledge that there is no one Judaism or feminism of which to speak. But we can look to Jewish and feminist teachings to find complementary lessons about the significance of language. From both we learn that *how* we say things matters because words are powerful, and that *what* we say matters because words can redeem and words can hurt.

Feminist Thought about Language

While an emphasis on language is embedded in both perspectives, it is probably more readily associated with feminism. One of

Rabbi Rebecca Alpert, ordained at the Reconstructionist Rabbinical College, is co-director of the Women's Studies Program, Temple University.

feminism's most public contributions has been to alter, radically, the language that we speak. No longer is "man" or "he" accepted as a generic term that refers both to men and women. "Ms." has become commonplace. Recently, when my daughter and I went to see a revival of the 1961 play "How to Succeed in Business Without Really Trying," I could not help but notice how glaringly anachronistic it was for a group of men to sing about a "great fraternity," the "brotherhood of man." Now we understand that the brotherhood of man did not include the sisterhood of women, that through language women have been excluded from any sense of belonging or power. Feminism has reclaimed that power for women by showing how words and deeds are interconnected. It has taught us the valuable lesson that words are more than symbolic, that they have the power to change the way we think and behave.

Feminism is also responsible for raising awareness of the way words hurt by defining sexual harassment as a crime. Sexual harassment is a harm done predominantly through speech that before feminist consciousness was never perceived to be hurtful. Accepting the notion that saying derogatory or threatening words to someone is wrong and that one is culpable for this kind of speech is a major change in our understanding of the power of language. It is remarkable to see a culture that popularized the aphorism "sticks and stones will break my bones, but words can never hurt me," begin to understand how much words can hurt someone. The typical victim of harassment may never be touched physically. But the words said to him or her may cause deep pain that can result in resigning from a job, dropping a college course, or a variety of emotional and even physical symptoms.

Jewish Perspectives on Language

While feminism is noted for redefining our understanding of language, Judaism is often seen, particularly in contrast to Christianity, as a religion of deed rather than creed. But as the people of the Book, Jews take words quite seriously. In the Bible, the Book of Leviticus focuses primarily on ritual behavior. Nevertheless, generations of Jewish teachers used Leviticus as a beginning point for understanding the power of words (BT *Arakhin* 15b).[1]

It is in Leviticus that we find the commandment to observe *Yom Kippur* (Day of Atonement) as a day of self-affliction and atonement. This atonement process begins with *Kol Nidre* (literally, "All Vows," the service on *Yom Kippur* eve). For most of us, the words to *Kol Nidre* are not as important as the moment itself. Perhaps we do not even know the meaning of the words we chant. The ancient melody, the *tallitot* (prayer shawls) worn in the evening, the beginning of a fast day, the presence of the Torah scrolls, and the enormous crowds of people surrounding us usually outweigh the impact of the words.

But the words are important, for they teach us about the supreme value of words in our tradition. "All vows that we will make in the coming year, may they be considered null and void."[2] Perhaps we ignore the words because they are beyond our simple comprehension. *Kol Nidre* is the opportunity our ancestors took to make sure that their words were not taken as a literal contract. They wrote this legal formula to affirm that they should not be held to vows that they would make. Our ancestors truly believed that their words meant something. If they made a vow, it had to be carried out regardless of the consequences. To understand this, think of the biblical Nazirite vow.[3] Only a prayer as solemn and heartfelt as *Kol Nidre* could provide an escape.

Because we no longer take our words as seriously, the idea behind *Kol Nidre* makes no sense to us. We are not as aware of a basic insight that our ancestors understood: That in certain circumstances, to say something is to do something. J.L. Austin, in his work *How to Do Things with Words* (Oxford University Press, 1970) clarified this concept when he coined the term "speech acts." Austin reminded us that through language we make things happen. The example he gives is saying "I do" at a wedding or "I swear" in a court of law. Jews, by the way, traditionally do neither of these acts. That has everything to do with our understanding of how powerful words can be.

But the idea of "speech acts" extends farther than Austin's examples. What we say creates a reality and changes the way the world works. So when we make a promise to do something, and we take that promise seriously, those words have the power to make something happen because we understand ourselves as responsible to turn our speech into action. Today, we cannot imagine being held to a promise simply because we utter it. Without this perspective, we fail to comprehend the power of speech for ancient Jews. Yet the power of the ritual itself reminds us of its original meaning, which should not be ignored.

So when Jewish feminists suggest, for example, that the names we call God are important, that referring to God only in masculine pronouns and images excludes women from seeing ourselves as created in God's image, we are not only echoing a feminist sentiment but are really thinking in concert with ancient Jewish tradition, which took the words we utter with utmost seriousness.

Our ancestors also understood that words are harmful. Leviticus 19:16 ("You shall not bear tales") is the origin of our concept of *lashon hara* (evil speech; gossip). Rashi's commentary on this verse asserts that evil talk has evil consequences for the perpetrator as well as the victim. According to him, people who participate in defamation are likely to become spies or engage in other hurtful activities. Slander is not a trivial offense. Words hurt.

Lessons for the Present

But, these days, we have come to ignore the wisdom we find in Jewish tradition. Mainstream society has rejected the idea that hate speech can be harmful to those toward whom it is directed, especially to those who lack the power to respond. Those who try not to offend through speech are demeaned as "politically correct."

By ignoring the lesson that words can hurt, our culture has replaced civility with a peculiar notion of free speech, which seems to mean that we have complete permission to say hurtful things about others. Free speech is a complex ideal. It should be thoughtful and bold; not hateful and undisciplined. Learning when to speak and when not to speak, what to say and what not to say, is a value in itself and an important corollary to the ancient Jewish prohibition of *lashon hara*.

What I have learned from Judaism and feminism is to respect the power of language, to care about what I say and how I say it and to know that the way we use words can change situations and alter feelings. These mutually reinforcing lessons make me listen and read, and speak and write with a great reverence for words, for the people who are communicating with those words, and for the traditions from which these insights derive.

Food and Sacrifice

The Altared Table: Women's Piety and Food in Judaism[1]

JODY ELIZABETH MYERS

*"When a person dies, the soul will arrive in the future world
and be asked, 'How did you occupy yourself?' If this soul says,
'I fed the hungry,' then they reply, 'This is the gate of the Lord;
all who feed the hungry may enter.'"*
                    —*MIDRASH* PSALMS ON PSALM 118:19

My first independent religious decision involved food. On Hiroshima Day, 1969, wanting no part of humanity's violence, I vowed to become a vegetarian. This was to be my way of honoring the sanctity of life. Since then, I have adopted many other food customs and rituals. Food is essential in how I find entertainment, show hospitality, give comfort, and solidify relationships. My political conscience is still stirred by the misuse of food sources and the task of feeding others. This focus on food is not just my own quirkiness—it is part of being Jewish. Food is a central factor in the formation of Jewish identity, and food-centeredness expresses itself with great intensity among Jewish women.

Food in the Bible

The Garden of Eden story (Gen. 2–3) teaches three crucial lessons about food and Jewish society. God allows all sorts of edibles for the first humans, but prohibits one, the fruit of the tree of knowledge. Attracted to the prohibited food because it promises

Dr. Jody Myers is director of the Jewish Studies Program at California State University, Northridge.

knowledge, the woman disobeys God and eats it. The man follows her example. As a consequence, finding sustenance becomes a chore ("By the sweat of your brow shall you get bread to eat" [Gen. 3:17]), and conflict between men and women is introduced into the world ("Your urge shall be for your husband, and he shall rule over you" [Gen. 3:16]). This story conveys that food plays a central role in the Jewish imagination. It provides for the first human interaction, the first conflict between God and humanity, and is a source of tension between women and men. Even God cares deeply about human food choices. These principles undergird the relationship between food and worship throughout the Bible.

Ancient Jews worshipped God through ritualized eating. The sacrifice of foodstuffs was considered the means to a harmonious relationship with God, and sacrificial rite skimped on language. We barely hear of prayers in biblical narratives; instead, people gave thanks and acknowledged the covenant by building an altar and offering sacrifices. Sacrifice was generally a silent ritual: Neither the priest nor the worshiper was required to say anything.[2] Prayers and psalms were recited outside sanctuaries or away from the altar of sacrifice. Words simply could not match the power of a whole-hearted offering of food.

Worship required eating, and the reverse was true as well: Eating required worship. Slaughtering an animal for its meat, picking the first fruits of a tree, harvesting the crops, and assessing the newborn of the herd at springtime were milestones that had to be honored by a religious offering. Sacrificial worship was also a means of limiting and sanctioning the human use and destruction of God's creation. According to the Torah, Eden was a vegetarian society. Meat-eating began on a widespread scale after the Flood (Gen. 9:2–3) as God's concession. Jews evinced a moral concern by restricting meat consumption with further prohibitions. Eating certain animals (Lev. 11), slaughtering cruelly or ingesting the life-blood of an animal (Gen. 9:4), killing the young before the eyes of its parent (Deut. 22:6–7), and cooking a young kid in its life-source, its mother's milk (Ex. 23:19), were all forbidden. But it was also wrong to be more stringent than the laws required, and following the vegetarian principles of Eden was considered a sign of mourning, indicating the mourner's distance from the vital life source. Permitted eating was sanctified eating—a form of divine service.[3]

In male-dominated society, women played a minimal role in the sacrificial food rites. Only men could become priests, and priestly status was transmitted patrilineally. Women could bring an offering to the priest (and were commanded to do so in some instances) and eat from consecrated foods, but priestly law judged their bodies more prone to ritual impurity than males, and so they were often barred from holy sites and consecrated food.

Was the absence of women from the rituals more than a reflection of their relative powerlessness? Could they have stayed away deliberately, or was their spirituality somehow less aggressive than men's? Remember that food is a source of tension between women and men in biblical society. Biblical narratives connect sacrifice to women's losses and men's gains: Hannah is granted a son upon promising to release him to priestly service (1 Samuel 1), the warrior Yiftaḥ's plea for victory was fulfilled and then paid for with the sacrifice of his daughter (Judges 11).[4] When Abraham prepared to sacrifice his wife Sarah's only child (Isaac), the boy survived, and Abraham was rewarded with further offspring; the next mention of Sarah, however, proclaims the news of her death (Gen. 22–23:1).[5] Perhaps many women rejected the sacrificial system, or perhaps they had their own worship, private ceremonies, prayers, and poetry (Ex. 15; 1 Samuel 1; Judges 5).

From Sacrifice to Sacred Table

Not surprisingly, biblical literature connects the end of sacrifice to the undue prominence of women. Foreign women are blamed for the introduction of pagan deities into the sanctuary (1 Kings 11, 16), and the prophet Jeremiah complains that women are baking cakes and bringing them as offerings to the Queen of Heaven (Jeremiah 7:18).

In addition, some prophets demanded that Jews abandon their narrow, fetishistic focus on the sacrifices. These prophets rejected punctilious observance of the sacrificial rituals in favor of pure conviction and deeds of social compassion.[6] Isaiah preached the following message:

> "What need have I of all your sacrifices?" says the Lord. "I am sated with burnt offerings of rams, and suet of fatlings,

and blood of bulls.... Trample My courts no more; bringing
oblations is futile, incense is offensive to Me. New moon and
Sabbath, proclaiming of solemnities, assemblies with iniquity,
I cannot abide.... Wash yourself clean; put your evil doings
away from My sight. Cease to do evil; learn to do good.
Devote yourselves to justice; aid the wronged. Uphold the
rights of the orphan; defend the cause of the widow." (Isaiah
1:11–17)

With the repeated destruction of local and central sanctuaries,
the power of the sacrificial system necessarily diminished. The
decline of sacrifice did not end Jewish concern with food, but channeled it in a different direction. Meat-eating became separated
from sacrifice, and non-sacrificial forms of worship flourished.

Rabbinic Judaism, the new form of Judaism established after
the destruction of the Second Temple in 70 CE, elevated non-
priestly and non-sacrificial values and institutions to central
importance. The primary avenues to God became Torah study,
prayer, deeds of lovingkindness, and fulfillment of the countless
ritual observances established by the Rabbis. These activities had
not been part of the hereditary priestly system and therefore were
not prohibited for women or non-priestly men. This change gave a
greater religious role to those who had stood on the periphery of
the religious order.

The Rabbis transformed the sacrificial rites of the Temple into
domestic table rituals. The Sabbath offerings were re-enacted in
three special meals, and Passover sacrifice became a family feast of
highly symbolic foods. Lifecycle ceremonies were followed by an
obligatory communal feast, the *se'udat mitzvah*. Every holiday's
designated Temple sacrifice was replaced by home and synagogue
rituals that were in some way symbolic of the sacrificial offering
for the occasion. The Rabbis composed dozens of *berakhot* (blessings) to be said over food and after eating. The holiness that was
previously contained within the sacred precinct of the Temple
extended into homes and community. Sanctified food, which once
referred to the food designated for sacrifice, now meant the food
prepared for every Jewish family's use.

Rabbinic Judaism's preoccupation with food rulings, rituals,
and interpretations was a replacement in kind of the sacrificial

system's preoccupation with hundreds of intricate laws, rituals, and nuances of cultic practice. Many Jewish dietary laws come from the early Rabbinic period. The Rabbis combined the sacrificial laws and the general prohibitions against cruel and wanton meat-eating and transformed them into the system we know today as *kashrut* (Jewish dietary laws). Another point of continuity with biblical food-centeredness was that voluntary food limitation, such as vegetarianism, continued to be regarded as a sign of mourning, self-chastisement, or personal arrogance, and was severely limited by Jewish law.[7]

Popular tradition teaches that Jews have been "the people of the book," prizing Torah study above all. This is only partly true. Rabbinic Judaism made us "the people of the table" as well. The table was at the center of every Jewish dwelling. Laden with food, with books stacked up in the empty spaces, it substituted for the altar.[8]

Women, Food, and Religious Expression

How did this change affect women and food? The domestication of religious ritual and the demise of priestly values and institutions resulted in new opportunities for women's religious expression. In the early Rabbinic era, women were active participants in the Jewish communal religious sphere.[9] Eventually they were excluded from the study houses and marginalized in the synagogues, but other opportunities were available to them. Women still had the domestic arena in which to express their religious feelings. They surely played a major role in shaping the dietary laws, for they controlled the kitchen. Although slaughtering was usually handled by men, the rest of the kashering of the animal, in addition to the food preparation, was in women's hands. Knowledge of these practices was handed down in the home from mother to daughter; even the Rabbis recognized that their halakhic discussions of these matters in their texts and academies were somewhat divorced from practical reality.[10] Women knew that their home-making involved holy acts and intricate knowledge of laws mandated by God, with potential for bringing divine providence into their families and communities.

Rabbinic Judaism continued substantially unchanged for centuries. In the late medieval period, an illustration of this continuity with regard to women and food can be found in the following prayer. Written by a woman, it was recited while fulfilling the Rabbinic commandment known as *ḥallah*, separating and burning a small piece of dough from the unbaked bread in symbolic reference to the priestly tithe:

> May my *ḥallah* be accepted as the sacrifice on the altar was accepted. May my *mizwah* be accepted just as if I had performed it properly. In ancient times, the high priest came and caused the sins to be forgiven; so also may my sins be forgiven with this. May I be like a newborn child. May I be able to honor my dear Sabbaths and holidays. May God bestow upon me that I and my husband and my children be able to nourish ourselves. Thus may my *mizwah* of *ḥallah* be accepted: That my children may be fed by the dear God, be blessed, with great mercy and great compassion. May this *mizwah* of *ḥallah* be accounted as if I had given the tithe. As I perform my *mizwah* of *ḥallah* with might and main, so my God, be blessed, guard me from anguish and pain.[11]

This prayer shows that more than a thousand years after its cessation, sacrifice was regarded by at least some women as the ideal vehicle of expiation and blessings. At the same time, they considered food that they personally prepared equivalent to the sacrifices, and they equated themselves to priests. I imagine that these women, standing over their stoves and urging family members to eat, saw themselves in the role of family priest, releasing divine blessings into their loved ones. Their rituals linked them to Jews of ages past. Although the bulk of women's hours were spent sustaining their families economically, they had a religious outlet in these and other domestic duties.[12]

Our Own Tables

For contemporary Jewish women, food-centeredness is more problematic, spiritually and emotionally, than in the pre-modern era. Contemporary Jewish women who observe the dietary laws relate to them in a more superficial way than did their ancestors: *Kashrut* is now largely determined outside of women's realm, because reliance on processed foods and state-controlled slaughtering has resulted in greater power to male Jewish legal authorities. Butchers, not housewives, kasher animals; bakers take *ḥallah* from the dough of baked goods, and many domestic rituals that were previously infused with sacred powers have been abandoned by even observant Jews. Modern women are nevertheless urged to become the (actually new) type of Jewish mother who does not economically support her family, but stays at home and, in some indefinable way, creates a Jewish environment for her family.

But what exactly does this mean? Women are no longer religious experts of the domestic realm, but primarily consumers who display the family's culinary largesse and arrange for material comforts. A considerable amount of their energy is now expended on planning the menus, preparing the foods, setting and cleaning the tables—and little, if any, of this is infused with religious content. Some of the tasks that our foremothers undertook were quite burdensome—kashering meat, for example—and we can be thankful that we are now freed from them. Yet contemporary Orthodox Jews have not filled this religious vacuum by encouraging women to observe traditionally male-dominated *mitzvot*, and pitifully few women in the non-Orthodox realm take these opportunities seriously.

The secularization of Jewish life also contributes to the separation of food and eating from religious values. Many Jews discount the spiritual context of food when they abandon Jewish observance, but the Jewish way of relating to food remains deeply ingrained in their attitudes and behavior. Food is tied to emotional sustenance, and it is also evocative of family. For many who wish to preserve familial and communal ties, the only vehicle they know is food. Thus, their Passover *seder* (ordered readings and meal) may consist of a family feast and a highly abbreviated recital of the *Haggadah* (text of the Passover *seder*), or a table ritual rendered without understanding, or no ceremony at all. A family feast like this may have symbolic meaning, but it invokes a shorter span of time and a smaller community than that recalled in the *Haggadah*. Observant Jews face quite a challenge when they attempt to transmit moral values while surveying platters of food around the table; it is even more difficult for secular Jews, who lack the prompting of religious texts and rituals.

Furthermore, in the modern era food is still a major source of identity struggle, conflict between women and men, and competition for power. Women who share households with men generally continue to bear the bulk of responsibility for preparing food, even when gendered divisions of labor are no longer rational or can no longer be sustained by satisfying explanations. We live in a society that is deeply divided over women's proper role; both men and women demand that women fulfill myriad and often contradictory expectations. This same society seeks the nurturing earth mother, but also obsesses over an idealized, slim female body shape. The eating disorders that today plague so many women are just one expression of deep confusion and dissatisfaction over their identity in the modern world.[13]

Judaism has the potential for a healthier perspective. It teaches that the body's sensual desires are normal and eating is a potentially sacred act. Jewish food rituals teach one how to redeem the world, rather than feel alien from it. We are fortunate that the central symbol of Jewish culture is a table! It allows us to associate food with showing gratitude to God for life, modeling respectful concern for nature, and sustaining community.

Like Jewish women and men in the distant and not so distant past, we can seek through our food to secure our harmonious relationship to God and society. We must shield our tables from the forces that threaten to desecrate them or simply render them meaningless. Setting our tables with care and concern, we can welcome holiness into our homes.

(Re)setting the Table: Some Practical Suggestions

How can we increase the social and religious importance of meals? Can we do a better job at making our meals with others a time of true communion, and make altars of our tables? Here are suggestions:

1. Think about ways to add to, or establish, the spiritual dimension of eating. What are some ways we can make our

food preparation and rituals an opportunity for learning about and teaching others the values represented by food?

2. Become more knowledgeable about the system of *kashrut* so that we can understand why generations of Jews have found it meaningful. If you have never kept the laws of *kashrut*, why not make a start? If you are experienced with keeping kosher, are there ways you can follow the laws in a more thoughtful manner? Do you get so focused on the details of daily and Passover-related *kashrut* that you lose sight of their social context?

3. Begin to integrate behaviors into *kashrut* that are presently external to them, and so make our observance more socially responsible. This might involve insisting on food that is nutritious and not overly-sumptuous (resisting the food-bingeing that often dominates our feasting); incorporating within our dietary laws concern for human labor (rejecting food that is produced at the expense of workers' health and making this known to food producers); showing respect for the natural environment through our food choices (limiting meat consumption, rejecting food that is produced through cruelty to animals, eating organic); and dividing the work of food preparation fairly. Could we mark these behaviors with a *berakhah* just as we would eating or other sacred deeds?

4. Commit ourselves to adopt food rituals that have social and environmental benefit: Collecting food for others, showing hospitality toward those who need it, teaching people how to sustain themselves, recycling food packaging, or maintaining a compost heap.

5. Learn how to make, from scratch, a Jewish dish from our own or another tradition, and share it with others.

American Dishes

MICHELLE NORDON

*"And the land shall yield her fruit, and you shall eat your fill,
and dwell therein in safety."*
—LEV. 25:19

*"'A person who brings a meal offering to God…' (Lev. 2:1).
[Read instead 'A person is brought as a meal offering to God,' as
the following story illustrates:] A woman once brought a handful of meal as an offering. The priest rejected it, saying, 'What
sort of offering is that? What is there in it for eating or for
sacrifice?' But in a dream it was said to the priest, 'Despise her
not; but reckon it as if she had offered* herself *as a sacrifice.'"*
—LEV. *RABBAH* 3:5

My mother never taught me how to cook, so when I moved out of
my parents' home, I thought I would starve. I didn't know how to
shop for food, either, and when I had to go to the market, my mind
swarmed with my mother's voice, saying *No, not that, no, that's the
wrong sort, no, that costs too much.* I would go home convinced my
money would run out, that I was slowly destroying whatever delicate nutritional balance my body had achieved. *You should be careful,* my mother would warn, *you're going to give yourself food
poisoning.* I knew she would rather cook my meals for me and simply have me deep-freeze them for later.

My mother nearly starved once in her life, but it took me a long
time to realize that her feelings about food, her fears about me,
emanated from that past. She thought I didn't eat enough and was
on the brink of withering (I *was* very skinny), even when dinner
was always waiting for me at her table. So I imagined I would
slowly disappear once I left her home and had to go through not
only the ordeal of eating, but that of providing food for myself.

It took me a few weeks of being on my own to discover freedom.
Liberation soon filled my new kitchen, with jars of home-made

---

Michelle Nordon, a native of Los Angeles, writes primarily short fiction and creative non-fiction and also works as an editor in the Los Angeles office of the
University of California Press.

honey, strings of garlic cloves, a few cookbooks I chose for the colors on their covers. I bought a whisk, a grapefruit knife, a steamer. I learned how to do things my mother in fact never did—how to crush garlic and simmer it slowly in olive oil, how to pick fresh dill, how to steep whole peppermint leaves in a silver-handled glass cup and drink in the herbs, the medicinal qualities of which she knew nothing.

Then there were some things I didn't learn until later; these were things my mother did know, deep ancestral secrets, but even so, I couldn't get recipes out of her. How do you make pickles? *With pickling spices.* Where do you get the spices? *You can get the spices anywhere.* (Anywhere? Where?) How many days do you leave the jar with the pickles out in the sun? She would laugh a little and shrug her shoulders, and I think she was actually a little embarrassed. *Just look at them*, she would say. *You'll know when they're ready.*

I wonder sometimes what kept my mother that thin line away from starvation—a crust of bread? a pickle? maybe an orange? She was herded with the rest of the women in the family out of their home and into the ghetto, then later marched through the town to the waiting trains. She passed their own house along the way, as it was next to the train station; that she and her mother and sisters, in their place in that line of people, would stop right there, in front of their house, was a miracle. A woman came through the wrought iron gate from the courtyard they shared as neighbors. She was the daughter of a priest; she brought milk out to feed my aunt's baby. She begged my mother's mother, begged her, whispering, *Let me take her, now, quickly*, but my grandmother would not let go of her youngest granddaughter. The miracle passed.

The next day the only ones left were my mother and one of her sisters, the only ones both "useful" and uncomplicated enough to be spared. She woke up and asked, *Where's my mother? Where's my older sister and her baby?* Someone pointed to smokestacks. My mother grew up literally overnight. A year later, she was nearly starving, but it all ended just in time, fortunately, in time, for her, and she was the only one of her family left. Her other sister, I am told, had refused to eat.

I am her family now, and at last I have proven I am not weak, or too thin (I have gained weight now that I can cook interesting things). I know where to get spices and honey and garlic, and I have even figured out how to make pickles. I touch the jar I have put in the sun as the spices go to work; it is warm and smooth, sitting there roundly, quietly. Though my mother was never much of a teacher, though she insisted on cooking for me herself, I have managed to learn anyway. I reassure her. I make her pasta, chicken, American dishes because I am an American kid, but I pickle cucumbers for her, and she smiles as she bites into one, her face wrinkled, but so vibrant.

Food and Love

BETH HUPPIN

"The stranger that lives among you shall be treated as the homeborn; you shall love the stranger as yourself, for you were strangers in the land of Egypt...."
—LEV. 19:34

"Hospitality is more important even than encountering God's Intimate Presence."
—BT *SHABBAT* 127A

My Grandma Marian and Grandpa Abe raised and fed their own three children, three of Grandma's sister's orphaned children, and Grandpa's orphaned baby brother. In addition, the neighbor children always ate at their house. "You'd think their parents never fed them!" Grandma would complain years later. I imagine they ate at her house because her food tasted better.

According to family lore, there was always a pot of soup cooking in the back of the family store. Anyone who came into the store hungry left satisfied. One time an unemployed watchmaker came in looking for work. When they learned he was sleeping on a

---

Beth Huppin is a Jewish educator and co-founder of the Seattle Jewish Coalition for Homeless People.

bench, my grandparents brought him home. Room was found for one more person. He stayed for five years, working in the store during the day and doing odd chores around the house in the evenings. "I don't know how I would have managed without him!" Grandma would say. My grandparents never considered taking the man in to be of great merit. He took care of them, even as they took care of him.

Every Jewish holiday meant a special meal made by Grandma, Aunt Norma, and my mother. As the women put the finishing touches on the meal, the men went to *shul* (synagogue). They always brought home a few guests who were passing through town for the holiday. The women set extra places in anticipation. Part of the pre-meal ritual was wondering aloud whom the "men" would find.

The men generally found the guests, but it was the women who fed them. As I think about it now years later, this gender distinction in my family becomes even clearer.

When a friend was dying of cancer, my father, a lawyer, took care of the family's financial and legal matters. He offered advice and comfort in tangible and important ways. But it was my mother who went to the hospital every day to feed our friend lunch so that his wife could have a few hours' break.

When someone in the community died, the men were counted in the *minyan* (prayer quorum) so that the mourner could say *Kaddish* (mourner's prayer), but it was the women who made sure that the mourner was provided with meals. Recently, when my grandfather died, I found out what it felt like to receive meals of comfort. It was Friday afternoon, and I was capable of cooking, but the gap caused by his death left me unmotivated to do anything. I had two small children, and *Shabbat* (Sabbath) was drawing near. Like a gift from heaven, the bell rang and four different friends appeared within minutes of each other, offering not only food, but comfort. That night, as we ate a *Shabbat* meal provided by the community, I found that the food itself comforted me. Food cooked by others assured me that I was not alone.

As my husband and I raise our three daughters, I look to my own family for female models for myself and for them. I see images of the women in my family nurturing others, welcoming them into our home, feeding and visiting them in times of sickness and distress. They are images that move me deeply because they provide profound messages about the true meaning of human kindness and connectedness. Now, in retrospect, I realize that loneliness did not seem to be part of these women's lives. They were too busy doing for others.

When my grandparents were old, they were not lonely. When they were ill, many people came to visit them. And when they died, many people came to bury and mourn them. I imagine them in the "next world" together. Grandpa is looking for lonely souls, and Grandma is feeding them. Her heavenly pistachio nut cake is always ready, and, in her wonderful old-country accent, she is encouraging them to try it. If they say they are not hungry, she will remind them that "You don't have to be hungry to eat cake." Hunger was never the issue. Even in heaven it is not good to be lonely.

Health and the Body

Health, Healing, and Holiness

VICKI HOLLANDER

*"And God spoke to Moses, saying, 'Have the children of Israel
bring to you the finest oil of the olive, transparent from the
pressing, that the light which burns continuously be ever lifted
upward.'"*

—LEV. 24:1–2

Health: A Loadstone

When I was a young girl there was a crystal fixture in the sun-
room. On sunny mornings the room was flooded with rainbows. I
loved putting my hands on the walls, seeing the rainbows on my
skin: The closest thing to catching one.

Defining health for women is like catching rainbows. What
does it look like? How does it feel? How do we know we have
it? Health flows from the convergence of our body, mind, heart,
and soul.

As a girl, I learned to use my mind and was taught its value. I
also learned to be uncomfortable about my body and its shape. My
grandmothers and her sisters, all from the Pale of Russia, were
short, large breasted women—bodies rounded, voices loud, far
from the cultural ideal. My young body was growing just like
theirs, but in a land where boyish was beautiful. I wore my father's
too big sweaters to cover myself. I felt bright but not pretty.

As a woman, I have sought within both myself and the Jewish
community a place where I can welcome my entirety, a place
where the knowledge of the spirit, intuition, body, and heart are as

---

Rabbi Vicki Hollander resides in Vancouver, B.C., where she weaves together
ritual, poetry, spiritual counseling, and retreats.

valued as the knowledge of the mind. I ask myself and others: How can we foster a sense of well-being?

A Prayer: Praised are You, our Source, Creator of the Universe, who has shaped me with wisdom, creating within me passages and vessels. It has been revealed and is known that should even if one of these be opened up or shut closed in the wrong hour, it would be impossible to exist, even to stand before You. Praised are You who heals all flesh, Doer of wonders (*traditional blessing over bladder and bowel function*).

A Verse: "Have the children of Israel **bring** to You **the finest oil of olive...**"

A Commentary: Bring yourselves. Bring your beautiful bodies that I created. Bring them forward to Me, proudly. Bring your sweet souls and full hearts, for they are the rich oil of the olive. In the celebration and the offering, you shall know gladness and peace.

Illness and Healing

Simply living with our rhythmic cycles, we feel the paradox of our bodies: How strong and hardy, how frail and vulnerable. I remember standing alone at the hospital window, watching the sun set, wondering if I too was going to sink and disappear from sight. Recently, the other woman rabbi in town had come in for the same surgery. She left with a hysterectomy and cancer diagnosis. I hadn't eaten enough pizza, hadn't dressed in enough wild clothing, or worn bright enough colors. I hadn't played enough, hadn't sunk my teeth into life deeply enough. I was thirty-one years old.

Illness sometimes means having to make significant treatment decisions. For some a terrible aloneness arises, as if no one else had ever faced this experience before. Fears come in the night, and you slip into bargaining, making grade-school deals with God. "If You just help me, give me...then I'll be good forever."

Another form of dis-ease: When you are physically well, but carry depression, grief, despair. A blurry line separates human emotions from mental illness, problems related to circumstance from those seemingly without cause.

Who decides which is health and which disease? Who names the boundaries? The question goes back to Adam. Who has the power to name: "This is reasonable. This is crazy." And then what do we do with that diagnosis: Ours and theirs? Whom can we tell and trust and ask for help?

A Prayer: My Source, Guide of my ancestors, support me as I walk. Help direct my steps and draw me closer to knowing wholeness. Aid me to travel where my heart longs and needs to go, that I may do so with life, surety, and inner peace. Save me from dangers that surround me without, and from my fears within. Let my decisions lead to wellness.

May Your kindness, compassion, and deep-seated loving surround me, and draw the same up from within me and from others who travel alongside me. Hear my call; be with me. Praised are You, Who hears the prayers of those who call upon You (*adapted from the traditional prayer for travelers*).

A Verse: "Have the children of Israel bring you the finest oil of the olive, transparent from the pressing, **that the light which burns continuously….**"

A Commentary: Your light within, your spirit, illuminates your body and carries your you-ness, even in the worst of times. It is your guide, and burns throughout the night, continually, signaling that you are not alone, that I am with you, near you, always.

Holiness

Traveling through the dark times: Times of grief, being bent backward, knocked flat on the ground, I deepened the most. I used to say I'd give it all up for happy innocence. But I wouldn't.

Only through being ill have I learned that my body speaks to me. I had ignored her messages, unopened letters. Now I try to be more tuned in, so that she need not shout and be dramatic to get me to hear. My body knows a lot. She holds wisdoms.

A Prayer: We give You our thanks…for our lives, which are in Your hands, for our souls, which are entrusted to You, for Your miracles, which surround us each and every day, and for Your wonders, the numerous forms of beauty with which You grace us in every season, at every time, evening, morning, and noon (*adapted from the* Amidah, *a series of blessings that is the centerpiece of every prayer service*).

A Verse: "Have the children of Israel bring to you the finest oil of the olive, transparent from the pressing, that the light which burns continuously **be ever lifted upward**."

A Commentary: Come to Me. For in approaching, in the offering, you shall feel holiness. We shall meet and join. And you shall know wholeness, well-being, and peace.

Shattered and Whole

DEBBIE FRIEDMAN

"I will place my sanctuary amidst you and my spirit will not reject you."
—LEV. 26:11

Debbie Friedman, runner, healthy eater, Pritikinite, no sugar, no drugs, no liquor—the one who takes such good care of her body. Then one day I went to bed with a headache and woke up two hours later, my life changed forever. My legs were like concrete pillars, limbs going every which way all at the same time; I had a severe seizure disorder. I had suddenly become an immigrant to my own world, my speech sometimes sounding as if I just arrived at Ellis Island.

I didn't know if I would ever walk again, or talk normally, or even live. The idea of "control" became a farce. All the people who spent time with me and had to see me in this condition were looking in a "mirror," knowing that this could happen to them.

Debbie Friedman is an internationally renowned composer, liturgist, teacher, and performer. Her recent release, "You are the One," is available from Sounds Write Productions.

Now, some days I just sit and think about things. At times I completely forget what I'm thinking. I go on in my mind attempting to remember words or ideas: I might get a glass of water that I fill with "winters" so that my drink is nice and cold or buy some "Octobers" to eat with my rice cakes. (Everyone I know uses "Octobers" to make guacamole.) I experience periodic loss of control of my body functions—from drooling, to being frozen in postures and unable to move, to incontinence. All these things have made me feel as though I am in the body of an old woman. It has taken me years really to feel the impact of what has happened and what is *still* happening.

Once, I was walking at the Dinah Shore Open, a women's golf tournament. There were masses of people, and I loved walking through the crowds at the golf course. I followed a player and walked the entire eighteen holes. When I needed to, I held on to a friend's arm for support.

Near the end of the day, two police officers stopped me and asked if I was all right. I told them I was fine and asked, "Why?" They replied that there was a report of a woman fitting my description who looked as if she were intoxicated. I said in my spastic, lisping mode of speech, "Oh, how I wish this were intoxication!" and hobbled away. For the few hours that I was walking the course, I had forgotten that I was physically different from most everyone else. After all, there I was, doing what everyone else was doing. Then, for a moment, I thought that it was raining, but I realized that mine was the only face that was dripping wet. The tears had finally begun to come.

I am flooded with memories. When I see old friends, I am reminded of the way I used to be with them. When I see people running or folk-dancing or riding bikes, I realize that those are all things I loved to do and will never do again.

The neurological problem with which I live has become a teacher for me. Every day, I more fully understand that it is not going to go away. This is the first time I have ever chosen to expose my affliction publicly. It is uncomfortable. I would much rather write about teaching Jewish music—I'd be happy to tell jokes. This is, for me, the ultimate self-disclosure. This is the place where I stand alone and unknowing, broken, vulnerable, hurting.

I don't want this impairment. I want it to go away. I don't want to end up demented. I don't want to have my cognitive function or my body function impaired to the point of losing my dignity. I do not want to die. There is no escaping it. I could try to be numb to it, avoid it, pretend it away. But this is my life.

We Are Not So Different

Once I began to accept that this dysfunction is part of me, I realized that I am not so different from anyone else. At some time, you too will say: Sometimes I can't stand up, sometimes I can't sit down, sometimes I can't hold on, sometimes I can't move, sometimes I can't talk, sometimes I can't find the right words, sometimes I say things that are inappropriate, and sometimes I want to throw in the towel because I get so tired. My life, my movement disorder, is a metaphor. Perhaps the physical manifestations are different, but every moment we live, our bodies keep us working and moving as they are dying and disintegrating.

The only real difference between us is that I am sitting *here* and you are sitting *there* and I am telling you *my* story. Neither of us is a stranger to torment, distress, fear, confusion, or internal conflict. Both of us will watch people dying in our arms and wonder when it is our turn.

Confrontation with death and suffering is part of what motivates us to be. Think about why we do the things we do. Ultimately we are driven by death to live. I do not mean that the fear of death drives us, but death itself, which paradoxically gives us the motivation for an authentic and meaningful life.

I find that I am alone. The fact that no one else in this world will ever *really* know what another feels or fears or wishes or dreams is both exquisite and terrifying. Each of us is unique and alone. Ironically, this is something that we have in common.

How to Address This Universal Condition?

I have a theory of *teshuvah* (repentance, return) that relates to the human confrontation with disability and death. I believe that *teshuvah* is about recognizing who we are as *neshamot tehorot* (pure souls). When the High Holidays come around, in order to accomplish *teshuvah*, we must take the time to come back to who we were before we learned about danger and the need for self-protection.

At the cost of abandoning our inner essence, our pure souls, most of us have chosen to protect ourselves with walls and barriers. Often, these not only keep dangers out, they also keep joy out; they keep our *selves* out. *Teshuvah* is coming home to the truest self, to, "I'm sorry I hurt you. I wasn't myself." It is an opportunity to peel off the facade and uncover the games we play in an effort to hide our most pure and vulnerable essence.

While concerned with the self, the process of *teshuvah* is not narcissistic. The annual call to *teshuvah* is a reminder that our time in this world is limited and that we must journey honestly, accepting that our gifts are not for us alone, but meant to be put forth in this world as a way of reconstructing the once whole, now shattered vessel whose shards, the mystics tell us, are scattered all over the universe. Returning to ourselves helps us engage in partnership with the world and with the One of all that is.

When our bodies, the sacks in which our *neshamot* are housed, begin to give way and we confront death, the psychological walls that we build for our protection also begin to give way. They make way for the soul to emerge, becoming accessible not only for self, but for everybody and everything around. Denial of our finitude would only feed the avoidance of our spiritual potential.

I am reminded of a *midrash* about the destruction of the Temple. The *Shekhinah* (close-dwelling presence of God, associated with the feminine), which dwelled in the Temple, went out and accompanied the prophets as they warned the people of the potential destruction for which their behavior was paving the way. Each time the prophets were rejected by the people and the *Shekhinah* saw that the people did not change, She withdrew further into the walls of the Temple. Finally, there was nowhere for her to go. The *Shekhinah* withdrew into the Holy of Holies, the core of the Temple. At that point, the Temple was destroyed.

As we build more walls for self-protection, there are fewer places for our souls to emerge. Confrontation with suffering can enable us to lower our walls and provide more space for our souls, but the ultimate liberation happens when we die, and our bodies, like the ancient Temple, turn to dust.

Suffering Can Teach Us

When a disaster befalls us, we have the option to withdraw or to attempt to transform the experience into a teacher for ourselves, our friends, our families, and our communities. Our personal disaster may not only be *our* gift, it may sometimes be another's gift as well. It is our obligation to discover these gifts and give them to others. A word, a thought, a touch may turn someone's life around and give meaning to their existence. And you may never know that you were responsible for that.

It is interesting that people tell me how different I am now from how I was before this happened. They tell me that I was arrogant and a prima donna. But from my perspective, I was always afraid to ask for what I needed. Even when I was performing, I was timid about asking for things.

In our society, it is somehow acceptable to ask to have your needs met when ill, but if you are well and ask to have your needs met, that is perceived as demanding or even "prima donnaesque." As a public person, I sometimes find myself the object of other people's projections. Many people whom I thought were my friends left me once they saw me in my disabled state. Ironically, other people who were "put off" by what they perceived as fame and stardom were now unafraid to approach me. Because I was in need of their help, I had now become accessible.

People assume that my song *"Mishberach"* was written after I became impaired. The fact is that I wrote this prayer for healing in 1986, eighteen months prior to the onset of my impairment. Even then I was in need of healing—though I did not know it. Once I was visibly vulnerable, people were better able to see me as vulnerable in other ways, as well. I, too, came to know my vulnerabilities.

Prayer as a Tool

I have found that prayer is a powerful tool for acknowledging and experiencing grief, anguish, anger, hope, love, and, consequently, healing. BT *Berakhot* (54a, 60a) teaches that it is incumbent upon us to bless what is good and also what is not good. To bless what is good is a cinch; to bless what is bad is hard. Blessing what is bad is the first step to admitting the adverse impact of events on our lives, and therefore, the first step towards healing.

I studied the *asher yatzar* (blessing over bladder and bowel function).[1] Those "vessels" and "holes" mentioned as opening and closing perfectly and allowing us to stand before God, are not, in fact, working properly in me. I wondered, "How is it possible to stand before God and pray if I am damaged goods?" I wept, finally concluding that if the *peshat* (simple, contextual meaning) assumed my body functioned flawlessly, then I would need to create a *midrash* (legend in the Rabbinic style) for myself. The literal meaning was unusable for me, so I found a spiritual message: If I do not open myself, if I am closed, if I do not give of myself, then is it possible to "stand," that is, to exist and pray, before God?

I have found that access to a concrete text like this one—whether it angers me, hurts me, lifts me, calms me, or does nothing but remind me that I am capable of thinking coherently—is essential to healing.

I pray that the pain I may experience will continue to teach me so that I may learn to be a source of someone else's comfort. My friends and family have been like angels. I have been enveloped with their gentleness and goodness. I pray that I be granted the physical strength to give as I have been given to, and to participate in the continued healing and well-being of all who touch my life. May I never forget that for every loss we experience, a thousand gifts will come, and the shattered vessels will be ever so slightly more whole than before.

Afterbirth

JUDITH GLASS

"Only he shall not go in unto the veil, not come nigh unto the altar, because he hath a blemish; that he profane not My holy places...."
—LEV. 21:23

"What we need...as women, is not experts on our lives, but the opportunity and the validation to name and describe the truths of our lives, as we have known them."
—ADRIENNE RICH, "MOTHERHOOD: THE CONTEM-
PORARY EMERGENCY AND THE QUANTUM LEAP"

I spent five years trying to get pregnant, five years that included basal thermometers, dilation and curettage, exploratory surgery, fertility drugs, pain, and disappointment. Finally, my husband and I gave up on the fertility clinic, filed for an adoption, bought a house, and went on with our lives. Two months later, I was pregnant, and obviously very happy. Our son was born with a very small left hand, which had three unformed fingers and two malformed but useable fingers. He was beautiful. And I could not stop crying.

All this happened in 1971. Twenty-five years later, my thinking has clarified on the many issues involved. I understand my own experience better, and I have some ideas about the cultural meanings of that experience. In this vignette I use both a personal voice and an analytic one to convey the interrelated layers of feelings and ideas. The personal is indeed political!

The Messages of Language

The sociologist Erving Goffman defines stigmatizing as a process that one group inflicts on another in an attempt to spoil identity.

Dr. Judith Glass has had a long and varied academic career and is now an independent consultant on organizational and gender issues. She is a member of the steering committee of the Los Angeles Jewish Feminist Center.

My story illustrates two different experiences of stigmatizing labels. The first is my experience of "barrenness," a label Judaism applies to childless women, a label connoting incompleteness, failure, unhappiness. And yet, childbearing is only one aspect of a woman's life and creative potential. At no time was my life "barren"; I have always been a teacher and an activist for social change, and I both give and receive much from others. It was feminism that sustained me and gave me tools to withstand the withering power of a patriarchal label that reduces a woman's worth to the fruit of her womb. Yes, I wanted a child, and, yes, I felt great pain each month that I did not conceive. But the need of my culture to "spoil my identity" exacerbated that pain instead of relieving it.

The second experience of stigma, of the attempt to spoil identity, is the language available to describe children like my son. Karl Kraus called language "the house in which the human spirit lives."[1] Language provides the context of our experience of others, of self, of the world. Consider the words: Birth defects, handicapped, crippled, or the currently in vogue terms exceptional, differently-abled, special. None of them is emotionally right, nor is any a description of him. Yet, if he were to take on these labels, surely his experience of himself would constrict the house of his spirit. I have come to say about him that he was born with certain anomalies, a term that is more neutral and therefore less labeling— not an ideal solution, but, at least, these are words that I can get out of my mouth.

Wholeness and Perfection: Transcending Duality

An anomaly is an element that does not fit a given set or series of expectations. Anomalies can be confronted either negatively or positively. Because recognition of anomaly leads to anxiety, we can respond negatively, by ignoring, denying, or condemning differences—rendering whatever is anomalous either invisible or stigmatized. However, we can also choose to confront anomalies positively, by creating a new pattern of reality in which the anomaly has a place, in which the anomaly enriches meaning by calling attention to other levels of existence. Life can be understood in broader terms and celebrated in its mystery and variety.[2]

Too often, both Judaic and Western culture have chosen the negative route. Leviticus 21:17 states that physical perfection is required of all things presented in the Temple and of the priests themselves. It is instructive, in this regard, to consider other tribal cultures in which the physically imperfect person is named *shaman* (holy one) precisely because of physical difference, a more positive confrontation with anomaly that points the way to expanded levels of meaning, embodiment, and belonging.

Many responses to the body and bodily anomaly exist in Judaism, and these can be in deep conflict with one another. One set of responses denigrates the importance of the body or the mind altogether and stresses instead purity of soul (Isaiah 40:6–8). Other responses honor the body as a temple and consider cleanliness a *mitzvah* (Lev. *Rabbah* 34:3). While Leviticus requires physical perfection of the priests and all things presented in the Temple, the Talmud describes the messiah as a leprous beggar (BT *Sanhedrin* 98a).

Over the last twenty years, through my embrace of feminism, I have understood yet another way of confronting anomaly: Rejecting a mind/body, spirit/matter duality. Within Western and Rabbinic thinking, both, there is an undeniably dualistic strain in which mind or spirit is separate from body or matter, whereas feminist thought stresses the unitary experience of oneself in the world as spirit embodied, and body inspirited.[3]

Dualistic thinking would have us believe that wholeness is a function of spiritual health, while physical perfection is quite another ideal. But none of us is physically perfect, and our inability to achieve this valued state damages our self-image and our spiritual life, thus belying the assumed duality. Feminism, in contrast, emphasizes the interconnection of mind, body, and spirit, which together affect our sense of self.

In this context, the greatest challenge in raising my son was to ensure that his self-esteem, his self-image, not be damaged by the prejudices or anxieties of others; that he grow up whole, anomalies and all. Accordingly, it was a very special moment when he came home from nursery school with a big tracing of his body, in which his hands were clearly visible. His willingness to be drawn, to have the drawing on the wall of his classroom with everyone else's, was a major sign that he, body and spirit, was okay in his own eyes. More recently, his girlfriend told him that she likes to hold his left hand because it is different than holding other hands, and so she always knows that it is he. For them both, this is an attitude and experience in which anomaly enriches meaning and in which bodily experience enhances spirit, and vice versa.

Another aspect of wholeness and self-esteem is the ability to cope with prejudice, which involves an understanding of who has the problem. Stigma and prejudice reside in the community at large, and both parents and stigmatized children need to know this. Shortly after my son's birth, my aunt expressed her surprise that I did not cover his hands. Yet, if my husband and I did that, and later taught him to hide his hands from the view of others, we would be conveying the message that he had something of which to be ashamed. Rather than do this, we taught him that people who stared at him, or children who asked him over and over what happened to his hand, were concerned about their own bodies, and that the problem was theirs, not his. Ironically, by treating his body and using his hands naturally, much less attention was called to them than would have been the case if he did keep them in his pockets. One year, his elementary school teacher told me it was Thanksgiving before she even noticed his fingers; and his art teacher in college, a man with an artificial arm, did not "see" his hand for over a year.

The Tyranny of Medical Expertise

Part of the path to learning and acceptance lay through doctors' offices. Practically the first words the obstetrician said to me after the birth were, "Oh, they do wonderful things these days." This was a man who was able to cope only by denying his emotions and mine, who could only suggest fixing the body. We did take our son to major hand surgeons on both coasts and received a wide range of advice, most of which we rejected. One incident was particularly revealing about the medical imagination and its approach to issues of anomaly.

A famous hand surgeon examined our son when he was a year old. He told us that he could transplant bones from the boy's toes into his hands, and while his anomalous hand would never look exactly like his other hand, it would look more like a "normal" hand than it did at the start. We have more bones in our toes than we need to walk on, so there was no problem there. How many surgeries were we talking about? Ten or twelve microsurgeries. Would there be a lot of pain? No.

My father, who had accompanied us to the surgeon's office, was much heartened by this visit. He heard that "the problem" could be solved. I was horrified, and totally sure that it was the wrong thing to do—that after ten or twelve surgeries, there would be nothing left of the child but his hand. We would have implicitly told him that he was not okay and that we had to "fix" him. In fact, we did nothing, a decision we have never regretted.

However, that moment was fraught with vulnerability. We are taught to respect medical advice, even as we have learned to get second opinions. (We did get second opinions, which reinforced our decision to reject surgery. But, even if the surgical advice had been reiterated, we would not have made that choice.) The issue here is that the doctor's focus was on what would advance his scientific knowledge; he saw our son as a body on which he could practice his experimental technique, a body separate from spirit. We had to decide on the basis of what would benefit the interconnected spirit and body of our child. It was our decision that what could have been done, should not be done; there was no technological fix. It was a lonely moment.

The Need for Blessing

I have thought long and hard about whether "differentness" should be acknowledged, celebrated, or go unremarked in birth ceremonies. The arrival of new life is so wondrous that the birth itself must be the focus of celebration. There are many anomalies that are not known at birth, and many kinds of differences, some of them stigmatized, that appear only later in life. Yet, the issue of wholeness and self-esteem is so significant, our achievement of these spiritual values so problematic, and community prejudice so widespread that some ritual attention is warranted. By understanding that physical "perfection" is available to no one, the entire community can be helped to new awareness.

Of course, birth itself or naming ceremonies are not the only appropriate moments for ritual around anomaly, nor are they the only occasions when special blessing is needed. There are many impacted times impact in the lives of parents or children. Some involve celebrating victories in difficult situations; others, healing from painful experiences. First days in school, camp, or after-school activities, or starting to date are examples of such times. So are occasions of giving or receiving comfort and support; acknowledging pain, fear, vulnerability, and love; exploring perfection and *shalom* (in this case, translated as wholeness); or evoking strength. Decisions to have surgery or other medical interventions—and decisions not to—are also appropriate occasions for the recitation of a blessing. *Shabbat* (Sabbath) is always only a few days away from such moments and, because it is a time when children are traditionally blessed by their parents, is an apt time for special blessing. Furthermore, because *Shabbat* is a time for learning, gathering as a community, and celebrating creation, it can also be used as an occasion for confronting prejudice.

I considered the traditional Jewish blessing, originally meant to be recited upon seeing someone who was unusual or anomalous in appearance. The blessing—*barukh attah adonai eloheinu melekh ha'olam meshanneh habriyyot*, Blessed are you, God, Ruler of the universe, who varies creation—was unacceptable to me because it distances the reciter from the person encountered, and turns that person into an Other. Imagine yourself hearing this blessing, maybe several times a day, all the time knowing the occasion for its recitation. Would you feel acknowledged and esteemed as a person? Or would you feel singled out as different—as a freak, albeit part of creation? Would you be inclined to seek out other people, or hide from them? It simply is not sufficient to acknowledge that creation is varied. It is necessary to bless it in an affirming voice, in a manner that enlarges a common space and builds personal identification with, and recognition of one's self in, another person—however anomalous or "typical" that person is.

With all this in mind, I have written a blessing that may serve to guide and center us. Like the *Sheheḥiyyanu* (blessing for reaching a new or momentous occasion), it is meant for use at multiple moments. The fact that it is appropriate for all children and not just children with anomalies helps to remind us that our standards of bodily or mental "perfection" usually serve to lessen self-esteem. Using a form introduced by Marcia Falk,[4] the blessing says:

נְבָרֵךְ אֶת מְקוֹר הַחַיִּים שֶׁבָּרָא אֶת צוּרוֹת הַחַיִּים לְמִינֵיהֶן, וְאֶת כֻּלָּנוּ שְׁלֵמִים, גַּם אִם לֹא מֻשְׁלָמִים.

Neverekh et mekor haḥayyim shebara et tzurot haḥayyim lemineihen, ve'et kulanu sheleimim, gam im lo mushlamim.

"Let us bless the Source of life in its infinite variety, that creates all of us whole, none of us perfect."[5]

Sexuality and Ritual Purity

When the Siren Stops Singing

JANE RACHEL LITMAN

"Thou shalt not lie with..."
—16 TIMES IN LEV. 18

"How wonderful you are, love, how much sweeter than all other pleasures."
—SONG OF SONGS 7:8

I like sex. There, I said it. I don't mean just kissing and cuddling, and not only the great spiritual moments when my ego boundaries drop and I become one with my beloved according to Kabbalistic (Jewish mystical) theory. I like the normal, non-supernatural, physical experience, the hot desire and electric sensations of my body, the feelings of...you know, sex.

But sex, particularly my own sexuality, is a not an easy topic about which to write.[1] As a woman rabbi, I am regarded as the rough equivalent of a Jewish nun, and so I feel that I must keep even the existence of my own sexuality a closely guarded secret. Speaking about sex, except in the most intellectual and theoretical terms, is the great taboo. Despite the sexual freedom that has been ours for the last thirty years, despite the AIDS crisis, increased sexual activity among young people, and media exploitation of sexual themes and imagery, people today, particularly adolescents, do not have much more information about sex than I did twenty years ago. Sex remains a veiled and mysterious topic; even the mechanics are barely explained.

Rabbi Jane Rachel Litman, co-editor of this volume in the *Lifecycles* series, is on the faculty of California State University, Northridge, and serves Congregation Kol Simcha of Orange County, California.

As a girl of about twelve or thirteen, I was desperately curious about sex. I wondered how one chose a partner, and how sexual activity might feel with a partner. Then, one evening as I was collecting donations at a political rally for peace in Vietnam, in one of those enthusiastic moments after a particularly uplifting and memorable speech (which, by now, I have completely forgotten), another of the volunteers, my good friend Michael, put his arm around my waist, leaned over, and kissed me. I was pleased and happily responded in kind.

Not all my early sexual experiences were as pleasant. Although many of them were gifted with the enthusiasm and eagerness of young love, others were disturbing or frightening. At a B'nai B'rith Girls beach party when I was about fifteen, my girlfriends literally had to pull a young man off me because he could not understand the word, "no."

Some incidents were just plain confusing. When I was sixteen, I went to Brotherhood Camp² for a summer to learn about ethnic diversity and social justice. There I met a brilliant, impassioned young activist, Alma. She and I became fast friends, exchanging ideas about how to redeem the world. One day after a long hike in the woods, arguing, citing this author, that poem, we sat talking on a log. As I gazed at Alma's beautiful animated brown face and blue eyes, I realized that she was the most lovely creature in all the world. Within me rose a feeling of intense physical desire.

My next feeling was one of equally intense disorientation. My world, though rich in literature, learning, and popular culture, had given me little enough information with which to interpret my strange, delightful gropings with adolescent boys in the back of darkened movie theaters. For my feelings about Alma on that summer day in the forest, I had no reference whatsoever. Certainly my Jewish education had given me nothing relevant to that moment. It was only years later that I could interpret what I had experienced.

My total confusion is neither a unique nor an isolated phenomenon. Women's inability to understand our own sexual feelings is a fairly common experience, whatever our sexual orientation or religious and social background. Whether we feel pressured to engage in sexual activities for which we feel no enthusiasm or we find that the erotic behavior in which we wish

to engage is stigmatized or forbidden, we are left dazed and confused. We are given too little information, few role models, mixed
messages.

Jewish tradition provides extensive guidance in a wide variety
of areas. We are told how and what to eat; how to allocate money;
how to fulfill our duties toward our children, families, communities. Why then does it give so little advice to women about how to
have a satisfying sexual life?[3] This is not all that difficult a question
to answer. Jewish religious norms and guidelines have been
shaped mostly by men, and, although men have traditionally considered women part of the Jewish community in terms of diet, holiday celebration, and even prayer (to a certain extent), women
have not been part of the sexual collectivity—rather, we are the
objects of it.

Jewish Woman as Siren[4]

Traditional Jewish thought views sexuality as an overpowering
male urge that must be tamed through legal injunction and religious discipline. The sexual constraints of Leviticus, rehearsed
every year on the Day of Atonement, the holiest day of the Jewish
calendar, are directed to men, not women. The biblical Book of
Proverbs warns *men* against the evil *woman*, a tempting "alien"
creature full of "smooth talk" (2:16–19).

Rabbinic Judaism emerged in an era when social and religious
gender segregation were more pervasive than in biblical times.
According to its cultural ideal, Jewish men spent their days in the
yeshivah (traditional academy of Jewish learning) in male homo-
social groups, passionately and erotically directed to the study of
text. Jewish women operated the domestic and, to a large extent,
economic life of the community. Sexual discourse, at least that
which has come down to us, was part of the male sphere.[5]

The texts that Jewish men wrote and studied give us some
insight into male sexuality, but provide very little guidance for
women. In fact, women were prohibited from studying these texts
specifically because it would give them ideas about, and perhaps
independence in, sexual behavior (BT *Sotah* 20a). When modern
women encounter these texts, we are often surprised by the male
sexual fantasies they contain.[6] Graphic stories of comparative

phallus size (BT *Baba Metzi'a* 84a), naked women almost seducing renowned scholars (BT *Kiddushin* 81b), homosexual temptation (BT *Baba Metzi'a* 84a), snakes crawling into women's vaginas (BT *Shabbat* 110), voyeuristic disciples hiding under their teachers' beds during intercourse (BT *Berakhot* 62a), and intercourse with animals (BT *Avodah Zarah* 22b) are woven into discussions of legal status, holiness, contracts, and torts. Later Jewish mystical material is even more redolent with male sex fantasy. The overflowing spring, the cosmology of the heavens, even the elongated birthing uterus and nursing breast are interpreted by Kabbalistic thought as representations of the divine phallus.[7]

Although the day-to-day reality of life varied greatly for each individual man, the symbolic system promoted by traditional text study heightened male sexual drive. The division of life into rigid gender roles also lessened opportunities for men to interact with women in non-sexual ways. From a male "gaze," women existed primarily in the sexual arena. According to Jewish law, the male sexual urge had only one legitimate outlet: A man could not legally masturbate; homosexual contact was taboo; nocturnal emission was discouraged by frightening stories of Lilith, and other female sexual demons who used semen to create demon children (*Zohar* I 54b). Sexual desire was to be fulfilled only in the marital bed. In addition, marital sex was restricted to two weeks in the month due to the laws of menstrual "purity." Women thus served as the objects of a considerable amount of pent up, repressed, and sublimated male sexual need. Women were not just desirable; according to Rabbinic thought, we were the powerful source of the male sexual drive. Our hair, arms, voices, legs could, according to cultural belief, inspire even the holiest man to forget his spiritual quest and become a mere puppet in thrall to the nearest woman.[8]

Each woman, just by virtue of being a woman, was the Siren, at least to her own husband. She didn't need to wear make-up or work out. She didn't have to go on diets and look like a fashion model; in fact, this Siren was supposed to wear concealing clothing and hide her hair in order to present a less compelling temptation to the poor men (other than her husband) who had to have contact with her. She was the most sexually powerful, alluring being on earth.

It may very well be that the role of fantasy Siren held some sexual fulfillment to many heterosexual Jewish women over the generations. Certainly, the enormous resources spent by women in our society to "look sexy" is evidence of the continued popularity of this sexual model. Numerous contemporary books of Orthodox literature about menstrual "purity" regulations still present this vision of sexuality, declaring the time of a woman's renewed purity, to be a monthly "honeymoon" and the *mikveh* (ritual bath) to be a kind of pampering women's spa.[9]

But the world of the Siren in Jewish culture relied on certain social structures that disappeared or diminished with the advent of modernity. Jewish men spend less time engaged in mystical text study. The *yeshivah* society and its literature has ceased to function as the overarching cultural norm for Jews. Other sexual outlets such as masturbation, adultery, sex with prostitutes, and homosexuality are decreasingly taboo for men. The vast majority of Jews no longer follow the menstrual "purity" laws. Symbolically and in actuality, male sexuality is less channeled to one specific source of desire.

Other Sexual Options

Modernity also opened up new options for Jewish female sexuality. Jewish women began to have the possibility of being sexual subjects, rather than elevated objects of male desire. With these new possibilities came an enormous Jewish silence. No longer limited to the role of Temptress, Jewish women looked to their tradition for a more broadly defined sexual wisdom, but found little direction.

Some women became "free thinkers," eschewing marriage. Jewish socialists, anarchists, communists, and Zionists attempted to articulate a new women's sexual ethic apart from traditional economic and familial roles.[10] Gertrude Stein wore pants, moved in with her Jewish lover Alice B. Toklas, and set up housekeeping. Emma Goldman publicly advocated birth control and free love. But the majority of Jewish women just quietly stopped going to the *mikveh*, stopped covering their hair, calves, and arms, and looked to secular culture to advise them about sexuality.

The postwar "sexual revolution" gave Jewish women even more choices. Today, unmarried heterosexual women are likely (even expected) to engage in sexual activity. Lesbianism is more accepted by the Jewish community, particularly in urban environments. Sexual behavior in general is extremely privatized, and non-public activity between consenting adults, including women, is generally tolerated. For non-Orthodox Jews, there is surprisingly little gossip, whispering, denunciation, or opprobrium in regard to women's sexual behavior. This is a situation unique in Jewish experience.

Current Jewish Thought on Sexuality

Most contemporary Jewish movements and leaders continue to respond to this unique situation with silence, or with theoretical positions completely out of touch with social reality.[11] Occasional discussions tend to be male-centered in both approach and content. Several popular articles explore contemporary Jewish sexual ethics as a "sliding scale" with monogamous marriage at one end and rape(!) at the other.[12] Never mind that to women rape isn't sexual at all—it is a violent assault—and that many women in monogamous marriages express little or no sexual desire. These articles merely reframe from a modern perspective the traditional Jewish view of sexuality as an overpowering male urge in need of control. Of course, in many ways this is a disingenuous subterfuge. Although the goal purports to be the control of male sexual drive, in reality the objects of control, both in the past and now, end up being women. It is women who must control how we dress, where we travel at night, with whom we talk at parties, etc.

The Jewish community's failure to speak out about women's sexuality, much less generate new ideas about it, is doubly unfortunate because, frankly, our secular society also offers very little to women in the way of sexual theory or practice. It advocates all the worst aspects of the Siren syndrome—objectification, superficiality, materialism, unrealistic expectations—with few of the more benign ones—passionate desire, sacred symbolism, loyalty, every woman as a vision of beauty. Judaism's lack of ideological evolution in regard to sexuality has left several generations of Jewish women foundering. Popular culture (often, like Rabbinical literature, dominated by Jewish men) gives confusing mixed messages: Sometimes Jewish women are "oversexed nymphomaniacs," otherwise we are mostly "frigid."[13] Jewish lesbians are essentially invisible. In general, there is little, if any, information about well-adjusted, self-loving, happily sexual Jewish women. Young Jewish women are left to embark alone on a difficult course of sexual experimentation. In the best of circumstances, this sexual experience serves as a foundation for self-understanding, communication, and respectful relationships that avoid the errors of previous encounters. In the worst of circumstances, it can lead to a devaluation of self, greater confusion, disease, and emotional distress.

A Sexual Vision in Line with Reality and Ideals

It was only after an unfortunate marriage at the age of twenty, and a very painful divorce six years later, that, as a single woman in my late twenties, I began that slow process of trial and error. After my divorce, I read modern feminist theory about sexuality, which asserts the view of women as agents rather than objects. Living in the San Francisco Bay Area brought me into contact with people engaged in a variety of sexual and lifestyle arrangements—gay, bisexual, lesbian, transgendered,[14] monogamous, non-monogamous, married, living together, communal households. I dated a number of people, including a rabbinical student who was committed to celibacy before marriage, but whose imaginative idea of what constituted celibacy differed greatly from my own! I found out that the different people I dated had wildly variant ideas about the appropriate timing, nature of, and approach to sexual issues. Slowly, I discovered what was right for me, how to communicate this to others, and how to set boundaries to protect my choices.

Although my academic field was Jewish Studies, I found nothing in Jewish literature, historic or contemporary that spoke to my personal reality. This essay is my contribution to a more informed and realistic Jewish approach to women's sexuality today.

Judaism must offer models of human sexuality other than ardent male lust for female Sirens that is in need of ever-vigilant social control. Extending this model by installing strictures to control *women's* lust would only be a step backward. Very few contemporary women experience our sexuality as an overwhelming urge which, if unchecked, would run wild. If anything, modern women need more permission in terms of our sexuality, not more control. Women must have the social support to refuse unwanted sexual activity *and* to pursue desired sexual expression. Judaism must acknowledge women as sexual beings with a variety of needs and passions. The central issue for women is less about the mechanics of sexuality than about sovereignty, choice, and self-respect. From women's perspective, sexuality is not manifest in a sliding scale between violent coercion and civilizing institutions such as marriage, but in a feeling within ourselves—our bodies and imaginations.[15] This is as true for women in long-term committed relationships or marriages as it is for single women in the dating world.

Empowerment and sovereignty help us pay more attention to the messages our bodies and minds deliver; nevertheless, impediments to self-knowledge persist. Lesbian and bisexual women often find it hard to understand or come to terms with the nature of our own desires. Heterosexual women are often so overwhelmed by male sexual demands that we cannot find space to know our own wishes. All of us at times bargain sex for love and acceptance, or even just being left in peace. Women's sexual desire remains an enormous taboo, a thing that "nice Jewish girls" are not really supposed to feel.

Yet, it turns out that Jewish sacred text, specifically the first chapter of Genesis and the Song of Songs, presents sexuality as a gift from God—not a scary, out-of-control drive requiring suppression. The Bible teaches us that we are holy, created in the divine image. Even Leviticus, for all its Thou-shalt-nots, regards sex as a particularly sacred act, and the Jewish mystical tradition clearly follows suit. There is certainly Jewish precedent for seeing sexuality as other than a terrifying inner *yetzer hara* (evil inclination).

In line with this understanding, it is important not to scapegoat sexuality for general human frailty. Obsessive antisocial sexual behaviors may be viewed on a par with other addictive behaviors, and sexuality itself should not be demonized. Similarly, sexual harassment is best viewed as a form of power abuse and discrimination, not a form of sex. Sexuality is not a bargaining chip. Ignoring or suppressing sexual feelings will not make a person a saint; neither can sex be effectively traded for love, security, or ego fulfillment. Sex can be powerful and chaotic, but this is true for other activities in our lives as well. Imagine if we approached driving an automobile with the same level of ignorance and terror we bring to sex; if there were as little agreement about the rules of the road as there is about appropriate sexual behavior, there would be nothing but accidents and wreckage.

Wisdom for the Future

Sexuality is a form of intimacy. Like other forms of intimacy, such as friendship, being part of a support group, mentoring, and parenting, there are risks associated with taking on too much too soon, as many a new step-parent finds out. In my experience, sexual relationships are most successful when we think through our desires and how best to satisfy them. Unsafe sex[16]—which can spread life-threatening diseases—clearly violates the Jewish religious affirmations of the sanctity of life. The larger Jewish wisdom about human relations—not to lie, cheat, manipulate, harm, coerce, or behave abusively—applies to the sexual realm. Self-knowledge, good communication, respect for others—spiritual goals encouraged by Jewish ethical values—are the most important tools for a healthy, satisfying sexual life. Lesbianism, bisexuality, and various other minority sexual preferences are within the range of normal human desire. They are not pathologies or inherently immoral, and do not require massive apologetics or justifications.

For Judaism to play a significant role in the ethical, physical, and spiritual development of Jewish women, it must deal with contemporary reality. Silence and denial will not serve the needs of Jewish women of all ages for moral guidance about sexuality or any other challenging life theme. One goal of religion is to awaken people to the sacred and meaningful in daily life. To do this, it is important that Jewish religious leaders and institutions articulate theories and models of sexuality that speak to the Jewish women of today.

"In Your Blood, Live": Re-Visions of a Theology of Purity

RACHEL ADLER

"Speak to the whole Israelite community and say to them: 'You shall all be holy, because I Adonai *your God am holy.'"*
—LEV. 19:2

This article deals with laws regarding menstruation and Levitical laws of ritual purity. Ritual "purity" is distinct from cleanliness or virtue; ritual "impurity" implies neither dirt nor misdeed. A primary source for purity laws is Leviticus 15. Men's and women's genital discharges, including menstruation, were regarded as impure. A menstruant was impure for seven days (including her time of flow), and contaminated anything she touched, and any man with whom she had intercourse. Following this seven-day period she returned to a state of purity. After the destruction of the Second Temple, the system of bodily contamination and purification fell into disuse except for the laws regarding menstruation and sexual relations. These were explicitly applied to the entire population. The Rabbis imposed additional days without sexual intercourse. At the end of the bloodless interval, purity was restored by immersion in a mikveh *(ritual bath). These regulations are euphemistically called* tohorat ha-mishpaḥah *(purity of the family), and constitute one of the three commandments directed specifically to women in the Rabbinic system.*[1] *—Eds.*

Twenty-five years ago, as a young Orthodox woman, I began what became an influential essay with the words, "All things die and are reborn continually."[2] I was wrong. Sometimes we cannot repeat ourselves. We can only transform ourselves. Yet our moral responsibility for that earlier self and its acts lives on. Twenty-five years later, as a feminist Reform theologian, I continue to be faced with an essay I wrote, an essay that continues to be quoted, cited, and reproduced, promulgating opinions and prescribing actions

---

Dr. Rachel Adler is a theologian and ethicist whose writings, including *Engendering Judaism* (Jewish Publication Society, 1997), discuss the intersection of Judaism and gender.

that I now cannot in good conscience endorse. My essay was called "*Tum'ah* and *Taharah*: Ends and Beginnings." It dealt with the ancient laws of purity whose major surviving form is the powerfully valanced body of law and custom concerning women's menstruation. Because this legislation governs sexual and social behavior and attitudes so pervasively, it can be said that menstrual impurity is constitutive of the religious selfhood of women in Orthodox Judaism. I undertook to justify this legislation by constructing around it a feminist theology of purity.

Confronting my essay, I have had to ask myself: What is the responsibility of a theologian when she no longer believes what she taught to others as Torah? Merely to recant is insufficient, because theologians are not just theorists. They exemplify ways to live out Jewish commitments with integrity. What I owe to those who read and were persuaded by my theology of purity is not merely to outline abstractly my revised conclusions, but to tell a richly detailed story about a particular process of rupture and transformation in a specific time and place.

My task is complicated by the fact that the earlier essay itself represents a kind of transformation—a reframing. Even the title is eloquent of that project: "*Tum'ah* and *Taharah*: Ends and Beginnings." It signals that I had defined my topic as a theological understanding of the entire ancient category, not just the part of it pertaining to women. The title evades the words "woman," "sex," "*niddah*" (menstrual impurity), "menstruation," and "*mikveh*" (ritual immersion by which purity is achieved). It also eschews the common euphemism "*tohorat hamishpahah*" (purity of the family), in which women are reduced to a nameless function whereby families are produced and maintained in purity.

Interpreting Impurity as Egalitarianism

In my essay of twenty-five years ago, I attempted to reframe the meaning of women's menstrual impurity by reintegrating it with the other purity regulations stipulated in Leviticus, rather than focusing upon it as a unique phenomenon.[3] I interpreted all these regulations as ritual expressions of a single theology of purity equally relevant to women and men. I now see clearly how this generalized reframing reflected my awareness of and hopefulness about egalitarianism as a value in secular society. Probably, it was the discrepancy between my sense of self-worth and entitlement as a participant in secular and in traditional Jewish contexts that heightened my experience of *niddah* as a source of gender stigma.

Egalitarianism seeks to normalize women by stressing their similarity to men. That is how I sought to neutralize the stigma of *niddah*: By emphasizing its kinship with the purity laws applicable to men. I maintained that all impurity ritual enacted a common set of meanings. Implicitly, this was a denial that any special "women's meaning" distinguished menstrual impurity from impurities contractable by men. The strategy I chose has been used extensively by secular jurisprudence to neutralize discrimination: Obscure or ignore the differences on which discrimination was predicated and stress instead the commonalities all are presumed to share.[4] That the laws of pollution had once applied to men was therefore indispensable to my argument, even though men had not observed them for many hundreds of years.

Women's Otherness and Menstrual Impurity

It is important to understand that my concerns were as much the-ological as social. Existing theological justifications of menstrual impurity did not help me to make sense of myself as a God-creat-ed creature. They treated me, to use Kantian terminology, as a means to someone else's end, rather than as an end in myself. To have the observance of *niddah* and *mikveh* justified to me as the instrumentality whereby my husband was entitled lawfully to cohabit was both inadequate and insulting.

Indeed, the otherness and the instrumentality of women were foundational presumptions of the men who wrote about these laws.[5] What was significant about menstruation for them was that it made women uniquely capable of causing men to sin by trans-mitting pollution to them. They never asked themselves how it would feel to be someone to whom such a capacity had been assigned or whether menstruation might have other meanings to those who menstruated. Their one educational goal was to per-suade or terrify women to keep their pollution to themselves.

Some sources threatened non-observers with death in child-birth or deformed children (BT *Shabbat* 32a–b). Others promised

observers a honeymoon every month in compensation for the
estrangement of *niddah,* on the dubious assumption that sex is
most satisfying when the participants are unfamiliar.[6] The only
rationale the sources did not offer was the rationale that motivates
all sincere piety, the one held out to men: That observing the commandments would make one holier and bring one closer to God.

I required an explanation that acknowledged my personhood
as intrinsically important and affirmed my capacity for spiritual
growth. Even more urgently, I needed to understand how a body
that menstruates, a body that pollutes, could be a holy body. The
male writers were concerned about how women were to comport
themselves in their impurity. I wanted to know what it might
mean to be pure.

Insights from Anthropology and Comparative Religion

Intuitively, I sensed that the classical texts by themselves would
yield no answers. The topic had not interested their creators
because women as spiritual subjects had not interested them.[7] I
took my questions into fields of secular learning: Anthropology,
literary criticism, comparative religion. These areas provided perspectives to focus upon the Jewish texts. They offered forms of discourse in which I could view myself as a subject and participant
rather than as an object to be passively defined. The classic anthropological work of Mary Douglas taught me a new way to understand the categories of purity and pollution.[8] Douglas argues that
the body may be viewed both as a symbol and as a mirror of society. Upon it are inscribed the categories that make sense of the universe. Protecting the demarcation lines of those categories protects
us from chaos or meaninglessness. Pollution is the punishment for
violating those boundaries, and thus endangering the coherent
world. Supplementing Douglas' theory of pollution with a literary
reading of the texts in Leviticus, I theorized in that article written
twenty-five years ago that the boundary crossed by all those who
incurred impurity was the boundary between life and death. I
maintained that all forms of impurity were regarded as encounters
with death and were associated with conditions imaged as
death-like or life-diminishing (menstruation, seminal emission,
and the erosive skin diseases the Bible calls *"tzara'at"*), or as nexus

situations that bridge the passage between life and death (e.g., childbirth and the purification ritual for corpse-impurity).

The comparative religion scholarship of Mircea Eliade provided me with an understanding of water as an ancient and universal symbol of regeneration and renewal, and of cycles as markers of sacred time and affirmations of restoration.[9] Using his formulation, I depicted the *mikveh* as the womb or the watery chaos from which Creation is elaborated, a life-giving fluidity in which forms can be repeatedly dissolved and made new.

Drawing on these sources, I relocated menstrual impurity and *mikveh* in a universal, cyclical process by which all creation endlessly rehearses its death and rebirth. In the context of this theology, menstruation was not only normalized, it acquired powerful spiritual significance. While the theology justified the laws of menstrual impurity and supported their observance, it sought to reframe their meaning, to remove their stigma, and to discover their spiritual value.

The sources I brought to my theology of purity, however, built their arguments upon assumptions very different from my own. In fact, some of the implications of these assumptions were incompatible with Orthodoxy: That diverse religions have comparable or analogous symbols, myths, and practices; that valuations such as pure and impure are socially constructed and not divinely proclaimed; that religious meanings are derived not merely from texts, but from how the words of the texts are lived out in communities. Rabbis who viewed my work as merely an effective apologia for getting educated women to use the *mikveh* had no interest in pursuing these disturbing implications. They regarded secular sources much the way they regarded women, as instruments, rather than as ends in themselves. But the more I came to understand the scholarly sources I had utilized, the deeper and more troubling were their implicit challenges to the work into which I had incorporated them.

Gender and the Social Facts of Impurity

What did it mean to formulate a theology of purity that was blind to gender difference and silent about gender stigma, when the only kind of impurity with behavioral consequences in Orthodox communities is gender-specific—menstrual impurity? What did it mean to claim that the theological meaning of *niddah* had to do with symbolisms of life and death, when its impact on women's lives was obviously and concretely sexual? What did it mean to describe *niddah* as part of a cycle when, in the public life of the communities in which it was observed, women were always treated as if they were impure?

The social facts about ritual impurity in living communities are about the impurity of women. Sexual relations with a *niddah* are forbidden (Lev. 18:19). Also forbidden are physical contacts and expressions of affection, on the grounds that they could lead to sexual relations.[10] In all but the most left-wing Orthodox circles, the general presumption of *niddah* status is a reason for denying women access to the Torah and for excluding them from conventional social courtesies like shaking hands.[11] In contrast, men experience themselves socially as pure. Although they may meet the qualifications for biblical impurity (having had a seminal emission, for instance, or contact with a corpse), there is no behavioral consequence. The only men who have to contend with impurity laws are *kohanim*, descendants of the priestly clan, who may not expose themselves to corpse impurity (Lev. 21:1–4). *Kohanim* who obey these laws, although they probably bear some second-hand impurity from polluted others, experience themselves as utterly pure. Socially, then, purity and impurity do not constitute a cycle through which all members of the society pass, as I argued in my essay. Instead, purity and impurity define a class system in which the most impure people are women.

A more rigorous literary analysis would have called into question my reading of biblical purity law. The word *niddah* describes a state that is neither socially nor morally neutral. *Niddah*, from the root *n.d.y*, connotes abhorrence and repulsion. In a recurring prophetic motif, it is associated with adultery, idolatry, and murder.[12] The icon for sinful Israel wallowing in its corruption is not the corpse-handler or the leper but the exposed *niddah*, her skirts stained with menstrual blood, shunned by passers-by (Lamentations 1:8, 17).

I explained that imagery away, interpreting it as an expression of prophetic despair and loathing at societal impurity that refuses to be cleansed. *Tum'ah* (impurity) is a stigma, I argued, only when it is divorced from the purification cycle. At some earlier time in Israel's history, I believed, there had been a Golden Age when the cycle had revolved smoothly and blamelessly for both women and men, when gender had not been a source of stigma. This belief informed my reading of the purity texts of Leviticus. But this belief is untenable.

Utilizing cross-cultural anthropology, Howard Eilberg-Schwartz argues convincingly that the stigma upon menstrual blood enables ancient Israelite religion to draw a crucial distinction between men's and women's capacities for holiness.[13] The uncontrolled blood flowing from women's genitals is blood that has the power to contaminate. Its antithesis is the blood of circumcision deliberately drawn from men's genitals, which has the power to create covenant. Mary Douglas' explanation of purity categorization is insufficient, Eilberg-Schwartz suggests, because the symbolism of the body and its fluids, embedded in categories and rules, does not merely reflect but is constitutive of the social structure within which it applies. The Israelite purity symbolism that associates masculinity with fertility and control, and femininity with death and disorder, constructs a culture in which men dominate women. This polarization of the symbolic meaning of gender is intensified by developments in Rabbinic and post-Rabbinic Judaism: Purity laws affecting men become atrophied, while those affecting women are elaborated and made more stringent.

My Apologetic Reinforced the System

My theology claimed that impurity was universal. The social reality, since the Rabbinic period at least, was that impurity was feminine. My theology claimed that impurity was normal and morally neutral. Literary and anthropological evidence, as well as contemporary social reality, identify impurity as deviant and a source of stigma and exclusion. All the meanings of menstrual impurity asserted by my former theology are explicitly disconfirmed by historical precedent, literary analysis, linguistic usage, and communal practice. And yet women embraced this theology with great fervor and felt transformed by it.

What I had succeeded in creating was a theology for the despised, reminiscent of certain strains of early Christianity, where worldly power went unchecked, the slave remained a slave, the poor stayed poor, the woman was subject to her husband, but the meaning of indignity was inverted and transfigured: Humiliation was triumph, rejection was salvation, and death, eternal life. My theology upheld the rules and practices that sustained women's impurity by holding out to the impure a never-before-experienced sense of purity. For women who were touched by this theology, *mikveh* became not merely the water that made one sexually accessible once more, but water that cleansed the soul.

It became acutely painful to me to meet these women at lectures and conferences and have them thank me for a theology I had come to believe is both intellectually and morally unjustifiable. It seemed inadequate to tell them I had changed my mind, now that my teaching had been so strongly integrated into their spiritual praxis. I did not know how to be accountable to the people who had learned from me. I had never heard a theologian say that he or she had been wrong. In addition, I was left with questions of faith and practice, some of which are still unresolved for me. Is the *mikveh* usable for women's ritual? Should we ritually acknowledge our menstruation? Can we continue to regard the Holiness Code of Leviticus as sacred text? What does it mean to be pure?

Transforming the Meaning of Purity

When Jewish women who were not Orthodox appropriated my reframing of immersion in the *mikveh* to mark occurrences for which no ritual expression had existed, they taught me an important lesson about the possibility of salvage. They began using the *mikveh* to purify themselves of events that had threatened their lives or left them feeling wounded or bereft or sullied as sexual beings: Ovarian tumors, hysterectomies, mastectomies, miscarriages, incest, rape.[14] In waters whose meaning they had transformed and made their own, they blessed God for renewed life. They imbued these rituals with a different understanding of what purity means.

Those who create and practice these rituals appear to agree with the writers of the ancient texts that impurity afflicts the embodied human self; it is not a malaise of disembodied soul. But for the feminist Jew, impurity seems to mean the violation of physical or sexual integrity, death by invasion. If purity is the mirroring of God's oneness in human wholeness, it is no less fragile and transitory than humankind itself. Our flesh is gnawed by disease, eroded by age, menaced by human violence and natural disasters. Our minds and souls are subject to intrusions, exploitations, indignities. We keep breaking or being breached. We keep knitting ourselves together, restoring ourselves, so we can once again reflect God's completeness in our female or male humanity.

When I was Orthodox, I thought that God's Torah was as complete as God: Inerrant, invulnerable, invariable truth. I thought that I, the erring, bleeding, mutable creature, had to bend myself to this truth. Whatever I was or saw that did not fit had to be cut off, had to be blocked out. The eye—or the I—was alone at fault. I tried to make a theology to uphold this truth, and as hard as I tried to make it truthful, it unfolded itself to me as a theology of lies.

I do not believe the laws of purity will ever be reinstated, nor should they be. The worlds reflected in such rules are not worlds we inhabit. Neither should we seek to replicate such worlds. They are unjust.

In the mind of God, according to a *midrash* (Rabbinic legend), is a Torah of black fire written on white fire (Deut. *Rabbah* 3:12). In the hands of Jews is a Torah written in gall on the skins of dead animals. And the miracle is that the fire of God's Torah flickers through our scroll. I continue to learn the purity texts, hoping for some yet-unglimpsed spark, but that is not enough. I must learn what purity can mean in my own world and in the most human world I can envision. For if ours is a Torah of and for human beings, it may be perfected only in the way that we perfect ourselves. We do not become more God-like by becoming less human, but by becoming more deeply, more broadly, more comprehensively human.

We must keep asking the Torah to speak to us in human language, this crude jargon studded with constraints and distortions, silences and brutalities, that is our only vessel for holiness and truth and peace. We must keep teaching each other, we and our study partner the Torah, all that it means to be human. Human is not whole. Human is full of holes. Human bleeds. Human births its worlds in agonies of blood and bellyaches. Human owns no perfect, timeless texts because human inhabits no perfect, timeless contexts. Human knows that what it weds need not be perfect to be infinitely dear.

Sacred need not mean inerrant; it is enough for the sacred to be inexhaustible. In the depths of Your Torah, I seek You out, *Eheyeh*, creator of a world of blood. I tear Your Torah verse from verse, until it is broken and bleeding just like me. Over and over I find You in the bloody fragments. Beneath even the woman-hating words of Ezekiel I hear You breathing, "In your blood, live."[15]

———◦《◉》◦———

4

Themes of Numbers/Bemidbar Rabbah: Creating Community in Times of Transition

——◦◉◦——

What is my place in the world?
How can I pass through the wilderness of my own life?
How shall I be part of a community,
and what sort of community do I hold as the ideal?

L ife and lifecycle have often been compared to a journey, with markers and milestones along the way. The image is complex. On the one hand, a life journey is rarely experienced as efficient; seldom if ever do we take the shortest and most direct line between two or more points. An individual life journey can be circuitous and wandering, with the path emerging as one walks. For all the traditional maps and popular modes of transport, there are no inevitable, preordained stations.

On the other hand, even the most wandering journey implies a purpose and a direction, a sense of destiny as well as destination. Likewise, "markers" and "milestones" imply a history. Certain trails have been worn and prepared by those who came before us. The Lonely Man myth notwithstanding, journeys are rarely solitary. Even trailblazers walk in and with community. Both of us have taken on pioneering roles with the support and friendship of others, including one another. If this book treads new ground in women's Bible study, it is thanks to a vision and workload shared by many.

Women writers have drawn heavily on the image of journeys. A survey of any feminist library or bookstore yields scores of books with the word "journey" in the title—everything from Ann Bannon's early lesbian novel *Journey to a Woman*; to Christine Downing's guide, *Journey Through Menopause*; to Nelle Morton's personal and theological reflections in *The Journey Is Home*. The fascination with journey stems from its multiple implications, all of which are relevant to contemporary life—that the process of getting where we are going is significant in its own right; that we are growing because of the transition; that there is a better place ahead; that each of us must find our own way even though we share the journey with others.

On the course of their journeys, many women have diverged from the beaten path—marrying later or not at all, exploring traditionally "male territory." Jewish women in particular have been at the forefront of union organizing, social work, and the feminist movement. Community remains vital—both for company on familiar paths and, especially, when breaking new ground.

The twin life themes of journey and community dominate and inform the Book of Numbers. Numbers, in Hebrew, *Bemidbar* (in the wilderness), traces the journey from slavery to redemption in geographic, temporal, and spiritual terms. The book begins in the wake of the revelation at Sinai and ends with the Hebrew tribes ready to invade the land of Israel. "These are the journeys of the Children of Israel" (33:1). Through formative experiences during their wanderings, a ragtag band of slaves is forged into a cohesive community.

The stories told in Numbers imply that it is not enough merely to be passively "freed"; psychological and communal maturation are part of an ongoing process of *becoming* free. Thus, the wilderness of the Sinai desert is both the setting of religious evolution and a metaphor for the inner wilderness of the Israelites in their quest for holiness. The desert is a place of danger and deprivation—hunger, thirst, raging fires, vicious animals—but also of miraculous growth and creativity—talking beasts (Num. 22:28–30); rocks that spurt water (20:8f); food that falls from the sky and comes up from the earth (11:6f). Numbers recounts an epic communal journey, from West to East, from one generation to the next, from slavery to security, from doubt to faith.

Major Thematic Divisions

The Book of Numbers can be divided into three sections: The prologue (Num. 1:1–10:10) covers an interval of nineteen days and is devoted to taking an accurate stock of resources before departing from Sinai. The central text (Num. 10:11–25:18) describes the people's wanderings and communal transitions in the desert over a period traditionally calculated at forty years. This section details rebellions, punishments, sacrificial instructions, the deaths of Miriam and Aaron, and confrontations with other nations, including the story of Bilam (Num. 22:1–24:25). An epilogue narrates a stay of a few months on the plains of Moab (26:1–36:13) during which the people prepare to implement the divine plan for conquest and life in the promised land. Included in this section are land apportionment, the sacred calendar and holidays, the appointment of Joshua as leader, laws of conquest, and boundaries and cities of refuge for the new land. The sections are highlighted by two main censuses, one at the onset of the book (hence its English name translated from the Greek) and one toward the end, in readiness for the conquest.

These exhaustive censuses mark the transition of the generations from the people born in Egypt to those who come of age in the wilderness. The first census counts the generation of the exodus, a group of people who repeatedly and publicly yearn to return to the land of slavery. The second census tallies a new generation, ready to fulfill the will of their God. The midpoint between the two is the incident of the spies in chapter thirteen, in which the elder generation proves itself psychologically incapable of entering the promised land. Numbers in many ways represents the "death of the old and the birth of the new,"[1] with the censuses serving as a frame for individual tales of several successive rebellions and reprisals. These rebellions stem from discomfort with the authority of Moses as well as the continuing insecurities of a people born into slavery. In the end, the challenges to Moses actually underscore his leadership, and bring forth a more united, cooperative generation, not socialized to the ways of life in Egypt.

The repeated insurrections involve core issues of communal life. They deal with concerns as basic as food and water (11:4–34; 20:5–13) and as contemporary as what constitutes appropriate familial relationships with non-Jews (25; 31:15f). The struggles take place over specific issues of content, but also encompass the very nature of the communal enterprise. Narratives of rebellion alternate with presentations of the law, as if to say that a people is built by means both of resisting and of accepting social structure. The various revolts raise questions about leadership, communal membership, legitimate authority, and due process (e.g., 12:1f; 16:1f; 25:1f). Many of the essays in this chapter grapple with similar issues in relation to communal identity.

Real vs. Romantic

A startling feature of Numbers is its bluntly self-critical portrayal of the fragilities and deficits of our ancestors. This contrasts starkly with the valorizing epics of most non-biblical literature of the period. Numbers does not intend to cast its protagonists in a heroic light, but rather to narrate a series of religious truths. Even God is shown in a less than completely flattering light; the God of Numbers can be punitive and narcissistic. The unflattering portrayals of Numbers imply that facing the present reality head-on is a necessary condition for growth and salvation.

This is an important model for our day when truth is too often subservient to the dictates of popular culture, "looking good," or market interests. In particular, women in our society are taught to evade unpleasant truths for fear of being "unladylike." Yet it is only when we fearlessly critique the behavior and values of our world, even of our Jewish community, that we open the possibility for redemption.

New Identities

Numbers explores the trepidation inherent in liberation. Freedom raises insecurity and fear because it generates new, unpredictable possibilities and choices for which each person must be responsible. As a newly liberated slave people, the Israelites validate psychotherapist Virginia Satir's generalization that people prefer the certainty of misery to the misery of uncertainty. Soon after the miracle of the parting of the Red Sea, the Israelites wish they had died in Egypt, rather than face hunger or thirst in the desert (Ex. 16:3).

Contemporary Jewish women continue to confront fears of being fully free. The old roles, however oppressive, were clear. Now, like the ancient Israelites, we must enter uncharted territory and grow into all sorts of new possibilities. As the Book of Numbers and this chapter make clear, the transition to a new system is not easy.

Transition brings the formation of a new identity, and the Torah uses a variety of symbols to convey this development. Numbers sees the evolution of a slave people and "mixed multitude" into orderly Israelite tribes named after, and—according to the story—descended from, the twelve sons of Jacob. Tribal identity is both concrete and metaphorical, representing worldly power and land distribution, as well as a spiritual connection to the clan narratives of Genesis. Group emblems in the form of banners, animal mascots, and blessings reenforce the tribal structure. The tribes are arrayed in a formal pattern, surrounding the sanctuary in the center of the camp. This arrangement conveys the notion that everything is in place: God in the tabernacle at the heart of the camp, tribes surrounding in perfect formation, (male) leaders at the head of their tribes.

Identity is not a fact of life, but a theme of life. It is created over time and space, in response to numerous life challenges. In Numbers, identity is repeatedly forged through deprivation and doubt, and faith is required to transcend the difficulties.

Although this message of growth and faith is certainly universal, on the whole, Numbers explicitly excludes women from its
major symbolic statements. Women are not tallied in either of the
censuses. They are neither counted nor their deeds much recounted. It is each *man* who stands before his own standard, in formation, according to the house of his fathers (2:17, 34). Women are not
only invisible as individuals, but also excluded from the patriarchal tribal identities of the *sons* of Jacob. There is no tribe of Dinah,
no namesake or lineage for Jacob's daughter.[2] Rabbinic *midrash*
makes an attempt to include women in some ways. *Sifrei Naso* 39
on Numbers 6:23, for example, explicitly reads women into the
(male-oriented) communal blessing. However, even when their
own language is more inclusive than that of the Bible, the Rabbis
justify not counting women:

> Why [does Num. 3:15 mention] "every male" [in the count-
> ing] without mentioning "every female"? Because the glory of
> the Holy One, blessed be God, results from males. King
> David said, "*sons* are a heritage of Adonai; the fruit of the
> womb is a reward" (Psalms 127:3). The "heritage of Adonai"
> refers to males (Num. *Rabbah* 3:8), but if females come, they
> are also a reward.

Women face a particular challenge in the formation of identity,
specifically because of this lack of religious equity. It is hard to find
our place in the encampment when we are not among those counted. Even so, an ability to live at the margins can be an advantage
during times of flux and transition. As Mary Catherine Bateson
puts it, "Women have always lived discontinuous and contingent
lives...which turns women's traditional adaptations into a
resource."[3]

Contemporary advocates of women's equality believe that,
whatever skills we have gained at the margins, it is important for
women to be enumerated in our own right. It is only if we count
that we can find our territory in the Jewish tradition. It may seem
obvious to us that women "count," but the fact is that women were
not numbered in *minyanim* (prayer quora) until about twenty years
ago—and Orthodox congregations still don't count women.
Married women's donations to many Jewish charities are still
counted under their husbands' names. Recent scholarship on

Jewish women's history and literature attempts to grant women their place in the communal cultural encampment by finding the ways in which women did count and contribute in the past.

Women's Marginalization: The Case of Miriam

Miriam is an active and important figure, a biblical hero to whom many have pointed as an example of women's leadership and empowerment. In Numbers 12, she and Aaron appear to engage in a rebellion against their brother, Moses. They question Moses' singular prophetic ability, asking "Has not God spoken through us also?" (Num. 12:2). It is significant that only Miriam, and not Aaron, is punished with a skin disease. Aaron and his male descendants retain their priestly status. Miriam and subsequent generations of women are marginalized, however. After Miriam, women seem to be excluded from officiating in public religious life. Women's leadership is thus delegitimated.

Miriam's unique status as prophet and leader underscores the absence of women in general. In Exodus, she appears to have a constituency of women (Ex. 15:20–21). In Numbers, she is a woman alone and suffers punishment alone. This is often the fate of the token woman who achieves unusual leadership or authority. Her experience is always other and odd, and when inevitable problems arise, her difference is frequently held to blame. In recent years, as Jewish women have taken on public leadership roles in politics and religion, the stigma of Miriam as lone woman is happily losing its grip.

Men Directing Women

It is difficult to imagine a great many women leaders and prophets in the legal context and atmosphere of Numbers. Chapter 30 inquires whether and under what circumstances women are capable of making sacred commitments. The vows of emancipated adult women—that is, divorced women and widows—are valid. Those of minor or married women are conditional, however, upon the affirmation of father or husband, respectively. This pattern clarifies that in terms of religious duties, women who are attached to men are regarded as quasi-property, in the category of supervised wards, people not entirely free to make their own choices.

Unfortunately, the societal annulment of women's commitments had practical as well as symbolic consequences. Following the biblical precedent, Rabbinic Judaism tended to prohibit women from acting as witnesses or signatories to contracts. Women were thus barred from concluding important legal and market activities. In effect, women were relegated to second class status in both religious duties and economic life.

Even more disturbing than the general disregard for women's oaths is the troubling description of the degrading ordeal imposed upon a woman suspected of sexual infidelity. As reported in Numbers 5, she is publicly forced to drink "bitter waters" in order to prove her innocence or uncover her guilt. In a move toward gender equity, the Rabbis theoretically extend punishment beyond a guilty woman to her lover and, under certain circumstances, to her husband (BT *Sotah* 28a; Num. *Rabbah* 9:35). Ultimately, they eliminate the ritual altogether (Mishnah *Sotah* 9:9). (Of course, Temple rituals were no longer practiced following the destruction of the Temple in 70 CE.) The Bible itself, however, offers no equivalent for men to this terrible humiliation—one of the very few instances in which a woman is at the center of ancient Hebrew religious life. The woman suspected of adultery is objectified as the sexual chattel of her husband and subjected to communal sanction. One can only speculate on the impact of this ritual on women's alienation from Israelite religious observance.[4]

Israel as God's Wife

Prophetic writings and Rabbinic *midrash* use the Torah's distrust of women's fidelity as part of their marital metaphor for the relationship between God and Israel (e.g., Hosea 1:2f, Num. *Rabbah* 9:45). The people Israel in the wilderness is personified as an adulterous woman:

> If at a time when God was angry at them, God showed them love, how much more kind will God be when pleased with them! What is this like? A king has become angry with his wife and said, "I will divorce her and have no pity on her

children. She is not my wife and I am not her husband."
However, he went to the marketplace, to the jeweler's, and
directed him to make some golden jewelry for his wife.... So
it is with the Holy One, blessed be, when He is angry at
Israel. (Num. *Rabbah* 2:15)

According to this *midrash*, the rebellions described in Numbers
erode the basic covenant, portrayed as a marriage between a male
God and his bride, Israel. Rebelliousness—adultery—is framed as
a female trait. The wrongful behavior of the entire community is
thus symbolically laid at the feet of its women. When sin is embodied as a female trait, real-life women are contaminated.[5]

The prophets and Sages also offer another picture of bridal
Israel. The time in the Sinai desert is presented as a nostalgic "honeymoon," when God was in the very midst of the camp, a pillar of
fire that all could see. In the *midrash* that opens this chapter, Rabbi
Vicki Hollander creatively translates the prophet Jeremiah in this
vein: "I remember how sweethearted you were in your youth, how
your pledges to Me shone with love, how you followed Me to an
unknown place far away into the desert, to a land filled with wildness, with no seed sown by human hand" (Jeremiah 2:2).
According to this view, Israel in the wilderness is a bride alone
with her beloved, without social obligations or institutions—no
Temple, no conquest, no land to apportion—to come between her
and her Mate. In this reading, the desert is a place where time and
normal affairs are suspended, a place of perpetual youth, innocence, and love.

Women's Place and Portion

In the Book of Numbers, Maḥlah, No'ah, Ḥoglah, Milkah, and
Tirtzah, daughters of Tzelofeḥad, lay claim to their property
rights as women.[6] According to the *Sifrei Pinḥas* 133 on Numbers
27:1, the sisters acted as they did because they perceived that
"God's compassion is not like human compassion. Humans are
more compassionate towards men than women, but the One-who-
spoke-and-the-world-came-into-being is not like that. God's compassion extends to both." The end result of the sisters' challenge is

that, as in the case of vows, women are in a liminal state, neither fully included nor fully excluded from the clan lineage.

The issue is raised twice in the biblical text (27:1–11 and 36:1–12). The daughters' request is brought directly before God by Moses, and results in the ruling that women whose fathers leave no sons behind may inherit land. A second request by the men of the tribe of Joseph—this one not reported to have been brought directly before God—results in a divine ruling, reported by Moses, that erodes the first: Brotherless women may inherit tribal territory from their fathers, but must marry within their father's tribe and family. This is because land, like tribal affiliation, follows the male line and will thus be lost to the daughters of Tzelofeḥad through marriage. Women's place and portion is dependent on their relationship to men—the Israelites who own and bequeath land, the Israelites who count and are counted.

Applying the Lessons of Numbers

It is sadly ironic that although Israel is described as emerging from the wilderness experience with a more mature, developed relationship to the divine, the women of Israel are largely excluded from this relationship during the desert wanderings. Women's tribal membership, leadership, vows, and connection to the land are all weak, compared with those of men. The text attempts to negotiate a path for women as dependent outsiders.

How then are we to form authentic Jewish communities that fully include women? Numbers highlights the centrality of territory, religious voice, and leadership in transforming a people. It leads us to ask: What is the appropriate Jewish "territory" for women? Is it in separate groups and organizations? Are women part of the central narrative and community or essentially marginal to them? How can women assert a religious voice? Are women worthy of trust? How can women successfully take on communal leadership and avoid being marginalized or tokenized?

The essays in this section address these and other related questions, even as they conform to the narrative direction of the biblical book. Rabbi Vicki Hollander opens the chapter with "The Gift of an Unsettled Habitat," a *midrash* on the nature of living in the wilderness. Employing the style of homiletical *midrash*, a traditional

Jewish textual genre, Hollander reveals some of the political and theological subtext of Numbers: Issues of control, power, freedom, covenant, and faith. The *midrash* leads into a complementary guided visualization.

In "Wilderness," poet Alicia Ostriker creates a lyrical blend of biblical and American metaphors to evoke the emotional essence of wandering in search of a promised land. Her work serves as a bridge between evaluation of available resources and actual movement—the same transitional shift that occurs in Numbers.

Social historian Dr. Martha Ackelsberg evaluates the intersection of traditional notions of community with the current communal enterprise. Ackelsberg presents an overview of Jewish communal life from the days of the Bible to the present, and discusses fundamental communal tensions such as concern for boundaries, struggles over leadership, and disagreement over behavioral standards.

In "Images of the Self in Moral Action and Community," psychotherapist Barbara Eve Breitman interweaves theories of development of self with the need for social action in the world. She explains how *tzedakah* (sacred practice of charity) and *gemilut hasadim* (practice of lovingkindness) create a moral sensibility of responsibility *and* of relation with others. This paradigm transcends current gender categories.

Biblicist Dr. Ora Horn Prouser examines the process of creating community during extended periods of change. Coming out of a traditional egalitarian perspective, she views the bewildering gender issues of our day in light of the Israelites' behavior in the desert.

Rabbi Margaret Holub speaks from her personal experience as a member of several diverse communities. Today's communal "murmurings" parallel the discord that was part of the development of the Hebrew tribes in the wilderness. Holub also offers advice on how to create positive, functional Jewish women's groups.

"Prayer in the Wilderness" by Rabbi Sheila Peltz Weinberg explores models of prayer in the creation of community, using her own worship experiences and the Book of Numbers as liturgical guidelines. She closes with inspirational meditations based on biblical verses.

Jewish activist Arlene Agus and novelist Esther Cameron end the chapter with prayers for the transitions in prayer itself: The beginning and conclusion of a service. Both authors reflect on the meeting of individual and group. The chapter as a whole, like the Book of Numbers, moves through wilderness toward the realization of divine covenant.

Dis/counting women presents a painful barrier between us and the promised land. The march toward redemption for women and for Judaism itself begins with a realistic evaluation of the history and nature of community. It culminates with the realization of a more sacred social order.

—J.R.L. AND D.O.

Wilderness

The Gift of an Unsettled Habitat: A *Midrash* on a *Midrash* on "In the Wilderness"

VICKI HOLLANDER

"God spoke to Moses in the wilderness (bemidbar) of Sinai, in the tent of meeting...."
                                                   —NUM. 1:1

In keeping with the style of classical homiletical midrashim, *this contemporary midrash focuses on a particular verse from the Torah, but then brings in a text from the Prophets or Writings to develop its ideas. Only after expounding and developing a theme is the circle completed: Each section ends with a quotation of or reference to the Torah text. The twist of this* midrash *is that it uses midrashic rather than Toraitic passages as its main texts — Numbers* Rabbah, *rather than Numbers. Thus, this is a* midrash *on a* midrash *on the Torah, rather than a* midrash *directly on the Torah. The text elaborated deals with the opening of the Book of Numbers (the epigraph above). When phrases from the main text are explicated in the body of the* midrash, *they are printed in bold. The meditation that follows the* midrash *explores the same themes in a different way.* —Eds.

Rabbi Vicki Hollander resides in Vancouver, B.C., where she weaves together ritual, poetry, spiritual counseling, and retreats.

—◈—

"'And God spoke to Moses in the wilderness of Sinai': Why in the wilderness of Sinai? Our sages have inferred from this that **Torah was given in accompaniment of three things: Fire, water, and wilderness.**"

—NUM. *RABBAH* 1:7

"Wondrous deeds before our ancients,
in the Land of Egypt, in the fields of Tzo'an.
Split sea and they passed through
Waters piled high in a heap
By cloud leading them during the day
Throughout night by the light of fire."

—PSALMS 78:12–14

Fire: Symbolizes wisdom, insight, passion.
Light was the first thing God created.
Fire enables us to see.
Fire warms us.
Fire helps us cook and eat.
Fire shields us from danger. Fire, in control.

Water: Symbolizes life, abundance, generosity.
Division of water was the second act of creation.
Our bodies consist mostly of water.
Our crops depend on water.
Water cleans. Water renews.
Through the waters of the Red Sea we passed
safely to touch land.
Water, in control.

Wilderness: Symbolizes freedom, wildness, a place where
    seekers find.
Wilderness, dry land, was God's third act of creation.

Wilderness, where bushes burn and are not consumed.
Wilderness, where mountains touch heaven,
Where firstborn sons are laid down for sacrifice and saved.
Wilderness, in control.

Torah was given with three things:
Fire: That we should burn with insight and wisdom. **Water:**
That we should be nourished and overflow with life.
Wilderness: That we should know our wildness and
approach, come forward, out of love.

Wilderness, Torah, and Freedom

" 'And God spoke to Moses in the wilderness of Sinai':
Why was the giving of Torah marked by these three
things? To indicate that as these are free to all
humankind, **so also are the words of Torah free.**"

—NUM. *RABBAH* 1:7

"Then laughter filled our mouth; on our tongues, joy...."

—PSALMS 126:2

Free: No one owns Torah.
It is available to all who seek.
Torah is owned by no group.
No money can buy it.
Torah's words, lessons, messages are open to all who draw
near.

Free: Torah's words cannot be totally captured by anyone.
There is always more to learn, to understand.

Free: There is always enough of it.
We can never get it all. There is always more.
Like fire, water, wilderness, Torah does not end.
Torah defies time.

Free: Torah is burning, fluid, wild, unfettered, pure, spirited, available
For us to come and drink from it.

Imitatio **Wilderness;** *Imitatio* **Torah**

"'And God spoke to Moses in the wilderness of Sinai.':
Anyone who does not **throw him/herself open to all
like a wilderness...**"

—Num. Rabbah 1:7

"Even the darkness is not too dark for You. The night shines
like day, the darkness is as light."

—PSALMS 139:12

Throwing oneself open: To life, to feeling, to experiencing
the mystery of living.
Our teachers saw how life can close us up,
    that sometimes just to survive we shut parts of ourselves
    off.
We close up feelings, money, loving, risks, adventures, spirit.
We are instructed:
Throw yourself open like a wilderness,
    for in the opening up, we can be touched in new ways.
In the opening up, we can hear Torah.
In the opening up, we can be transformed.

Wilderness and Covenant: Receiving Torah

"'And God spoke to Moses in the wilderness of Sinai.':
Anyone who does not throw him/herself open to all
like a wilderness cannot **acquire wisdom and Torah**."

—Num. Rabbah 1:7

"My soul thirsts for you, my flesh longs for you
in a tired and dry land where there is no water."
—PSALMS 63:2

Our people stood in wilderness, amidst
    fire, clouds of water, and God.
Our people stood beneath the *ḥuppah* (wedding canopy).

We, wizened by the world, toughened,
We, made of fire, water, and wilderness,
    are also invited to approach.

Touched by life's winds, chaffed,
Standing in the wild places,
We are enjoined to choose God freely.
We, closed by the harsh cuff of experience,
    are urged to throw ourselves open to feel,
To enter into relationship,
    under *ḥuppah* as did our people long ago,
To taste the sweet taste of Torah,
    like manna on our tongues,
To dance, to celebrate
To meet our Partner
In the wilderness.

"I remember how sweethearted you were in your youth,
how your pledges to Me shone with love,
how you followed Me to an unknown place
Far away into the wilderness
to a land filled with wildness
with no seed sown by human hand."
—AFTER JEREMIAH 2:2

Guided Imagery on the Gift of a Continuing Story in an Unsettled Habitat

Relax. Breath deeply. Imagine yourself going back in time, back to the old country, through the streets of Spain, back to Babylonia, to Canaan, to the desert.

The desert, your birthplace. You were born after the crossing of the Red Sea, and your tribe treasured children. They looked for signs of each child's spirit-task.

You were taught many things as a child. You learned to build and tend **fire**. You respected its power.

You learned how to listen for **water**, how to feel its call, watch the earth, dig for it. Water was life.

All the ways of living in the **wilderness** were taught you: How to read the stars; how to tell if a storm approached; what herbs were used for healing, and where you could find them.

Each night, sitting around the fire, the women and men told stories. Stories of the Beginnings, the great Flood, the ancestors. Stories interspersed with messengers suddenly appearing, guiding us on our way. Stories of journeys into the unknown. The elders of the tribe, women and men, taught each youth whose soul was drawn to them. Now your elder calls you: It is time to take your place in the circle by the fire.

Stories may come to you in dreams, or rise up within you when it is their time to come into the light again. You will learn the mysteries threaded like beads through the teachings. You, memory carrier, story holder, shall bear our ancestor-wisdoms, giving them life, freeing them. They will light the way as you walk ahead into unseen land.

If you have any questions you wish to ask your elder, ask them now. Listen for the answer. Listen for any other message your elder has for you. Ask if your elder has something to give you to take with you on your way. Then, say goodbye to your elder.

Sit quietly in the desert. The sun is about to set. It is time to leave this place. Ready yourself for returning. Leave the wilderness, travel through the streets of Jerusalem, by the waters of Babylon, on to golden Spain, back to the old country. To the place where you now sit. Breathe deeply. And open your eyes.

Wilderness

ALICIA OSTRIKER

*"According to the number of the days in which you spied out
the land, even forty days, each day for a year, shall you bear
your iniquities, namely, forty years, and you shall know My
displeasure."*

—NUM. 14:34

*"And you shall be My people and I shall be your God, that I
may uphold the oath I swore to your ancestors, to give them a
land flowing with milk and honey..."*

—JEREMIAH 11:4–5

We wander the wilderness. Can we ever remember a time when
it was not so? Always a remnant recounts the story,
intoxicated by time future. Next year in Jerusalem. Soon
the promised land.
What is the promised land, that the Almighty drives us to it?
A child runs by the oceanside, dashes barefoot into the surf,
runs giggling to the mother. The grandmother hitches her
pruning hook over a long branch. In the evening the man
under his fig tree and the man under his vine get together to
discuss the next election. The wives join them and nobody
makes them afraid.
Milk and honey, the desert blooms, spacious skies.

The promised land really exists, it really doesn't, are we
there yet. Borders unspecified, we will know when we've
arrived. Profusely fertile, agriculturally a heartland;
good also for grazing; room for cities. Are we there yet?
The land of opportunity, these truths to be self-evident, it is
necessarily elsewhere, from sea to shining sea. No more
auction block. Take this hammer, carry it to the captain,
tell him I'm gone. Emancipate yourself from mental slavery.

Alicia Ostriker is a poet and critic; her most recent book is *The Nakedness of the
Fathers: Biblical Visions and Revisions* (Rutgers University Press, 1994).

If you are not for yourself who is for you, if you are for
yourself alone what are you, and if not now, when? Keep your
hand on that plow, hold on. No more sin and suffering, no
pharaoh, no king, one man one vote, are we there yet, no
grinding the faces of the poor, are we there yet, no bribing
of judges, are we there yet.
An impossible place, let freedom ring in it. We've been to
the mountain. We've seen the land: A terrain of the
imagination, its hills skipping for joy. How long, we say,
we know our failure in advance, nobody alive will set foot in it.

Definitions and Ideals of Community

Reclaiming the Fragments: Rethinking Jewish Community from a Feminist Perspective

MARTHA ACKELSBERG

"'Thus shall you bless the sons of Israel' (Num. 6:23): This teaches only about a priestly blessing for the free men born of Israel. But what of women, converts, and slaves? The scripture states, 'I will bless them' [Num. 6:27]...implying: The priests will bless the free men born of Israel, but God will bless them all—the entire community of Israel."

—NUM. *RABBAH* 11:8

"Face to face the Lord spoke to you on the mountain out of the fire."

—DEUT. 5:4

"R. Yohanan said: A statue—a thousand people look at it, each and every one of whom says, 'It is looking at me.' Even so the Holy One made each and every person in Israel feel that God was looking at him [or her], saying, I am the Lord thy God. In another comment, the verse is read, The Lord spoke with you face after face on the Mount.... R. Levi said: God faced them in many guises. To one He appeared standing, and to one seated; to one as [a] young [man], and to one as [an] old [man]...."

—*PESIKTA RABBATI* 21, 6 ON DEUT. 5:4

As the above passages suggest, community is composed of diverse individuals—people with differing needs, sensibilities, and perspectives. Even those present at the revelation at Sinai—the

---

Martha Ackelsberg, Professor of Government and Women's Studies at Smith College, was a founding member of Ezrat Nashim and of B'not Esh, and lectures and writes on Jewish feminism, Jewish community, and Jewish families.

defining, if not constitutive, event of the community of Israel—
may well have had very different experiences of it. Questions of
sameness and difference have been with the Jewish people since
our beginnings.

Although community has always been fraught with conflicts
and difficulties, it has always been an essential Jewish value.
Indeed, Judaism is fundamentally communal. Jewish spirituality is
often most fully realized in community: Certain significant
prayers, for example, require a *minyan* (prayer quorum); they cannot be said in the ascetic isolation so valued in many other traditions. Not only prayer, but Jewish study has also been communal:
We are enjoined to find others with whom to learn (*Avot Derabbi
Natan* 8:3).

Jews have shared a communal history, a common fate, and a
commitment to a collective mission, however differently we may
have defined it, of realizing God's reign on earth. To those ends,
we have organized ourselves in communities; cared for the sick,
weak, and poor among us; tended to the education of the young;
and otherwise dedicated ourselves to developing and maintaining
bonds of solidarity.

Yet questions of who defines and makes rules for "the Jewish
community" have perplexed Jews for generations. Over the years,
conflicts over community have focused on three major areas: What
determines membership status in the community; what constitutes
standards of behavior for members; and who exercises authority,
and on what grounds. Debates on each of these questions have
flourished, even despite the relatively narrow limits (for most of
Jewish history) on who could participate in the discussion—
women, the poor, and the uneducated were excluded. These issues
of community have been a focus of special concern for contemporary Jewish women.

The power of the communal bond is often cited by traditionalists as a reason for limiting innovation, particularly around questions of women's status. For many years, women were not
honored with *aliyot* (honor of reciting blessings before and after
the Torah is read). If a reason for that exclusion was given—other
than "it just isn't done"—it was the Talmudic phrase, *mipnei kevod
hatzibbur* (because of the honor of the congregation/community
[BT *Megillah* 23a])—a phrase still cited in Orthodox and some

Conservative communities. The implication was that *aliyot* for women would reflect badly on the larger community—it would look as though there were not enough men capable of assuming the responsibility. Furthermore, as women came to an awareness of our subordination within Judaism, many of us were told by rabbis or other leaders that we ought not air our concerns about male dominance in Judaism too loudly, because that might "reflect badly on the community." Or, similarly, that we ought not demand full and equal rights for women in Judaism because the "continuity of the community" depended on women's maintenance of home and family.

In terms of gender and in general, Jewish communal boundaries have rarely been more contested than they are today. Is membership in the community to be defined by birth to a Jewish mother or conversion, or is there a place for patrilineal descent? Should the non-Jewish partners of intermarried couples be members of synagogues? May they have *aliyot* at family celebrations? May women constitute a prayer group? The answers to such questions are almost as varied as the number of synagogues in the United States. There is, in fact, no agreement among contemporary Jews as to what "Jewish community" means. That diversity of perspectives is a reflection of the fact that we are not *a* Jewish community, but a *multiplicity* of Jewish community groups, each claiming authority and legitimacy. In this context, many perceive diversity as divisiveness. The question is: How might we use diversity for our betterment?

As Old as the Bible Itself

While communal themes recur throughout Hebrew scripture, Numbers is one of the fullest treatments of the topic. Tensions among Moses, Aaron, Miriam, and the Israelites are commonly seen as power struggles, but they can also be understood as conflicts over what the community was to be and who had the right to claim authority. This is illustrated in the rebellion against Moses by Miriam and Aaron (Num. 12:2–15). Asking "Has the Lord spoken only through Moses? Has He not spoken through us as well?" Miriam and Aaron challenge the legitimacy of Moses' claim to solitary leadership. God sharply defends Moses' special status, and Miriam is stricken with "snow-white scales" (12:10).

It is interesting that "the people did not march on until Miriam was readmitted" to the camp, after her scales were healed (Num. 12:15). Evidently, God's will with respect to leadership was not necessarily that of the community of Israel. In addition, only Miriam was punished, not Aaron. While many explanations for this apparent inequity are plausible, it may be that, in the context of the emerging patriarchal community, insubordination on the part of Miriam, a woman, called for swifter and more visible punishment than for Aaron.

Korah's rebellion (Num. 16), like that of Aaron and Miriam before him, was a challenge to the authority of Moses (and Aaron) over the community. But Korah's challenge went even further: Korah and his followers "combined against Moses and Aaron and said to them, 'You have gone too far! For all the community are holy, all of them, and the Lord is in their midst. Why, then, do you raise yourselves above the Lord's congregation?'" (16:3). God intervened, Korah and his followers were destroyed, and Moses' authority was reasserted. But the repetition of such stories makes clear that at least some members of the community objected to the given hierarchical structure of leadership and to their exclusion from participation in setting and carrying out communal goals.

Beyond the Bible as Well

In the first centuries of the Common Era, newly developing Rabbinic Judaism recognized the significance of these conflicts, and attempted to address them through *midrash*. In some *midrashim*, the Rabbis validated the notion of diversity of views in the community. The *midrash* from *Pesikta Rabbati* quoted at the start of this essay is one example. While some Rabbinic texts seem to advocate a pluralistic vision of community, the Rabbis themselves asserted their own authority as the sole legitimate interpreters of both law and community standards. If some *midrashim* defended individuality and pluralism, others promoted the legitimacy of Rabbinic authority even over direct revelation from God (BT *Baba Metzi'ah* 59b).

Differences between the Rabbi's situation and that of Aaron, Miriam, and Koraḥ are striking. In the biblical cases, Moses' authority was upheld by God, apparently against the wishes of a substantial number of the people. By contrast, Rabbis who claimed their authority through the community (even if they were not "elected" by it in the modern democratic sense) successfully asserted that authority against God's objection. Such stories are usually cited as examples of struggles over authority, but they also have much to tell us about the constitution of community: Specifically, the Rabbis argue that it is, to a considerable degree, up to members of the community—rather than God—to determine what community membership and leadership entail.

During the medieval and early modern periods, Jews in Central and Eastern Europe lived in separate communities (ghettos), and Jewish communal authorities regulated most daily activities. Those authorities were often chosen by (at least some) community members—usually the learned and/or wealthy males—although their formal grant of powers typically came from the local gentile ruler. In the context of a world where communal membership was the basis of all "rights," the hold of a community over its members was powerful. Although only the learned and/or wealthy males could participate in setting codes of conduct for the community, all members were obliged to follow them. Jewish communal leaders could maintain a high degree of control by threatening recalcitrant members with shunning, and/or banishment. The only real option open to those who would challenge communal authority was to leave the community, an option that became increasingly available in the modern world.

During the same time period, structures of governance were somewhat different within Sephardic Jewish communities (created by refugees from the Spanish expulsion/Inquisition). Patterns of participation were similarly gendered, if perhaps less restrictive along class lines. Both in Morocco and throughout the Ottoman Empire, Jewish communities (as all non-Muslim communities) were granted considerable communal autonomy, in exchange for the payment of taxes to the regime. In Morocco, for example, Jewish communities were governed by Castillian *takkanot* (regulations) derived from Rabbinic law. These *takkanot* were written by

scholars and read in the synagogue on a holiday before they could
be put into effect. Such readings provided the men in the community with an opportunity to appeal or propose modifications.[1]

After Emancipation in Western Europe, individual Jews were
accorded citizenship and further conflicts arose over power,
authority, and obligation within the community. Jewish creativity
flourished, resulting in a growing variety of bases for community:
E.g., Jewish socialism, Zionism, Reform, neo-Orthodoxy. Each of
these movements represented a challenge to conventional understandings of who constituted the Jewish community and held
authority within it, and what defined the obligations of its
members.

Now, in Our Day

Today, the term "community" is still sometimes used inclusively,
to refer to all Jews, regardless of affiliation or observance. It is that
holistic Jewish community, or "Jewish people," that is invoked in
the face of crisis—the Holocaust, the problems of Russian Jews, the
Six Day War. But on a day-to-day lived basis, Jewish communities
since the Emancipation are necessarily partial, precisely because
we no longer have universally acknowledged structures of authority. There is no one who can speak definitively for all Jews.

This fragmentation creates a unique opportunity for Jewish
women struggling to redefine Jewish communal life along more
egalitarian lines. The absence of authoritative communal structures brings to the surface tensions between what has been and
what might be, while highlighting questions of community and
difference. What do we mean now when we speak of "Jewish communities"?

One set of tensions revolves about communal standards of
behavior. Many Jews, including some feminist Jews, feel nostalgically drawn to the simplicity of a life governed by strict sex roles,
a romanticized "Fiddler on the Roof" old country in which everyone knew his or her place, and there was little need to worry about
status. I remember as a college student, participating in a weekend
study session on life in the *shtetl*, the small, largely self-contained
communities in which most Eastern European Jews lived. I came
home to my dorm, thinking how beautiful and simple such a life

might be. At the same time (and particularly in retrospect, with my since-developed feminist consciousness) my nostalgia was tempered by awareness that *shtetl* life was extremely difficult for most of its inhabitants and that its world was one in which all power—political, religious, economic, social—was centralized in the hands of a few men. It might have been simple, but it was surely not democratic; nor did it provide room for the kinds of self-development and -expression that most contemporary Jews take for granted.

A similar tension between love of tradition and respect for a contemporary/feminist consciousness confronts us in regard to standards and authority within Jewish communities. On the one hand—and particularly in the context of an American society increasingly characterized by fragmentation, alienation, and loss of a sense of roots—we often find ourselves craving a deep and uncomplicated sense of belonging, a connection that affiliation with Jewish communal institutions seems to promise. Yet, as our awareness has developed and grown over the years, we are less and less willing to belong at the price of our own humanity.

When I was a college student, I hesitated to take on new roles and lead *Shabbat* (Sabbath) services. I bought the line that if women became the equals of men in the public/ritual arena, it would mean the abandonment of children and home, and the Jewish future would be threatened. Now I find such a position appalling: Jewish continuity cannot be dependent upon women denying our own potential for service, participation, and growth. Communities that depend for their existence on stifling the development of half their members are of questionable value.

Toward a New Understanding of Community

What is at issue is the relationship between group identity and diversity. For generations, Jews have defined ourselves over against the outside world: We are different from "the heathen." The unstated implication of such a definition is that "we" are the same, so that those within can, in fact, be distinguished from those without. But, as we have seen, the question of what that homogeneity consisted has been contested from the start, and even more in recent years. In any case, even if we ever were homogeneous as

Jews, we certainly are not now. Whether with regard to religious versus secular orientation, religious affiliation, relationship to Zionism, or a host of other possible fault lines, Jewish life is varied and multiform. Estimates reveal that over half of those who identify as Jewish in the United States, for example, are unaffiliated in any significant way with Jewish communal institutions.[2] In such a context, does it make any sense to speak of *a* or *the* Jewish community?

The critical question becomes: How do we imagine collectivities that are open to, and inclusive of, our differences, rather than threatened by, and excluding of, them? This reconceptualization must begin with the image of collectivities characterized by multiplicities of Jews and ways of being—collectivities that even God speaks to not as a homogeneous unity, but "face after face," in all our diversity and particularity. Such communities must respect the differences among us, as men and women; adults and children; coupled and uncoupled; heterosexual, gay, lesbian, bisexual; wealthy and poor; ill and healthy; Sephardic or Ashkenazic; Reform, Orthodox, Conservative, Reconstructionist, Jewish renewal-affiliated, or unaffiliated; Zionist, non-Zionist, or anti-Zionist. Members of each of these sub-communities are Jews; and each may have much to offer to the Jewish people.

This perspective differs, of course, from that of some members of the Orthodox and Ḥasidic communities, who argue that there is no room for pluralism in this sense and that there are simple answers to the questions I have raised. My point, however, is that this position is belied by contemporary reality: Jewish communities are already diverse and plural. The only question is whether we attempt to ignore or deny that reality or to confront it as an opportunity for growth.

Re-defined communities must respect the multiple facets of the identity of each of us: As a woman, a teacher, a lesbian, a person in a number of different types of relationships with a number of different children; one who is affiliated with a Conservative synagogue, but who finds her primary spiritual home in *ḥavurot* (Jewish worship/study fellowships) and in a once-yearly Jewish feminist spirituality collective; and as one who has long struggled with her relationship to Zionism and Israel, I cannot often fit myself into simple categories. No one really can. Communities must recognize, acknowledge, and celebrate not only the diversity among members, but the multiplicity of each member's commitments and identities. Such multiple connections enrich each of us and the Jewish people as a whole.

Guidelines for Action

What does this mean, practically speaking? It means that Jewish communal institutions ought to support members in all their variety. Organizations need to offer their resources to all those who would be part of them, adjusting membership or affiliation fees to people's ability to pay; offering flexible time schedules to Jewish communal workers and child-care at all events; accommodating the differently-abled so that all who wish to participate may do so. It means celebrating relationships other than traditional marriages and providing contexts for mourning the loss of relationships other than those of spouses, siblings, parents, or children. It means overcoming the assumption that all Jews are Ashkenazic and developing school, youth, and adult education programs to explore the many Jewish cultures around the world. It means enriching our communities by learning from the varieties of Jewish culture and experience and by welcoming Jews of various backgrounds into our community. It means ceasing to organize communal or synagogue memberships around heterosexually constructed nuclear families and ensuring that both children and adults in single-parent and/or gay or lesbian families feel "normal" and wanted. To pin all our hopes for Jewish continuity on the health and safety of a particular and limited model of family life is both shortsighted and foolish.[3]

Taking Jewish community seriously means thinking creatively about what resources (artistic, spiritual, economic, political, social, medical, educational, or otherwise) are available among all those who are Jews, and inviting all who have those resources to share them with larger collectivities. The invitation to contribute should in no way depend on people's economic or social standing, level of (formal) Jewish education, ties to Israel, or relationships of intimacy. In short, engaging in struggles over what the boundaries of our communities should be, or over who should have the right to exercise authority over them—particularly attempting to find an

answer that will serve for all contemporary Jewish communities—
is both fruitless and unnecessary. Rather than seeing our contemporary fragmentation as a problem, we can claim it as fertile
ground for innovation and growth. We should not forget that the
same fragmentation which appears as a lack of "standards" has
already provided the context for a tremendous flowering of Jewish
creativity—both individual and communal—since Emancipation.

The Jewish people is composed of many Jewish communities,
reflecting the complex needs and identities of increasingly diverse
groups of Jews. Let us celebrate our diversity, just as the *midrash*
with which this essay begins celebrates the diversity of the ways
the Israelites experienced the divine. While such a model does not
provide us with a way to resolve disputes, it suggests that living
communities encompass conflict and tension, as well as agreement
and harmony. It is only openness to difference and diversity—
rather than fear of it—that will contribute to the ultimate growth
and continuity of Judaism. To that end, I offer a *berakhah* (blessing)
I wrote some years ago to celebrate the power and presence of my
vital, growing (and often conflictual) Jewish feminist community.
May it give us the power and the courage to live not only with differences, but with the creativity that can come of uncertainty,
drawing on the strength of our common commitments:

יִתְרוֹמֵם לִבֵּנוּ בְּדִבּוּק חֶבְרָתֵנוּ.

Yitromem libbenu bedibbuk ḥevratenu.

May our hearts be uplifted with the joy of community.

Images of the Self in Moral Action and Community: Reflections on *Tzedakah* and *Gemilut Ḥasadim*

BARBARA EVE BREITMAN

"Within the community there will be one way for both you and the stranger. It is an eternal law throughout your generations: You and the stranger are alike before God."
                                                    —NUM. 15:15

"The world stands on three pillars: On Torah, on service [of God], and on deeds of lovingkindness."
                          —SIMON THE JUST (SHIMON HATZADDIK),
                                        MISHNAH *AVOT* 1:2

I had an experience when I was twenty-two that I rarely tell anyone about. It was the year my father died. I had moved to a strange, new city where I had neither friends nor relatives, to begin a graduate program in the Department of Religion. I was isolated and alone, cut off from significant relationships after suffering a major loss, deeply depressed, and sometimes troubled with suicidal thoughts. At night I would crawl up like a snail and lay in the center of a mattress on the floor of my bedroom.

In the spring semester, after racking up several incompletes, I signed up for a seminar on Buber and Tillich. I was grateful to find myself capable of immersion in this class and to discover, finally, some meaning in my studies. For weeks I sat in the window-lined library reading room, in an encounter with Buber, desperate to find the Courage to Be. One warm afternoon, as I paused to raise my eyes from the page and gaze outdoors, the world dropped its veil of corporeality. Trees, flowers, grass, and people on that green campus transformed into a gold flickering light in which the world revealed itself. Every living creature retained its shape, but appeared glowing, outlined by sparkling threads and veined by

---

Barbara Breitman is a feminist therapist in private practice in Philadelphia, an instructor at the University of Pennsylvania School of Social Work and at the Reconstructionist Rabbinical College in pastoral counseling, a long-time activist in Jewish renewal, and a board member of Aleph.

light. In that instant, a knowing entered my heart speaking this wisdom: I am connected with every living creature, and every creature is connected with every other creature, all made of the same glowing stuff of life, precious and sacred, all One. "All life is Holy." A moment later, the world clothed itself again in its material form, and the scene resumed its familiar outlines.

Somehow, at this time of intense isolation, when my connection with the father who had participated in giving me life was ruptured, when I was separated by emotional and physical distance from my mother and all others I had been close to, I was given the gift of an experience that reconnected me in a deep and profound way with life. I do not try to explain it. I just know the experience was as real as, more real than, anything else that has ever happened to me. The knowing from that afternoon has informed my life ever since.

The totally white, male, mostly Christian faculty of the Department of Religion was in the thrall of Logical Positivism in those days. Jacket covers of books I was assigned to read typically announced themselves to be the "first-rate antidote for fuzzy thought and muddled writing."[1] The inside pages proudly proclaimed:

> If a mystic admits that the object of his [sic] vision is something which cannot be described, then he must admit that he is bound to talk nonsense when he describes it.... We conclude, therefore, that the argument from religious experience is altogether fallacious.[2]

Even then, I knew better than to divulge my afternoon vision to anyone; still, in class, I persisted in a scholarly interest in religious experience and posed questions about the nature of morality that might be derived this way. To me it seemed self-evident that a deep experience of the interconnectedness of all life could only lead to a morality rooted in an acute consciousness of the sacredness of the other, from which would naturally derive injunctions against hurting other living beings. My thinking was considered uninteresting and immature and was met with the silence reserved for the fuzzy-headed.

In my second year of graduate school, a scholar of Jewish mysticism was hired, and I was excited by the prospect of studying with him. However, like so many daughters of Jews striving to be "American," I lacked a formal Jewish education. For me, the labyrinth of Jewish mysticism, which required extensive prior knowledge, remained an all but impenetrable maze.

Ironically, during a summer cracking my teeth on Aramaic and trying to study Jewish texts in the basement of The Jewish Theological Seminary, I felt increasingly cut-off from the sources of my own spirituality. I yearned to bathe in the ocean and feel the sun on my face. A cultural and psychological chasm existed between me and the Rabbis and kabbalists (Jewish mystics), a chasm created by time and history, by anti-Semitism and accommodation, and by gender.

After two-and-a-half years, I dropped out of graduate school and went to work in a rural psychiatric hospital where I hoped to take religious experience more seriously than in the Department of Religion. I yearned to breathe fresh air.

Images of Self in Feminist Theory

Modern Western psychology has posited a correlation between one's vision of self and one's moral action. The dominant view of mature moral development is that of the autonomous self. The ideal independent agent exercises a capacity for detachment, perspective, objectivity, and rationality in moral decision-making, applying concepts of abstract justice in situations of human choice. In this model, others are experienced as individuals distinct and separate from the self, who are entitled to certain rights, and toward whom one applies the criteria of justice objectively, through reason, to arrive at appropriate moral judgments and decisions.[3]

In recent years, a growing body of feminist psychological theory, rooted in an analysis of women's lives, has begun to question the connection between images of self and conceptions of moral development. This work in psychology has been paralleled by similar work in fields of feminist philosophical ethics, social theory, and theology.[4]

The dominant Western model, which for decades had been assumed to be universally applicable, was recognized by feminists as androcentric, overwhelmingly founded on the experiences of boys and men. As women scholars formulated theories of development based on girl's and women's experience, a second model emerged: A relational self interconnected with other contiguous selves. In this view, moral decisions are based on an ethic of care in relationship, rather than objectively weighing rights. Decisions derive from capacity for empathy, rather than capacity for perspective. Others are experienced as subjects, however different from the self, with whom one is embedded in empathic relationship.

Feminists debate why women seem to have a more highly developed capacity for empathy. Psychoanalytic theorists believe that women's sense of self differs from men's because girls usually grow up with a primary caretaker of their own gender, unlike boys. Girls experience similarity with their mothers and often identify with them. This leads girls to develop relatively fluid permeable boundaries around the self and to experience the development of the self as inseparable from, and always in the context of, relationship. Boys, however, must disidentify with mother in order to establish a mature identity. They form bounded, distinct, and separate senses of self. The psychologist Nancy Chodorow hypothesizes that the mother also experiences her son as more "different" than a daughter, so promoting the son's view of himself as distinct from mother.[5]

Socialist feminists look beyond the intra-psychic realm and attribute the illusion of the autonomous individual to the economic system of capitalism. Women's greater capacities for empathy reflect gender role socialization that has allocated the affective realm to women. Women, who have the primary responsibility for providing emotional "goods" necessary to sustain men and children, have thus become experts in the "production" of caring.

One socialist feminist philosopher, Sandra Bartky, extends Marx's concept of surplus labor into the realm of the family. According to Marx, the capitalist exploits the worker by paying only a fraction of what the laborer's work produces, pocketing the difference, or surplus, between what a product costs and what a worker is paid. Bartky coins a new term—surplus nurturance—to describe the output of women's energy through emotional support given to men in unequal, non-reciprocal affective exchanges. Implicit in Bartky's concept is the idea that men sustain an *illusion* of autonomy precisely because women already satisfy their emotional needs.[6]

Social constructionists and postmodernists eschew any attempt to attribute essential or immutable characteristics to women or men. They insist that the self is socially constructed and seek to understand how the development of self occurs within specific organizations of cultural and material life at particular times and locations in history.[7] They look at how the self-as-separate schema or the self-as-connected schema develops as a function of culture, history, ethnicity, and class as well as gender.[8] Cultures that value self-reliance and independence develop and reinforce self-schemata as separate and autonomous; by contrast, cultures that value collective responsibility and interdependence favor self-as-connected schema.

Many thinkers additionally emphasize how differences in social standing affect the development of self-concept. For example, "majority" groups (i.e., men, whites, upper- and middle- class people) enjoy material conditions and social power that are consonant with an ideology of individualism and an image of the autonomous self. People with less authority (i.e., women, blacks, poor and lower-class people), whose individual and group survival may depend on being-in-relation, are disposed to notions of self as relational and social.

Images of Self in Jewish Culture

Within Judaism, there are two different but interrelated concepts of moral action and behavior: *Tzedakah* (sacred practice of charity) and *gemilut ḥasadim* (sacred practice of lovingkindness). Jewish tradition distinguishes between them in several ways. The essential difference is already evident in the roots of the words: *Tzedakah* derives from *tzedek* (justice, righteousness), and *gemilut ḥasadim* derives from *ḥesed* (lovingkindness, grace, steadfast love).

"Charity" is understood by the Sages to be an obligation on the part of the donor, and a right on the part of the needy. *Tzedakah* is neither discretionary nor subjective. It is a *mitzvah* (commandment, sacred obligation) regulated by law. *Tzedakah* is a core component of social justice. In fact, Rabbinic courts may compel someone who refuses to give charity not only to give, but to give according to the court's assessment of her/his means. The Rabbis delineated the mechanics of this *mitzvah*, according to strict and specific rules: Who must give, who may receive, how much should be given, and in what manner. According to the Talmudic Sages, the highest form of *tzedakah* is mutually anonymous: "Which is the *tzedakah* that saves from a strange death? That in which the giver does not know to whom he has given nor the recipient from whom he has received" (BT *Baba Batra* 10a–10b). Anonymous giving is intended to prevent the recipient from feeling undeserved shame and the donor from feeling exaggerated pride. According to Maimonides' famous hierarchy of giving, the penultimate level of giving preserves the identities of donor and recipient as secret. The most virtuous form of *tzedakah*, however, is to promote self-sufficiency by offering employment or entering into a partnership with the person in need.[9]

The practice of *gemilut ḥasadim* traditionally covers a wide range of activities through which people can embody God's *ḥesed* in their behavior toward one another.[10] The Rabbis labeled all of the following practices as examples of *gemilut ḥasadim*: Visiting the sick, providing shelter and food for the wayfarer or the homeless, being sensitive to the needs of the disabled and caring for them, accompanying the dead until they are lowered into the grave. *Gemilut ḥasadim* included all acts of the heart, deeds flowing from the compassion of one person toward another. So important was *gemilut ḥasadim* as a value, it was considered one of the distinguishing characteristics of the Jew. The denial of the duty of *gemilut ḥasadim* was considered by the Rabbis to be a denial of what is fundamental to Judaism.[11]

According to the Talmud and Rashi, the duty to the dead was regarded as the quintessential act of *ḥesed* because there is no possibility of the gift ever being returned (Rashi on Gen. 47:29). During the ritual washing of a corpse, members of a *ḥevra kaddisha* (burial society) are instructed to engage in a deep cleansing of the body of the deceased, to purify all the orifices, even to clean under the nails. There is a sacred and extraordinary intimacy and physical contact that occurs between the living and the dead. Vulnerability, shared humanity, and a deeper understanding of the fragility of life emerge from the experience of this ritual preparation when it is done with consciousness and intention.

Tzedakah and *gemilut ḥasadim* each lead to different experiences of self. *Tzedakah* supports the image of a separate, individuated, autonomous self, giving aid to an other. There is a purposeful distance maintained between donor and recipient. The two ideally never touch nor meet. The exchange between them is primarily an exchange of material goods. There is no opportunity for the donor or the recipient to be changed by a personal encounter with the other. There is no opportunity or necessity for empathy. At the same time, the obligatory nature of *tzedakah* recognizes the necessity for each individual to fulfill the social contract of caring for one another. It demands that each Jew commit to a sacred code of economic and social justice, including a principle of regular redistribution of material resources.

Gemilut ḥasadim involves a giving not only of one's material wealth but of oneself. The desirability of anonymity between donor and recipient, so meticulously prescribed in the giving of *tzedakah*, does not apply. Because the exchange is not material, the giving can cross class lines: The poor may have as much to give as the rich. It is an offering of self that transcends even the boundaries between life and death.

The Talmud explains that *gemilut ḥasadim* can be superior to *tzedakah*:

> In three ways is *gemilut ḥasadim* superior to *tzedakah*: Charity can be done only with one's money. *Gemilut ḥasadim* can be done with one's person and one's money. Charity can be given only to the poor. *Gemilut ḥasadim* both to rich and poor. Charity can be given only to the living. *Gemilut ḥasadim* can be done to the living and to the dead. (BT *Sukkot* 49b)

How are we to understand this passage? The Rabbis seem to be saying that while the giving of *tzedakah* is imperative, it is not enough; the empathic meeting between people is essential to a fully ethical life. The intention of *gemilut ḥasadim* is precisely for an exchange of self between the people involved, for genuine meeting and empathy, for psychological and social distance between self and other to be bridged, for people to meet as subjects.

Empathy is essential to *gemilut ḥasadim*. It is not necessary for *tzedakah*.

While *tzedakah* and *gemilut ḥasadim* prescribe different relational styles and support different experiences of self, they both assert and derive from the interconnectedness of life lived in community. The intensely communal experience of Jews enabled (and perhaps required) the Rabbis to develop two complementary values: A concept of moral action based on justice, sacred obligation, and autonomy; and a concept of moral action based on love, empathy, and relation. The use of these two strategies and relational styles by Jewish tradition transcends the strict gender division of modern Western thought, which postmodern feminists critique. The Jewish sensibility of connection derives from our communal experience, not our genderedness. What Jews and contemporary North American women have in common is the value we place on collective experience from which we extend our sense of self and capacity for empathy.

Jews in North America have developed elaborate mechanisms and institutions for raising and distributing charity to others. This perpetrates the tradition of *tzedakah* and also accommodates a Western cultural emphasis on the separate individual. But *tzedakah* was never meant to be the sole expression of charitable or moral action in the world. We have lost the opportunity for self-transformation that is possible through the practice of *gemilut ḥasadim*. We have all but forgotten the centrality of *gemilut ḥasadim* to being a Jew.

Gemilut Ḥasadim and Building Community

In tight-knit, self-regulating communities, Jews bonded together for survival, creating a network of social welfare institutions to care for one another: Collecting alms for the poor, burying the dead, visiting the sick. Both *tzedakah* and *gemilut ḥasadim* were modes of moral action grounded in organic communities. The challenge to our generation is both to revive such institutions in the Jewish community and to apply these concepts to diverse groups of people, deepening our empathy for others different than ourselves.

In the closing decades of the twentieth century in the United States, our definitions of community have changed dramatically. In some ways, our community, the social matrix in which our lives are embedded, has expanded; in others ways, it has contracted. In an open, democratic society, many of us live in neighborhoods with people who are not Jewish, belong to communal and social organizations with non-Jews, and count among our friends people who are not Jewish. We also participate in the oft-cited "global village." On the other hand, we live in an excessively privatized culture. Traditional forms and sites of community—the neighborhood, the nearby extended family—have all but broken down. We live in "community" only if we have made the effort, consciously and conscientiously, to reconstitute some form of communal life.

A similar statement could be made about diversity. Even in this democratic and diverse society, most of us spend our lives in groups of people deemed similar to ourselves. Most white people do not visit to the homes of black families on the grounds of friendship. Many heterosexual parents are hesitant to allow their children to become close friends with the children of lesbian or gay parents. Most Christians have not set foot in a synagogue, and many suburban dwellers have not walked the streets of the inner city. Most hearing people do not make the effort to include deaf people among their friends. Even young and old are often segregated from one another.

In our efforts at acculturating to the highly individualistic ideology of American Protestant culture, we have cut ourselves off from deeply communal experiences. Both Judaism and feminism share a commitment to life lived in community and understand that the process of becoming whole can only occur in mutual, caring relationship with others.[12] Serious practice of *ḥesed* has the effect of transforming each individual self through empathy with others. Restoring *gemilut ḥasadim* to its proper place as a "pillar of the world," equal in importance to Torah and *avodah* (worship), has the power to transform.

As a member of Mishkan Shalom, an activist congregation in Philadelphia, Rabbi Nancy Fuchs-Kreimer organized people in the congregation to reawaken "*gemilut ḥasadim* consciousness." In this endeavor, she had to confront our society's excessive sensitivity to boundaries before even beginning the work of *gemilut ḥasadim*. Members of the nascent committee had to be reassured that they were not being intrusive, for example, when they visited a grieving family to offer comfort. The volunteers experienced a conceptual breakthrough once they understood that they constituted a *minyan* (prayer quorum) necessary to enable the bereaved to say *Kaddish* (mourner's prayer) at home. At least initially, they needed the Torah of obligation to lower boundaries and create the possibility for the Torah of empathy. The human contact Rabbi Fuchs fostered eventually led to a change in community consciousness, because differences of various kinds were transcended by empathy and caring.[13]

Extending, or Dropping, the Boundaries

It is not easy to promote exchanges of self among people of different races, genders, sexual orientations, abilities, and even religions, though that is the implied intention of *gemilut hasadim* as I see it.

For several years, I worked as the white member of a bi-racial team attempting to promote racial understanding among teachers in an urban, desegregated school. I was humbled in the face of how difficult it is for people of different races to develop empathy for each others' experiences; particularly how difficult it is for white people to understand and empathize with the suffering of African-Americans. In the aftermath of the Rodney King verdict, which showed how many white Americans were capable of denying what they saw with their own eyes, I was reminded of the chilling scenes from the movie *Shoah*, in which concentration camp guards denied that Jews were murdered in the camps. Racism, anti-Semitism, homophobia, and sexism all objectify others so as to block our capacity to see and experience them as real people—different in some aspects, but essentially and significantly like their antagonists.

To have empathy for the pain of others, *especially empathy for pain we have had some part in causing*, we must be capable of facing the evil in ourselves. We must acknowledge our capacity to hurt others and simultaneously forgive ourselves for it. If we are too self-punitive, then we do not allow ourselves to accept our harmful behavior, and we can never take responsibility for the hurt we cause. We split off the evil in ourselves and project it onto others. Empathy helps us reclaim the split-off parts of ourselves.

The practice of *gemilut ḥasadim* in our extended community requires that we "reconstitute the objectified other as a subject."[14] Every time we expand ourselves to include the joy or pain of someone (seemingly) different we transform and expand ourselves. We do not just add the other to our understanding of self; we reintegrate a fragmented part of our own souls. We break through the denial of our ultimate and inexorable inter-connectedness. If all human beings have been created *betzelem elohim* (in God's own image), then, even in the most distant other, we must be able to recognize the self.

Preserving the Planet

In transcending the boundaries between living and dead, *gemilut ḥasadim* encourages concern for generations still to be born, as well as for those who have died. Thus, empathy expands to include the natural world and its non-human creatures, so necessary to the preservation of the earth for future generations. Robert Jay Lifton, the renowned psychiatrist and anti-nuclear activist, has named an emerging image of self, the "species self." Among twentieth-century human beings living under the threat of global annihilation and species suicide, Lifton sees "self-concept inseparable from other human selves in sharing with them the ultimate questions of life and death" on the planet.[15] The development of this inclusive sense of self may be crucial if diverse nations are to make the commitment necessary to sustain the world.

Simon the Just teaches that the *world* stands—or, implicitly, topples—on three pillars: Torah, service [of God], and *gemilut ḥasadim*. *The continued existence of the world depends on our expanding capacity for empathy, ever broadening, with no prescribed limit, to include wider and wider circles of diverse others within the experience of our self.* The only way to develop that empathy is to have direct experiences with those others. We must bridge social, economic, cultural, and psychological distances.

Moral behavior, politics and social action grounded in empathy are different than social action guided by justice. *In an unredeemed world, we need both.*[16] We cannot rely on the achievement of empathy alone to make progress in the arena of social and economic justice. We need a sense of obligation to guide us, whether or not we have achieved empathy for another. But the survival of the world may stand or fall on a pillar of just action grounded in empathy, one that opens our hearts to embrace ever-expanding circles of diverse people and beings into our experience of Self.

Since that afternoon in the library many years ago, I have experienced the sacred in my life mainly in community, through shared tasks, empathy, and relationship, not in private, radiant visions. But I stand always before the mystery of that day.

The Process of Building Community

Living in Transition:
A Biblical Perspective

ORA HORN PROUSER

"The whole community, all of them are holy, and God is in their midst...."

—NUM. 16:3

Many of us who now take our egalitarian synagogues for granted grew up in a Jewish world dominated by male roles and voices. We are raising our children in a society in many ways unimagined and unimaginable by our mothers and grandmothers. Women's roles in Judaism and in society at large have changed tremendously—and continue in an extended period of change. While much still needs to be accomplished, an amazing transformation has taken place in just one generation.

The Book of Numbers finds the Israelite people living out an experience that is similar to ours in key ways. The period of desert wanderings, like our own, was one of transition. In forty years, a group of terrified slaves was replaced by a community poised to conquer the land of Canaan. The people learned to live and act as a unified free community in a covenantal relationship with God. Israelites of the wilderness period were adjusting to an interim lifestyle. They never intended to create a permanent, nomadic desert community. It is an essential element of the text that their generation would not enter the promised land.

Many situations in the Book of Numbers parallel our own Jewish communal dynamics. Some of them can also be read as

Dr. Ora Horn Prouser serves as Visiting Assistant Professor of Bible at The Jewish Theological Seminary.

paradigms for dealing with those dynamics. Numbers acknowledges the struggles and contentiousness that often accompany change, even as it sounds a plea for tolerance, cooperation, and patience.

Going Forward with Trust

Change is by nature unsettling. Many changes and innovations in a short period of time can be frightening and uncomfortable. Likewise, large goals are intimidating. This has often led—both for the desert generation and for our own—to focusing on obstacles rather than maintaining a steady course.

Early in the desert experience, twelve spies were sent to scout out the promised land (Num. 13–14). Upon their return, they unanimously described the land as a "land of milk and honey" (13:27). Ten of them, however, went on to characterize the inhabitants of the land as powerful giants whom the Israelites could never defeat. This led to a revolt during which the Israelites sought to stone their leaders and return to Egypt. As punishment for their rebellion, that generation of Israelites was doomed to die wandering in the desert, while their children would inherit the land.

The purpose of spying was to reassure the Israelites that, by God's grace, they were going forward to a wonderful place. So understood, the Israelites' rejection of the Land of Israel becomes especially scandalous.[1] They saw the promised land, tasted of its goodness, and still rejected the possibility of inhabiting it. The tragedy of the spies was that their close-knit "*minyan*" (quorum) was granted a rare fore-taste of a bright future in the promised land; however, they were too fearful of the obstacles to extend that experience beyond their own privileged few.

The spies' reaction can be made more easily comprehensible to us when seen in light of our situation as a transitional generation. There are those among us who have been lucky enough to live in egalitarian and participatory religious communities such as the Upper West Side of New York, non-Orthodox seminaries, egalitarian summer camps, and *ḥavurot* (Jewish study/prayer fellowships). We should see ourselves as modern-day spies, able to see and taste of the "promised land." We must focus on our goals and not the obstacles to their attainment so that, like the Israelites, we do not need to wait another generation for our vision to become a widespread reality.

Leading with Help and with Patience

Leadership roles in times of transition are extremely demanding. Responsibilities can include preparing the people for change both personally and educationally, training new leaders, and catering to those who think the transformations are either too extensive/fast-paced or too limited/slow. A leader needs to monitor the pulse of his or her community so that some balance is maintained and the community can remain whole. Leaders must protect themselves from placing the cause over the community.

Moses struggled to maintain this balance during the desert wanderings. As he pushed the people forward to prepare them for a new life, they, still used to Egyptian slavery, were afraid and insecure. Moses encouraged them, inspired them, interceded to God on their behalf, and occasionally despaired of their ability to change. During one of many rebellions, the Israelites cried out for food. Their complaint was not based on starvation but was, rather, a specific demand for meat. God and Moses' reactions to this are telling: "God was exceedingly angry," but Moses' vision was so distorted by impatience and exhaustion that it was "evil" in his eyes (Num. 11:10). Moses complained to God that his job was simply too difficult for one man. In response, God instructed him to gather seventy elders among whom would be spread some of the divine "spirit" (11:16–17). God understood the enormity of Moses' task, recognized his pain, and enabled him to continue productively.

It is enlightening to contrast this scene with Numbers 20, in which God directed Moses and Aaron to speak to a rock in order to produce water. In an act of frustration or impatience, Moses struck the rock instead. God provided the water, but punished Moses and Aaron by not allowing them to enter the land of Israel. The punishment was quite severe, and the motivations, of both God and Moses, are difficult to discern. It is clear, however, that God did not see this as merely another example of Moses' need for support and indulgence. There are legitimate responses to the stress of one's life's work. Leaders may feel lonely and frustrated, they may need help, but they cannot simply change all the rules because of their own impatience, preference, or insight.

We have among our leaders those who, like Moses, are impatient with their communities' rejection of new realities. They want their synagogues to embrace full women's participation, changes in liturgy, and/or new rituals. However, a leader who is progressive and insightful can sense where the community is and then slowly lead the people to new and fulfilling experiences. When this is done with sensitivity, patience, and vision, people grow as individuals and as a community. Women can find new avenues of religious expression even when a lack had not previously been felt. Men can find new resources of spiritual energy in addition to the joy of seeing their wives, mothers, and daughters spiritually fulfilled. However, this scenario is often played out in a less than ideal fashion. There are leaders who do not tolerate the slow process of transition. Imposing too many changes or expectations on their communities too quickly, they fail to show sufficient respect and sensitivity. This often leads to a backlash against any change at all and anger on all sides. Any promised land that a given generation envisions is going to negotiate its boundaries over time, naturally, on its own.

Respecting What Came Before

Our degree of success in struggling with transition depends on the wisdom to know what to change and how to go about changing it. There are those who want simply to throw out traditional conventions in favor of modern sensibilities. Others believe that almost no changes are acceptable since they might offend those who are resistant. Anyone in transition must attempt to distinguish and navigate a path between appropriate development and unfortunate and unnecessary rejection of the past.

In Numbers 16–17, Korah and his followers attempt an unsuccessful coup against the leadership of Moses and Aaron. On one level, their failure is easily understood: Moses, not they, was chosen by God. However, why should Korah not have been able to gain power? Moses made it clear several times that he was willing to share power and that he needed assistance. Korah's flaw was not his goal, but his method. He rejected the leadership of Moses and Aaron outright, and sought to oust and replace them. This stands in opposition to the biblical model for the transfer of power, which requires continuity. For example, when Aaron died, his leadership role was passed on to his son, Elazar. The transition was enacted publicly, when Moses took Aaron's cloak and placed it on his son (Num. 20:23–29). There could be no doubt that Elazar's leadership was an extension of Aaron's authority. Similarly, the transfer of authority from Moses to Joshua involved a public display of Moses placing his hands on Joshua and commissioning him as the next leader (Num. 27:18–23).

We learn from the Book of Numbers that each generation needs to keep faith with the past by building on predecessors and precedents as the source of its own authority and legitimacy. Change must be an outgrowth of inherited values and ideas, not an act of their total undoing. Leaders must work within the system they seek to shape.

We are not the first generation to see the need for change, and we will not be the last. Moreover, there is widespread disagreement over what transformations are desirable. What may and must be preserved of older models in dealing with women's roles? If we see fit to make a "clean break" with the past and start afresh, then in a very short time we will have many sects, disjointed from the past and unrecognizable to one another. One of the responsibilities of making changes in gender roles is to maintain the connection between our actions and ideals and those of our ancestors, to choose and frame what we do in terms of Jewish values (like justice), traditions (like continuing to write liturgy), and methods (like responsa literature and other legal means). Only if we follow such a path through the wilderness of transition can we reach the promised land as one people.

Responding to the Status Quo

In periods of transition, new realities arise and need to be addressed—including realities specifically related to women's rights. Such a situation was handled effectively in the case of the daughters of Tzelofeḥad (Num. 26:33; 27 and 36). These women came before Moses to press property rights: Their late father's estate was going to be lost to the family because he had no sons to inherit his land. Since this was a new legal scenario, Moses brought the case before God, who instructed that the daughters inherit the land and later added the provision that they marry within the tribe.

This text is emblematic of the Book of Numbers and the wisdom it offers to today's readers. It carries an elegant message of the hopeful possibilities for successful and comfortable change. There is also a message here, both for the members of the community and for communal leaders, in how to act responsibly and effectively. The sisters are appropriately respectful *and* outspoken in redressing a lack in the legal system they otherwise affirm. Their plea is not considered threatening in any way. In turn, their leader and the tradition itself show them respect. The sisters are individually mentioned by name more than once as a sign of the recognition that is their due.

Most of the change in the status of women in contemporary Judaism has come about because women sensed a need and acted upon it. Some members of the community have responded like Moses, recognizing that an injustice needs to be addressed, opening themselves to changes in sex-roles, and helping others to adjust to the newness. They were not threatened when women wanted to take on such traditionally male roles as having *aliyot* (honors of reciting the blessings before and after the Torah is read), counting in the *minyan*, or serving as rabbis and cantors.

An equally constructive communal force has been those who, in a spirit of theological humility, respect and support religious expressions with which they personally disagree. For example, a Talmud professor at the Jewish Theological Seminary found in the emerging trend of female students wearing *tallit* and *tefillin* (prayer shawl and phylacteries) a threat to the continued prevalence of the traditionalism he endorsed; nevertheless, he regarded their behavior as a sincere religious expression to be respected. Like Moses, he responded with encouragement and acceptance.

Our own generation must be willing to step forward like the daughters of Tzelofeḥad and to redress wrongs. We also must be willing, like Moses, to accept that change is inevitable. New situations, challenges, and solutions are the natural outgrowth of a vital, living tradition. Such evolution does not threaten our tradition, but rather, strengthens and solidifies it.

Marching On

Like the Israelites in the desert, we are a generation in transition. Again like them, many among us would prefer to return to the familiar ways of the past. Numbers provides us with models of appropriate behavior, for leaders and laypeople, in overcoming those fears and making gradual changes, to take us step by step to a better place. In the meantime, there is nothing wrong with where we are. It is not a holding station, but a place of growth and, if we make it so, a place of civility.

The Good, the Bad, and the Possible: Some Thoughts on Jewish Women Making Community

MARGARET HOLUB

"Moses and Aaron came away from the congregation to the Tent of Meeting and fell on their faces...."
—NUM. 20:6

Like many of us, I have a long and checkered career in the enterprise of community. Community has brought me the best and worst moments of my life. There was the community where we lived together on Skid Row, paying ourselves five dollars a week and eating food we "trashed" out of dumpsters while we ran a soup kitchen, a shelter, two clinics, a daycare center and protested the arms race—all on self-righteousness, youth, and adrenaline. There was the "yuppie commune" of six sharing a mansion and pool along with the vicissitudes of our love and work lives; we eventually disintegrated over undone dishes. I've been part of various *minyanim* (prayer quora), joined the so-called community of

---

Rabbi Margaret Holub is the spiritual leader of a rural, alternative *shtetl* on the North Coast of California.

my rabbinical school, met monthly in a hot tub/*mikveh* (ritual bath) with five other Jewish women, read *Tikkun* magazine (thereby, I suppose, being part of the "*Tikkun* community"). I am also a family member, a neighbor, a voter, and, nowadays, a Jew in a rural area.

I particularly love being in community with Jewish women. But I haven't always had the easiest time there, and I don't think I'm alone in that. Jewish women's groups are often inspiring and nourishing. They can also be hideously contentious. They can enervate the vigorous and obliterate the tentative. In a host of ways, they can suck more life out of us than they renew. This is not because we conform to terrible stereotypes of Jews or women. Rather, much of the problem lies in assumptions that we make about community when we come together. Like the Israelites wandering the desert in Numbers, we suffer, complain, and are often difficult because of the enormous transition we are making. Those who assume positions of leadership can be overwhelmed by the needs of the people, as Moses was in his day. Like him, today's leaders need extensive support systems (Num. 11:11f).

Why Jewish Women Are Wonderful to Be With

Jewish women gathering has always been precious. Whether we are dancing to Miriam's timbrel, baking cholent in a medieval collective oven, or planning a Hadassah fundraiser, our coming together has an element of celebration and a dynamic of sisterhood. But there is an element of pain as well. Each of us could tell some chapter of the same story. Our births were never blessed. We weren't taught the same things our brothers were. We weren't expected, or even allowed, to celebrate our coming of age. We grew up without the realistic possibility of becoming rabbis. We were slapped when we began menstruating. We were told that God is male. We had never touched a Torah. In short, we were wounded by the misogyny of traditional Judaism. We were not intimate with its texts and rituals, and we looked with envy and hunger, or repulsion upon those who were.

If this litany looks familiar, it is because over the past twenty years there has been a great outpouring from the collective mind and heart of Jewish women. Both in the impressive achievements of Jewish feminists and in the painful awareness of what remains to be done, these are heightened times. Whether we get together to do what men have always done but we never have, or we meet to do what Jewish men have never done—every meeting is a historic event.

This is not the first explosion of Jewish women's energy, and I expect that much more is yet to come. But over the past two decades there has been a remarkable flowering of Jewish women's workshops, retreats, conferences, and scholarly consortia. Books of Jewish feminist thought are proliferating. Magazines like *LILITH* and *Bridges*, as well as Internet conversations, draw Jewish women together all over the world. There is nothing like being gathered with so many others like ourselves who are releasing the balloons into the air, letting the snake out of the can, passing around the apple so that we can all take a bite. It is a fantastic time to be a Jewish woman.

But the Bad News Is...

Too many of these groups turn contentious and unhappy. After one conference I attended, a difference of opinion about a small amount of money became so bitter that participants threatened to sue each other. Communities split over whether or not to include children, lesbians' non-Jewish partners, different "flavors" of women rabbis. They collapse in a debate over which prayerbook will be used, or what program to do first. There are some good reasons for these arguments, not the least of which is that the issues are sometimes important in themselves. But that is not the whole story. I have seen certain dynamics assert themselves over and over in Jewish women's groups, irrespective of content or surface issues:

- Women to whom no one has listened are desperate finally to be heard—even more than we are desperate to listen to others or let our programs succeed. We go on and on, interrupt, drag things down, struggle to win our point rather than just state it, and create a bristly and unhappy environment.

- Jewish women writers, artists, rabbis, liturgists, etc. rarely get the academic and professional recognition we deserve. So we ought to be footnoted, thanked, and paid fairly when our work is used. It burns when we are not.

- We've all schlepped, scrubbed, and served everybody in our lives up to now. So why should we be the ones to type labels/work in the kitchen/make phone calls for this Jewish women's group? Or, conversely, "We're doing the work, and you aren't doing your share. So we own the group, and you owe us."

- Our childcare has fallen through. Our grant was turned down. We have deadlines. We have had a headache for a month and don't have time to go to the doctor. We are stressed and impatient and uncivil. And, damn it, we deserve to be!

There is a common denominator: Jewish women's lives are hard. We have to suck it in and "behave" in various other settings. Jewish women's groups are supposed to be the one place where we can be our unchained, glorious, brilliant, impassioned selves. Restraint, quiet, patience, courtesy, deference, modesty—these are the very tools of our oppression. Women's community should be unfettered by these constraints. Women should be able to work things out without having to hold ourselves in.

But sometimes we do not work things out among ourselves effectively, and it can be exhausting and depressing to gather with other women and be shouted at, castigated, badgered, and belea- guered by the fierceness of everyone's feelings and thoughts. I recently received a ten-page letter from a woman summarizing her reaction to an occurrence at a local, annual Jewish women's retreat. I read the letter sympathetically, but was overwhelmed by the strength of its emotional charge. My first impulse was to tell her, "This retreat happens for three days a year. It doesn't much mat- ter whether or not your needs are fully met there." Our little retreat is a weak vessel for the potency of her need.

Most single-issue, part-time communities are weak vessels for the affiliative needs of their participants. They are fragile by nature, depending on an almost miraculous convergence of

members' desires and abilities. There is nothing wrong with this—
as long as we diversify our community portfolio. My own local
Jewish community is richly textured and satisfying, as are the
goings-on in the town where I live. If I go to that Jewish women's
retreat once a year, and it doesn't work for me, I will be disappointed. I might not go back, but it will not be my whole web of
community.

I recently talked with a rural-lesbian-Jewish-tradeswoman-
environmentalist-intellectual friend about community. She said,
"Well, there's the Jewish community. And then there is the lesbian
community. And even within the lesbian community, there are the
lesbians who live in Fort Bragg, and the ones who live in Albion,
and there are the older lesbians and the young lesbians. And there
is the lesbian book group and the ones into spiritual stuff and the
ones into the trades." I added: "And within the local Jewish community there is the *minyan* crowd, and the New Age Jews, and the
Rosh Ḥodesh (New Moon Festival) women, and the Jewish lesbians,
the people who are more into *tzedakah* (sacred practice of charity),
the ones who just like a good party, and the ones who are absorbed
with their kids, and...." We laughed about our rich and overlap-
ping experience of community. We have worked at it, and we are
lucky.

But for so many Jewish women this is not so at all. They may
belong to a lot of groups, but they are starved for real community,
for a setting in which they can do the deep work of life in company with others. Urban life militates against community for a host
of reasons. And sometimes we find ourselves in situations that
make it still harder to connect—home with young children or
elders, working long hours, responding to a private muse.
Personal choices and priorities can also run against the grain of
community—the pursuit of wealth, renown, or extraordinary
achievement; the habits of individualism; and the protection of
privacy all make life in community harder to attain. My
tradeswoman friend has made significant life decisions based on
the importance to her of community, as have I. At the end of our
lives we may look back and see that our professional achievements
were fewer, that we had less material comfort than we might have,
that we didn't write the novel we had dreamed of or spend a year

in India. But we will have lived our lives in community. It is our most important value.

I see many of my contemporaries realizing in midlife that they are starved for community, for sharing the pursuit of meaning with others. Suddenly they are furious with their affiliative groups and organizations for leaving them so hungry. They try to create in that once-a-year conference, that *ḥavurah* (Jewish worship/study fellowship), that women's group, a community that will be able to hold all that feeling, all that hunger. When it works, it is dazzling. But sometimes it just explodes.

Part of the Solution: Diversification

The greater benefit lies not in creating one perfect vessel but, rather, in going back to the less precisely perfect communities in which we find ourselves and investing ourselves there as well. I think back on the ways that I, along with other Jewish feminists, fought the battle of gendered language in prayer. We formed our own *minyanim* and davened (prayed) out of our own prayerbooks. My personal Jewish community was hand-picked to exclude any hearing or speaking of "King" or "Lord" and, consequently, any people who used those terms. I still dislike masculine prayer language, and I still think that it causes some measure of actual harm. I am delighted to see that the work we did is beginning to infiltrate and influence more mainstream Jewish settings. But I have undergone a personal shift. Today, I am willing to trade an occasional *"melekh"* ("king") for the company of people who disagree with me on that front. How much I would trade is up for grabs—or at least for compromise. I have my boundaries, as we all do. But it usually works out "somewhere in the middle," and that is increasingly fine with me. The more we diversify, the more community will be in our lives.

People who are looking for Jewish community might benefit by choosing the most diverse setting rather than the one that most reinforces their own passions. Maybe those exciting edges that thrill some people and outrage others can be explored in small groups, rather than foisted on everyone. Maybe each of us can trade a little less satisfaction out on those edges for the sake of the whole. Maybe it is sometimes worth giving in on matters of ideology for the sake of getting along—maybe or maybe not.

It is worth bearing in mind that even communities which seem very different offer one gift in common: Community itself. External differences do not override the essential endowment. Perhaps that can be read as an explanation for why each of the different ancient tribes of Israel, with its distinctive heritage, banners, and leaders, brought exactly the same gift to dedicate the altar (Num. 7:12–89).

We may not fit in at our neighborhood synagogue. We may have nothing in common with our neighbors or the parents of our kids' classmates. We may not even like the people with whom we work. But those are our communities, too. The more we bring women's needs, perspectives, and history into communities that are not focused on these—the more we listen to, appreciate, and try to enjoy people whose histories and needs differ from our own—the sooner we can feel at home. Then, when we do experience those precious moments of meeting others whose interests and hearts are one with ours, we won't be so pent up with frustration that we destroy that for which we longed.

Part of the Solution: *Derekh Eretz*

Derekh eretz is the closest Rabbinic term to "etiquette." It means "doing the right thing" or "simple decency." Let me propose some principles of *derekh eretz* for Jewish women's community:

1. We need to take care of our personal stuff at home—not take it into or out on the group. If I am stressed, unhappy, underpaid, or overtired, it is my responsibility to talk with a relative, rabbi, therapist, shaman, or friend—or to pray or meditate about it. We need the calm of a community in which each of us takes responsibility for what we bring to the circle.

2. It helps to remember that the loudest people are usually the most vulnerable, not the least. They need tenderness and concern, even though they provoke just the opposite. This is equally true, maybe more so, if I disagree with the content of what they are saying.

3. There is nothing retrograde in being kind, thoughtful, or even polite. No interrupting, no yelling, no storming out— no matter what.

4. When conflict arises, everyone concerned should take a deep breath and a long perspective. Yes, the personal is political, but not every issue is the deathwatch at Masada. Will this issue still matter in a week? In five years? Is this important to me because of what is concretely at issue, and/or because it reopens old wounds?

5. At the same time, when conflict legitimately arises, it should be dealt with, not pushed under the proverbial rug. We need ways to resolve conflict that are serious and effective as well as egalitarian and sensitive to the needs of others. My own community has begun using a *beit din* (Jewish court) model when conflicts arise. Our local Quaker community conducts "threshing sessions" to "seek out the Light" in order to resolve problems in a spiritually-informed way. Rabbi Leah Novick has spoken of a tradition in some Jewish communities of meeting monthly before *Rosh Ḥodesh* to examine the community, as one traditionally examines one's own soul on each *Yom Kippur Katan* (mini-Day of Atonement, another name for *Rosh Ḥodesh*). We need to be inventive.

Finally, let's remember why community is important to us. A clue comes from my tradeswoman friend. When I asked her about her most powerful experience of community, she answered, without skipping a beat, "the canoe rescue!" A couple of winters ago, she and three friends set out to run the Navarro River. But the river was not as high as they expected, and they were not able to get to the end before dark. So they got out of the boat midway and huddled on shore, prepared to spend a freezing night. When they didn't arrive back home, one's housemate called another's lover, who called a neighbor who knew the river well, who brought his partner. And they all, gay, straight, male, female, Jewish and non-, searched along the river bank until they found the canoeists at 3:30 in the morning, and warmed them with brandy, dry clothes, and love.

This is community at its best. All of us need to know that someone will come after us if we are stuck in the dark. Community is
more than friends, more than people with common beliefs or a
shared agenda. It is people who will notice if you are not there,
who will search for you and warm you when they find you. It is
this awareness, more than a hunger for ideological soulmates, that
I sense is missing for many of my Jewish friends who complain
they lack community.

Life is not easy for anyone, and we all need companions to
sweeten its passage. But connecting is not always easy, either.
However abrasive any of us may be, however confused, however
misguided, we are all in community together because we really
need each other, though not always for the reasons we think. I
advocate a gentler approach to Jewish women's community, a
lighter hand, a bit of spreading out, and, yes, a little holding back.
The rage, exhaustion, and despair that any of us might bring to
community are no doubt wholly justified. But if they break the
vessel, all is lost, including the pleasure and the solace that is
absolutely possible in community with other Jewish women.

Personal Exercises and Reflections

1. Draw a map with yourself (and your family, if you wish) in
   the center, and all your communal affiliations in concentric
   rings around you. Put closest to yourself the affiliations
   that feel closest, most intense, most satisfying; then in more
   distant rings place more peripheral affiliations. Do you feel
   understood and free to express yourself in these various
   groups? Are you satisfied with this map? With the levels of
   commonality and diversity in your communal life? With
   the role of Judaism and Jewish groups? With the role of
   women and women's groups? What changes would you
   like to make?

2. What do you need most in terms of (Jewish) community?
   What keeps you from having what you need?

3. If you were ill for several months and could not take care
   of yourself, are there people who would bring you meals,

visit regularly, comfort and assist your family or close circle of support, keep you connected to Jewish life? Are there
members of your (wider) community for whom you would
do the same?

4. Imagine the community of your dreams—the people you
would most like to relate to, the activities you would do
together, the expectations you would have of each other. Is
your ideal community made up of like-minded people or a
spectrum? What surprises you about this utopian vision?
What might you implement?

Prayer in the Wilderness

SHEILA PELTZ WEINBERG

"Thus shall you bless the people of Israel. Say to them: 'May Adonai *bless you and protect you! May* Adonai *deal kindly and graciously with you! May* Adonai *bestow favor upon you and grant you peace!'"*

—NUM. 6:23–26

"Moses cried out to Adonai, *'Please God, pray heal her.'"*

—NUM. 12:13

"Then Israel sang this song: 'Spring up, O well, and sing to it!'"

—NUM. 21:17

"As Bilam looked up and saw Israel...the spirit of God came upon him....: 'How good are your tents, O Jacob, your dwellings, O Israel!'"

—NUM. 24:2–5

Israel's trek through the wilderness has a certain momentum and direction toward the promised land, despite the inertia and resistance that are ever-present. It is managed through a multiplicity of activities—powerful signs and portents; dramatic rituals involving objects such as trumpets and fringes; rebellion and grumbling. In Numbers, it is not a set liturgy or prayer, but rather the prodding of Moses and the persistent calling of the divine promise, the Land, and the narrative, which guide, lead, and inspire.

Contemporary Women's Prayer

What is true for the generation of the desert is also true of women's contemporary trek through the landscape of Jewish observance. We experiment, create, write, and sing. We produce compelling and dramatic ritual. We grumble and rebel, but no fixed liturgy has yet emerged. We are too busy fighting inner and

---

Sheila Peltz Weinberg is a Reconstructionist who serves the congregation known as the Jewish Community of Amherst.

outer demons, gathering, healing ourselves and each other. New rites, roles, and forms are born willy-nilly. They keep us busy and allay our doubts. We lack one Moses to keep and chart our direction, but our communities grow from the secrets, risks, and triumphs we share. They are watered by our tears of sadness and joy.

Formal communal prayer in this wilderness phase of Jewish women's spirituality is an iffy proposition. It can be great or terrible. It can bridge the gaps of self and other, unique and same, acceptance of reality and visionary hope. It can articulate a common language that energizes us even in our private struggles. It can also be dull, banal, confusing, alienating. It can leave us feeling alone and let down. I have participated in communal prayer experiences where different people experienced both extremes at the same time.

I have seen fights break out around prayer. These reflect the underlying issues of building transformative communities—issues of inclusion and exclusion, of competition and leadership, of trust and honesty. I also have seen great vulnerability around aesthetic sensibilities, style, and taste. These moments spur me to ask: How can prayer serve a healing and uniting function in our communal lives? How can prayer move us forward in the wilderness toward greater clarity and compassion for ourselves and each other? How can prayer help us deepen our appreciation of our differences *and* recognize the inviolability of our interconnectedness? How can we rely on prayer without it becoming rote? It is understandable that more questions abide in the wilderness than answers. Perhaps our prayer, too, needs to be more interrogative than declaratory.

Personal Prayer

Prayer has been enormously important in my personal life, not only in community but as a path through my own internal wilderness of noise, conflict, and distraction. When I pray, I utilize the ancient words encoded in the Jewish prayer book, words from other new and old sources, my words and no words, stillness and movement. What is essential is regularity. I need to devote at least some moments of prayer upon rising and before going to sleep.

The main content of personal prayer is asking for help and saying thank you. My major goal is to admit that I am not fully in control of what goes on in my day, but can rely on the power of the Creator/Liberator to lead me forward. I pray to the "inner" and the "deeper" more than to the "higher." I pray as a way of declaring my intentions to be fully present to what life brings. I pray for the knowledge of God's will for me and the power to carry it out. By this I mean I pray for the next step in the path through the wilderness. I pray for wisdom and courage. Prayer can help uncover dishonesty, and it can enable me to gain serenity about some of life's problems. I pray that my prayer isn't disconnected from my actions, never a substitute for paying attention, speaking up, making changes, taking risks, caring for myself and those I love.

Prayer is about lightness, although it is often seen as somber. It is about loosening bonds that chain me to my own self-importance, whether expressed in self-congratulation or self-deprecation. Prayer helps me be less attached to having things my way and more willing to be aware of what leads to freedom, health, and peace. Prayer is an extraordinary gift for living a happy life as long as I pray for what can be granted by prayer—things like honesty, courage, willingness, and patience. Not the lottery or the reversal of a fortune that is set or of my own making. Prayer is free. Perhaps that is why it is so devalued in our culture.

Prayer Questions

Who can pray? In the wilderness of Sinai, Moses prays, Aaron offers the priestly blessing, Israel sings a prayer, and Bilam (Balaam), a non-Jew, offers a blessing instead of a curse. Prayer is accessible to all the men. Today, women seek to enfranchise ourselves and to make up for the deficiency of female voices in the text. The power that prays is the divine power within us, it is the voice that soars above the habitual, the clouded and absent. In it, we express our longing for presence and connection. We need to locate the voice of prayer, the inner Moses/Aaron/Miriam/Bilam, the divine voice of wisdom, authenticity, honesty.

To Whom do we pray? In Numbers, Moses speaks to God, but the people of Israel beseech a well to rise up and respond. I pray to what I cannot control. I have no fixed image of the recipient of my prayers. This is the wilderness. We need continually to ask each other and ourselves this wonderful question about the recipient of our prayer. The biblical image of a well is significant, especially in light of its midrashic connection to Miriam (Num. *Rabbah* 1:2). Well, source of living waters, quenches our thirst and craving, keeps us alive as we take the next step and the next.

What is the content of prayer? The biblical prayers in the wilderness are concerned with protection and safety, clarity, light, grace, peace (Num. 6:22–26); the dispersion of our enemies or difficulties and distractions (10:35–36); healing (12:13); receiving water (21:17–18); and affirming our strengths and envisioning our triumphs (24:5–9). The content of prayer is universal. Ultimately, prayer draws its purpose from the wilderness, the place of transformation.

It is noteworthy that some of the prayer texts in Numbers have been included in the traditional liturgy, while others have not. Aaron's priestly benediction is used in the *Amidah* (series of blessings that is the centerpiece of every prayer service) and for personal blessings at weddings, *Bnei Mitzvah* (coming of age ceremonies), and Sabbath tables. Bilam's blessing for the Israelites is incorporated into morning services as *Ma Tovu*. Moses' prayer for Miriam's healing is frequently sung in Jewish renewal circles.

Our challenge in this generation of transition to full equality for women is to articulate our prayers—new and old—and to connect them with our stories, longings, visions, hopes, and fears. Our task is to weave together our personal discoveries with our collective efforts, to make our voices strong and clear and liberating.

Meditations on Prayer

The Bilam Prayer (Num. 24:1–9) Imagine you, like Bilam the prophet, are standing at a mountaintop overlooking the Jewish community (your synagogue or *ḥavurah* [Jewish worship/study fellowship], the larger Jewish community in your hometown, or another group that comes to mind). You have been given prophetic powers to see clearly and hear accurately from far away. What do you see? Where are most Jews spending their time? What is the center of the activity and excitement in the community? What are the sources of strife and conflict? What are the areas of confusion and yearning? Look closely and focus on the leadership of your community. What are their driving passions? Where are they directing the energy of the group?

If you could speak a few sentences of prophesy, of inspiration, of blessing—what would you say?

Yevarekhekha/The Priestly Blessing (Num. 6:22–26) Sit in a comfortable position. Relax your body as you breathe deeply and fully from your belly. Beginning with your toes and moving to your scalp, relax each muscle in your body. Notice any tension. Allow it to dissolve and float away. Continue to breathe slowly and deeply. Count slowly from 10 back to 1, allowing your body to relax more and more.

Now imagine you are surrounded by a golden light of blessing. This light comes from an infinite Place of light, healing, and blessing. It flows around you and offers you safety and protection. Feel the golden light around you... Feel the safety... Rest in it... Enjoy it... Feel the blessing... Feel the protection.

Breathe slowly and deeply into your own heart. Imagine that each breath is filling you up inside with that golden light of love and caring. Feel the light of compassion fill your heart. Imagine you are being held and embraced by a being of infinite love. You see a face of limitless compassion smiling at you with boundless tenderness and sweetness. Take into your heart all the light that is shining upon you... Feel it deeply... Rest in it... Enjoy it... Send blessings of love to your self, to your loved ones, your friends and neighbors, to all who dwell on earth.

Allow the golden radiance to continue to surround you. You are light. You are whole. You are connected to the Source of all blessing, and the energy of love flows through you and around you. You are one with all that is, was, and will be... You feel harmony... Feel it deeply... Rest in it... Enjoy it... Send blessings of peace to your self, to your loved ones, to your friends and neighbors, to all who dwell on earth.

Women's Communal Prayers

ARLENE AGUS AND ESTHER CAMERON

"Thus you shall bless the children of Israel...."
                                                    —NUM. 6:23

The following are meditations and prayers about praying. The first was written to inaugurate a prayer service for Jewish women of diverse backgrounds. It can be adapted to any women's meeting. The second was created for use at the end of a women's gathering. —Eds.

Tkhine: A Meditation for Praying at a Women's Gathering

Arlene Agus

We gather here, in the presence of others, to embark on the
     most solitary of journeys, into our thoughts, our dreams,
     our fears, our needs, our vulnerabilities, and our aspira-
     tions.
We grant each other silence and surround each other with
     quiet murmurings to lend strength without diminishing
     strength.
We strain toward the deepest, most honest, authentic parts of
     our selves.
And there we find You.
We are the women of Your people.

And, like the points of the star that bears our identity, we
     radiate outward in many directions.
Some of us reach out, seeking Your presence in sacred texts
     and rituals.

Arlene Agus is senior associate at Ukeles Associates, Inc.
Esther Cameron converted to Judaism in 1978 and lived from 1979-1990 in Israel;
an excerpt from her memoir-novel, *c, or the Autoanalysis of a Golem*, appears in
Roberta Kalechovsky's *Global Anthology of Women Writers* (Micah, 1990).

Some of us reach deep inside, seeking their destiny in inner-most calling of the spirit.
Others of us develop Your acts of creation with the brush, the pen, the voice, the needle, the stage.

We turn to You today to make us worthy of that star, to help us focus not on our differences, but on our commonalities.

Remind us that the divergent rays of that star draw their incandescence from the luminous common source at their center. In that center blaze our past, our purpose, and our promise, the ultimate redemption of our people.

Clear our vision to see in others what You see in us.

Quiet our fears of difference, dissolve our harsh judgments, eliminate the labels that limit our compassion, so we may encourage one another in our strivings as well as in our failures.

The six points of our star bear witness to the six women who gave birth to our nation:

Sarah	Leah
Rebecca	Bilhah
Rachel	Zilpah

Refine our appreciation of the models who preceded us as well as those of our own generation.

And here we stand, alone with our thoughts.

The higher-pitched murmurs distinguish our congregation from others, yet in ways we cannot define.

Help us to harness the special qualities we share as women and apply them usefully to the questions we have gathered today to address.

O God, endow this day with dignity and accomplishment. Let us bring together the best of our selves in prayer, in study, and in consultation.

And let our star reflect Your light
"for by that light did You teach us our way of life, the love of righteousness, justice, blessing, mercy, and wholeness" (after the prayer *Sim Shalom*).

Closing Prayer

Esther Cameron

We go now from this place
Where we have spoken of our shared concerns,
Invoked the wisdom of our common mind,
To seek each their own way within a world
That's not yet ruled by Understanding's law.
Spirit of community, now grant
That we may keep, while on our separate ways,
The presence of Your mind, the strength that flows
From the common bond, that we may see the world
With tranquil sight, discerning everywhere
The sparks of holiness that we must raise,
Resisting importunities of fear,
Supporting one another where we can.
Make smooth our way back to the meeting place,
Help us to find the others we must bring
To this expanding circle of Your light,
That when we meet again we see more clearly
The vision of a world that's whole, and Yours.

5

Themes of Deuteronomy/ Devarim Rabbah: Second Law, New Visions

———— ❦ ————

What are the most important lessons I have learned—
from my ancestors and in my own experience?
How can I remember these and pass them on?

So much of life is a repetition—not only of what our parents and ancestors did, not only of the great and grand patterns of human existence, but of what *we* do. We experience birth, coming of age, marriage, mid-life, and then re-experience these passages through the next generation. We cycle through familiar holidays and Torah readings. We revisit the core issues and themes of our individual lives. Similar questions, lessons, and personal patterns present themselves over and over, in different guises and levels of profundity. I see myself in the same mirror, but from a new perspective, and, over time, it is hoped, with a greater depth of vision.

Deuteronomy is, as the Greek-derived name implies, a repetition of the law.[1] Formulated as addresses by Moses to the generation about to enter the promised land, this fifth book of the Torah repeats a significant portion of the history and laws already presented in the previous four. It reviews information in the hope that the younger generation(s) will truly hear and enact the word of God.[2] At first glance, Deuteronomy seems the least likely of the five books of Moses to impassion contemporary Jewish women. There is no obvious connection between Jewish women's encounter with tradition and Moses' biblically grounded call to obedience.

Yet, Deuteronomy not only summarizes the messages previously given by God to the Jewish people, it adds to and interprets the corpus for future generations. In this sense, Deuteronomy is both a review and a re-viewing. Like a feminist "click story,"[3] this biblical book recalls and reframes an inheritance so familiar that it is in danger of becoming stagnant or invisible. Suddenly, reader and text, vision and visibility, are noticed and honored with new awareness. This paves the way for fresh interpretations and deeper explorations of meaning. It introduces the possibility of change—even within a fixed and eternal document. Thus, the book of the Torah that may appear to be nothing more than a repetitive exhortation to obey God's law, actually raises issues that both reflect and inform the concerns of our own generation, and especially of Jewish women.

Primary among these concerns is the question of how we relate to the inherited traditions of the past. Continuity was a key theme for Moses in the Book of Deuteronomy, as it remains a watchword for Jewish leadership today. Issues of (dis)continuity are also vitally relevant for all contemporary women, who are, in some ways, so like our mothers, and yet, in other regards, so different from them.

In American and Jewish cultures, both recently and over time, circumstances and values have changed. These changes have in turn led to innovations in leadership, law, and communal priorities—some of the most dramatic of which have involved women taking on public roles. Not coincidentally, developments in leadership, law, and a shared communal vision are major themes in the Book of Deuteronomy—and in this chapter.

How to Create Unity Across the Generations?

Today, many Jews feel nostalgia and genuine admiration for the people and values of the past, even though they would never wish to return to the patriarchal practices of our ancestors. Deuteronomy introduces the possibility—and difficulty—of successful adaptation that maintains connection and integrity with the past. Such adaptation implies two concerns: Authenticity—upholding our heritage, and relevance—addressing new circumstances. The problem of choice and balance can be posed in terms of extremes: Of what use is a "Torah-true" Judaism that fails to take cognizance of the lives of contemporary Jews? Of what value is a Judaism driven only by the needs of the moment?

In its deep structure, if not always on the surface, Deuteronomy takes the reality of change for granted. Constancy is more problematic—even unattainable. Much of Deuteronomy is concerned with how, in light of ongoing change, the Israelites might meaningfully preserve tradition. This inquiry is of particular interest in our fast-changing times.

Deuteronomy is predicated on the assumption that Moses can speak to all the people—of his generation and of generations to follow. Moses preached a unity of purpose and belief, even to the extent of overriding or ignoring tribal and class distinctions.[4] Yet unity and continuity were, as they remain, scarce commodities and elusive ideals. Moses' frequent insistence that nothing must change is belied by the context of Deuteronomy: Everything was changing, and he—predicting disobedience, punishment, and exile—was hardly sanguine. A new generation was entering a new land with a new leader. Whether we read Deuteronomy as a coherent unit of Moses' last speeches or in the historical context suggested by biblical criticism,[5] society was in transition. Plurality, even division, were in evidence.

Lately, the Jewish community has been absorbed with the question of continuity, both in terms of how we educate the next generation and in terms of sheer survival. Deuteronomy is concerned not merely with continuity as such, but with continuity that is *meaningful* to both the elder and younger generations. The last book of Moses presumes that, especially for those who have not personally witnessed the miracles of Egypt and Sinai, the reasons behind the commandments are essential. According to Deuteronomy, proper motivations for observance include love and awe of God, remembrance of divine grace, aspirations toward holiness, and the personal rewards of a *mitzvah*-centered existence.[6]

Bridging the Gap 1: Growth and Change in the Law

Deuteronomy provides at least three broad strategies for bridging the gap between generations, all of which have specific relevance for women and feminists. They are centered, respectively, around law, story, and time.

Perhaps the simplest bridge-builder is the introduction of new laws, as well as variations on established ones. While some apparent changes between Deuteronomy and earlier books could be attributed to the preservation of competing traditions, others represent clear choices and evolutions. The fact that the people are entering a new land prompts a detailed pronouncement of commandments and expectations relevant to the new setting. The prohibition against intermarriage (Deut. 7:3), the focus on urban as well as rural settings (Ex. 23:10–11 vs. Deut. 15:1f), and the centralization of the sacrificial cult (Deut. 12:1ff, 16:2ff) are among the best-known innovations that reflect new circumstances. As we shall see, many changes in the law also promote social justice.[7] Laws regarding slaves, for example, are more liberal in Deuteronomy than in Exodus.

More fundamental than any specific change is the underlying assumption that law can and does change. Overtly, change is prohibited. The Israelites must neither add to nor take away from the commanded word (4:2, 13:1), turn neither right nor left from God's demands (5:29, 28:14). Yet, it is the leaders of future generations who will rightly decide and interpret the law (16:18, 17:8f). Moreover, their judgment, in exact parallel to the word of God, shall not be deviated from, "to the right or left" (17:11). In some ways, the past is the ultimate, unsurpassed value: There will never be another prophet like Moses (34:10). On another level, however, the future overrides the past: Another prophet, who *is* like Moses, will replace—even supplant—him (18:15f, 34:9).

In the laws and paradoxical legal theory of Deuteronomy, the Torah itself introduces the possibility that Torah can be interpreted, expanded, and even revised. Deuteronomy reveals not only the ability of the tradition to change, but also the traditionality of such development. In effect, Deuteronomy is the first extended commentary on the Torah. By its example, it invites the reader to respond to Torah as a living, and therefore evolving, document.

Women and the Law Of all the many controversies and concerns in the Jewish world since the Enlightenment, women's issues have been among the most prominent in testing the balance between stability and adaptability. Whether, how, and when women study Talmud, cover their hair, lead services, chant from the Torah, or become rabbis affects the nature of Jewish community dramatically, fundamentally, and in numerous practical details.

It is by now a cliché among liberal Jews to assert that *halakhah* (Jewish law) has always responded to the values, insights, and realities of the day. Deuteronomy is a core text for that claim and specifically for feminist perspectives on *halakhah*. It portrays Law as a conversation across generations, incorporating, and even demanding, responses from the Jews of every era.[8]

Bridging the Gap 2: Reading Ourselves into Promises and Stories

Non-legal material likewise unites Jews of different eras. Deuteronomy subtly weaves together the disparate stories and promises of different generations, demonstrating how ancient traditions can be successfully combined with newer ones. For example, the covenant with the patriarchs and the covenant at Sinai/Horeb are rendered into one.[9] It may seem obvious to us that they are both part of one long tradition, but this perception exists largely because Deuteronomy, along with other texts, makes and repeatedly reinforces that connection (7:8). The new, combined national narrative becomes a bridge between generations.

A related means of linking past and future is education—a key Deuteronomic value taken up by Rabbi Emily Feigenson in this chapter. Parents are enjoined to teach children the story of their people (6:7, 20; 11:19). Deuteronomy supports a shared literary heritage by demanding that the laws for the kings and the people of Israel be recorded, studied, and recited (17:18, 27:8, 31:11). Moreover, the shared text of Deuteronomy itself provides a connection among Jews of different periods.

Jewish women have a special interest and need to read ourselves into the central covenants and stories of our people. When women relate to the covenant God made with our fathers [sic] or to the story of our people and the usual emphases of its transmission, we automatically do what Deuteronomy does—we build a bridge between that history and our own identity. We make connections and compensations so quickly and subtly that we overcome, or cover over, significant differences.[10] Becoming conscious of this process can help us critique our own marginality and develop intentional tools to transcend it. It can also offer the community at large a model for continuing the dialogue with texts from which individuals or whole generations may be estranged. People have many different moral and theological struggles with the Bible and Rabbinic literature. Feminism gives Judaism a gift when it brings the general problem of alienation into particular and vivid focus. To wrestle with problematic texts—woman-centered or not—is to take both ourselves and the tradition seriously.

The "engaged alienation" I describe raises fundamental issues of meaning. To ask why women are not represented in certain texts or public honors is to probe the texts and honors themselves, not just the exclusions or exemptions. For example, when we ask why women have not traditionally chanted from the Torah, we raise important questions about the whys and wherefores of public Torah reading, about what it means for *anyone* to chant from the Torah and to represent the community in doing so. (Vanessa L. Ochs explores such questions in her essay, "*Leynen*.") Continuing the dialogue with tradition can also uncover or forge unexpected connections between ancient and contemporary perspectives. In this chapter, for example, Rabbi Shohama Harris Wiener discovers a model and endorsement for women's leadership styles in the Jewish mystical tradition.

Bridging the Gap 3: Transcending the Barriers of Time

It is not just laws and stories, but our very relationship with time that allows for continuity between generations. Throughout Deuteronomy, Moses' flowing speech is periodically "interrupt-ed" by a narrator.[11] Both Moses and this narrator seem to con-fuse—or at least conflate—chronology. Moses speaks of past, present, and future in such a way as to address several generations at once. For example, he warns:

> When you shall bear children, and children's children and
> you shall have remained long in the land, and shall deal cor-
> ruptly...I call heaven and earth to witness against you this
> day that you will surely perish quickly off the land into
> which you go over the Jordan to possess it... (Deut. 4:25–26)

Who is the "you" that shall perish? It seems to be some confla-tion of the future sinners and the ones who are witness, along with heaven and earth, this day, of the warning. Which day is "this"? This day of Moses' speaking, surely; but also *this* day of the read-ing of the text. If we are speaking of the generation of children's children, it is far into the future. Yet the responsibility is immedi-ate. The same message applies to the generation that will enter the land, the generation(s) that will attempt to hold on to it, and the generation(s) that will need to regain it.

A disruption of our usual sense of "the now" occurs through-out Deuteronomy when the (obviously later) narrator comments, and mixes in, on Moses' message.[12] We flip between perspectives, now looking back on our ancestors, now being present among Moses' congregation. Repeated references to *"hayom"* (today / this day), *"ba'et hahi"* (at that time), *"ad hayom hazeh"* (to this very day), *"bayom hahu"* (on that day) fall in on one another, especially when the message of "today," given to Moses earlier (in Exodus) and tes-tified to by past experience, is meant to be applied to future situa-tions (4:14, 7:17–18). In the end, varied and contradictory expressions of timing are overridden by the decisive *"kayom/kehay-om hazeh"* (as it is / remains this day—4:38, 6:24, 10:15, 29:27). The phrase links the past, present, and future Israel in a dynamic unity.

This conflation is more than sleight of hand, masterful redaction, or a worried father speaking simultaneously to immediate and distant descendants. It represents a theological assertion relevant to contemporary Jews who wish to link themselves to an ancient heritage: Neither Moses, nor God, nor the Torah itself speaks "once and for all." The giving of Torah took—and takes—place at an eternal moment, which knows the bounds of no periodization. "This commandment that I command you this day" (30:11) is the commandment enjoined upon us every day, newly (*Sifrei Va'ethanan* 33 on Deut. 6:6). "Not with our ancestors did *Adonai* make this covenant [at Sinai/Horeb], but with us—we, who are all alive here today" (Deut. 5:3).

Including the One Who Is Not Here This last quotation points to a compatibility between contemporary women's needs and Deuteronomy's politics of inclusion. In Exodus, Moses excluded women with the warning that "all" the people "stay away from a woman" in preparation for the Sinai experience (Ex. 19:15). In Deuteronomy, declarations regarding Sinai/Horeb transcend gender, as well as time. The phrase "we who are all alive here today" allows for women's inclusion. Other wording explicitly includes all the people—children, *wives/women*, and strangers in the camp—in a reiteration of the covenant (Deut. 29:9–11). Even if women were excluded at first, they are included at last. The priestly classes are to read the Law aloud every seven years to "all Israel" (the phrase appears twice): "Gather the people together, the men and the women and the children and the stranger who is within your gates, that they may hear and that they may learn" (31:12).

In Deuteronomy more than any other book of the Torah, women are potentially and actually part of a national "we" (Deut. 16:11, Ex. 34:23). Moreover, to the extent that women are alienated, we fit right in! Everyone is distanced and even alienated from the past—that is the collective, essential problem addressed by Deuteronomy.

Transcending the Barriers within a Generation

In harmony with its inclusive strain, Deuteronomy expresses a populist concern for the "underdog." To build a just society, those who are most privileged must give up some short-term gains and advantages—thus, tithing (Deut. 14:28–29), forgiving debts (15:2), paying a worker's salary expeditiously (24:14–15). Even people who have lost a possession are especially well protected in Deuteronomy (Ex. 23:4, Deut. 22:1–3). Care for the poor, strangers, slaves, widows, and orphans is a value throughout the Torah, but especially so in its final book, where providing for Levites, the unlanded tribe, is also emphasized.[13]

Deuteronomy acknowledges the humanity of the underprivileged and oppressed. In a number of places, it even focuses on their perspectives. For example, Exodus 22:24–26 prohibits taking a garment overnight in pledge for a loan, since the borrower might sleep in it. Deuteronomy 24:10–13 adds that one may not enter a borrower's home to retrieve a pledge, thus guarding the dignity, as well as the property, of the borrower.

The experience of having been a slave obligates one to be fair and compassionate to the less fortunate (Deut. 15:13–15, 24:17–22). Moreover, compassion is a divine trait and thus helps to mold holy, Godlike people: "[God] does justice for the orphan and the widow, and loves the stranger[s], to give [them] food and clothing. And you shall love the stranger, for you were strangers in the land of Egypt" (10:18–19).[14] The *midrash* picks up on this empathic strain when it interprets the verse "And [God] will give you mercy" (13:18) to mean that God bestows as a gift the quality of being merciful (Deut. *Rabbah* 3:7; see also 5:7).

Deuteronomic empathy finds a parallel in the ethic of care and caring identified and endorsed by feminist theorists.[15] Some contend that relatedness and empathy toward others is typical of female psychological and moral development—a subject explored below. Feminists, like Jews, have identified with and advocated for the Other, the disenfranchised. Clearly, the brand of empathic social justice so central to Deuteronomy has motivated feminist Jews. As Rabbi Susan Schnur implies later in this chapter, women's inclusion is a matter of *din* (strict justice), as well as *raḥamim* (compassion, mercy). Along these same lines, Rabbi Dianne O. Esses regards the humanism of Deuteronomy as a model and mandate for how to treat Jewish women.

To Which Generation Do We Belong? The Numbers chapter argues that contemporary Jewish women are wanderers in the desert, no longer enslaved, and not yet able to assume ownership of our own territory; we are a sometimes recalcitrant group, in the process of building and (re)defining community. This Deuteronomy chapter takes a different, but not necessarily contradictory position: That *all* generations are transitional. Our generation—like the one Moses addressed, like every other—is both parent and child. We are the elders, teaching our youth new insights born of women's inclusion and perspectives, hoping they will carry on with these lessons and complete the journey to the Promised Land. And we are the heirs to a sacred heritage, entrusted to preserve the precious stories, boundaries, and guidelines of our ancestors.

The founders of the Jewish feminist movement are the Moses of our generation; they have recalled the principles of the foremothers (just as Moses invoked and relied on the forefathers), resisted oppression (even as he did in Egypt), and led exhilarating breakthroughs to new freedoms (as in the exodus). Feminist pioneers, like Moses, must teach and relate to a generation that may not remember the struggles, but benefits from them. At best, these elders, again like Moses, will overlook the promised land from a distant mountaintop—unable to control or even to witness exactly how changes in leadership, law, and daily living will play out in the new community. According to Rabbi Jane Rachel Litman's essay on destiny, feminist pacesetters may not even reach the mountaintop, being still engaged in desert wanderings. In any case, the generations that eventually enter the Land will be guided by visions such as those articulated by Esses, Feigenson, Litman, Schnur, and Gloria Steinem.

The Value of Being Different

Deuteronomy is unique among the books of the Torah in its focus on Israel's election as a nation. Yet, the book is ambivalent on the subject. Mostly, Israel is pictured as lovingly, particularly, and even uniquely chosen by God "from among all the peoples on the face of the earth" (Deut. 7:6). However, in one instance, Israel's election is considered an insult and punishment to other nations, rather than a compliment to our own (9:4–6). Israel is also likened to other nations, and God acknowledges the special inheritances of many peoples—not Israel alone.[16] Deuteronomy leads one to ask:

How and how much is Israel different from other nations?[17] How might distinctiveness feed the arrogance against which God warns? How might we instead use what sets us apart to sanctify our relationship with God and Torah? *K.d.sh.*, after all, means both "holy" and "set apart."

These questions are relevant not only to ancient Israelites and contemporary Jews, but also to the debate within the women's movement about gender differences. At one time, difference per se was perceived as negative, because it had so often been the excuse for undermining women. What was designated as typically female often stood in opposition to more respected "male" qualities. Today, many feminist researchers and theorists understand women to have distinctive methods of relating and regard those relational styles as a positive value—no matter how oppressive the circumstances under which they were acquired, and no matter how women's distinctiveness was demeaned in the past.[18] It may look to the world that women were "chosen" to be oppressed; the same claim has been made about Jews. But these theorists believe that, in part *because* of past mistreatment and other shared experiences, such as motherhood, women have a special message, a Torah of empathy, to teach. This is not unlike the claim that having been a slave in the land of Egypt causes, or should cause, former slaves to treat the underprivileged with kindness.

Some feminists refute the existence of significant gender differences (outside of basic biological distinctions). They oppose the data or research methods that attest to difference, or agree that there are differences, but posit that these are the result of a power differential; similar patterns might be observed for blacks in relation to whites, Jews in relation to gentiles, or lower classes in relation to the rich. Many in this camp argue that emphasis on gender obscures individual differences, which are both greater and more influential than differences between men and women as groups. Indeed, some question the usefulness of "gender talk," which may reenforce our socially-constructed identities and make them seem fixed or even natural.

Most feminists fall somewhere in the middle, between understanding an ethic of care as peculiarly, if not uniquely, female, and denying that there are sufficient gender differences to merit exploration of "female" or "male" styles. Everyone faces the challenge of discussing gender differences without polarizing the sexes, reinforcing old stereotypes, or creating new ones.

To the extent that we can agree on naming, understanding, or theorizing differences—be they biological, developmental, sociological, relational, linguistic, psychological, evolutionary, experiential—the question then becomes: "So what?" Is our ideal separate spheres? Androgyny? Shall we validate both "male" and "female" qualities, perhaps advocating a balance among such qualities in each individual or in society as a whole? Shall we (temporarily) compensate for historic prejudice by giving greater voice and attention to women's styles, perspectives, and habits? Is it our ideological choice to favor women's relational style as the preferred (or even superior) norm? My own ideal is to cultivate *all* beneficial modes of human expression appropriate to their circumstances and, ultimately, to cease labeling them by gender—not even calling them "classically" or "historically" male or female. However, it would be foolish to imagine that this ideal could be realized without first exploring the very real differences in experience and perspectives between men and women, as groups. We have a great deal to learn from one another. And if we seek full human expression, we will have to make a special effort to hear and incorporate women's muted voices.

Essay Themes and Their Relation to Chosen-ness

Like the other chapters, this one begins with a textual reading in a woman's voice. Dr. Alice Shalvi re-tells the story of receiving the Torah on Mt. Sinai from Miriam's point of view. Her *midrash* asks: Where was Miriam while Moses was on the mountaintop and Aaron was building the golden calf?

Contributors to the Deuteronomy chapter pursue three main themes. Shalvi, Steinem, Wiener, and Rabbi Elizabeth Weiss Stern all cover the topic of leadership—a subject important to Deuteronomy in light of Moses' maturation as a leader and transfer of authority to the next generation. These contributors reflect a spectrum of views on what it is that women (perhaps uniquely) have to offer as leaders.

Esses, Ochs, and Barbara D. Holender examine the transmission of the Law from different viewpoints. Esses regards transmission of law and narrative in paradoxical terms. Every authority simultaneously validates and supplants the inheritance from previous authorities, in the same manner that Deuteronomy repeats the law—but with a twist. Ochs explores the ritual relationship we have to law, and the issues that are raised when women chant words of Torah. Holender's poem puts into words the multiplicity and ineffability of Torah.

Schnur, Feigenson, and Litman conclude the chapter with visionary essays. All three presuppose that while we have already experienced tremendous changes, we—like the generation of freed Israelite slaves, poised to enter a new land—stand on the verge of still greater transformations. For these authors, "women's participation" means not only access to formerly male bastions, but also influence on their development. Such influence will have both concrete and far-reaching impact, affecting even our basic understanding of such topics as justice (Schnur), education (Feigenson), and the Jewish future (Litman).

The essays in this chapter represent a wide range of the various possible approaches to gender difference. In Steinem's ideal, leadership styles are expanded for all people, even as social norms are infused with what has been women's separate and devalued sphere. Stern questions how much we really know about gender difference and disputes the existence of a female rabbinical style. Esses specifically rejects separate spheres for men and women—a central feature of the Syrian-Jewish community in which she was raised. In contrast, Feigenson advocates separatism, at least as a short-term strategy for helping women find their voices. Schnur sees Jewish women as advocates for both strict justice/rule-orientation and partiality/relationship-orientation, playing out the two approaches in an intricate dance. Thus, she implicitly refutes the association of the former to men and the latter to women.

In many ways, the women's movement has been stuck on the question of difference. One way to transcend repetitious and predictable debates about the source(s), nature, and extent of gender difference is to reframe the issue in terms of chosen-ness. In this paradigm, the focus is on the positive uses of difference—the "so what?"—more than difference itself. In its purest form, biblically and midrashically, chosen-ness implies distinctiveness and holiness without a sense of superiority.[19] Jews are chosen not because we are better, but because we received the Torah and brought it to the world. Jewish women's contribution, like that of Judaism in general, must be particular in its source and universal in its significance. What Torah are women bringing—or might we bring—the world? How can women apply our distinctive history and experiences to the service of God and people? These are meta-questions of this book. Similar questions need to be asked by men, who are beginning now to explore gender issues and who differently embody the image of God. We benefit most by leaving such questions open, even as we pursue answers. We are not yet in the promised land, but still on our way; we do not yet have perfect justice, perfect gender-balancing, or even perfect consensus about our differences, commonalities, identities, or goals. But what could be more Rabbinic than encouraging further dialogue, than answering the question of difference with a new set of questions?

—D.O.

Leadership

Another Mountain, Another Reading

ALICE SHALVI

*"The Holy One, blessed be God, said: 'When you stood at Sinai
and received the Torah, I wrote that I love you, as it is said,
"But because Adonai loved you...."'"*
— EX. *RABBAH* 32:2 AND DEUT. 7:8

*"And I [Moses] looked and, behold, you had sinned against
Adonai your God and had made a molten calf; you had turned
aside quickly out of the way that Adonai commanded you.
And I took the two tablets and cast them out of my two hands,
and broke them before your eyes.... Thereupon Adonai said to
me, 'Carve out two tablets of stone like the first, and come up to
me on the mountain; and make an ark of wood. I will inscribe on
the tablets the commandments that were on the first tablets that
you smashed, and you shall deposit them in the ark.'"*
— DEUT. 9:16–17, 10:1–2

*"Rabbi Joseph taught: Both the tablets and the fragments of the
tablets were deposited in the holy ark."*
— BT *BABA BATRA* 14B; BT *MENAKHOT* 99A

*According to traditional Jewish belief, the Torah is the word of God, tran-
scribed by Moses the prophet. God spoke; Moses wrote. What he wrote is
what he heard, and he heard with the ear of a man of his time, no matter
how great a man or how momentous the time. What has for many years
exercised my mind and imagination is not so much whether God is male
or female, since God is clearly inconceivable, ineffable, and non-corporeal.*

Dr. Alice Shalvi was born in Germany in 1926, educated in England, and since
1949 has lived in Jerusalem. She taught at Hebrew University for forty years,
served as a school principal for fifteen years and, since 1984, has been the
founding chairwoman of the Israel Women's Network.

Far more relevant is the sex of God's messenger and interpreter, of the one who transmitted the Torah to the children of Israel.

A well-known feminist essay by Virginia Woolf entitled "Shakespeare's Sister" sought to explain the paucity of great women writers. What I offer here is a re-reading that hints at a different religious sensibility, a different history that might have been born had Moses' sister, along with or instead of Moses, been destined to encode the word of God.

This re-reading addresses a number of interesting textual questions: What motives can we ascribe to Moses to explain his breaking of the tablets? How do we understand the sibling relationships among Miriam, Aaron, and Moses, especially in light of the elliptical and confusing episode in which Miriam seems to be scapegoated (Num. 12:1–16)? If Miriam is a prophet so beloved by the people that they will not move on without her (Num. 12:15), why is her story so truncated, and how might we reconstruct it?

The text is formatted as two parallel girsa'ot *(versions, variant readings). The left column represents the Miriam* girsa, *the right column, that of Moses. Moses' text does not read as a continuous narrative, but in sparse fragments. This is the reverse of the "normal" situation, in which it is women's stories that are only partly known.*

The Tablets of Stone

She labored up the steep mountain in the darkness, breathing hard with the effort, her feet occasionally stumbling, her sandals hardly serving to protect her from the sharp shards of rock that hampered her climb. She knew she must reach the summit before sunrise. That was the mission imposed on her by the Voice that had called her the previous day, the same Voice that, years earlier, had bidden her remain in the tall rushes on the river bank long after her mother had deposited the newborn infant, bundled in the cloth-lined basket, in the shallow water among the reeds. The same Voice had prompted her, encouraged her, to step forward when the elegant princess stooped to pick up the basket, and offer to bring a woman to nurse the pretty boy child.

A slim crescent glowed pale in the desert sky to light her way; the stars were brilliant and the cold night air refreshed her.

At last she reached the top of the mountain and sat down to rest. The intense dark was that which precedes the dawn. She realized that the sacred hour was at hand, that at any moment she would once again hear the Voice.

And suddenly it came— calling her name tenderly, as her mother used to call it when she was young and they were alone in the unmanned house. She sprang to her feet and listened.

"Miriam, Miriam," came the Voice.

"I am here," she replied, "*hinneni.*"

"Know, I have chosen you this day to carry My message to the people. You, the singer,

God called to him, "Moses, Moses."

He answered, *"Hinneni,* Here I am."

the dancer, who took the cymbals and led the women in praise-giving when I delivered Israel from the terrible pursuit and brought them safely across the parted waters.

"The people are restless, they are divided, frustrated, led out of bondage into a wilderness fraught with danger and hardship. To become a nation, this ragtag of tribes requires a common goal, a common code, an ethos that will unite them—an ideal that will guide them.

"Go down and carry My message to them. Bid them love each other, bid them love the earth that I created, the creatures that fill the earth, the human beings who people it. Bid them love Me, for I will always love them and protect them, sending rain to make the earth fruitful, bringing light each dawn as an assurance that after suffering comfort will always follow. Go down and gather them around you, take up your cymbal and sing to them, sing to them of love and of *Shekhinah*" [close-dwelling presence of God, associated with the feminine].

As the Voice ceased, Miriam saw the first gleams of

sunrise, the sun lighting the bare desert landscape, dark brown shadows marking the clefts and crevices between the mountain peaks. She felt the divine presence, and it gave her strength to fulfill her task.

But what words would she use? How would she speak to the people? What song would come from her throat?

To help her remember, she picked up two flints and sought out a large, flat stone. On it she hammered out one word: לֶאֱהֹב, *le'ehov* (to love).

By the time she had finished, working rapidly, the sun was high in the sky. She began the descent, slipping occasionally as loose rocks rolled from under her feet. She cradled the tablet of stone in her arms as she had cradled the baby Moses when they laid him among the rushes.

Suddenly, she became aware that she was not alone.

Coming down the mountain, walking toward her, was her brother, staff in hand, climbing steadily and firmly, a strong man at the height of manhood. She waited to surprise him, eager to tell him of her night on the mountain, to share with him the divine message. She would ask him

Moses went down the mountain, for his people whom he had brought up out of Egypt had become corrupt.[1]

to come down with her, to help gather the people.

Together they would stand, the two brothers and the sister,[2] the acknowledged leaders of this band of freed slaves, the children of Yokheved and Amram—and she would deliver the message. She would sing them the Word, she would teach them to love.

But her brother's eyes were cold with anger as he began to speak:

"They don't deserve God's Word."

Suddenly he wrested the tablet of stone from her arms. In a blind fury, without reading the Word, he raised the tablet above his head, shattering it with full force on the rock in front of him, smashing it to pieces.[3]

As she cried out in alarm, he thrust her from his path and hastened down the mountain.

For a long time she sat on the mountainside, collecting the shards, trying to piece them together, but she realized this was a hopeless task. What was she to do? She descended the mountain and crept under the shade of the large heavy cloth that served as the family tent. Despair filled her heart. She felt

he raised the tablet above his head, shattering it with full force on the rock in front of him, smashing it to pieces.[3]

unequal to fighting with this brother, this powerful creature who was the people's hero, who had enshrined himself as their leader.

But as she sat downcast, the Voice came to her again: "Do not despair. You too have a share in the miracle. You have heard me speak. You have beheld me face to face. I am the *Shekhinah* that guided you, and I will not forsake you.

"Be strong and of good courage.[4]

"Be strong and of good courage."[4]

"You too shall be written in the annals of my people. Take heart and heed what I have to say. I will speak, and you will write, and the day will surely come when your story is told in all the tents of Israel, wherever women gather..."

So Miriam took up a flint, she found a large tablet of stone, and she listened. And as she listened, she wrote: בְּרֵאשִׁית בָּרְאָה ...
"In the beginning, She created...."[5]

"In the beginning...."[5]

Women, Leadership, and *Tikkun Olam*

ALICE SHALVI

With the Book of Deuteronomy, the Five Books of Moses come to a remarkable close, a final act that is all the more astonishing when we realize that it comprises a virtual soliloquy. Save a few interruptions by God and a narrator, the "words," the *devarim*, are those of Moses himself—the same man who resisted God's bidding to speak to Pharaoh, claiming that he was "slow of speech and slow of tongue" (Ex. 4:10).

Deuteronomy is an impressive blend of exhortation and prophecy, historical summary and legislative rulings, threats and promises, blessings and curses. The range of subject matter is framed by geographical surveys, describing, at the outset, the territory roamed by the Israelites after their exodus from Egypt, and, at the end, the promised land that they—but not Moses—are about to enter.

The muster-roll of proper names conjures up a vast region (Deut. 1:1–2), yet it is one which, by a direct route, should take only eleven days to cover. It has taken the Children of Israel forty years! From the summit of Pisgah, on Mount Nebo, Moses is shown "the whole land" (34:1–3). Yet, having seen its full extent and beauty, he is doomed never to enter it, even though he is still physically at the height of his power, "his eyes undimmed and his vigor unabated" (34:7). He must write his own epitaph and remain on the other side of the Jordan.

The paradoxes and ironies encoded in Deuteronomy may be seen as paradigmatic of Moses' own character, which is a wholly human blend of virtues and faults, despite the semi-divine qualities that distinguish him from other mortals. Moses can be quick to anger, often impetuously unreflecting in his responses. The most memorable examples of this tendency are the smiting of the

---

Dr. Alice Shalvi was born in Germany in 1926, educated in England, and since 1949 has lived in Jerusalem. She taught at Hebrew University for forty years, served as a school principal for fifteen years and, since 1984, has been the founding chairwoman of the Israel Women's Network.

Egyptian (Ex. 2:12), which necessitates his fleeing to the desert; the breaking of the tablets (Ten Commandments) when he descends from Mount Sinai and finds the Israelites worshipping the Golden Calf (Ex. 32:19); and the striking of the rock at Mei-Merivah (Num. 20:11)—the act that is the explicit cause of his being barred from entry to the promised land. All these actions, human and understandable as they are, can nevertheless be perceived as hubristic, leading to reversal of the desired outcome: Exile rather than assistance; postponement in delivering God's commandments; delay rather than expedition; exclusion from redemption.

God's miracles help Moses in the practical tasks of leadership and also elevate him in stature. God works great wonders, but it is usually Moses who interprets the words of God. Moreover, it is Moses who acts or speaks to precipitate and call attention to the miracles. God dictates the Ten Commandments, but it is Moses who inscribes the second set of these on the tablets of stone and brings them down from the mountaintop (Ex. 34:28). Moses is the only human permitted to speak to the divine "mouth to mouth" (Num. 12:8). He awed and dazzled Aaron and all the Israelites; "his face was [so] radiant" that he had to veil himself after each direct encounter with God (Ex. 34:29–35). Little wonder that the closing eulogy proclaims "Never again did there arise in Israel a prophet like Moses" (Deut. 34:10).

Combining human talents and foibles with prophetic and nearly divine qualities, Moses is a leader par excellence. He drags a reluctant raggle-taggle of tribes out of bondage and into nationhood. He guides them to accept not only the one God but an entire innovative moral code based on the oneness of God and the comparable, parallel, oneness of Israel. Moses' leadership style is the prototype of the Maccabean: A clarion call that has become the byword of Israel Defense Force commanders—"*Aharai*! Follow me!" Indeed, the *midrash* puts this very word in Moses' mouth (Deut. *Rabbah* 1:2). He possesses what is probably the most vital aspect of leadership: He is able to persuade others to follow him.

Time and again, as the people's spirits droop, as they express fear, doubt, dismay, despair, he is able to rally them, either with words of anger and reproach, or with promises, reassurances, and encouragement. Knowing when to chide and when to encourage, evaluating situations and gauging people's physical and psychological responses—these too are essential to leadership. Stern in judgment and punishment, yet constantly concerned with the welfare of the people, Moses repeatedly intercedes on their behalf when God threatens to annihilate them. His constancy of purpose is a further essential quality of leadership. In the course of forty years, with guidance from God, but little assistance from any mortal, he prepares a generation for freedom. Using his talents, charisma, and authority, he leads the Israelites out of Egypt and introduces them to the commandments.

Do Women Fit the Mosaic Model?

When women think of leadership, we can, clearly, look to Moses—and other male figures—for inspiration. However, the hierarchical mode of leadership, which Moses so brilliantly exemplifies and which is prevalent in all patriarchal societies, has coincided with, if not led to, an almost universal subjugation of women. Furthermore, there is obvious value—to the reclamation of women's history and the shoring up of women's self-esteem—in finding female role models.

Many Jewish women naturally seek these models in the Torah and other sacred writings. But our search more often than not results in dismay, for as the history of early humankind and then of the patriarchs and matriarchs and of the Children of Jacob unfolds, the role and influence of women significantly decline. The protagonists of Genesis include a number of outstanding women who played a vital role in determining the course of events, for good or for ill. Eve eats the forbidden fruit; Sarah persuades Abraham to cast out Hagar and Ishmael; Dinah becomes a *casus belli* for her brothers, bringing about mass slaughter. However, the matriarchs tend to act primarily, if not exclusively, within house and family, and their power is clearly limited. Much of women's so-called "deceit" throughout the Bible can be attributed to their inability to achieve or act directly.

Miriam, a more likely heroine in the eyes of modern women, at first plays an active and critical role: She ensures the survival of Moses, displaying both concern for his fate and quick-wittedness in offering the boy's own mother as a wet nurse (Ex. 2:4–9). After the Children of Israel cross the Sea of Reeds, she leads the women in a song of praise, indicating that she stands in relation to her own sex rather as Moses stands to the entire people. But thereafter she is barely mentioned, reappearing only in the strange episode relating to the Cushite woman whom Moses had married (Num. 12), where she is distinguished by a punishment for hubris in questioning Moses' authority—a punishment more severe than that meted out to Aaron, her accomplice.

The diminution of Miriam's role is of a piece with the definition of women's legal status in Leviticus and Numbers. Daughters are under their father's authority until they marry; thereafter, they are under that of their husbands. This trend serves as a foregrounding factor for the only significant female figures in the penultimate book of the Pentateuch (there are none at all in Deuteronomy), namely the five daughters of Tzelofeḥad. It is in them that we can perhaps discern women's distinct and different mode of action—a difference that may serve as explanation not only for the absence of a female equivalent to Moses, but also for the fact that even today, when women almost everywhere have been enfranchised, there are still very few outstanding women leaders in the political, Mosaic sense.[1]

Five Daughters and an Alternative Model

Although the daughters of Tzelofeḥad are all individually named (Maḥlah, No'ah, Ḥoglah, Milkah, and Tirtzah), the initial identification accorded them is exclusively and emphatically through the *male* line of descent: Their father was "the son of Ḥefer, son of Gilead, son of Makhir, son of Manasseh, son of Joseph" (Num. 27:1). Faced with the family's loss of inheritance because their father had no male heir, they courageously bring their case before Moses in the most public place possible. "They stood before Moses, Elazar the priest, the chieftains, and the whole assembly, at the entrance of the Tent of Meeting" (Num. 27:2). They present their case briefly and cogently, questioning the principle of inheritance solely through the male line, which Moses has just proclaimed. They act collectively to rectify the injustice and illogic they discern in the ruling. None seeks any advantage over her sisters. Significantly, this is one of the few occasions when Moses the lawgiver lacks a clear answer. He has to consult God, and God's reply is unequivocal: *"ken benot tzelofeḥad dovrot"* (Num. 27:7). "Just (or right) is the plea of Tzelofeḥad's daughters." The emphatic opening monosyllable of that reply, with its two hard consonants, reverses normal syntax, and makes the response even more forceful. The sisters raised an issue that, apparently, neither God nor Moses had so far foreseen or provided for; they set a legal precedent as well as winning their own case.[2]

The collective mode of action *by* a group and *for* a group is characteristic of women's political leadership and organizing. Other ways women tend to operate include a non-confrontational and subtle strategic style. Having established their father's innocence ("He was not one of…Koraḥ's faction" [Num. 27:3]), the daughters plead that *his* name not be lost to his clan. In other words, the claim is not presented in terms of their personal gain, though such gain will clearly result if they are heeded, but in terms of potential loss or shame to a (dead) *man*. Later, faced with loss of lands should women "marry out," the (male) heads of the family speak up (Num. 36:1–12)!

Tzelofeḥad's daughters were not leaders in the same sense that Moses was, but they *were* precedent-setters, models, exemplars. These sisters, rather than the matriarchs who acted in the domestic sphere, provide appropriate role models for women who seek empowerment and equality in the public arena, but who most emphatically do not see Moses as a figure to emulate because they find the hierarchical mode uncongenial and prefer to work collaboratively.[3]

Gender Difference and Leadership

Contemporary feminist theory is divided on the question of gender difference in moral judgment. Carol Gilligan's pioneering work distinguishes between typically male and typically female relational styles—the former being rules- and rights-oriented and the latter, oriented toward relationships, obligations, and empathy.[4] While Gilligan's conclusions strike a chord in the hearts and minds of many women, they have been attacked as "essentialist" and as legitimizing distinctions that ultimately perpetuate detrimental stereotypes. Her critics maintain that what she (and others) identify as gender-different patterns may not, in fact, be consistent, or, if so, may be the result of millennia of social conditioning that could (and should) be eliminated by re-education, affirmative action, and other means.[5]

My own work since 1975, both as principal of Pelech, an experimental high school for religious girls in Jerusalem, and as chairwoman of the Israel Women's Network, has been primarily with females. Much of my social as well as my professional life proves, upon examination, to consist of daily contact, interaction, and collaboration with girls and women. Nevertheless, as a political and social activist, I am also in touch with many men, most of whom occupy positions of authority in government, senior management, and other areas of decision-making and policy formulation.

Experience has led me to conclude that—at least for the present and despite the significant examples of women who have achieved and exercised power in authoritarian and confrontational ways typical of male competitiveness—women's "way of thinking," modes of decision-making, and norms of action are, on the whole, distinct from those of men. We are more collaborative, more inclined to seek consensus and to care for others rather than focusing on vanquishing opponents or prevailing in our approach. We prefer "win/win" to "win/lose," "both/and" to "either/or." We sit in circles, facing and relating to each other as equals, rather than in serried ranks gazing up at a charismatic leader. We even work together in what is usually considered a highly individual area of human activity—artistic creation—as has been shown, for example, in *The Dinner Party*.[6]

I have witnessed these female tendencies exemplified over and over again: In the encouragement and personal investment of time and sympathy displayed by teachers to their students; among women delegates from various parties to the Knesset Committee on the Status of Women; between the Israeli and Palestinian women of the Jerusalem Link, a collaborative organization established in the wake of a peace dialogue held in Brussels in 1989; and, most memorably, at that dialogue itself. A turning point resulted from one Palestinian's expression of empathy with Jewish victims of the Holocaust and her exhortation to fellow Palestinians to follow suit. This readiness to see the "enemy's" point of view effectively put an end to the mutual recriminations that had preceded her appeal.

My own experiences, then, have convinced me that women's mode of action is usually distinct from the mode of leadership that Moses so well exemplifies. But is it capable of bringing about as significant a transformation as that achieved by Moses? Does it have the power to transform a band of unruly slaves into an autonomous, independent, law-abiding nation? I believe it does, and my belief seems to find corroboration in yet another personal experience.

The Influence of Role Models vs. the Power of Leaders

Since 1992, the World Union of Jewish Students has held an annual seminar on women's leadership. Participants come from all over the world. Each year I have conducted the opening session, in which I attempt to reach a group definition of leadership and a consensus on the required qualifications for a leader.

I begin by asking the participants to name an individual whom they perceive as a leader. The responses are as varied as the women's backgrounds, but the majority of those named are men, with Golda Meir as the most frequent exception.

My second question is phrased so as to avoid the word "leader": Who is the person you most admire and would like to emulate? This time, virtually every participant names a woman, frequently one with whom she is personally acquainted, and, in 1994, to my astonishment, the vast majority named their mothers. Women's choices, as well their educational and professional achievements, have expanded exponentially since I was a student; young women today can perceive their mothers not only as objects of love (as I did) but also (as I and my contemporaries on the whole did not) as objects of admiration, as role models. Thus do attitudes and traditions change and evolve.

My models were "women who dared," women who—like the daughters of Tzelofeḥad—challenged and sought to break down the barriers of discrimination, who took risks and exposed themselves to ridicule, opprobrium, and even physical violence in order to assert what they perceived as their inalienable rights.

I think with admiration of the Pankhursts and other British suffragists who chained themselves to the railings at Downing Street. One threw herself under the king's horse at Ascot

race-course and was trampled to death; others endured the cruelties of force-feeding rather than break their hunger strike.

I think of the women who preceded me at Cambridge
University and who proved to the all-male establishment that
women too could excel at mathematics and logic; their (officially
unrecorded) examination results were better than those of their
male colleagues. In 1951—almost a hundred years after the pioneers had first challenged male preconceptions and authority—
women were finally formally accepted as full members of the
University.

All these women were pioneers and precursors. They worked
as groups rather than individuals, so that few names are remembered. Apart from one or two suffragists, they did not make fiery
speeches nor explicitly exhort others to follow them. They were, in
many respects, "ordinary people" with whom we can identify.
They acted, in the first instance, for themselves, for their own
advantage; but in doing so they challenged long-unquestioned
stereotypes, thus bringing about profound social change and helping to create a more just society. Privileges previously confined to
a select few were extended to a far wider social group—one that
included women.

The outstanding characteristics I have discerned among
women with whom I have been privileged to work—characteristics I have tried to describe in this essay—are commitment to a
cause, concern for others, and an attempt to achieve consensus.

Above all, women seem to be prepared to listen. In Hebrew,
the term for understanding a language is not "to know" (*lada'at*),
but *"lishmo'a,"* literally, "to hear." We cannot really comprehend
or internalize values unless we listen and hear. This to my mind
explains the frequent use by Moses in Deuteronomy, his final
exhortation to the people, of the phrase "Hear, O Israel," an adju-
ration that has become Judaism's cardinal credo and declaration of
faith. It is not just that, like any teacher or leader, he wants to be
sure that he has the full attention of his audience. He is calling for
understanding.

Women may not be temperamentally inclined—or socially
adequately empowered—to become leaders of the Moses type (a
task that, in any case, is limited in its potential because, as the text
tells us, never again will there be such a person). Many probably

do not wish to be military commanders like Joshua. But we can and do—consciously and unconsciously—serve as role models, mentors, and nurturing influences. This style of leadership need not supplant nor *be* supplanted by any other. It must, however, expand both our discussion and our definition of "leadership."

Women's values and modes of action—care, concern, commitment, connection, collaboration, communication, and consensus—could be integrated into contemporary systems of government by ensuring equal representation of women in every forum where policy is determined and critical decisions taken—that is, by implementing precisely that principle of equality which impelled the daughters of Tzelofeḥad, the suffragists, and the university pioneers. In this way, we could ensure that women's voices be heard and could expect them to be heeded, listened to. In consequence, I am convinced, the world would be a better place for all humankind.

Women and Leadership

GLORIA STEINEM

"...You shall value the spiritual leaders of your generation."
—ADAPTED FROM BT *ROSH HASHANAH* 25B
ON DEUT. 17:9

We do what we see, not what we're told. That is why the most effective leadership is leadership by example. That is why role models are so important.

We need to remember how far behind women start when it comes to leadership. We have relatively few public role models. Unlike men who are actually praised for leaving their families to

Gloria Steinem is a writer, activist, and feminist organizer who is the consulting editor of *Ms.*, the magazine she co-founded in 1972; president of Voters for Choice, a pro-choice political action committee; and author of several books—most recently, *Moving Beyond Words* (Simon and Schuster, 1995).

fight for what they believe in—no matter how distant or arcane their cause—women are called selfish if we fail to sacrifice *everything* for our families or if we even speak up for ourselves. We are urged to be much more concerned with the welfare of others than with our own. In fact, "co-dependent," the term invented by twelve-step groups, is really just a well-socialized woman.

This double standard applies not only to individuals, but to categories of learning; indeed, to the very way we categorize. For instance, what happens to men is called "politics." What happens to women is called "culture"—as in, "You can't change that— that's culture." Because women are "natural," successful women leaders are called "lucky" or even "motherly."[1] Because male leaders are "intellectual," they are called "courageous" and "great." If God looks like the ruling class, it's a "religion," but if God is female, or even if the religion has female leaders, it is often called "spiritualism," "paganism"—or worse.[2] Male God-language is monotheistic, but female God-language is not.

In an ideal but achievable world, women will be leaders as often as men, men will take care of the children as much as women, and childrearing itself will be valued as a crucial form of leadership. That is the only way we can ever overturn gender roles, develop all the human qualities within us, and become whole people. As we seek to build that world, we must admit that many of us have been successfully socialized under the current system; some women feel that women cannot be leaders—and that the reverse holds true as well. Just as some men punish the weak member of their group, some women punish the strong one. That is the way gender roles are policed.

Yet women are being transformed by gaining footholds in public leadership, and leadership is being transformed by women. We are developing the strength, daring, and ability to deal with conflict. We are also bringing with us values like empathy, linking instead of ranking, and giving credit as well as taking it. We are not only learning from men, but learning we have something to teach men—something the world badly needs.

Women's Teachings

When we say "power," for instance, we are likely to mean power over our own lives, not power over others. When we say "success," we are likely to mean the empowerment of others, not their *dis*empowerment. (After all, our model is the family, where the ideal is to help children become independent, not to keep them under our thumb—if only because that thumb gets very tired.) When we say "structure," we are more likely to mean a circle than a hierarchy, cooperation not domination. After all, domination hasn't done much to change our minds. We tend not to have faith in it.

We are also less likely than men to be divided from each other by conventional political labels. For twenty years, I have been quoting my friend, the actor and director Lee Grant, who explained the phenomenon this way. "I've been married to one Marxist and one fascist," she said, "and neither one took out the garbage."[3] Since we are dealing with patriarchy and with societies in which men are central and women are peripheral, our concerns go far deeper than the superficial political labels that overlay patriarchal assumptions. Although each human being is a unique miracle, in societies that value most that which is associated with men, female human beings share similar experiences that allow us to build bridges between and among apparently divided groups. Women have been leaders in Israeli-Palestinian and interfaith dialogue, for example, just as the Irish Peace Women were often the only bridge between warring Protestants and Catholics in their country.

Women also tend to lead by the power of persuasion—if only because we are so penalized for giving anything that resembles an order. In the long run, persuasion is the only kind of power that honors the power of others. What we value most in a leader is the ability to posit a vision of what could be—for without a vision of change, there can be none—and to phrase it in an inspirational and persuasive way that brings people together, that resolves conflict instead of creating it.

Men and women alike prefer leadership that guides and persuades by hope, rather than rules and dictates by fear. Like prayer and other forms of thought that provide an organizing principle for reality, hope is a form of planning. This means that the future vision we put forth must be a positive one, for it is also a self-ful-filling prophecy. Why would we want to perpetuate a chain of destruction? I see in women leaders today a great concentration of hope—and that is a very precious commodity for us all.

Men tend to be rebellious in youth, and become more conserv-ative as they grow older. Women tend to be conservative in youth—when we haven't yet experienced the injustices of the labor force; of childrearing, which men don't yet share equally (to put it mildly); and of the double standard of aging. Only after hav-ing some of those experiences, as we grow older, do we tend to become more active and rebellious on our own behalf. Since life expectancy has increased in industrialized countries by thirty years since 1900, we now have a lot more time to rebel—and to lead.

With all the changes in recent years, and with women and men informing each other's experience, we have before us a new image of leadership. It blends experience *and* a radical vision, wisdom *and* hope, self-understanding *and* activism. But it won't be com-plete until men are raising children as much as women are, and women are making political decisions as much as men are.

Practical Realities of Religious Leadership

ELIZABETH WEISS STERN

"And Miriam was shut out from the camp seven days, and the people did not journey until Miriam was again brought into the fold."

—NUM. 12:15

"...Miriam died [in Kadesh] and was buried there. And there was no water for the congregation..."

—NUM. 20:1–2

"...I sent before you Moses, Aaron, and Miriam."

—MICAH 6:4

What was so compelling about Miriam that the congregation would not go on without her? How did her living example somehow slake their physical and spiritual thirst? We know so much about Moses and, to a lesser extent, Aaron. Miriam is a mystery. Though she is a role model for women, I can only imagine what qualities of leadership she brought. Was there something distinctive about her leadership *as a woman*?

Not long ago, a colleague called and invited me to speak at a conference for women rabbis on the subject "Defining a Successful Rabbinate." When the phone call came, I had a twin in each arm. I don't remember exactly what the other three kids were doing, but since I had just completed my daily hour-and-a-half carpool circuit, I assume that Jonah was doing his homework and Sarah Leah was taking advantage of my being on the phone to sneak upstairs and watch television, her brother Aaron in hot pursuit. I wondered: Is this the "balance" we talk about? Or is "balance" just a euphemism for the seesaw between competing loyalties to

Rabbi Elizabeth Weiss Stern, ordained at Hebrew Union College-Jewish Institute of Religion in 1984, currently serves at Temple Shalom, Dallas, Texas. She is the mother of five children.

personal and professional demands, the ambivalent attempt to do everything at once and well?

Women rabbis, like other women who have entered professions that were considered "male," often argue that we do not want traditional "success." Many of us are unwilling to serve in large congregations and key leadership roles of major institutions because we perceive that service to be at the cost of family and balance. Women can point to many ways in which we have helped to transform the rabbinic model. We have different kinds of successes to our credit: Gender-sensitive worship experiences; more participation and leadership by lay women; *Rosh Ḥodesh* (New Moon Festival) celebrations; empowerment of lay people; a growing appreciation among Jews—rabbis and congregants alike—of the benefits of smaller, more intimate congregations and of the rabbi's need for a personal life.

We have yet to develop, however, a convincing and coherent model for success that can replace or compete with the traditional, hierarchical, workaholic, (male) model. Perhaps this is because we still want what "the boys" have and believe ourselves to be capable of handling it (better) once we get it. After all, we are a self-selected group: There are plenty of other healing and Jewish professions we could have entered. We chose the rabbinate even with—and maybe, in some ways, because of—the power and leadership style that typically define its success. And even if I don't want to pursue that model myself, I want twenty or fifty of my colleagues to do so—because it is primarily on traditional (male) turf that the battle for legitimacy can be won. Ironically, then, my definition of personal success is at odds with my definition of success for the collective body of women in the rabbinate. I want my sisters and daughters to succeed in the very hierarchical model I reject, because, like it or not, that is our ticket to full inclusion and, thereafter, to the power we need to effect change in the mainstream. With all due respect for the more feminized models of the rabbinate, we entered what was essentially a boy's club, with a model of success that seduces us even as we try to transform it. The transformations Gloria Steinem writes of in this volume will not, I am afraid, become normative in our lifetime. For practical reasons, we must engage and become fluent in established (male) models. We must recognize, too, that for most working people, feminist values and worldly ambitions support each other in some ways and contradict each other in others.

What Do Women (Rabbis) Want?

Women rabbis are striving for balance, intimacy, empathy, and empowerment. Who wouldn't want those things? Who wouldn't want to be *portrayed* as wanting them? We distinguish ourselves in our congregations as presenting a model other than the senior rabbi or the male rabbi who preceded us. The "women's model" focuses on being compassionate, sensitive, easily accessible, flexible.

But we want other things, as well: Things that may not be as politically correct as "balance," "empowerment," and "intimacy"; things like power—pure and simple—prestige, respect, influence.

The clichéd sex-role distinction is that, while all rabbis are spiritual leaders, men tend to emphasize leadership, and women, spirituality. Men are rule-oriented; women, relationship-oriented. But I do not believe that women have the corner on the sensitivity market. Moreover, I would challenge the presumption that powerful leadership is the exclusive purview of men. First and foremost, I challenge women to claim our own power. We need to get over our ambivalence, our excessive need for permission and approval. We must overcome the instinct that power isn't "lady-like," that it isn't spiritual, that it necessarily evokes the male hierarchical model instead of Carol Gilligan's interconnective web.[1] Must it be either/or? Of course, accumulating power is not the point of religious leadership. But unabashedly using our power is sometimes a critical and courageous tool. As I consider women's professional concerns in the rabbinate—unequal pay, unequal opportunities, lack of female leadership in the seminaries, mistreatment, sexual harassment—I recognize that these issues are all expressive of our own powerlessness.

A while back, my husband and I had dinner with an individual who had been invited to Dallas as a scholar-in-residence for a local Jewish organization. I was excited about meeting this person and looked forward to the opportunity of getting to know him.

Dinner was a disappointment. Our guest barely glanced in my direction. Even when I asked a question, he directed his answer to my husband. He talked about his work, about rabbis he has known, about his travels. At the end of the dinner, as we rose to leave, I said, "Dr. So-and-so, I am sorry I will have to miss your lecture this evening, but I have a class to teach." "Oh?" he replied, "and what do you do? Are you a teacher?" For a split second, I was embarrassed for us both. "I'm a rabbi," I said. And I couldn't resist adding, "In fact, you will probably see my picture on the wall of the synagogue where you're giving your talk." He was clearly horrified by his own *faux pas*. I watched his face as he did a mental rerun of the evening's conversation. Here I was, a rabbi, and he had treated me like a...a...*rebbitzin* (rabbi's wife)! "Oh! I'm sorry!" he stammered. "I didn't know!"

I was tempted to remind our guest of the experience of the Ḥafetz Ḥayyim, a rabbi known for his writings on respectful language, when he travelled by train to a neighboring town to deliver a lecture. On the same train were some of his disciples. Unfortunately, they did not recognize him. They did not realize that the old man whom they pushed out of the way as they took their seats was, indeed, their beloved *rebbe* (rabbi). When the train pulled into the station, and the disciples saw a crowd of dignitaries meet the old man, they immediately realized their error. Mortified, they rushed over to apologize. "Rebbe," they said, "Please forgive our rudeness on the train!" "Don't apologize to me," the Ḥafetz Ḥayyim replied. "Me, your Rebbe, you didn't offend. You offended some nameless, insignificant old man. Go find him and apologize."

I wanted to say to our dinner guest: "Me, the rabbi, you didn't offend. Go apologize to that woman with no title." I realized, at that moment, how accustomed I have become to being treated as a rabbi—with respect, as someone worth listening to, taken seriously. For that moment when I was treated like "just" a woman, "just" a wife, I didn't like it. All women deserve better. The title "rabbi" is so familiar to me that I have come to take for granted the authority and respect that is conferred with it. I really don't want to give that up. There is a magic to the title "rabbi" that called to every person who has said, "I want to be a rabbi."

Relating to Gender Difference

I am proud of the qualities that women bring to the title "rabbi." And I understand full well that, regardless of what we do or don't do, people will see us, still, as "women rabbis." I entered the rabbinate under the mistaken assumption that I was becoming a rabbi, not a woman rabbi. "If I put on a robe," I thought, "no one will notice." That is simply not so. And it isn't all bad.

When I was an associate at another temple, the preschool children would refer to me as the "Mommy Rabbi" or Mrs. Rabbi Zimmerman. I (sort of) didn't mind. I understood the security those titles conveyed. After all, isn't a congregation a family? And don't we still have as our idealized family model the mommy and the daddy? Especially with the disappearance of the traditional *rebbitzin*, female associate rabbis have become, in many large congregations, the female authority figures—the nurturing, unconditionally loving, compassionate mothers. For me—and, I suspect, for others—success in the associate position was achieved not only by honing rabbinic skills such as sermon delivery and hospital visitation, not only by learning to do what your senior rabbi did, but also by learning to do what the senior/male *didn't* do: By becoming, indeed, the woman rabbi.

Such gender typing has its insidious side. The senior rabbi of the congregation I served urged everyone to call him Shelly, while I opted to be called "Rabbi." It was obvious to me that congregants said "Shelly" and thought "Rabbi," but said "Rabbi" and thought "Liza." He had to urge people to dispense with titles; that is a problem—and opportunity—women rabbis rarely have.

There *are* gender differences. Sometimes those differences piss me off; sometimes they enable me to be my most effective. Will gender ever be irrelevant? Do we want it to be? I can't answer those questions. I can only report that after twenty years in the rabbinate, women are just beginning to appreciate the ways in which our femaleness works for and against us.

Do we have any power over the way in which our gender impacts our profession? Rabbi Laura Geller has suggested that women will truly find our place as religious leaders when we fully "shift the paradigm from the equality between men and women to the transformation of Judaism itself."[2] Until that transformation takes place—or, perhaps, in order to empower ourselves to effect change, we must claim all types of power. We must learn, for example, to take a position without apology. If women are paid less or otherwise treated as inferior to our male colleagues, then it is because people are taking advantage of our own discomfort with making demands or appearing "unspiritual." In order to exert power—at the negotiating table or in an established position of spiritual leadership—we have to be willing to be disliked and disagreed with, to assert our decisions and take the attendant risks.

Women's continued success in the rabbinate may in part hinge on our willingness to affirm and pursue, not only balance, intimacy, and empowerment, but also recognition, compensation, respect, and power. We must grant ourselves permission to express ourselves in the full variety of our individual and collective voices. We must learn to speak as Aaron spoke to the people and to Pharoah; as Moses spoke to the rock, against Israel's enemies, and before God. And we must (re)discover how Miriam addressed Pharaoh's daughter (Ex. 2:7), murmured against Moses (Num. 12:1), and sang at the Sea (Ex. 15:21).

Love Is the Answer: A New Paradigm

SHOHAMA HARRIS WIENER

"And you shall love..."
                                                        —DEUT. 6:5

*"The reward for one who performs out of love is doubled and
redoubled."*
            —AFTER *SIFREI VA'ETHANAN* 32 ON DEUT. 6:5

I shall begin by sharing on the personal level, because the most
powerful form of leadership is setting an example.

A Universal Vision, a Personal Story

A vision: There is a realm of life where the heart sings, the eyes
feel, and the hands hear. Where souls embrace each other without
touching, and love is the breath of life. Where all living beings
emanate the brilliance of the light of holiness, and every thought
manifests into a creation of lovingkindness.

This vision is a mystical one, rooted in Rabbinic lore about *olam
haba* (the world-to-come) and *gan eden* (the Garden of Eden). I
see it in my mind's eye when I meditate on the meaning of
Deuteronomy 6:5, *"ve'ahavta,* and you shall love..." It is for me a
model of what I envision at my seminary, The Academy for Jewish
Religion. I have always believed in visions, although this spiritual
vision is for me fairly recent.

My earlier visions also revolved around love, but within the
context of a woman's traditional role. I saw myself as a support for
my husband in his career, a nurturer for my children and community, and a part-time educator. My worldview shifted in my thir-
ties due to illness in the family, and in desperation I tried to find
spiritual support. I said to God, "I do not know if you exist, but I
will pray for one hour as if you do." God responded to my plea,

Rabbi Shohama Harris Wiener, D. Min., is President of The Academy for Jewish
Religion, a pluralistic seminary for rabbis and cantors in New York, and a teacher
of Jewish spirituality and healing.

and, four years later, I entered The Academy for Jewish Religion as a rabbinical student. I felt I had come home and loved the Academy as I had never loved my Ivy League alma maters.

As ordination approached, I was asked to stay on as assistant dean. This came as a great surprise, since I planned to serve in a pulpit. However, it felt *bashert* (destined by the good will of Providence), and I accepted the position. Shortly after, the dean left, and I asked for his position.

For seven years, I was dean and CEO of my seminary, keeping an eye out for the "right man" to come along and be President. In the first few years, I felt very inadequate, carrying a role for which I had no suitable model,[1] and little formal training. I prayed very hard, asked a lot of questions, and enrolled in a doctoral program at New York Theological Seminary in administration and spirituality. I bonded with and enlisted the help of the Academy's students, faculty, alumni/ae, and board, as well as others I felt drawn to in the Jewish world. My family, especially my adult daughters, also became my advisors.

At the end of the seventh year, it dawned on me that I was doing very well as CEO. The model of leadership I had instituted due to my "insufficiency" was actually responsible for the Academy's dramatic growth and success. Not only was there was no "right man," but I was the right woman. How shocking. How ironic. And how empowering. With this new understanding, I asked to be President, and was met with total support. I still struggle with fears of inadequacy, but I know that I am doing what is meant for me to do.

Kabbalah (Jewish Mysticism) and Leadership

While my style of leadership evolved out of experience rather than theory, I see in it a contemporary kabbalistic model that fits my feminist needs. Its basic premise is that female is as important as male, and as powerful.[2]

Kabbalah is a holistic theory, a way of understanding the interplay of divine energies with creation and sustenance of the universe. It is a way of seeing that everything in the cosmos is interrelated, and that sparks of God reside in everyone and everything. While the system is extremely complex, comprising ten *sefirot* (energy centers) and a number of worlds or universes, a simple explanation is sufficient for seeing its relevance to my ideas on leadership.[3]

Wholeness and blessing come from a balance of and flow between the receptive energies, which are called female, and the active energies, which are called male. This does not mean that women are receptive and men are active, but that both men and women have female and male *sefirot* and need to keep them in balance. For example, being a strong leader means balancing right-brain wisdom (*ḥokhmah*) and left-brain knowing (*binah*), and balancing the unconditional love of respect and caring (*ḥesed*) with the tough love of expectations (*gevurah*).[4] A successful leader must have persistence and drive (*netzaḥ*) as well as the capacity for empathy (*hod*). The center *sefirot*, the places of balance, are the crown (*keter*) where Spirit enters, the heart (*tiferet*) where love resides, foundation (*yesod*) where sexual energies collect, and rulership (*malkhut*), the center of speech and action. *Kabbalah* understands that all people in a system have distinct expertise to offer and that collaborative interchange is essential to success.

In *kabbalah*, the four worlds of Spirit (*Atzilut*), Thought (*Bri'ah*), Emotion (*Yetzirah*), and Action (*Asiyyah*) are equally important, and energy must flow freely among them for the world to be repaired and healed. This is different from a hierarchical model, which holds that Thought and Action are the only worlds in which leadership operates. The kabbalist is in contact with Spirit and Emotion as well; these worlds influence thoughts and actions.

While kabbalistic theory can be seen as feminist, it is beyond gender and applies equally well to both men and women. Both sexes need to work on expanding and balancing their energies in a healthy way.

How do I live this theory? I consciously spend time each day in the world of Spirit, connecting with higher energies, and asking that they guide my thoughts, emotions, and actions. Sometimes I visualize/feel/hear them as *Shekhinah*, the divine feminine presence; sometimes, as an emanation of *Hakadosh Barukh Hu*, the divine masculine presence; and, sometimes, as angels or spirit guides.[5] Knowing that I am on a continuing personal journey of spiritual growth is essential to my feeling worthy to be a rabbi to emerging rabbis and cantors. Leadership for the coming of age must be led, and fed, by Spirit.

Opposition as an Opportunity for Love

While I recognize that women face oppression and discrimination in many areas, I choose not to see these as opposition. That would draw me into negativity, and I would expend energy uselessly. Lasting change will come when we draw our power and vision from the highest Source. The beginning of change is personal spiritual practice and attitude adjustment.[6]

I choose to believe that there are no difficult people; there are only people in difficulty because they are in need of spiritual light and healing. Therefore, for me, prayer, meditation, and visualization are essential tools of leadership. If I am dealing with someone who seems particularly difficult, I may spend weeks praying and meditating on the situation. Even less problematic situations merit spiritual preparation. Never do I go into a meeting without first sending light and love to the room and the people who will be in it. I share these practices with those I teach at the Academy and in workshops around the country. My students and I find that it has positive effects, both on the one praying and the ones who are blessed with prayer.

For example, a cantor came to me for advice. She was having a terrible time with her rabbi. He used every opportunity to put her down and had no respect for her wishes or opinions. She was ready to quit. I told her that she had to find a way to pray sincerely for the rabbi. I would pray for her to find the strength to do this. A month later, the situation had shifted dramatically, and the rabbi was being appreciative. A year later, and the two of them are continuing in a mutually supportive relationship.

Love is the new paradigm. Women who have been raised to be nurturers already carry the most important attribute for being successful as leaders. We have been in a school without walls or degrees, but it is a school nonetheless. We must continue to network, to support each other, and to engage the hearts of the growing numbers of men who share our vision. Those who lead and serve out of love will flourish. This is God's will.

Transmitting the Law

Paradoxes of Authority

DIANNE O. ESSES

"Love therefore the stranger, for you were strangers in the land of Egypt."
                                                        —DEUT. 10:19

When I was nineteen years old, I left the traditional Syrian Jewish community where I had grown up—a community where I did not feel free to be who I was—in order to find the voice I needed to speak. It is a community that hardly anyone leaves. My own private Exodus. I tried to give it all up at once: Any semblance of authority, community, tradition, religion, or identity determined by anything outside myself.

In the Syrian Jewish community of Brooklyn, the authority of "the-way-things-were" defined the very different spheres of men and women. The unquestioned natural order of things was a compelling mandate in this immigrant community.

Jews from Syria settled in New York in the first quarter of this century. With a surprising tenacity—in sharp contrast to the assimilation of European Jews—they held on to their Middle-Eastern worldview and traditions. It's not, of course, that they didn't change; rather, they used American culture in ways that enhanced their cohesiveness and, at the same time, promoted their success. For example, Syrian Jews have used their success in American business to fund synagogues, schools, community centers, and *mikva'ot* (ritual baths), thus preserving a traditional insular community in the heart of Flatbush, Brooklyn.

Rabbi Dianne O. Esses, the first Syrian-Jewish woman to be ordained, graduated from The Jewish Theological Seminary and is an associate of CLAL (the Center for Jewish Learning and Leadership).

Within this world set apart, men and women play distinct roles. Bearing and nurturing children are women's primary tasks; thus, they spend their lives in the private sphere. Their days consist of managing the household, cooking and shopping, preparing for the Sabbath, holidays, and life-cycle events—often with the help of housekeepers. They play cards with other Syrian Jewish women almost daily, in an afternoon ritual that also includes storytelling, eating, and exchanging news.

Men live mostly in a man's world. Upon graduation from high school, sons usually enter their fathers' businesses, spending long hours working with other Syrian Jewish men. Many complete a business degree at the same time. A few nights a week, they also play cards with their male friends. The women provide refreshments.

Syrian synagogues reflect this divided world, thereby linking the authority of the-way-things-are to the authority of Judaism itself. Not only are women physically distant from the men and the Torah, but they also remain silent. The men raise their voices in the Middle-Eastern sing-song chants of the liturgy; the women mouth their prayers—as silent as Hannah (1 Samuel 1:13).[1]

Eluding My Role

Growing up with this stark separation between male and female, public and private, paid and unpaid work, I felt myself a person divided. To be part of this world required that one live a life determined by gender. One was either male or female; there was no choice but to act one's part. Despite my female body, I did not fit the image of a young Syrian Jewish girl. I was not elegant and could not imagine marrying and "playing house" within a few years of high school. On the other hand, neither was I anything like a Syrian male. I had no affinity for business, yet I envied the power of the male world. Despite the messages I was sent regarding who I was supposed to be, somehow, I kept eluding the required role—or perhaps it eluded me. Either way, I became alienated from the authority structures of my own community.

When I left home to go to college—unheard of for most Syrian girls—I tried to strip myself of Syrian culture and Judaism. I tried to strip myself of history itself. In fact, when people asked me about my religion, I would say disdainfully, "Well, I was born Jewish, but now I'm nothing." I thought that liberation meant rejecting the past and the hold it had over me.

But I felt utterly impoverished, empty. If I was so free, I wondered, then why was I so unhappy? I could not shake the shackles of the past so easily.

Repetition

And then, for the second time, Judaism came—and this time took hold. I began to study religion with a professor at New York University, James Carse, who taught each tradition as if it had something important to say to and about the human condition. I learned that Judaism could be construed as a liberating and radical tradition. I could hardly believe that what I was studying in college was the same tradition I had known growing up.

After college, I directed an oral history project and interviewed scores of Syrian Jewish immigrants. The complex picture that emerged—a story full of pain and fear, sacrifice and humor and culture—made it impossible for me to maintain my old simplistic understanding. Words like "patriarchy" and "victim" eclipsed both who they were and who I was. To other Syrians, precisely what I had experienced as chains of bondage were chains of continuity, connection, and relationship.

I spent years studying and slowly becoming observant again. Finally, I decided to go to rabbinical school. I wanted a chance to appropriate my own tradition fully, to step into the circle and center of power from which I had been excluded. In 1989, I entered the Rabbinical School of the Jewish Theological Seminary. While I was certainly entering a new world and a vastly different culture, I was to discover, much to my dismay, that my struggle would be the same in many ways.

While the Seminary welcomed me as a prospective rabbi, it has little awareness of the variety of ethnicities within Judaism. Thus, paradoxically, rabbinical school was the wrong place to find my way back to my own heritage. Furthermore, though the institution, in most senses, accepts the equality of women in Judaism, it has difficulty making room for a different voice—the unique culture and heritage of women, forged by a long history of marginalization.

In rabbinical seminaries today, women are free to study and appropriate texts written by and for men, which objectify and have authority over women. I left the confining world of my childhood only to discover the source of those constraints! Here were texts that separate male from female, public from private—here was the basis for those sharp divisions in Jewish life and that narrow the definition of being a woman. Whether as a non-Ashkenazic Jew or as a woman, I had no way to sanctify the inheritance of my mother, grandmothers, and aunts. Again, I could not express the full range of who I was. Once more, I found myself struggling with authority, with gender questions, and with hierarchy.

At JTS, I finally realized that I could not succeed by leaving again. One major exodus is enough. I knew that I would at some point have to choose a community, an ideology, a path, and just wrestle. It was time to enter the land—almost any land—and live there. Nothing would be perfect; nothing would be pure Liberation. The Conservative movement, like most every institution—including the Syrian community—both liberates and binds. If I leave, I will find the same narrowness in a different form. Today I choose to remain what I am and what I have become: A Syrian Jew, a woman, and a Conservative rabbi. I stand in this place, and I wrestle.

Learning and becoming fluent in the classical sources of Judaism brought me to the point where I am now able to question those sources credibly and intelligently. I am emotionally *and* scholastically able to address the central question confronting all Jewish feminists: What authority can we give a tradition that marginalizes and often demeans women?[2] Can we allow to have any authority or power over us a tradition that bars women as witnesses and allows men to "acquire" them in marriage? If ancient texts are meant to ground us in a certain identity, what kind of identity are we shaping, actively or by default, in response to them?

Untying the Knot

Part of the answer lies in repetition, in retelling our story—a process essential to the Jewish tradition. Deuteronomy is the biblical book that retells the story of the Israelites wandering through the desert and receiving revelation at Mt. Sinai. Moses recasts the laws revealed to him at Sinai for all the Israelites to hear in the plains of Moab. He commands them to teach these laws, to repeat them to their children (Deut. 6:7). Thus, not only is Deuteronomy the book that repeats, not only is it the *mishneh torah* (second Torah), it is the book that *commands* repetition and transmission.

But this emphasis on repetition can be deceiving. The secret and power behind repetition is that it is not truly repetition at all. The laws *change* in transmission to the people, as does the communal story. Social laws are expanded with an emphasis on caring for the distressed and not oppressing the stranger.

Whereas laws in Exodus show concern for both the slave's and the master's rights, Deuteronomy's laws are concerned only with the rights of the slave. Furthermore, it is in Deuteronomy that the maidservant becomes co-equal with the male slave, gaining a degree of independence. In fact, there is an overall humanizing principle that distinguishes this book from the preceding books in the Torah.[3]

This principle, if continuously and vigilantly applied beyond Deuteronomy, could produce a concern for women equal to that expressed for men. Deuteronomy is not, by any means, a feminist work. Yet perhaps this progression of a biblical source of authority toward greater concern for the individual and especially the downtrodden points toward a feminist vision. To obey the command not to "oppress the stranger" in its fullest sense might require transforming Torah study into a process that does not alienate women, either from the Torah or from themselves.

Repeating the story is a subversive act if done correctly. While it may look like I am merely telling the story again, if I do it with my whole being, "the" story will necessarily be transformed by who I am, by my story.

> "[Torah] is not in heaven...." [Israel] said to [Moses]: "Our teacher Moses, you say to us, 'It is not in heaven, neither is it beyond the sea,' then where is it?" He answered them: "It is in a very near place, 'in your mouth, and in your heart, that you may do it,' and it is not far from you, it is near to you." (Deut. *Rabbah* 8:6 on Deut. 30:12–14)

In the process of transmission, *I* am telling the story right *now*, in this moment of history to *you*. If the "I" or the "you" or the "now" is lost, it is not truly transmission.

The "creative betrayal"[4] of transmission becomes most apparent when those who were marginalized by the tradition grant themselves the authority to stand in the center and tell the story.[5] Thus my becoming a rabbi appears to my Syrian community as a betrayal. I "betray" its system of authority by assuming authority myself. So, too, a gay or lesbian Jew becoming a rabbi might look to most of the Jewish community like heresy. And I would agree: These are the finest betrayals, the most precious of heresies that Judaism commands. They shatter idols.

It is my prayer that all Jews take the commandment to transmit the tradition, the commandment to "betray" the past, as the holiest of obligations—thereby perpetually transforming the tradition into a living and wild thing.

Heresies

I wonder how the story might continue to betray itself. I can only imagine my distant future as a wizened rabbi, a wise old hag who peers through a large magnifying glass at the Bible and Talmud, at the poetry of Adrienne Rich and Audre Lorde, teaching the ways of manifold "*torot*" (plural of Torah). I imagine that I will be asked to tell the story of my life, as old people should be asked, and I might, in a voice quivering with age, tell the following story:

Do you remember how Abraham left everything he knew and then Rebecca left her entire family never to see them again, and Jacob ran away from home and then ran away again from his father-in-law's household, and Rachel and Leah ran away from home with Jacob—Rachel stealing the holy objects that belonged to her father? And that eventually all the Jews left Egypt and wandered in the desert and went to the promised land? And then they were chased out of the land of Israel and went to Babylon and beyond, and the Jews scattered all over the world—to places like Yemen and India and Syria and even Europe? And do you remember how in modern times they left those lands and went to the North and South Americas and created a state in Israel and how most Syrian Jews

settled in New York and became a thriving clan that multiplied and mul-
tiplied?

Well at some point it was time for me to leave, to join all those others
who had left—not in order to become different—but truly to become a
Jew. I lived out the Jewish story by leaving, by wandering, by journeying,
by becoming a stranger. I traveled far from all the things that were famil-
iar to me and settled in the foreign land where the European Jews did not
understand or even know the ways of Eastern Jews. It was my job to try
to explain it to them, to tell the story of my exodus and make them under-
stand why I left that world, and how it was so different and full of so
many treasures that they couldn't ever imagine. Yet I left behind all those
treasures that I was trying so hard to keep and to pass on to the European
Jews. And I tried to tell the European strangers that their ways weren't
the only Jewish ways in the world and neither were they the best, because
as soon as you believe that, your world becomes Egypt, and it's time to
leave again.

And so I left again and again, exodus upon exodus. It is the way of
the Jews to become strangers in the world perpetually.

(Re)telling Your Own (Heretical) Story Using my story as a
model, tell your life story in terms of your evolving relationship to
authority. Name the authorities that you had as a child and the
sources of authority you relate to now. Trace your evolution, and
then try to envision where you would like to go with this issue in
the future. Do you want to be more of an authority yourself? What
sources of authority would you like to draw on? How would you
ideally like to wield authority? Answers to these questions will
both revise and revitalize our ancestral history.

Leynen

VANESSA L. OCHS

"When all Israel is come to appear before Adonai, *your God, in the place God will choose, you shall read this Torah before all Israel in their full hearing."*

—DEUT. 31:11

My grandfather, Nathan Yablin, chanted from the Torah each week in his synagogue in Watertown, New York. He was a *ba'al koreh*, a master in chanting the verses of the Torah according to ancient melodies passed down as oral tradition. Although my grandfather knew the verses and their melodies by heart from so many years of practice, he reviewed the Torah text before each week's reading, familiarizing himself with the melodies assigned to each word. This activity of chanting the Torah is called *leynen* (Yiddish, meaning "to read"). To my grandfather, and to many Jews today, this is logical enough, for reading the Torah during public prayer means singing it in the traditional way.

As a child, this is how I knew that chanting Torah—*leynen*— was an important job: When someone led the prayers or chanted from the Prophets, he or she just ploughed ahead, even if s/he had made a mistake and the people listening had noticed. But when a man chanted Torah (and in those days, it could only have been a man), he was flanked by two knowledgeable proctors called *gabba'im*. Their sole task was to correct his pronunciation even if he goofed slightly, even though it meant calling attention to his mistake in front of the entire congregation.

At twelve, I was permitted to learn to chant *Haftarah* (prophetic reading) for my Bat Mitzvah (coming of age ceremony for girls). The girls in my Hebrew School class were not taught to chant from the Torah but, for that matter, neither were the boys. We were all

---

Vanessa L. Ochs, author of *Words on Fire: One Woman's Journey Into The Sacred* (Harcourt Brace Jovanovich, 1990) and *Safe and Sound: Protecting Your Child in an Unpredictable World* (Penguin, 1995), teaches religion and writing at Drew University, Madison, New Jersey, and is on the faculty of CLAL (the Center for Jewish Learning and Leadership).

discouraged from learning. The retired rabbi who taught us how to chant *Haftarah* used to say that if we thought the *Haftarah* chant was hard to learn, just imagine learning to *leyn*!

To chant from the Torah, we were told, you had to memorize the pronunciation and the musical notes for every word. You needed the aid of a *tikkun*, a Torah reader's study guide. In this book, each page is divided into two halves. On one side of the page are the words of the Torah along with vowel marks to aid in pronouncing each word. There are punctuation marks and demarcations that separate sentences and sections, along with little dots, dashes, and squiggles that indicate how to sing the words.

On the other side of a *tikkun* page, "*leyn*"ers encounter the Torah text just as it appears on the parchment: Without vowel marks, demarcations, or musical signs. The retired rabbi never showed us a *tikkun*, nor did he show us the opened scroll—but he told us that the words in the scroll did not have even the slimmest resemblance to the Hebrew print we knew. The letters, he said, looked like Chinese.

If we behaved and sang our *Haftarah* chant without horsing around, he permitted us this game: We would flip to any phrase in the Torah (except for the many versions of "And God said to Moses") and he would chant the rest of the sentence for us. We were amazed and begged him to do it again and again until he confirmed that he could not be stumped. What I saw convinced me that chanting was possible only for an elder like this retired rabbi or my grandfather—men gifted with fabulous, photographic memories.

I respected this man's virtuosity, as I respected my grandfather's, but I cannot say that I aspired to chant Torah—even if it had been possible for girls—any more than I wanted to know how to load a piano up on a pulley and hoist it up to a fifth-floor window. I knew some boys at camp, rabbis' sons or Jewish day school students, who knew how to *leyn*. Since I had heard how hard this was, I was impressed. When a boy had procrastinated too long and failed to prepare adequately, a buddy would accompany him to the *bimah* (pulpit) and make hand signals representing the musical notes. My girlfriends and I thought the boys who could read on the spot in this way were particularly dreamy.

Torah Reading Through Adult Eyes

Years later, I was teaching at a college in the boondocks. By that time, more and more women were leading various parts of the prayer service. Not a single Jewish professor or student at this college knew how to *leyn*. It was September, the beginning of the academic year. In a very short time, it would be *Rosh Hashanah* (New Year). Clearly, there was no time for anyone to learn how to chant. But I could sing, and I knew Hebrew, so I seemed the logical person to memorize the melody of a chapter of Torah from a tape. I reluctantly agreed to a makeshift arrangement: At the service, while I chanted the passage from my holiday prayerbook, someone else would scan the verses in the actual Torah scroll, so at least it would seem as though the Torah were being properly read. I felt there was something very wrong about this reading, and not just because I was not chanting from the scroll itself. In order to come and chant that morning, I had left my new baby with a sitter for the first time. As I chanted the passage, only a small portion of my mind was on the notes and words (ironically, about Sarah weaning Isaac). Much more of my mind was on my own baby: Was she all right? Would she take the bottle I had left with the sitter? I felt that my limited concentration made my reading a sham. I did not have the focused attention that my grandfather had—or, at least, appeared to have.

And what if I had been menstruating at the time? I, ever intolerant of the notions of a menstruating wife contaminating her husband with impurity, found myself wondering if a menstruant contaminated a Torah scroll. Later, I would learn that the Torah is immune to any state of ritual impurity, male or female. So here in the boondocks, where no one even thought to disqualify me from reading because I was a mother or a woman, I was more than willing to take over society's usual job of rendering a woman doubtful, awkward, and inept.

In the decade that followed, I decided to learn to *leyn* properly. I did not ever want to find myself in a Jewish community in which the Torah needed to be chanted and no one had the skills to do the job. I was also inspired by a conversation with my former high school Talmud teacher, Professor Judith Hauptman. She told me that she had finally learned to chant Torah and was doing so regularly in a congregation that was open to women filling this role.[1] Professor Hauptman described chanting as "the quintessential Jewish act." How could this be, I wondered? She, who prayed and studied so much, who performed so many *mitzvot* (commandments, sacred obligations), found this particular liturgical act ultimately riveting. I, not a seeker of ultimate thrills like skydiving or hang gliding, was curious. Though I feared I was an old dog beyond learning new tricks, I thought I—after all, the granddaughter of Watertown's *ba'al koreh*—just might be able to learn to read Torah.

I began by asking my friend and cousin Cantor Henry Rosenblum to make me a tape of the trope, the various melodic patterns. I played that tape in my car as I drove for a full summer, singing along with my daughters. I made little flashcards of the notes, trying to keep all the melodies straight. Studying on my own in this way, I would surely have given up. But, thankfully, Cantor Maimon Attias of the Morristown Jewish Center formed a Torah reading society. For half an hour a week, a handful of students squeezed into little Hebrew school chairs and learned to chant from the *tikkunim* we had purchased. First a word at a time, then a phrase, then a line, then a full verse. Cantor Attias would have us cover up the annotated side of the page and look only at the side that represented the words as they would appear in the scroll. (Contrary to what the retired rabbi had taught, the words did not remotely resemble Chinese. They looked more like fancy Hebrew calligraphy.) Each session, I would complain, "I can't do it." It seemed impossibly difficult to all of us. Cantor Attias would cheerlead, "You *can* do it. Listen, you just did it." Of course, he was right.

At the end of two months, those who had not dropped out had become some of the world's more tentative Torah readers. We men and women stumbled along. If our skills did not bring much honor to Torah, I would like to think that the genuineness of our effort did. We could only improve, and in time, we did. We would also be joined, as the months went along, by others who noted what we had accomplished and felt that if we could chant Torah, even limpingly, they could too.

I confess that I had once resented hearing the Torah read by novices, particularly when I heard adult women bumbling through public readings at some of the earliest egalitarian services. At the time, I thought that if women were going to be performing rituals for the first time, they should at least practice some more before making their debut. I feared they would give "ammunition" to the opposition, who could now would remark, "This is what happens when women do it." Over the years, my attitude changed: It struck me that if women waited until our new liturgical skills were perfected, we would wait forever.

The Experience of Reading Torah

Torah reading now holds an honored place in my life. Each month, I receive a letter from Cantor Attias indicating the next Sabbath on which I will chant. I try to arrange my schedule to fit this date, for it is a compelling engagement. No later than the Wednesday preceding my assigned Sabbath, I open my *tikkun* and begin to practice for about ten minutes a day. I usually do this in my office. It is a break I take as a reward for having graded a set of students' papers or having sketched out the draft of an article. I begin my preparation by reading the verses aloud in Hebrew. If I do not know what every word means, I open up my Hebrew-English Bible and check. If the broader context of the verses does not immediately come back to me, I review the portion of the week. Then I sing and sing and sing until I remember. When my daughters are home and hear me chanting in my office, they do not interrupt. They have determined that this must be truly important.

I have been chanting Torah for several years now, and each time I begin to tackle a new portion, I doubt that I will ever commit the verses to memory. Each time the verses eventually do stay in my head. Sabbath morning I scan the reading one last time and hope for the best. I have become less anxious as I wait for my turn to come up front to the *bimah* to chant. My heart rarely thumps in panic now, nor do I fret that I have prepared the wrong verses.

When I chant, I put on a *kippah* and *tallit* (skullcap and prayer shawl), liturgical gear I now wear. The week before I was to chant Torah for the first time, I called to ask my teacher, Professor Hauptman, if she covered her head and wore a *tallit* when she chanted. She asked if I were taking a poll in order to decide what to do. No, I told her, I had given thought and learning time to the issues of a woman's "liturgical garb," and was still ambivalent. Following the custom of observing the tradition of one's "parent's house," I decided that for the time being at least, I would do whatever Professor Hauptman did. She said she covered her head and wore a *tallit*. So, for the time being, I do, too, even though I am still not altogether comfortable wearing liturgical garb that has been worn primarily by men.

When I go up to the *bimah* to chant and take my place at the lectern, Cantor Attias hands me a *yad* (pointer). While the person who has been called to the Torah is reciting the blessing said before the Torah is read, I pray that my reading will bring honor to the congregation. I take a deep, natural childbirth breath and tell myself: "You will remember." Each word I point to in the text stretches up to greet me. My concentration is intense. The only realities I acknowledge are the words, the sound my voice makes, and the concentration of the two *gabba'im* who stand on each side of the Torah and check to be certain I have read perfectly. I do not experience the presence of these *gabba'im* as critical or potentially embarrassing. Rather, I think of them as friends holding a safety net under my tightrope. Their concentration intensifies my own: We are all thinking about these same words of Torah, syllable by syllable, letter by letter. In a world where we so often speak without thinking and hear without listening, this purposiveness, this shared attentiveness moves me powerfully. When I finish, I am relieved—not so much because the tricky task is done, but because the intense concentration can be broken. And I am proud. When the people on the *bimah* shake my hand and others greet me as I return to my seat, I gladly accept their acknowledgment in a way I rarely accept praise. Women often stop me and whisper that when they hear the text sung in a woman's voice, they hear the words in a new way. An older gentleman in the congregation once confided, "I never thought I could get used to the idea of a woman chanting the Torah, but when I listen to you each month, I think, maybe I have gotten used to it already."

Now I, too, see reading Torah as the quintessential Jewish act. Curiously, this became most clear to me when I first prepared to *leyn* passages that exasperate me as a woman. I asked myself how I could chant a passage that denigrated women? Why would I take part in perpetuating these troubling words, singing them in a sweet, clear voice? And I discovered this answer: These words are a component of our tradition. In the rest of my life as a Jew—when I am a mother and a teacher and a learner—I enter into dialogue with the text and confront it and jostle with it. As a Torah chanter, my task is to transmit the words of our people, to keep them in our minds and hearts so that they can be viscerally important to us, important enough to encounter and consider deeply.

For the few moments that I chant, I am an unconflicted vessel, a conduit for God's word.

Torah

BARBARA D. HOLENDER

*"You shall love Adonai your God with all your mind, with all
your strength, with all your being. Set these words, which I
command you this day, upon your heart."*
—DEUT. 6:5, 6

Even when you hold it in your arms,
you have not grasped it.
Wrapped and turned in upon itself
the scroll says, Not yet.

Even when you take them into your eyes,
you have not seen them; elegant
in their crowns the letters stand aloof.

Even when you taste them in your mouth
and roll them on your tongue
or bite the sharp unyielding strokes
they say, Not yet.

And when the sounds pour from your throat
and reach deep into your lungs for breath,
even then the words say, Not quite.

But when your heart knows its own hunger
and your mind is seized and shaken,
and in the narrow space between the lines
your soul builds its nest,

Now, says Torah, now
you begin to understand.

Barbara D. Holender is the author of *Shivah Poems: Poems of Mourning* (Andrew
Mountain, 1986), *Ladies of Genesis* (Jewish Women's Resource Center, 1991), and
Is This the Way to Athens? (Quarterly Review of Literature, 1996).

Looking Toward the Promised Land

Justice

SUSAN SCHNUR

"You shall not judge unfairly. You shall show no partiality."
—DEUT. 16:19

The Hebrews, more than any people, cared deeply about justice, and this earned them at times (peculiarly, one might think) a negative reputation. "Those Jews, you know, so narrowly legalistic."

Partiality Tempers and Elevates Justice

But there's a grain of truth in many accusations, and this one's no exception. Obsessive justice-hunting—untempered by "partiality"—can take on a life of its own, can even lead, oddly, to injustice. Some contemporary halakhic (Jewish legal) stances—in relation to justice for women, for example—are cases in point. For example, a girlfriend of mine was grossly insulted when she was told she was not "allowed" to recite *Kaddish* (mourner's prayer) for her father. In response, the local Orthodox rabbi informed her that law and even custom took precedence over her feelings.

"Partiality," of course, means those loyalties in our lives that cause us to turn a blind eye to justice. Camus, for example, said, "I believe in justice, but I will defend my mother before justice."[1]

Partiality is affirmative action.

Aren't we commanded, indeed, to be always "partial" to our Hebrew God—despite the vagaries of Her justice? And isn't the binding of Isaac powerful precisely *because* Abraham chose partiality to God over justice? And isn't the Jewish *brit* (covenant) itself based on loyalty, not justice?

Rabbi Susan Schnur is editor of *LILITH* magazine and a writer.

"All other things on issues being roughly equal," wrote the columnist William Safire, "women should strongly support women until some parity [i.e., equal representation in political office] is reached. Then, secure in a system in balance, they can throw the rascals out, regardless of sex."[2]

Partiality Endangers Justice, Too

But partiality can be misused as a mere slogan and a tool for manipulating public opinion. As both women and Jews, we are wise in the ways of disprivilege, having developed, over centuries, a hard-bitten, doubly earned reality principle. Mercy shmercy, we say (we've too often been the one-way benefactors of it). Only "justice" is to be trusted in this deeply flawed world. Apologists use partiality to explain why women have been exempted and then excluded from daily prayer with a *minyan*. Women are so spiritually elevated, they argue, that we do not *need* to pray at specified hours. Or, our contributions on the home front are so essential that we cannot be spared to lead in the public arena, as well.

Partiality as a Component of Justice

Whatever its limits or abuses, Jewish women value partiality as a core element of justice. For who among us would care about justice at all if we didn't, at base, have a certain transcendent attachment to others? We hold justice and partiality in tension, but, in the larger picture, partiality is an essential part of justice.

Jewish women—minorities times two—are ideally suited to model the crucial maturity required by this moral dialectic. In relation to Judaism, we have learned both to criticize and to defend. If we weren't "partial" to it (and to Israel as well), we would be at risk, at times, of throwing the whole thing out. And, on the other hand, if we were *only* partial, then we would court danger. Standing excessively by our institution, our community, our state, our partner—we turn virtue into vice.

We are privileged to have this hard-earned wisdom: Absolute partiality deprives us of our good judgment, but absolute justice deprives us of our human tenderness. We've learned this from our lives.

And so we mold Judaism's brightest future—keeping in balance, always, a love for our parochial selves and a vision of global justice—sometimes one declaring trump, and sometimes the other. It is worthwhile to discuss and infer the "rules of the game," to name criteria for deciding when and to what degree partiality or pure justice should prevail. Yet, in the end, the dialectic is too sophisticated for any calculus.

So when, in the future, some Empress somewhere is found, yet again, to have no clothes, we will be neither exclusively crowd nor exclusively child. Rather, we will hold our two responses in harmonic tension, responding with both justice *and* partiality. Loyal to the Empress, we will not shame Her. Yet we will not collude with Her either. We will speak truth to power—because we share power. Demanding justice, we will also love.

It is a messianic task for which we are perfectly suited.

Re-Visioning Jewish Education

EMILY FEIGENSON

"And these words that I command you this day shall be upon your heart. You shall repeat them continually to your young, and speak about them when you sit down in your home and when you are walking along the way, whenever you lie down and whenever you get up."

—DEUT. 6:6–7

The Torah's lofty portrayal of Jewish learning—continual, intimate, and pervasive—contrasts sharply with the scratchy reality of contemporary Jewish schooling. I have experienced Jewish education on many levels and in many settings and continue to yearn

Rabbi Emily Feigenson has graduate degrees in Jewish Education and Philosophies of Judaism and has served in a wide variety of Jewish educational settings.

for what is described in the Torah. In Sunday school, *ulpan* (immersion program in Hebrew language), university, and two seminaries, I was asked to gain greater expertise in order to ascend the hierarchy of knowledge. The information I collected left me intrigued, wanting to know more, and lonely. All along, I longed for what the Torah describes—bondedness in learning rather than competition, inspiration more than analysis, religious and communal fellowship more than intellectual precision. I wanted learning and pursued schooling. I craved a mentor and surrounded myself with experts. I desired to become a mentor and instead learned how to teach.

One may wonder how we as a people went from the Torah's sacred vision of learning as an intimate, individual, continual process to today's norm of schooling. Teachers, and not parents, do the bulk of formal childhood education. Educators, parents, and students have concerns that seem far removed from the commands to love God and convey the tradition. As in the secular classroom, questions of class size, subject, budget, motivation, and varied capabilities dominate. When most Jewish educators lie down, and when they rise up, they confront the gap between ideal and real achievements; they doubt whether love of the tradition— much less of God—was "caught" by the students. How did we get here from there?

The following Talmudic passage presents a chronology of developments in Jewish education.

> In former times, the child who had a father received instruction from his father, for the Bible states, "And *you* shall teach [words of Torah] to your children" (Deut. 11:19). But the fatherless child did not study Torah at all. Later, an ordinance was instituted that teachers for the children were to be appointed in Jerusalem; for the Bible states, "Out of Zion shall go forth the Torah and the word of *Adonai* from Jerusalem" [Isaiah 2:3]. After that ordinance was made, fatherless [boys were] not brought to Jerusalem. It was therefore decreed that schools for primary instruction should be established in the principal communities of each province. Even so, boys were sometimes brought for study when they were already sixteen or seventeen years old.... Finally, Rabbi

Joshua ben Gamla decreed that primary schools should be established even in the small towns, and that boys should be sent to school at the age of six or seven. (BT *Baba Batra* 21a)

Regardless of the historical accuracy of this account, the Talmud reflects some important Rabbinic perspectives. The Rabbis faced parents who were unqualified, in their eyes, to school their own children in Judaism. They wanted to place schooling in the hands of qualified teachers. In contrast to our contemporary situation, the Talmud understands the commandment to teach children as applying only to boys.[1]

The exclusion of girls and women from the mainstream of study was especially tragic, because it was in classrooms and studyhouses that the vast bulk of Jewish legal and literary tradition developed. Women were, no doubt, engaged in serious religious and spiritual activities, but the lack of documentation has largely erased their creativity from the annals of Jewish history. Much of what has been passed down was developed without the obvious input of women.

With the rise of feminism, women now seek our own place in the process of studying, teaching, and creatively interacting with the tradition. As we do so, we are challenged by both the *content* and the *methods* of learning. We seek to expand the Jewish canon and curriculum, as well as to affirm the value of a personal, intimate educational process.

What and How We Study

Women's mere presence in previously male institutions of learning often prompts a re-examination of the curriculum. This volume and others provide many examples of women studying traditional content, but asking new questions and yielding new interpretations. Still, even if we are committed to evaluating ancient content in light of fresh perspectives, we must admit that as we redefine the curriculum and canon we are embedded in a complex web of ideas, attitudes, and assumed procedures. Struggling to affect its overall shape and texture, we feel pulled by that sticky, complex web at every turn. In a way, the simplest and most accessible piece of this complexity is content—what to study. More difficult is the question of process—how we study.

Too often, our interaction with tradition is handicapped by an over-emphasis on technical and scientific expertise. Mastering content—of any subject, including feminist Bible reading—has become the overriding goal of formal study, rather than one goal among a precious cluster.[2] This system typically judges different methods of learning and analytical skills purely as means to the end of mastery. If women's entry into Jewish educational institutions results only in including new topics and curricula, we may begin to feel as though we are putting on clothes that don't quite fit. We are affecting what is discussed to some degree, but not really deepening or changing the nature of the discussion.

Intimacy in Learning

As more Jewish women pursue *talmud torah* (Jewish learning; Jewish text study), we seek not only mastery but also intimacy during the learning process. This desire for "learning intimacy" shows itself in a variety of ways: Seeking a mentor, studying for nourishment rather than expertise, valuing personal disclosure by teachers and fellow students in the course of learning. Intimacy emphasizes the way a subject is studied, more than the breadth or depth of material. Knowledge is necessary, but not sufficient. Translating a Hebrew passage may not culminate in feeling closer to the poem's message; studying Jewish history may not help a student feel an integral part of its unfolding.

Personal connection in learning is certainly not new in the Jewish tradition.[3] Nowadays, a renewed desire for the personal element in study exists among men, but in my experience it is more common, and perhaps more essential, among women. Possibly, Jewish women's desire for personal encounter in learning arises from past exclusion. Women may need to establish a personal relationship with the teacher who is in the classroom, since we may not be able to construct a closeness to the teachers—almost always male, sometimes misogynist—described in our texts. We welcome the views and personal narratives of women teachers and classmates because, studying traditional texts, ours are the only women's voices we hear.

Some theorists have argued that men's outlook is—by nature or social design—fundamentally more congruent with "teacher as authoritative expert," while women see the ideal teacher as a mentor or nurturer. Not only the role of the teacher, but also the very goals of learning are affected, with men viewing the material as objective, and women emphasizing the subjective aspects or personal nuances of the material.[4]

Intimacy in Formal and Informal Schooling Regardless of its etiology, the desire for intimacy and personal narrative in learning promotes certain methods. Ideally, these facilitate personal encounters and, at the same time, help create new literary traditions. Keeping a journal, acting out a traditional narrative, interjecting a personal *midrash* (legend in the Rabbinic style) move students from reading about something to interacting with it. Affective educational methods help students to internalize the external material. The problem is that today's emphasis on mastery often leads to the use of such techniques as "tricks" to get the student's attention; then, the teacher quickly moves on to the actual agenda of external mastery.

Many of us realize that personal moments are not mere transition points or "hooks"; they are the core of learning. However, we who have been schooled with the emphasis on mastery find it difficult to break away from that mindset. We may erroneously imagine that interaction is something people can do "on their own time." But student interaction with text and with others is not only worth the time and effort, it is, in itself, valuable content.

Tomorrow's teachers of Jewish women need to recognize that these students are endeavoring to find, and provide, the female voices of 2,000 years of tradition: Teachers must consistently communicate that the woman who is struggling to become part of a conversation from which she has been excluded is an authentic and critical part of the course subject. Formal schooling needs to incorporate women's voices, even at the risk of slowing down the rate at which women gain skills and expertise.

The incorporation of personal story into the focus of the class is important from the teacher's end, as well as the students'. Otherwise, we risk implying that intimacy is needed and appropriate only among developing learners. Previous generations assumed that students learn from the whole person, and in fact students generally knew their teacher: He was an integral part of their own community. Today, it is generally considered unprofessional for a teacher to reveal much personal information. Yet, as women pursue *talmud torah*, many of us look to the teacher's personal wisdom, story, or puzzlement as much as to that teacher's expertise in a given skill or subject. Thinking of the teachers who have influenced me the most, I am more aware of their character than their curricula. The personal connection was more lasting and instructive than the details of any lesson.

There are some informal settings where intimate mingling of learners, teachers, and subjects happens more naturally, and this accounts for their success. Summer camps, weekend retreats, New Moon celebrations, *havurot* (Jewish worship/study fellowships)— all emphasize social interaction among learners and with the teacher, and often obscure boundaries between teachers and students. They also generally include subjective exploration of a given topic. Synagogues and community centers—which often offer dozens of formal courses that are poorly attended—would do well to experiment with this kind of learning. For instance, organized family-to-family hospitality—*hakhnasat orhim*—may become a crucial vehicle for learning, as families who feel strong in their Judaism reach out to those less sure. Synagogues and federations can organize mentoring or *havruta* (paired study) programs. Rather than attending a course, two people commit to meet periodically, for study and personal reflection.

In recent years, Jewish education has seen the growth of parent-participation days, family camp, and the like. Ironically, Jewish leaders today seek to involve parents, while, according to the quotation from *Baba Batra*, the Rabbis of centuries ago excluded them. "Family education programs" may well enrich the quality of Jewish schooling—for parents and children, students and teachers, women and men. The emphasis on family, however, is actually irrelevant. The main ingredient for success is intimate learning. Each program is successful only to the degree that it provides a vehicle for learning in an intimate style, sharing personal narratives, and integrating those stories into the chain of tradition.

Women's Voices, Women's Contributions

Can these changes—the expansion of Jewish education's content and the fundamental shift in emphasis from expertise to intimacy—be accomplished in a coeducational setting? Eventually, they will have to be, but women-only settings will help tremendously in the meantime. Studies show that girls and women are less apt to voice their thoughts and questions in mixed settings and more apt to be interrupted than boys and men.[5] Leaders of co-educational schools have not yet responded to this research by providing alternative educational groupings. But the success of women-only retreats as well as Passover and New Moon celebrations suggests that sustained homogeneous classes may be a step forward for Jewish girls and women.

Contemporary ambivalence about Judaism does not arise from ignorance or even from discomfort over incompetence with specific skills. Current schooling can provide remedies, but many are uninterested. Broad theological innovation must address frankly the gap people feel between the tradition and their present crisis of meaning. Key tools in bridging that gap include: Telling our own stories as part of interacting with ancient law and narrative; deepening and personalizing student-teacher relationships; broadening the definition of content (and even Torah) to include the self, especially the female self.

Women's presence and influence in contemporary Houses of Study set the stage for a revolutionary theological innovation. Half the Jewish people has recently joined the inter-generational, and now cross-gender, conversation. Our personal stories, questions, and conversations need to be recorded, as were the debates and thoughts of male rabbis in the past. Just as men's study and commentary produced multiple layers of Jewish literary tradition over the last fifteen centuries, so women's interaction with Jewish learning will inevitably affect and contribute to that corpus. In this rapid and unwieldy period of expansion, a new layer of tradition is evolving. Like many past innovations, it will ultimately be codified, made manageable, and incorporated into tradition in ways we cannot foretell.

Women's cries form the text of new psalms; women's experiences lead to new insights on the meaning of justice and to new legal traditions; women's yearnings give birth to new and amended prayers for our people. Perhaps most importantly, a new facet of the Holy will be seen and revealed. A holy product—larger, differently ordered, enriched by women's perspectives—will be gifted to our people as in the past. This literary and theological tradition will be born out of the interaction between *talmud torah* and women's hearts. It will revitalize and rebirth Judaism.

Destiny

JANE RACHEL LITMAN

"Adonai *said, 'This is the land of which I swore to Abraham, Isaac, and Jacob, "I will give it to your offspring." I have let you see it with your own eyes, but you shall not cross there.'"*
—DEUT. 34:4

"Your...daughters shall prophesy; your elders shall dream dreams...."
—JOEL 3:1

The future often holds out a tantalizing promise of better times. If, as Jews, we are on a pilgrimage from creation to the Messianic age, then each moment brings us one step closer to redemption. Yet knowing that we have a destiny is not the same as knowing what it is. As Jewish women in a period of great change, it isn't easy to predict the destination of our journey. When we stand and gaze, like Moses, into the distance, what do we see? Can we discern the contours and textures of our promised land?

Rabbi Jane Rachel Litman, co-editor of this volume in the *Lifecycles* series, is on the faculty of California State University, Northridge, and serves Congregation Kol Simcha of Orange County, California.

Even this question seems somewhat premature. In reality, the contemporary Jewish women's movement isn't at the dramatic climax of an arduous trek, poised to sweep away all challenge and occupy the territory of our dreams. The communal evolution of the Jewish people in the Sinai desert took forty years.[1] Ours is a movement of approximately twenty years; in the Torah's terms we are only about halfway, very much still *Bemidbar*, in the Wilderness. The generation of Jews that takes women's religious leadership for granted, the generation comfortable praying in gender-free God-language, the generation accustomed to reading about women's stories—this generation is not even of age. My eight-year old daughter's startling electric blue ribbon-bedecked *kippah* (skull cap) is only the external symbol of her confident sense of empowered Jewish female identity. The internal dimensions of this sensibility are more profound.

The most far-reaching cultural changes occur in the second generation of a social movement, since the construction of culture is a group endeavor, not an individual achievement. Individuals with vision begin the process of change, but only a group can institutionalize it. For example, specific reformers in Central Europe initiated a set of aesthetic innovations designed to "modernize" Jewish worship, to bring it closer to the forms then used in Protestant churches. Music, vernacular praying, decorum—these were social, rather than ideological alterations. It was only when the generation of young people educated in the newly created Reform institutions came of age that far-reaching theoretical positions were promulgated. The Hasidic movement, too, required two generations before it established an ideological foundation and gained widespread popularity.

The Jewish women's movement is barely into its second generation. I was in my late teens in the early seventies when the current wave of Jewish feminism began. According to the Torah's system, I am of the generation that matured in the desert. Women older than myself experienced an "Egypt" they could not even discuss—words and concepts such as sexism, androcentrism, and marginalization were not part of the popular vocabulary. By the time I was ready to pay serious attention to Jewish issues of gender, there already existed a theoretical framework for my ideas. Mine is the generation of struggle.

Out of Egypt

Over the last twenty years, I have seen the idea of women's equality become increasingly mainstream and institutionalized in the Jewish world. In every venue—leadership, education, ritual, communal life, theology, the arts—the Jewish women's movement has made impressive gains in North America, Europe, and Israel. There was a time, long since past, when I knew every woman rabbi personally. I vividly remember when a woman rabbi was viewed as a freak; once, on a ski lift in the mid-seventies, a man asked me what I did for a living. When I said that I was a rabbinical student, he actually fell off the lift. I decided that for the sake of *piku'ah nefesh* (the principle that saving a life takes precedence), I would in future just say I was a teacher. That time has also passed. Rarely am I any person's "first woman rabbi" anymore.

The changes have been subtle and pervasive. They have unfolded in stages. The first goal was equity: Equal access to Jewish religious life and institutions. The most obvious success in this vein is the complete acceptance of the Bat Mitzvah (coming of age ceremony for girls) in liberal and even some Orthodox circles. A generation ago, it was rare for a young Jewish woman to publicly have an *aliyah* (honor of reciting blessings before and after the Torah is read). Now in the United States, it is expected. In many ways, this "add women and stir" approach is the best recipe for success. For modern Jews, adding women to traditional practices strengthens the hold of tradition as well as the position of women. It is so eminently just, that it is difficult to protest. However, even such a modest alteration in the tradition leads to far-reaching changes.

The basic concept of Bat Mitzvah, ritual equity for girls, inspired a desire for female baby-naming or covenant ceremonies. Obviously these could not have the exact content of a *Brit Milah* (covenant of circumcision ritual). Equity thus required innovation, and innovation generated opportunities for and legitimated further ritual change. Creative ritual has since become one of the most developed areas of women's participation in Judaism. This may be because until recently ritual wasn't taken very seriously, or perhaps—particularly in liberal circles—women's rituals fill a great void left by decades of religious rationalism, as well as women's exclusion. Whatever the cause for their creation, there are now libraries of Jewish women's rituals.

It is naive to suppose that such major innovations will not change the very nature of our communal activity. Increasingly empowered in religious life, Jewish women have not been content with equal access alone. There followed a demand for Jewish activities specifically geared to the newly discovered spiritual needs of women. The last ten years have witnessed an explosion of women's *minyanim* (prayer quora), *Rosh Ḥodesh* (New Moon Festival) groups, Torah study circles, and retreats. These women-only venues became the wellspring of an enormous outflow of new liturgy, ritual, theology, and ideas for restructuring mixed-gender communal endeavors.

Liturgy and Bible study have also seen dramatic change. The Reform and Reconstructionist movements have published gender-inclusive prayerbooks that present a non-gendered God and are directed to a mixed-gendered congregation. Many liberal synagogues are beginning to experiment with the Hebrew liturgy, and it is not uncommon to see the biblical matriarchs included with the patriarchs in the appropriate Hebrew prayers. Jewish renewal groups are exploring new names and images for God. Recently, Bible scholarship and study have produced a plethora of works by and about women, this volume among them. Many of these commentaries "counter-read" the stories of Torah from the position of the women involved. This process yields powerful new insights about history and morality. Women's viewpoint has also sparked a trend toward personalization of text, a reading of scripture for the insights it brings to our lives, rather than as an historical source about society in ancient Israel. In general, there are many more resources about the lives of earlier generations of Jewish women. As a Jewish Studies major in the early seventies, I struggled with one male professor after another (there were no female professors) merely in order to do research on Jewish women. It wasn't considered a serious topic. Now the college course I teach on women in Jewish history is only one of many at universities throughout North America, Europe, and Israel.

The issues emerging from both the equal gender access and separate Jewish women's venues cannot, should not, and will not remain "women's" issues. The full empowerment of women will transform the nature of Jewish discourse. The thorough inclusion of women's voices and experience at every level will contribute to structural change in the character of Judaism. "Add women and stir" is a one-generation phenomenon.

Approaching the Promised Land

Where are we going as a movement? Ironically, on a personal level I have found that with the passage of time my ability to envision what *could* be is gradually supplanted by my power to effectuate what *can* be. My thought has become less utopian as I focus on the next significant change possible in the here and now. For the present, Jewish women leaders are the spies told about in Numbers 13, those who foray briefly into the mythic territory of the future. In many ways our primary task is to build a consensus among the community remaining in the desert.

I imagine that changes in liturgy, education, and social organization will be more far-reaching in the future, not less so. Struggles over equity will be behind us, and we will formulate radical new ways of engaging God and Jewish tradition. Gender, in and of itself, will be less of an issue as a new generation of women come to Judaism without feeling a profound sense of injustice and disenfranchisement. Because of this, gender will be of less significance to women than now, but of more significance to men, since they will no longer be able to avoid or discount the issue.

There will be ongoing incursions into fields previously restricted from women, particularly Rabbinic writings, including *halakhah* (Jewish law). As we have done and are still doing with ritual and Bible study, women will lay full claim to the Jewish textual tradition. There will be more works by women that both critique and co-opt what historically has been a male endeavor. Women are now using *midrash* (Rabbinic genre of lore, often based on biblical texts) as a method of appropriating traditional Jewish forms, and we are beginning to see a similar pattern in such fields as mysticism and Jewish law as they are reconstructed by feminists. Women will constitute our own *betei din* (Jewish courts) and write *halakhah*.

The glass ceiling will continue to fragment and chip away. In my lifetime there will be a woman head of United Synagogue, of the American Jewish Committee, and of the Jewish Federations in average mid-size American cities.[2] Eventually such women will not be tokens, but will be among many women assuming full leadership in the Jewish community. Drawing upon their experience as women, these leaders will change the way things are done in ways that are explored by some of the essays in this volume, and in ways we can barely imagine.

We are becoming increasingly international and diverse. The Jewish women's movement in Israel spans the spectrum of ideological belief, and often the most radical demands there (e.g. equal funding for religious education for young women) emerge from the Orthodox women's community. Jewish women's networks are meeting in Ukraine and Russia.[3] Great Britain has hosted several conferences devoted to Jewish feminism that were widely attended by European women. New technologies are our allies: Internet groups[4] create community across previously insurmountable geographic boundaries.

Kelal yisrael (totality of the Jewish People) will take on a new meaning in terms of broad inclusivity. Feminist insights about accessibility will be generalized to marginalized groups other than women, including disabled, poor, non-Askenazi, gay, and converted Jews. In twenty years, the Jewish community will have transformed its outreach process, producing a more richly textured public face of Judaism.

The shift from the desert to the promised land is a transition from sojourning to owning. Women, in partnership with men (and God), will own Judaism. Ownership has prerogatives, but also responsibilities. Women's increasing authority and "buy-in" will serve as a self-regulating feedback mechanism against change that threatens the well-being of the Jewish people.

As with the generation striving to reach and cross the Jordan, change will not be effortless, nor without resistance. However, it is important to remember that we have already accomplished the most difficult part of the journey, finding within ourselves the image of a better way. We have only to stay on course to enter the Promised Land.

Afterword: Engaging with Torah

DEBRA ORENSTEIN AND JANE RACHEL LITMAN

"The Bible is a seed, God is the sun, but we are the soil. Every generation is expected to bring forth new understanding and new realization."
—ABRAHAM JOSHUA HESCHEL, *GOD IN SEARCH OF MAN: A PHILOSOPHY OF JUDAISM*

"Blessed are You, Adonai, Our God, Ruler of the universe, who has sanctified us with Your commandments and commanded us to involve ourselves with words of Torah."
—TRADITIONAL BLESSING FOR TORAH STUDY

 All of us approach Torah study with some trepidation. We may imagine that, by rights, direct engagement with the Bible is only for "experts." But Torah is the sacred heritage of Jews and the world.

One axiom of *talmud torah* (Jewish learning; Jewish text study) is that it never stops. No one ever "graduates." The most learned Torah scholar is called a *talmid*

Rabbi Debra Orenstein, creator of the *Lifecycles* series, co-editor of this volume, and senior fellow of the Wilstein Institute, regularly writes and speaks on Jewish spirituality and gender studies. **Rabbi Jane Rachel Litman**, co-editor of this volume, is on the faculty of California State University, Northridge, and serves Congregation Kol Simcha of Orange County, California.

02ḥakham(im) (student of the Sage[s]). *Talmud torah* also presupposes the enduring relevance of the tradition and the abiding importance of each student. These
assumptions are central both to the themes and to the method of this book. Torah
learning, like the original revelation of the Torah to the Israelites on Mt. Sinai,
occurs in the meeting between student and sacred content.

In pursuing Torah study, it is helpful to be aware of the variety of frameworks and methods available. Below is some basic information about Torah, followed by an introduction to six broad (though far from exhaustive) approaches:
Theological, historical, mythic, literary, traditional, and feminist. The essay concludes with an invitation to continue the interpretive tradition by creating your
own *midrash* (legend in the Rabbinic style), as many contributors have done in
this book.

Admittedly, there is a certain artificiality in analyzing six separate approaches to Torah study. The traditional viewpoint incorporates mythic and literary elements. Theological beliefs influence writings primarily associated with each of
the other categories. Feminist approaches, and certainly our approach in this
book, take account of the other categories, incorporate models and lessons from
each, and attempt, as well, to influence how they are carried out. Thus, a reader
need not and cannot choose among the frameworks presented; they complement
each other and overlap.

Definitions, Settings, and Understandings of Torah

"Torah" may refer to: The Pentateuch or five books of Moses; the scroll in the ark;
Jewish tradition; sacred learning in its broadest sense. Sometimes, the whole Bible
is casually called "Torah." Bible, *Tanakh*, is an anthology, made up of three major
divisions: Torah (Pentateuch), Prophets, and Writings. This "one book" is collection of texts with various datings, literary characteristics, and theological viewpoints. Similarly, the Pentateach itself is a kind of anthology.

The contexts for Torah study are many and varied, as are the insights pro-
voked or facilitated by the different settings. The five books of Moses are traditionally read in synagogue four times per week, according to a yearly cycle that
includes sequential weekly portions, as well as thematic holiday readings. Torah
may be studied during prayer services, on one's own, on the Internet, or with a
study partner (*ḥavruta*). Common settings are university and adult education
classes, lay-led study sessions, and *Rosh Ḥodesh* (New Moon Festival) groups.

One can study the Torah in order (beginning with Genesis and continuing
through Deuteronomy), biographically (following a character), or thematically
(e.g., examining all laws that are concerned with food; looking at slavery, trick-
sters, or rebelliousness). A variety of supplementary sources, from ancient
midrash to medieval commentaries to contemporary essays, are available as study
aids. (Consult the Suggested Readings.)

As much as studying a biblical text in light of various commentaries and
approaches enriches one's understanding, it cannot replace a personal and
unmediated relationship with the text. Engaging the Bible directly is an essential
yet often neglected method of study. It requires clearing one's mind of all associations and assumptions, and reading the text as if for the first time. People who

may feel ignorant of the Bible or intimidated by it should know that an unencumbered and curious attitude toward the text is tremendously fruitful. Scholars regularly attempt to cultivate a "second naiveté" in service of fresh eyes and new readings.

We may think that we know the simple meaning of a text, but often what we call "plot" is clouded by layers of interpretation. It is good to ask: If I didn't know how I was "supposed" to feel about God/Ishmael/Lot's daughters/Moses, how might I react? An entertaining and useful exercise is to read various versions of a particular Bible story in children's books.[1] This reminds us where we got many of our assumptions, and also demonstrates the diversity of (not always conscious) interpretation.

Revelation and the Torah

A theological orientation assumes that Torah is holy and timeless, that it has something to tell each of us about who we are and how God wants us to be. For the "theological" reader, Torah sheds light on what it means to be human, as much as it illuminates the nature of the divine. It makes demands of people, along with claims about God.

Those who look to the Bible for moral or behavioral guidance are using a theological/revelation approach, even if they do not profess a belief in God. This approach asks: If you focused on this Bible/law/story as a divine message and wished to incorporate it into your life, how would you change your thinking, speech, and behavior? One tool for drawing out theological and moral meaning is to notice "forks" in the story where things could have gone otherwise, and then play them out. How would the message be different? This clarifies the moral(s) of the canonical story.

The theological stance assumes that the revelation at Mt. Sinai continues today through the Torah text. Various practices, common and obscure, are based on this approach: E.g., reading psalms during times of illness, delivering and hearing sermons, naming children after biblical figures whom it is hoped they will emulate, bibliomancy (opening the text at "random" and interpreting the particular verse spotted as a personal message). Some advocates of the "theological approach" understand each word of Torah to be holy and full of (sometimes hidden) purpose.

The framework of revelation is equally available to those with traditional ideas about how the Bible was created and transmitted, and those who endorse the historical approach of biblical criticism. "Revelation" does not necessarily mean "revelation of the entire Torah by God to Moses on Mount Sinai in discrete words and letters." Once biblical scholars developed the theory that the Bible emerged from many sources, which were edited over time, Jews were forced to consider whether a revelation transmitted and informed by many generations might be further hallowed, rather than muddied, by such participation; whether a Bible not literally or historically "correct" and verifiable could be mythically and morally true; whether, lacking a univocal Commander whose exact words are transcribed and known, we can discover or invent a legitimate source of commandedness and authority; whether we can continue to meet God and sustain a holy covenant, even though the record of our paradigmatic meeting and covenant at Sinai is not a literal transcript.[2]

Contributors to this book answer mainly in the affirmative. In general, *Lifecycles 2* is predicated on a theology of progressive revelation; i.e., it considers questions of meaning and matters of daily living in light of the Torah text and its ongoing revelations.

The Historical Approach

Most contemporary Bible readers, with the exception of fundamentalists and some Orthodox, agree that the Bible contains multiple historical layers. Various oral traditions, most likely of different schools, were recorded and edited over time, and eventually combined to form a single text.[3] Historians use clues within the Bible to unravel the mystery of ancient Israelite society. Laws and narratives can reveal the author(s)' agenda, shed light on the intended audience, provide details about customs and locations.

Certain texts reflect, and perhaps presuppose, particular societal structures. The narratives in Genesis, for example, have persuaded scholars that the ancient Israelites were a semi-nomadic people. Sometimes, a text provides clues to the political interests of its author(s). Thus, biblical passages that favor the needs and services of the priests have been labelled "priestly" documents.

The historical setting of a document can illuminate its culturally cued meanings and assumptions. Dating biblical texts—usually a controversial matter—can therefore be of great importance in their interpretation. For example, most scholars agree that Deuteronomy was edited *after* its predictions of expulsion and disaster were already a reality. Historical circumstances shaped the book, even as they affect our reading today.

Some of what historians do is creative aetiology—inventing likely contexts from which texts might have emerged. For example, perhaps laws were issued against the worship of the goddess Ashera precisely because she was being worshipped (2 Kings 23:6). In fact, this is born out by archaeological findings, which have uncovered goddess figurines even in priests' dwellings near ritual baths.

In general, extrabiblical evidence—in the form of ancient Near Eastern law codes, royal records, or archaeological findings—is useful for understanding the Bible in historical context. Thus, the law demanding an eye for an eye (Ex. 21:24; Lev. 24:20) is illuminated by contrast to the ancient law code of Hammurapi, which assesses different penalties, depending on the relative social standings of victim and offender (#196–199). In that light, the biblical law is less about vengeance than equality: A slave's eye is not worth less than a master's.

Historical reconstructions of biblical society are necessarily speculative. Robert Alter has credited the historical approach with "the courage of conjecture," but, like Edmund Leach, he sees less advantage in "unscrambling the [biblical] omelette," than in tasting and savoring the, probably inseparable, mix of ingredients that form the dish.[4] In general, contributors to this book are likewise more interested in the consequences and uses of the Bible than in its origins and settings.

The Bible as Literature

Since most contemporary Jews have some general liberal arts education, and since so much Western literature draws on biblical themes and allusions, a literary approach can be a relatively easy mode of access to Bible studies. This method is also important from a traditional perspective. Close textual analysis is a key element not only among literary critics but also, and first, in Rabbinic commentaries and *midrashim*.[5]

The following techniques, tools, and questions are useful in reading the Bible:

- *Identify literary genres and structures.* Is the text narrative, legal, poetic? Are there competing or complementary trends—e.g. comic elements mixed with tragic or ironic? Is the story/law presented in parts? In a chiasm/mirror image (a b c b' a')? Is an introductory prophecy or outline played out in the rest of the text? Does the text include overturned expectations or reversals?

- *Address the characters and narrator.* What do a character's actions and inactions tell you? How does dialogue illuminate character and status? What do characters know, and what don't they know? Is their affiliation or nationality important? Is the meaning of a Hebrew name significant? In what ways does a character change over time, and in what ways is s/he consistent?

  Distinguish the narrator's voice. How does the narrator color or identify with characters or situations? How and when does a narrator intervene? Does the narration speed up (covering a lot of ground at once) or slow down (intensively exploring a shorter interval), and what do the changes in narrative pace indicate?

- *Explore repetitions and omissions.* What is the effect and message of repeating a situation, Hebrew root, or word? Examine both the continuity and the changes, when an idea, law, or pattern is restated or roughly repeated. For example, biblical poetry has a parallel structure, in which an idea is reiterated in different words. What do those different words reenforce and what do they add? Or, how does a "type-story," such as the story of a barren woman who gives birth to a "chosen" son, both repeat and unfold newly in each case? Notice, too, what is missing from a text. What is left unclear, unsaid, or unexplained? Is the overt message of a passage either enhanced or undermined by the silences?

- *Investigate words that are unusual, distinctive, difficult to understand, or key to a particular passage.* Consult a concordance or CD-ROM of the Bible and compare the usage of an unusual or key word in different biblical passages. For example, the word *hinneni* generally conveys not just its literal translation of "here I am," but its contextual meaning of full spiritual presence and readiness.

- *Learn from context and juxtapositions.* How do laws and narratives that follow one another also inform one another?[6] How does the placement of certain information affect the way it is evaluated? Debra's essay on Jewish memory in the Genesis chapter notes that the story of Tamar affects and is affected by that of Joseph, in part because it is sandwiched between two halves of the Joseph narrative.

- *Look at the larger picture.* Is this part of the Bible serving to illuminate some other? For example, angels intervene when Lot volunteers to give his daughters to rapists in place of the male houseguests they demand (Gen. 19). This parallels and also condemns the male host and houseguest who are willing to give over their daughter and concubine to local rapists in order to prevent the rape of a male guest (Judges 19).

Individual essays take a literary approach when they consider structure, form, themes, and characters, as in Leora Zeitlin's treatment of the brothers in Genesis or Dr. Alice Shalvi's discussion of Moses' character and the foil offered by Tzelofeḥad's daughters. In general, the literary orientation of this book is quite strong. The literary term and concept "theme" is the basis for the chapter divisions, and is used to connect women's lives to Torah.

Myth—Not Fiction

In religious terms, a myth is an "organizing story" told by and to a community. It creates a context that shapes how people understand the world and how they read all other stories, including their own life history. Myths are so powerful that they even determine what stories and realities we can relate to, in the first place. Myths have been compared to frameworks, pairs of glasses, prisms, paradigms. Neil Gillman has defined the biblical myth as "a master story, a story on a grand scale which explains why things are distinctively as they are, for me, my people, humanity, and the cosmos as a whole." "It is also *my* story," he adds, "It tells me who I am."[7] Like the theological approach, the mythic is concerned with questions of ultimate meaning. The exodus, for example, is a myth about what it means to be free and to have a Savior.

Myths are not accurate—or inaccurate; they are truthful without being literal. Aetiologies and cosmologies—myths that explain origins of various phenomena and of the cosmos—are closer to poetry than to science, though the distinction between those two is blurring with the advances in quantum physics.

While myths can be neither proved nor disproved, they can be assessed. One way to measure the effectiveness of a myth is its longevity; another is the effect it has on an individual's thinking and behavior; a third is its ability to create, sustain, and influence community; and a fourth is the myth's propensity for generating new stories and myths in response to it. By all those measures, the Bible contains profound and effective mythical stories and is, in its totality, a myth of enduring influence.

Comparisons can be made between Israelite and other ancient myths, in order to assess, as with literary and historical differences, what elements are relatively universal, and what elements are unique or distinctive within a pattern.

The Bible can be read mythically in another sense of that word—i.e., in terms of mythic paradigms that exist outside the Bible. For example, the sibling rivalry stories of Genesis can be read through the prism of psychoanalysis—a myth, by the definition provided, in its own right. The mythic system of *kabbalah* (Jewish mysticism) can be used to interpret the story of creation. In this book, such authors as Zilla Jane Goodman (Genesis chapter) and Rabbi Shirley Idelson (Leviticus chapter) respond to biblical texts by providing alternative myths.

Traditional Methods for Torah Interpretation

The tradition certainly makes use of theological and literary approaches. At times, medieval commentators even attempt a certain type of historical approach by using the Bible to establish a chronology of record. Yet there is a distinctive Rabbinic approach to Torah study. A description of midrashic methods is included in Debra's "Stories Intersect: Jewish Women Read the Bible." The Rabbis use a similar interpretive style in other genres, notably *parshanut* (biblical commentary) and *kabbalah*.

In truth, there are countless traditional approaches to the text—and, indeed, various numbered lists of Rabbinic textual methods.[8] More than the Rabbis carry out interpretation based on rules of the game, however, the rules of the game are derived from what it is that Rabbis do. Perhaps the most famous list of methods comes in the form of an acronym—*pa.r.de.s* (orchard or paradise). The four methods represented in that word are *peshat* (simple, contextual meaning); *remez* (interpretation of hints in the text, through the use, e.g., of numerology, allegory, or acronyms); *derash* (homiletical interpretation); *sod* (interpretation of secrets in the text, involving esoteric and mystical approaches).[9]

One key and overarching principle of traditional Torah interpretation is that "interpretation" comes as a package with Torah. The *torah shebikhtav* (written Torah) is complemented by the *torah shebe'al peh* (oral Torah—i.e., Rabbinic literature, and specifically the Talmud). Naming the Talmud a kind of Torah elevates the authority of Rabbinic interpretation, and also "fixes" the Torah as our central text to which everything else refers. This is no accident: According to traditional teaching, both the written and the oral Torah were given at Mt. Sinai. "All future interpretations ever to be derived were already made known to Moses at Sinai" (after JT *Megillah* 1:9; Lev. *Rabbah* 22:1).

Traditional *midrashim* and commentaries can be used in a variety of ways. Reading many comments on a single passage expands and enriches one's understanding of the text; reading a single work on an entire section or book acquaints one more deeply with the commentator's orientation and more broadly with the Bible itself. Two important clues for reading both *midrash* and commentary:

1. Imagine that the Rabbinic text is providing you with an answer, and it is up to you to derive the question. (Debra calls this the "*Jeopardy* rule.") Often, the question is subtle and would have gone unnoticed by you, if not for the "answer" provided. Sometimes, there are layers of questions. For example, the answer to a superficial grammatical difficulty in the biblical text may also resolve a moral concern.

2. The ancient Rabbis often quote from the Bible to demonstrate and authenticate a point. These quotations or "prooftexts" are usually taken from a text other than the one under investigation. Often, the context of a prooftext will convey a subtle message about the main passage being studied. Therefore, it can significantly enhance your understanding of the Rabbinic interpretative process, the Rabbis' often playful associations, and the Torah itself.

Feminist Approaches to Textual Interpretation

Like Rabbinic interpretation, feminist critique is used throughout this book and includes a wide spectrum of opinion and exegetical techniques. In general, this interdisciplinary approach is built on several basic assumptions and commitments:

- That clues in the text can be used to recover or imaginatively reconstruct traditions about women, the circumstances of women's lives in the biblical period, and even the perspectives and opinions of ancient women.

- That the entire Bible—especially, but not only, those texts that relate specifically to women—can be illuminated by exploring the viewpoints of the women in the texts and / or of the women affected by them, down to our own day.

- That gender is a useful category of analysis for male as well as female characters and readers.

- That both major and minor female characters, as well as the details of women's lives and customs, should be fully explored. (In the past, biblical women have often been neglected, marginalized, or assessed primarily in relation to men.)

- That it is necessary to distinguish, wherever possible, the message of the text, the message of any discernible editorial hand(s), and the message of conventional interpretations. That the original text, without interpretive overlay, is often more favorable to women than we might suppose.

- That positive female role models and imagery, along with texts otherwise empowering to women, should be widely taught. That these texts should be read with a "hermeneutic of remembrance," an acknowledgment that while Israelite women were sometimes objects of patriarchal oppression, they were also agents in their own right and active participants in the formation of our religion.

- That egalitarian emphases in texts emerging from a patriarchal society are likely to be historically reliable, precisely because they run counter to a trend.

- That women's absence or voicelessness in certain texts should be noted as a phenomenon, rather than becoming transparent. That awareness of the historical context of the Bible does not justify deeming women's exclusion a part of the natural order of things.

- That the Bible is in certain ways oppressive toward women, and that misogynist texts and tendencies should be named for what they are. That we should apply a "hermeneutics of suspicion" to the overt and hidden power politics of the Bible and its interpreters.[10]

- That even misogynist texts can be plumbed for teachable messages about power and its (mis)uses, as well as Torah, holiness, theology, and gender. That such texts can be recounted "in memoriam," and in order to sensitize the contemporary reader.[11]

- That we can write dissenting or empowering postscripts to such texts, imaginatively reconstructing women's lives and perspectives.

- That texts can be read in combination and/or "against the grain" to recapture lost elements and question their face-value messages and meanings. That such readings yield feminist counter-traditions and (sub)versions.[12]

- That the Bible has been influential as a source and prooftext for redemption and liberation, as well as subjugation and oppression. That it is meaningful, worthwhile, and in the best interests of human advancement to remain engaged with this text.[13]

Florence Howe, founder of the Feminist Press, asks of every text she meets: "Where are the women?"[14] This question can "shake up" our default relationship with the text, highlight subtle gaps in the story of which we might not otherwise be aware, and yield new, more inclusive interpretations. Where was Rachel on Leah and Jacob's wedding night? Where were the women when "the people" (men) avoided them in ritual preparation for receiving the Torah (Ex. 19:15f)? Ancient and modern authors alike have addressed such questions.[15]

One good technique for reading the plot from an un(der)-represented perspective is to "suppose." If we accept the traditional reading that Dinah was raped (Gen. 34), how do we suppose she would feel about all that happened afterwards? Assuming she was not raped, as some have posited,[16] what effect would her brothers' actions, and her father's inaction, have on her then? Often, all suppositions lead to the same conclusion, so that an indefinite plot has definite consequences. (In this case, either way, Dinah was abused.) Even so, a number of plot-based possibilities remain. One can re-tell and retain all the alternate versions, or else choose a favored possibility on the basis of its logic, elegance, or moral implications.

How to Create a Contemporary *Midrash*

Any of the six categories discussed is a good avenue for beginning or continuing Torah study. These approaches also provide entry points into contemporary *midrash*, the creation of new narratives based on a reader's reaction and relationship to the Bible. The more you study a biblical text on its own terms and in light of various techniques, the richer the *midrash* you will be able to create. By the same token, writing a *midrash* creates the opportunity and incentive for study, and, in both our ideal and our experience, generally returns a person to the text.

Midrash-writing, like more conventional forms of engagement with Torah, can be undertaken on your own or in a group. You can write a *midrash* on any genre—law, narrative, poetry, even genealogy. Choose something that moves you or makes you curious. Texts with a great deal of ambiguity or confusion especially lend themselves to *midrash*, since the best *midrashim* tell a story that is coherent in itself and implicitly answers a textual question or problem. A *midrash* is considered especially elegant when, in presenting a story or idea, it can solve several questions or problems at once.

Read your chosen text and supplementary sources carefully and repeatedly, with an eye to uncovering questions. List anything and everything that strikes you as unusual, puzzling, or provocative. Ask questions based on theological, literary, mythic, historical, Rabbinic, feminist, and other concerns. Even questions that at first seem "silly" can yield interesting discussions and interpretations.

Play the story out step by step, and isolate what is at issue and what the dynamics are in each beat of the scenario. What are the pivotal moments, and who is in control then? How are the "snapshots" of this episode related to the surrounding text? What are the moral problems and messages? How do men and women relate to each other and to God? What problem(s) and motivation(s) does each character have? What problem(s) is the larger story or law itself addressing, both on and below the surface? What would happen if a similar event transpired now or a similar law were in force? What situations are analogous to the one described? Review questions asked by traditional commentators and midrashists. What answers do they provide? What additional answers come to mind? What other questions would you ask?

One way of getting at interesting ambiguities and problems is to describe in detail what is happening (present tense) at a specific, pivotal moment in the playing out of a law, song, or narrative. For example, describe the motivations, expectations, and emotions of those involved, as Eve, incited by the snake, extends the fruit to Adam (Gen. 3:6). Or imagine the setting and feelings at the moment when the midwives, summoned by Pharoah, open their mouths to explain why they have violated his orders (Ex. 1:18).

Entering into the Text Many traditional *midrashim* adopt the point of view of the various characters in a story. Try personalizing your *midrash* by using the first person singular to relate a story or law from the perspective of each person included in it. At first, be sure to mention only—and all—those parts of the picture to which your character has access. For example, "It was after these things that I, Abraham, was told to sacrifice my beloved son, Isaac" (Gen. 22:1). *But* "I, Isaac, suddenly found myself going along with my father, early in the morning, on the way to a destination I was ignorant of, without any explanation" (22:3). This will help you discern the narrator's voice and keep the various viewpoints distinct. It will also uncover gaps and discontinuous perspectives in the story, which your *midrash* can then fill or elaborate. For example, you might imagine a conversation between Abraham and Isaac (not reported in the Bible), after Abraham woke his son on the morning they set out together.

You can also report a law or narrative—again, in the first person—from the perspective of (1) animals or inanimate objects; (2) characters who are *not* present, though they appear in the larger story cycle; and (3) figures who are mysterious or underdeveloped. In the story of the binding of Isaac, these three types of perspectives are represented, respectively, by (1) the ram Abraham sacrifices in lieu of Isaac, along with the altar itself; (2) the absent Ishmael, Hagar, and Sarah; Satan, who dares God to test Abraham, according to *midrash*; and (3) the mysterious figures of God and the angel, as well as the relatively obscure servants who travel with Abraham and Isaac.

A similar technique, drawn from psychodrama, is to role-play different characters and speak their "secret thoughts," unarticulated in the text. Notice how the versions fit or don't fit together. Then, write a *midrash* that communicates one perspective, or somehow combines several, perhaps in a dialogue—another technique of traditional *midrash*. Or, play out what you would do—in the original setting or in a transposed, but similar contemporary situation—if you were in the same position as a particular character. Explore how you identify with different figures.[17]

Having studied the story of Hagar and Sarah, for example, you can enter into it by completing the blanks, below. (If doing this with a group, go around in a circle and let everyone fill in each blank a few times.)

I am like Hagar in that/because/when _____

I reject Hagar in that/because/when _____

I embrace Hagar in that/because/when _____

I am like Sarah in that/because/when _____

I reject Sarah in that/because/when _____

I embrace Sarah in that/because/when _____

This technique will help you understand the biblical figures—and yourself— better.

Another "right-brained" technique is synectics, a game of analogies. What are your associations to trees and "tree-like" qualities? How does this inform your understanding of Torah as a "tree of life" (Proverbs 3:18)?[18]

Poetry is also a wonderful tool for personalizing the themes and characters of the Bible.[19] Many women have written midrashic poems as part of an effort to reclaim women's stories.[20] Such poetry can emerge from group or individual interaction with the biblical text. When writing in/as a group, it is helpful to use specific structures and rules; these focus creativity, yield interesting poems, and decrease the pressure that some might feel. To explore Sarah and Hagar's relationship, each participant might write a single line of poetry from the perspective of either woman, using the format "I seem to...but really I...." and incorporating at least one verb other than "to be." Individual lines could then be ordered and juxtaposed so as to create a midrashic poem. Another simple, but powerful design is to begin each line of a poem about the Bible with the words "I wish."

Imagine, for example, using this guideline to write a poem entitled "Sodom and Gomorrah." Other possibilities: Incorporate sensory elements, metaphors, colors, or geographic locations in an assigned pattern. Such techniques are drawn from the work of Kenneth Koch, who pioneered group poetry writing among children and the elderly.[21]

The primary goal is not to create beautiful poetry, though that often does emerge. Rather, the goal is to discover new avenues of creativity and interpretation, to link individual and communal stories of today with our ancient, sacred teachings.

Non-verbal expressions—especially drawing and dance—have also been used to produce midrashic interpretations. In a technique called "hand-made midrash," each participant creates a picture of a key concept or story in the Bible by tearing and pasting colored paper.[22] This levels the artistic playing field and, more importantly, encourages symbolic representations of relationships and ideas. Often, it is helpful to ask everyone to portray at least one figure who does not appear in the text. Thus, a representation of Esther jeopardizing her life by entering the king's court might depict other heros and (near-)martyrs from our history, the artist him/herself, Haman, Mordecai, and God (Esther 5:1f). By crafting and explaining pictures in a group, you can notice your own interpretive assumptions, literally *see* those of others, and invent new *midrashim*.

Dance is another group activity that can be used to create, explore, and express personal, midrashic interpretations. With dance, as with hand-made *midrash* and poetry writing, it is important to make the exercise user-friendly for those who are not experienced in the art form. In creating a dance *midrash* on the story of Isaac's birth, participants could move their hands to represent the way Sarah laughed when she heard she was to become a mother at age ninety (Gen. 18:12). Hands might shake dismissively, wave uproariously, or spiral upward prayerfully, in different interpretations of the story. Dancers might speak words from the Torah, the traditional *midrash*, or their own commentary as they move. This exercise is useful in itself. In addition, books and workshops on midrashic dance teach how such "motivating movements" as these hand-dances can be incorporated into a choreographed piece.[23]

With midrashic poetry, drawing, and dance, *text study should precede and/or follow the artistic activities*, and group discussion of the creative product is illuminating. New insights can be captured in written reflections on the artistic/group/interpretive process. Many times, a (group) poem, picture, or dance will "work" as an artistic and midrashic expression; if not, it may well inspire new poems, pictures, dances, or expository *midrashim*.

"*Zil Gemor*—Go and Learn" (BT *Shabbat* 31a)

No matter what method is used in the creation of *midrash*, it is essential to connect the invention back to the biblical text. Otherwise, you may have created an interesting essay, poem, or performance, but not necessarily a *midrash*. "Connecting the invention back to the text" can mean using some of the Bible's language in your *midrash*, or even citing prooftexts for your interpretation, from the passage that gave rise to it or from another biblical text. If you generate a *midrash* from questions or perspectives that are textually based, you will not have difficulty "completing the circle."

In a particularly apt formulation, Paul Ricoeur provides a question and answer frequently discussed among literary critics. "What is indeed to be understood—and consequently appropriated—in a text?" Something much larger and more influential than we might assume: "The direction of thought opened up by the text...nothing other than the power of disclosing a world that constitutes the reference of the text."[24] The Bible is not just a text; it is a world. Indeed, for many students of the Bible, that world is the reference for *all* texts and experiences—not the Bible alone. Engaging in Torah study, therefore, can be a way of mapping the universe.[25]

Selected Readings on Women, Bible, Midrash, and Life Themes

Alter, Robert. *The Art of Biblical Narrative*. New York: Basic Books, 1981.

Alter, Robert, and Frank Kermode, eds. *The Literary Guide to the Bible*. Cambridge, Mass.: Harvard University Press, 1987.

Bach, Alice, ed. *The Pleasure of Her Text: Feminist Readings of Biblical and Historical Texts*. Philadelphia: Trinity, 1990.

Bal, Mieke. *Anti-Covenant: Counter-Reading Women's Lives in the Hebrew Bible*. Sheffield, England: Almond, 1989.

___. *Lethal Love: Feminist Literary Readings of Biblical Love Stories*. Bloomington, Ind.: Indiana University Press, 1987.

Bateson, Mary Catherine. *Composing a Life*. New York: Atlantic Monthly Press, 1988.

Bellis, Alice Ogden. *Helpmates, Harlots, and Heroes: Women's Stories In the Bible*. Louisville, Ky.: Westminster/John Knox Press, 1994.

Berlin, Adele. *Poetics and Interpretation of Biblical Narrative*. Sheffield, England: Almond, 1983.

Bible and Culture Collective. *The Postmodern Bible*. New Haven, Ct.: Yale University Press, 1995.

Boyarin, Daniel. *Intertextuality and the Reading of Midrash*. Bloomington, Ind.: Indiana University Press, 1994.

Brenner, Athalya, ed. *A Feminist Companion of Exodus to Deuteronomy*. Sheffield, England: Sheffield Academic Press, 1994.

___. *A Feminist Companion to Genesis.* Sheffield, England: Sheffield Academic Press, 1993.

___. *The Israelite Woman: Social Role and Literary Type in Biblical Narrative.* Sheffield, England: JOST Press, 1985.

___, and Fokkelien van Dijk-Hemmes. *On Gendering Texts: Female and Male Voices in the Hebrew Bible.* New York: E.J. Brill, 1993.

Bronner, Leila Leah. *From Eve to Esther: Rabbinic Reconstructions of Biblical Women.* Louisville, Ky.: Westminster/John Knox Press, 1995.

Brown, Cheryl Anne. *No Longer Be Silent: First Century Jewish Portraits of Biblical Women.* Louisville, Ky.: Westminster/John Knox Press, 1992.

Büchmann, Christina, and Celina Spiegel, eds., *Out of the Garden: Women Writers on the Bible.* New York: Fawcett Columbine, 1994.

Calloway, Mary. *Sing O Barren One: A Study in Comparative Midrash.* Atlanta: Scholars Press, 1986.

Camp, Claudia V. *Wisdom and the Feminine in the Book of Proverbs.* Decatur, Ga.: Almond Press, 1985.

Cohen, Norman J. *Self, Struggle, and Change: Family Conflict Stories in Genesis and Their Healing Insights for Our Lives.* Woodstock, Vt.: Jewish Lights, 1995.

Collins, Adela Yarbro, ed. *Feminist Perspectives on Biblical Scholarship.* Chico, Calif.: Scholars Press, 1985.

Curzon, David, ed. *Modern Poems on the Bible: An Anthology.* Philadelphia: Jewish Publication Society, 1994.

Darr, Katheryn Pfisterer. *Far More Precious than Jewels: Perspectives on Biblical Women.* Louisville, Ky.: Westminster/John Knox Press, 1991.

Davidman, Lynn, and Shelly Tenenbaum, eds. *Feminist Perspectives on Jewish Studies.* New Haven, Conn.: Yale University Press, 1994.

Day, Peggy L., ed. *Gender and Difference in Ancient Israel.* Philadelphia: Fortress, 1989.

Demers, Patricia. *Women as Interpreters of the Bible.* New York: Paulist Press, 1992.

Exum, J. Cheryl. *Fragmented Women: Feminist (Sub)Versions of Biblical Narratives.* Valley Forge, Pa.: Trinity,1993.

Fewell, Danna Nolan, ed. *Reading Between Texts: Intertextuality and the Hebrew Bible.* Louisville, Ky.: Westminster/John Knox Press, 1992.

Fiorenza, Elisabeth Schüssler. *Bread Not Stone: The Challenge of Feminist Biblical Interpretation.* Boston: Beacon Press, 1992.

Fishbane, Michael, ed. *The Midrashic Imagination: Jewish Exegesis, Thought, and History.* Albany: State University of New York Press, 1993.

___. *The Garments of Torah.* Bloomington: Indiana University Press, 1989.

Fraade, Steven D. *From Tradition to Commentary: Torah and Its Interpretation in the Midrash Sifre to Deuteronomy.* Albany: State University of New York Press, 1991.

Frymer-Kensky, Tikva. *In the Wake of the Goddesses: Women, Culture, and the Biblical Transformation of Pagan Myth.* New York: Free Press, 1992.

Ginzberg, Louis. *The Legends of the Jews* 7 vols. Philadelphia: Jewish Publication Society, 1938.

Goldberg, Michael. *Jews and Christians: Getting Our Story Straight.* Nashville, Tenn.: Abingdon, 1985.

___. *Theology and Narrative: A Critical Introduction*. Nashville, Tenn.: Abingdon, 1982.

Goldin, Judah. *Studies in Midrash and Related Literature*. Philadelphia: Jewish Publication Society, 1988.

Graetz, Naomi. *S/He Created Them: Feminist Retellings of Biblical Stories*. Teaneck, N.J.: Professional Press, 1993.

Handleman, Susan A. *The Slayers of Moses: The Emergence of Rabbinic Interpretation in Modern Literary Theory*. New York: State University of New York Press, 1982.

Hartman, Geoffrey H., and Sanford Budick, eds. *Midrash and Literature*. New Haven, Conn.: Yale University Press, 1986.

Heilbrun, Carolyn. *Writing a Woman's Life*. New York: Ballantine, 1988.

Holtz, Barry W. *Finding Our Way: Jewish Texts and the Lives We Lead Today*. New York: Schocken, 1990.

___, ed. *Back to the Sources: Reading the Classic Jewish Texts*. New York: Summit Books, 1984.

Jeansonne, Sharon Pace. *The Women of Genesis: From Sarah to Potiphar's Wife*. Minneapolis: Fortress, 1989

Kates, Judith, and Gail Twersky Reimer, eds. *Reading Ruth*. New York: Ballantine, 1994.

Kaufman, Sharon R. *The Ageless Self*. Madison, Wisc.: University of Wisconsin Press, 1986.

Kraemer, Ross S. *Her Share of the Blessings: Women's Religions among Pagans, Jews, and Christians in the Greco-Roman World*. New York: Oxford University Press, 1992.

Kushner, Lawrence. *God Was in This Place and I, i Did Not Know*. Woodstock, Vt.: Jewish Lights, 1991.

Lepon, Shoshana. *No Greater Treasure: Stories of Extraordinary Women Drawn from the Talmud and Midrash*. Southfield, Mich.: Targum Press, 1990.

Levine, Amy-Jill, ed. *"Women Like This": New Perspectives on Jewish Women In the Greco-Roman World*. Atlanta: Scholars Press, 1991.

Meyers, Carol. *Discovering Eve: Ancient Israelite Women in Context*. New York: Oxford University Press, 1988.

McClendon, James Wm., Jr. *Biography as Theology: How Life Stories Can Remake Today's Theology*. New York: Abingdon Press, 1974.

Milgrom, Jo. *Handmade Midrash: Workshops in Visual Theology: A Guide for Teachers, Rabbis, and Lay Leaders*. Philadelphia: Jewish Publication Society, 1992.

Millett, Craig Ballard. *Archetypes of Women in Scripture: In God's Image*. San Diego: LuraMedia, 1989.

Mollenkott, Virginia Ramey. *The Divine Feminine: The Biblical Imagery of God as Female*. New York: Crossroad, 1983.

Neusner, Jacob. *Introduction to Rabbinic Literature*. New York: Doubleday, 1994.

Newsom, Carol A., and Sharon H. Ringe. *The Women's Bible Commentary*. Louisville, Ky.: Westminster/John Knox Press, 1992.

Ochs, Carol. *Song of the Self: Biblical Spirituality and Human Holiness*. Valley Forge, Penn.: Trinity, 1994.

___. *The Noah Paradox: Time as Burden, Time as Blessing*. Notre Dame: University of Notre Dame Press.

Ochs, Vanessa. *Words on Fire: One Woman's Journey into the Sacred.* San Diego: Harcourt Brace Jovanovich, 1990.

Olyan, Saul. *Asherah and the Cult of Yahweh in Israel.* Atlanta, Ga.: Scholars Press, 1988.

Ostriker, Alicia Suskin. *The Nakedness of the Fathers: Biblical Visions and Revisions.* New Brunswick, N.J.: Rutgers University Press, 1994.

Personal Narratives Group. *Interpreting Women's Lives: Feminist Theory and Personal Narratives.* Bloomington: Indiana University Press, 1989.

Public Affairs Television. *Talking About Genesis: A Resource Guide.* New York: Doubleday, 1996.

Pardes, Ilana. *Countertraditions in the Bible: A Feminist Approach.* Cambridge, Mass.: Harvard University Press, 1992.

Pitzele, Peter. *Our Fathers' Wells: A Personal Encounter with the Myths of Genesis.* San Francisco: Harper Collins, 1995.

Ruether, Rosemary Radford. *Sexism and God-Talk: Toward a Feminist Theology.* Boston: Beacon Press, 1983.

Russell, Letty M. *Household of Freedom: Authority in Feminist Theology.* Philadelphia: Westminster Press, 1987.

___, ed. *Feminist Interpretation of the Bible.* Philadelphia: Westminster Press, 1985.

Sarton, May. *Journal of a Solitude.* New York: Norton and Company, 1992.

Sheehy, Gail. *New Passages: Mapping Your Life Across Time.* New York: Random House, 1995.

Simpkinson, Charles, and Anna Simpkinson, eds. *Sacred Stories: A Celebration of the Power of Stories to Transform and Heal.* San Francisco: Harper Collins, 1993.

Sprague, Jane, ed. *But She Said: Feminist Practices of Biblical Interpretation.* Boston: Beacon Press, 1992.

___. *Taking the Fruit: Modern Women's Tales of the Bible.* San Diego: Women's Institute for Continuing Jewish Education, 1989.

Teubal, Savina. *Hagar the Egyptian: The Lost Tradition of the Matriarchs.* San Francisco: Harper & Row, 1990.

___. *Sarah the Priestess.* Athens, Ohio: Swallow Press, 1984.

Tolbert, Mary Ann. *The Bible and Feminist Hermeneutics.* Atlanta, Ga.: Scholars Press, 1983.

Trible, Phyllis. *Texts of Terror: Literary Feminist Readings of Biblical Narratives.* Philadelphia: Fortress, 1984.

___. *God and the Rhetoric of Sexuality.* Philadelphia: Fortress, 1978.

Visotzky, Burton L. *The Genesis of Ethics: How the Dysfunctional Family of Genesis Leads Us to Moral Development.* New York: Crown, 1996.

___. *Reading the Book: Making the Bible a Timeless Text.* New York: Anchor, 1991.

Waskow, Arthur. *Godwrestling—Round 2: Ancient Wisdom, Future Paths.* Woodstock, Vt.: Jewish Lights, 1996.

___. *Down-to-Earth Judaism: Food, Money, Sex, and the Rest of Life.* New York: William Morrow, 1995.

___. *Godwrestling.* New York: Schocken Books, 1978.

Walzer, Michael. *Exodus and Revolution.* New York: Basic Books, 1985.

Weems, Renita J. *Just a Sister Away: A Womanist Vision of Women's Relationships in the Bible.* San Diego: LuraMedia, 1988.

Williams, James G. *Women Recounted: Narrative Thinking and the God of Israel*. Sheffield, England: Almond, 1982.

Zolty, Shoshana Pantel. *"And All Your Children Shall Be Learned": Women and the Study of Torah in Jewish Law and History*. Northvale, N.J.: Jason Aronson, 1993.

Zornberg, Avivah Gottlieb. *Genesis: The Beginning of Desire*. Philadelphia: Jewish Publication Society, 1995.

For bibliographies of *midrash* in English translation see Neusner, *Introduction to Rabbinic Literature*; Goldin, *Studies in Midrash and Related Literature*; and Francine Klagsbrun, *Voices of Wisdom: Jewish Ideals and Ethics for Everyday Living* (Middle Village, N.Y.: Jonathan David, 1980).

Glossary

aggadah: Jewish lore

agunah (plural *agunot*): Women chained to dead marriages

aliyah (plural *aliyot*): Honor of reciting blessings before and after the Torah is read; the blessings themselves; the segments of the Torah read. Making *aliyah* to Israel is immigrating to Israel.

Amidah: Standing (prayer), because the prayer is said while standing; series of blessings that is the centerpiece of every prayer service.

bashert: Destined by the good will of providence

Bat Mitzvah: Coming of age ceremony for Jewish girls

beit din: Rabbinical court

beit midrash: House of study, study hall

berakhah (plural *berakhot*): Blessing

brit: Covenant

brit milah: Covenant of circumcision

daven: Pray

gemilut ḥasidim: Sacred practice of lovingkindness

Haggadah (plural *Haggadot*): Text of the Passover *seder**

hakhnasat orḥim: Welcoming guests

halakhah (plural *halakhot*): Jewish law

* This word appears in the glossary.

ḥallah (plural *ḥallot*): Loaf of bread, often braided egg bread; eaten especially on
     Sabbaths and holidays
havdallah: Distinction-making ritual that separates Sabbath or holiday from
     weekday
ḥavurah: Jewish worship/study fellowship
ḥavruta: Study partner; paired study
kabbalah: Jewish mysticism
Kaddish: A prayer sanctifying God's name; popularly, mourner's prayer
kashrut: Jewish dietary laws
kavvanah: Intentionality, especially in prayer
kippah (plural *kippot*): Skullcap
matzah (plural *matzot*): Unleavened bread eaten at Passover
meḥitzah: Dividing wall between women and men in prayer
mezuzah: Box on doorpost containing the *Shema** prayer; doorpost
midrash (plural *midrashim*): Rabbinic genre of lore often based on biblical texts;
     Rabbinic legend(s); legend in the Rabbinic style
mikveh (plural *mikva'ot*): Ritual bath; ritual immersion
minyan (plural *minyanim*): (Prayer) quorum
mishkan: Tabernacle
mitzvah (plural *mitzvot*): Commandment; sacred obligation
niddah: State of menstrual impurity; menstruating woman
Rosh Ḥodesh: New Moon Festival; first day of the month
Rosh Hashanah: New Year
seder: Ordered readings and meal at Passover; order
Shabbat (plural *Shabbatot*): Sabbath
Shavu'ot: Festival of the Giving of the Torah
Shekhinah: Close-dwelling presence of God, associated with the feminine
Shema: Central prayer that declares God's oneness
shtetl: Small, largely self-contained community in which most Eastern European
     Jews lived
shul: Synagogue
siddur: Prayerbook
tallit: Prayer shawl
talmud torah: Jewish learning; study of Jewish texts
tefillin: Phylacteries
teshuvah: Repentance; return
tkhine (plural *tkhines*): Petitionary prayers for and/or by women, traditionally
     written in Yiddish
tzedakah: Sacred practice of charity
tzelem elohim: Image of God; value-concept of being created in the image of God
yeshivah (plural *yeshivot*): Traditional academy of Jewish learning
yetzer hara: Evil inclination; a common Rabbinic term for human passion and
     sexuality
Yom Kippur: Day of Atonement

* This word appears in the glossary.

Notes

———◦⟨◉⟩◦———

Stories Intersect

1. Mystics attempt to bridge any separation and ultimately to *be* Torah. Cf. Martin Buber, *Tales of the Hasidim: The Early Masters* (New York: Schocken, 1975), 107.

2. Sharon R. Kaufman, *The Ageless Self: Sources of Meaning in Late Life* (Madison: University of Wisconsin Press, 1986), 25.

3. Aphorism in Erich Heller, ed., *The Basic Kafka* (New York: Pocket Books, 1979), 237. Cf. Elana Rosenfeld Berkowitz, "At Age Fourteen," in *Lifecycles 1: Jewish Women on Life Passages and Personal Milestones*, ed. Debra Orenstein (Woodstock, Vt.: Jewish Lights Publishing, 1994), 87.

4. Nelle Morton, *The Journey Is Home* (Boston: Beacon Press, 1985), 202f; Carol P. Christ, *Diving Deep and Surfacing* (Boston: Beacon Press, 1980). According to some of the psychological research, *personal* storytelling plays an especially important role in women's communication. Deborah Tannen, *You Just Don't Understand: Women and Men in Conversation* (New York: William Morrow, 1990), 245–254; Mary Field Belenky, et al., *Women's Ways of Knowing: The Development of Self, Voice, and Mind* (New York: Basic Books, 1986), 101f, 200.

5. Carolyn G. Heilbrun, *Writing a Woman's Life* (New York: Ballantine, 1988); Mary Catherine Bateson, *Composing a Life* (New York: Atlantic Monthly Press, 1989); Janet Sternburg, *The Writer on Her Work* 2 vols. (New York: W.W. Norton, 1980, 1991); Personal Narratives Group, *Interpreting Women's Lives: Feminist Theory and Personal Narratives* (Bloomington: Indiana University Press, 1989).

6. Wendy Martin, *We Are the Stories We Tell: The Best Short Stories by North American Women Since 1945* (New York: Pantheon Books, 1990).

7. James Wm. McClendon, Jr., *Biography as Theology: How Life Stories Can Remake Today's Theology* (New York: Abingdon Press, 1974). Michael Goldberg differentiates among various kinds of stories in *Theology and Narrative: A Critical Introduction* (Nashville, Tenn.: Abingdon, 1982), 39–61.

8. Michael Novak, *Ascent of the Mountain, Flight of the Dove: An Invitation to Religious Studies* (New York: Harper and Row, 1971), 45.

9. Many authors no longer attempt a dictionary style definition, but rather name a set of family characteristics or functions typical of *midrash*. For a review article, see Gary G. Porton, "Defining Midrash," in *The Study of Ancient Judaism*, vol. 1, ed. Jacob Neusner (Leiden, Netherlands: E. J. Brill, 1995), 55–92. For a classic essay: Joseph Heinemann, "The Nature of the Aggadah," trans. Marc Bregman, in *Midrash and Literature*, ed. Geoffrey Hartman and Sanford Budick (New Haven, Conn.: Yale University Press, 1986). For especially accessible treatments: Renee Bloch, "Midrash," in *Approaches to Ancient Judaism: Theory and Practice*, ed. William Scott Green (Missoula, Mont.: Scholars Press, 1978), 36f; Barry W. Holtz, "Midrash," in *Back to the Sources: Reading the Classic Jewish Texts*, ed. Barry W. Holtz (New York: Summit Books, 1984), 178–211; James Kugel, "Two Introductions to Midrash," *Prooftexts* 3, no. 2 (May 1983): 131–155 (also reprinted in *Midrash and Literature*); Burton L. Visotzky, *Reading the Book: Making the Bible a Timeless Text* (New York: Anchor Books, 1991), 10f.

10. James B. Wiggins, "Within and Without Stories," in *Religion As Story* (New York: Harper and Row, 1975), 20.

11. See endnote 9 and David Stern, *Parables in Midrash: Narrative and Exegesis in Rabbinic Literature* (Cambridge, Mass.: Harvard University Press, 1991).

12. *Midrash* has been likened to postmodernist interpretations, which tend to focus on the multiplicity and "undecidability" of texts. For the value and limits of the comparison: Betty Roitman, "Sacred Language and Open Text," Hartman and Budick, *Midrash and Literature*, 159; Daniel Boyarin, *Intertextuality and The Reading of Midrash* (Bloomington: Indiana University Press, 1994), 1–21; David Stern, "Midrash and Indeterminacy," *Critical Inquiry* 15 (fall 1988): 132–61; Visotzky, *Reading the Book*, 228.

13. Michael Fishbane, *Biblical Interpretation in Ancient Israel* (Oxford: Clarendon Press, 1985); Michael Fishbane, "Inner Biblical Exegesis," in Hartman and Budick, *Midrash and Literature*, 21f; Phyllis Trible, *God and the Rhetoric of Sexuality* (Philadelphia: Fortress Press, 1978), 2–5, 38ff; Mary Callaway, *Sing, O Barren One: A Study in Comparative Midrash* (Atlanta: Scholars Press, 1986), 7f; Yair Zakovitch, *And You Shall Tell Your Son: The Concept of the Exodus in the Bible* (Jerusalem: Magnes Press, 1991); Visotzky, *Reading the Book*, 10f; Gerald R. Bruns, "Midrash and Allegory: The Beginnings of Scriptural Interpretation," in *The Literary Guide to the Bible*, ed. Robert Alter and Frank Kermode (Cambridge, Mass.: Harvard University Press, 1987), 626f.

14. Menaḥem Mendel Torum of Rymanov cited in Gershom G. Scholem, *On the Kabbalah and Its Symbolism*, trans. Ralph Manheim (New York: Schocken, 1965), 29–31. Cf. Franz Rosenzweig's letter to Martin Buber in *On Jewish*

Learning, ed. N.N. Glatzer (New York: Schocken, 1965), 117–18; Abraham Joshua Heschel, *God in Search of Man: A Philosophy of Judaism* (New York: Farrar, Straus, and Cudahy, 1955), 185f. Of course, the usual traditionalist stance is that God wrote and explicitly gave the complete Torah to Moses. Some say that the Prophets, Writings, and Oral Law were also given in "discrete words and letters." However, many traditionalists would agree that the prophets interpreted Torah (e.g., Jeremiah 2, Micah 6).

15. Rabbi Neil Gillman in a private conversation, October 22, 1995. Cf. Visotzky, *Reading the Book*, 224. See Ex. *Rabbah* 5:9 for a traditional understanding of how revelation is heard differently—and designed to be heard differently—depending on the listener.

16. Kaufmann, *The Ageless Self*, 162.

17. Some held that he was resurrected. Shalom Spiegel, *The Last Trial*, trans. Judah Goldin (Woodstock, Vt.: Jewish Lights Publishing, 1993), 30f, 47, 130.

18. Ibid., 7f, 21f, 46f, 102.

19. Jane Sprague Zones, ed., *Taking the Fruit: Modern Women's Tales of the Bible* (San Diego, Calif.: Woman's Institute for Continuing Jewish Education, 1991); Penina V. Adelman, *Miriam's Well: Rituals for Jewish Women Around the Year* (New York: Biblio Press, 1990).

20. E.g., Ellen M. Umansky, "Revisioning Sarah: A *Midrash* on Genesis 22," in *Four Centuries of Jewish Women's Spirituality: A Sourcebook*, ed. Ellen M. Umansky and Dianne Ashton (Boston: Beacon, 1992), 235; Bradley Shavit Artson, "A Midrash: And God Tested Sarah," *Women's League Outlook* (fall 1995): 25–26; Burton L. Visotzky, *The Genesis of Ethics: How the Dysfunctional Family of Genesis Leads Us to Moral Development* (New York: Crown, 1996), 110–111.

21. Thanks to Rabbi Nina Beth Cardin for this formulation.

22. E.g., Gen. 34 (Dinah); Ex. 2, 4, 18 (Tzipporah); 1 Kings 1–2 (Avishag the Shunammite).

23. *Ha'eshkol* 2, 47, attributed to Rav Sherira Gaon (tenth century).

24. On differentiating feminism and women's perspectives as they relate to Jewish studies: Debra Orenstein, "Introduction," in Orenstein, *Lifecycles 1*, xxiii–xxvii.

25. Of course, feminist criticism, unlike Rabbinic *midrash*, makes use of such extra-biblical input as ancient near eastern historical sources and archaeological discoveries.

26. Holtz, "Midrash," 179.

27. The Bible mentions 1,426 named individuals, of whom 1,315 are men. Carol Meyers, "Everyday Life: Women in the Period of the Hebrew Bible" in *The Women's Bible Commentary*, ed. Carol A. Newsom and Sharon H. Ringe (Louisville, Ky.: Westminster/John Knox Press, 1992), 245.

28. Judith A. Kates and Gail Twersky Reimer, *Reading Ruth: Contemporary Women Reclaim a Sacred Story* (New York: Ballantine Books, 1994). Inter- and trans-disciplinary approaches abound in feminist writings. The work of various scholars is summarized in Alice Ogden Bellins, *Helpmates, Harlots, and Heroes:*

Women's Stories in the Hebrew Bible (Louisville, Ky: Westminster/John Knox Press, 1994).

29. See pages 12–16; 17–18; 46–50; 64–65.

30. See pages 287–293.

31. Ilana Pardes, *Countertraditions in the Bible: A Feminist Approach* (Cambridge, Mass.: Harvard University Press, 1992); J. Cheryl Exum, *Fragmented Women: Feminist (Sub)versions of Biblical Narratives* (Philadelphia: Trinity, 1993); Alice Bach, ed., *The Pleasure of Her Text: Feminist Readings of Biblical and Historical Texts* (Philadelphia: Trinity Press, 1990), especially the title essay.

32. E.g., Exum, *Fragmented Women*, 16f, 170f.

33. Rosemary Radford Ruether, *Sexism and God-Talk: Toward a Feminist Theology* (Boston: Beacon Press, 1983), 23f.

34. Carolyn De Swarte Gifford, "American Women and The Bible: The Nature of Woman as a Hermeneutical Issue," in *Feminist Perspectives on Biblical Scholarship*, ed. Adela Yarbro Collins (Chico, Calif.: Scholars Press, 1985), 17.

35. Esther Ticktin, "A Modest Beginning," in *The Jewish Woman: New Perspectives*, ed. Elizabeth Koltun (New York: Schocken, 1976), 131f; Judith Plaskow, *Standing Again At Sinai: Judaism From A Feminist Perspective* (San Francisco: Harper and Row, 1990), 65, 72f. This view was also championed by Trible, *God and the Rhetoric of Sexuality*, 12f.

36. Elizabeth Schüssler Fiorenza, *In Memory of Her: A Feminist Theological Reconstruction of Christian Origins* (New York: Crossroad, 1994), 32f.

37. Cf. Nancy Fuchs-Kreimer, "Feminism and Scriptural Interpretation: A Contemporary Jewish Critique," *Journal of Ecumenical Studies* 20, no. 4 (fall 1983): 540.

38. Fiorenza identifies five hermeneutical strategies, one of which favors "timeless" texts over those that speak to a particular historical situation.

39. On Rabbinic standards, see pages 353 and 391, n. 8.

40. Susan Brooks Thistlethwaite, "Every Two Minutes: Battered Women and Feminist Interpretation," in *Feminist Interpretation of the Bible*, Letty M. Russell (Philadelphia: Westminster Press, 1985), 98.

41. Rosemary Radford Ruether, "Feminist Interpretation: A Method of Correlation," in Russell, *Feminist Interpretation of the Bible*, 112.

42. On restrictions: Debra Orenstein, "Invisible Life Passages," in Orenstein, *Lifecycles 1*, 118.

43. The recent wave includes: Kates and Reimer, *Reading Ruth*; Alicia Suskin Ostriker, *The Nakedness of the Fathers: Biblical Visions and Revisions* (New Brunswick, N.J.: Rutgers University Press, 1994); Jewish women's writing in Christina Büchmann and Celina Spiegel, eds., *Out of the Garden: Women Writers on the Bible* (New York: Fawcett Columbine, 1994); Elyse Goldstein, *Feminist Analysis of Five Major Themes in the Torah* (Toronto: Lester, 1997); Ellen Frankel, *The Five Books of Miriam* (New York: Putnam, 1996), among others. Recent books without a specifically feminist focus also address the relationship between self and biblical text. E.g., Carol Ochs, *Song of The Self: Biblical Spirituality and Human Holiness* (Valley Forge, Penn.: Trinity Press, 1994); Norman J. Cohen, *Self, Struggle, and Change: Family Conflict Stories in Genesis and Their Healing Insights*

for Our Lives (Woodstock, Vt.: Jewish Lights, 1995); Peter Pitzele, *Our Fathers' Wells* (San Francisco: Harper Collins, 1995); Visotzky, *The Genesis of Ethics*.

44. "Introduction," *The Liberating Word: A Guide to Nonsexist Interpretation of the Bible*, ed. Letty M. Russell (Philadelphia: Westminster Press, 1976), 9.

45. Adelman, *Miriam's Well*.

46. Rabbis Norman Cohen, Elliot Dorff, Neil Gillman, Zalman Schacter, Burton Visotzky, and Arthur Waskow are among the many men who have shown leadership in this area.

47. There was a strain in the tradition that disallowed Torah study for women. However, if we believe that women should or even *may* study, then the logic of the tradition's interpretive process dictates that women *must* study.

48. Bateson, *Composing a Life*, 17.

49. The enlightenment of Torah interpretation is compared by the Rabbis to the many sparks given off by a hammer when it hits metal (BT *Shabbat* 88b based on Jeremiah 23:29; Cf. *Sanhedrin* 34a).

Claiming Textuality

1. Rashi envisions Huldah as a Sage, teaching oral law to her generation (Rashi on 2 Kings 22:14).

2. Medieval Northern Europe; Spanish aristocracy in the "Golden Age"; Renaissance Italy; and eighteenth-century Germany.

3. Bernadette Brooten, *Women Leaders in the Ancient Synagogue* (Chico, Calif.: Scholars Press, 1982); Ross Kraemer, "Jewish Women in the Diaspora World of Late Antiquity," in *Jewish Women in Historical Perspective*, ed. Judith Baskin (Detroit: Wayne State University Press, 1991), 43–67.

4. Nahum Glatzer, ed., *The Essential Philo* (New York: Schocken, 1971), 311–330.

5. Judith Abrams, *The Women of the Talmud* (Northvale, N.J.: Jason Aronson, 1995).

6. Rachel Adler, "The Virgin in the Brothel and Other Anomalies: Character and Context in the Legend of Beruriah," *Tikkun* 3, no. 6 (November/December 1988): 28–32; 102–105. Shoshana Kaminsky, "My Mother Told Me: Abaye's Mother as Paradigmatic Jewish Folk Healer," unpublished graduate paper, Reconstructionist Rabbinical College, 1992.

7. Judith Romney Wegner, *Chattel or Person? The Status of Women in the Mishnah* (New York: Oxford University Press, 1988).

8. Such as Rashi's daughters.

9. Emil Kraeling, *The Brooklyn Museum Aramaic Papyri* (New Haven, Conn.: Yale University Press, 1953); Bezalel Porten, *Archives from Elephantine* (Berkeley: University of California Press, 1968).

10. Naphtali Lewis, ed., *The Documents from the Bar Kokhba Period in the Cave of Letters* (Jerusalem: Judean Desert Studies, 1989).

11. Ross Kraemer, ed., *Maenids, Martyrs, Matrons, Monastics* (Philadelphia: Fortress Press, 1988); Michael Adler, "The Jewish Woman in Medieval England," in *The Jews of Medieval England* (London: Oxford University Press, 1939).

12. Solomon Goitein, *A Mediterranean Society* (series) (Berkeley: University of California Press, 1967–1983); Franz Kobler, *Letters of Jews Through the Ages* (Philadelphia: Jewish Publication Society, 1954).

13. Shoshanna Gershenzon and Jane Litman, "The Bloody 'Hands of Compassionate Women': Portrayals of Heroic Women in the Hebrew Crusade Chronicles," in *Crisis and Reaction: The Hero in Jewish History*, ed. Menachem Mor (Omaha, Nebr.: Creighton University Press, 1995).

14. Shoshana Pantel Zolty, *And All Your Children Shall Be Learned: Women and the Study of Torah in Jewish Law and History* (Northvale, N.J.: Jason Aronson, 1993), 145; Sondra Henry and Emily Taitz, *Written Out of History* (New York: Bloch Publishing, 1978), 115.

15. Ivan Marcus, "Mothers, Martyrs, and Moneymakers: Some Jewish Women in Medieval Europe," *Conservative Judaism* 38 (1986): 45.

16. Howard Adelman, "Italian Jewish Women," in Baskin, *Jewish Women in Historical Perspective*, 135–158.

17. Zolty, *And All Your Children*, 137–143.

18. James Mansfield Nichols, "The Arabic Verses of Qasmuna Bint Ismail Ibn Bagdalah," *International Journal of Middle East Studies* 13 (1981): 155–158.

19. E. Fleischer, "On Dunash ibn Labrat, His Wife and Son: New Light on the Beginnings of the Hebrew-Spanish School," *Jerusalem Studies in Hebrew Literature* 5 (1984): 189–202.

20. Zolty, *And All Your Children*, 152.

21. Solomon Goitein, *Jews and Arabs: Their Contacts Through the Ages* (New York: Schocken, 1955), 186.

22. Adelman, "Italian Jewish Women," 140; Kobler, *Letters of Jews*, 442–447.

23. Marvin Lowenthal, trans., *The Memoirs of Gluckel of Hameln* (New York: Schocken, 1977). Gluckel's male translators have abridged her writing, but Bertha Pappenheim, Gluckel's descendant and Jewish feminist leader in pre-Nazi Germany, made an unedited translation.

24. Moses Shulvass, *The Jews in the World of the Renaissance* (Chicago: E.J. Brill, 1973), 224–230.

25. Abraham Habermann, *Nashim Ivriyot*, quoted in Zolty, *And All Your Children*, 214.

26. Henry and Taitz, *Written Out of History*, 114–124.

27. Shmuel Niger, "Yiddish Literature and the Female Reader," in *Women of the Word: Jewish Women and Jewish Writing*, ed. Judith R. Baskin (Detroit: Wayne State University Press, 1994), 70–90.

28. Frieda Forman, Ethel Raicus, Sarah Silberstein Swarz, and Margie Wolfe, eds., *Found Treasures: Stories by Yiddish Women Writers* (Toronto: Second Story Press, 1994).

Introduction to Genesis

1. The Talmud says, "When is a woman suspected of an affair? When the women who spin by moonlight talk about her" (Mishnah *Sotah* 6:1).

2. In our world, men too must guard against revealing themselves.

3. From "Kathe Kollwitz," in *A Muriel Rukeyser Reader*, ed. Jan Heller Levi (W. W. Norton and Company: New York, 1994), 217.

4. *Elohei Shem* (Gen. 9:26); *El Elyon* (14:19); *Adonai*, God on High (14:22); *El Roi* (16:13); *Elohei Shamayim* (24:7); *El Shaddai* (28:1); *El Beth El* (31:13); *Pahad Yitzhak* (31:42).

5. Joshua 24 may describe this event.

6. The earliest Hebrews were not monotheists, but henotheists. They followed one tribal God, but did not deny the existence of other gods.

7. Phyllis Trible and others, following Rabbinic *midrash*, assert the original Adam was not male, but androgynous, and that God's surgery separated this androgynous human into male and female. Phyllis Trible, *God and the Rhetoric of Sexuality* (Philadelphia: Fortress, 1978).

8. Catholic doctrine posits that Adam and Eve were innocent and without sin until the incident of the fruit. At this point, sex and biological reproduction were introduced into the world. Every human born through this process carries original sin.

9. Many feminists have observed that when men deceive, it's considered clever, but when women do, it's manipulative.

10. Gen. 4:1; 16:11–12; 21:6; 25:22–27; 29:32–35; 30:5–13; 30:17–24; 35:18.

11. Michael Adler, "The Jewish Woman in Medieval England," in *The Jews of Medieval England* (London: Oxford University Press, 1939); Renee Levine Melammed, "Medieval and Early Modern Sephardi Women," in *Jewish Women in Historical Perspective*, ed. Judith Baskin (Detroit: Wayne State University Press, 1991), 116.

12. This custom may be from ancient Mesopotamia, and demonstrates a cultural conflict between Mesopotamian and emergent Hebrew social norms. See A.E. Speiser, *Genesis: Introduction, Translation, and Notes* (Garden City, N.Y.: Doubleday, 1964). A feminist reading is Savina Teubal, *Sarah the Priestess* (Athens, Ohio: Swallow Press, 1984).

"'For Life, God Sent Me'"

1. Wilstein Institute Lecture at the University of Judaism, Los Angeles, Calif., January 26, 1992.

2. Respectively, Ex. 20:8, 13:3; Deut. 7:18, 24:9, 8:18, 25:17, 8:2.

3. BT *Shabbat* 127a. Brevard Childs, *Memory and Tradition in Israel* (London: SCM Press, 1962), 75.

4. Ibid., 78. This approach can be linked midrashically to the wordings "Remember" (Ex. 20:8) and "Keep" (Deut. 5:12) the Sabbath.

5. The Sabbath is called a *memorial* to creation, a *remembrance* of the exodus, and a *sign* of the relationship between God and Israel.

6. Both the lessons of memory and the punishment of being forgotten are paradoxically upheld by the injunction: "Blot out the name of Amalek—do not forget" (Deut. 25:19; cf. Ex. 17:14).

7. See pages xxii and 369, n. 27.

8. E.g., Gen. 6:18, 19:15, 38:2, 39:7; Ex. 2:5; Num. 12:1, 16:27; Judges 11:34, 13:2, 14:1, 19:2, 24; 2 Samuel 20:16; 1 Kings 3:16.

9. See pages xxix–xxxix.

10. Most scholars agree that the shared root is derived from two different sources. *Contra,* Rachel Adler, "A Question of Boundaries: Toward a Jewish Feminist Theology of Self and Other," *Tikkun* 6, no. 3: 46. While I disagree with her linguistic conclusions, her language and larger argument are elegant. For an interesting overstatement of the connection between maleness and memory, see Michael Medved, "You Must Remember This: Jewish Men and Jewish Memory," *Sh'ma* 25, no. 486 (January 20, 1995/19 Shevat 5755): 3–4.

11. Sondra Henry and Emily Taitz, *Written Out of History: A Hidden Legacy of Jewish Women Revealed Through Their Writings and Letters* (New York: Bloch Publishing Company, 1978).

12. Cited in Lawrence L. Langer, *Admitting the Holocaust: Collected Essays* (New York: Oxford University Press, 1995), 14.

13. Yosef Hayim Yerushalmi, *Zakhor: Jewish History and Jewish Memory* (New York: Schocken Books, 1989), 10f, 94f. Dominick LaCapra, *Representing the Holocaust: History, Theory, Trauma* (Ithaca, N.Y.: Cornell University Press, 1994), 12.

14. Yerushalmi, *Zakhor,* 10f, 95. LaCapra strives for a "telling" of the past that stands the test of critical judgment (identified with history), as well as religious need (identified with collective memory).

15. The root *z.k.r* appears more often in the Joseph story than in any other Genesis narrative. "To remember" is both a theme and a *leitwort.*

16. Cf. Gen. 37:30, 42:36.

17. After BT *Sotah* 10b; Cf. Gen. *Rabbah* 85:12.

18. According to the *Zohar* (1 188a–b), Tamar acted out of deep knowledge and wisdom.

19. Phyllis Trible, *Texts of Terror: Literary Feminist Readings of Biblical Narratives* (Philadelphia: Fortress Press, 1978).

20. See pages 12–16; 17–18; 63; 64–66; 147–152.

21. Edmon Jabes, "The Key," in *Midrash and Literature,* ed. Geoffrey H. Hartman and Sanford Budick (New Haven, Conn.: Yale University Press, 1986), 356. Cf. Psalms 97:11; BT *Ta'anit* 8b.

22. Yerushalmi, *Zakhor,* 113.

23. Paula Hyman, "The Jewish Family: Looking for a Usable Past," in *On Being a Jewish Feminist: A Reader,* ed. Susannah Heschel (New York: Schocken, 1983), 19–26. Cf. the section "On Story: Creating a Usable History" in Deena Metzger, *Writing for Your Life: A Guide and Companion to the Inner Worlds* (San Francisco: HarperCollins, 1992), 73f.

24. A *midrash* on 50:20. *Lehahayot am-rav* can be translated "to save the lives of many people" (the plain-sense meaning in the biblical text) or "to revive a great nation."

25. Leonard Fein, *Where Are We?* (New York: Harper and Row, 1988), 58–75.

26. Feminist readers of the Bible have commonly employed a "hermeneutic of suspicion" against patriarchal bias. Biblicist Tamara Cohen Eskenazi has

suggested using a hermeneutic of *ḥesed* for the Book of Ruth. Talk at the Assembly of the Women Rabbis of Los Angeles, Encino, Calif., spring 1995.

A Light Returns to Sarah's Tent

1. See my "The Palace of Pearls," in *Gates to the New City*, ed. Howard Schwartz (New Jersey: Jason Aronson, 1991), 439–444.

2. Francis Brown, S. R. Driver, and Charles A. Briggs, eds., *A Hebrew and English Lexicon of the Old Testament*, 1st ed. (New York: Oxford University Press, 1979), 13–15.

3. This is in the tradition of previous generations of women. Chava Weissler, "The Traditional Piety of Ashkenazic Women," in *Jewish Spirituality from the Sixteenth-Century Revival to the Present*, ed. Arthur Green (New York: Crossroad, 1987).

4. Aryeh Kaplan, *Jewish Meditation* (New York: Schocken Books, 1985); Thich Nhat Hanh, *The Miracle of Mindfulness* (Boston: Beacon Press, 1987).

Returning to Zion

1. Aaron David Gordon, "An Open Letter to Joseph Chaim Brenner," *Selected Writings* (in Hebrew) (Jerusalem: Zionist Library, 1982) 196f.

At Home with God

1. In some families, children hide the *afikomen*; in others, they seek it.

2. The leaven found during *bedikat ḥametz* is burned the next morning.

3. Gershom Scholem, "Kabbalah," in *Encyclopedia Judaica*, vol. 10 (Jerusalem: Keter, 1972), 594–601.

4. Martin Buber, *Tales of the Hasidim: The Early Masters* (New York: Schocken, 1947), 97.

5. Cf. Martin Buber, *Tales of the Hasidim: The Later Masters* (New York: Schocken, 1948), 277.

Eve: A Model for All Partners

1. Other translations: "A helpmate" or "a help against him."

2. See David R. Freedman, "Woman, a Power Equal to Man: Translation of Woman as a 'Fit Helpmate' for Man Is Questioned," *Biblical Archaeological Review* 9, no. 1 (January/February 1993): 56–58.

3. E.g., Psalms 54:6, 119: 175, 121:1–2; 1 Chronicles 12:19; 2 Chronicles 18:31.

4. The prime example of when it does signify conflict is in Gen. *Rabbah* 17:3: "If a man is worthy, his spouse will support him, and if he is not worthy, she will be his opponent."

Re-Reading Genesis and Our Lives

1. For Ilana Lapid.

2. *Pirkei deRabbi Eliezer* 25; Gen. *Rabbah* 50; *Yalkut Shimoni, Vayyera*. Renita J. Weems, *Just a Sister Away: A Womanist Vision of Women's Relationships in the Bible* (San Diego: LuraMedia, 1988), 129–140; Merle Feld, "Lotswife," *Tikkun* 9, no. 5 (September/October 1994): 1.

Family
   1. This piece is for him, and for the children.

Seeking Women's Friendship
   1. Judith Plaskow, "The Coming of Lilith," in *Four Centuries of Jewish Spirituality*, ed. Ellen M. Umansky and Diane Ashton (Boston: Beacon Press, 1992), 215–216.
   2. Ellen M. Umansky, "Genesis 34," in Jane Sprague, ed., *Taking the Fruit: Modern Women's Tales of the Bible* (San Diego, Calif.: Woman's Institute for Continuing Jewish Education, 1989), 69–70.
   3. *Pirkei deRabbi Eliezer* 25; Gen. *Rabbah* 50:4, 51:5; Naḥmanides on Gen. 19:26; and *Yalkut Shimoni, Vayyera*. Renita J. Weems, *Just a Sister Away: A Womanist Vision of Women's Relationships in the Bible* (San Diego: LuraMedia, 1988), 129–140; Merle Feld, "Lotswife," *Tikkun* 9, no. 5 (September/October 1994): 1.
   4. J. Cheryl Exum, "Murder They Wrote: Ideology and the Manipulation of Female Presence in Biblical Narrative," in *The Pleasure of Her Text: Feminist Readings of Biblical and Historical Texts*, ed. Alice Bach (Philadelphia: Trinity, 1990), 45–67.

An Ethical Will
   1. A guide for writing one's own ethical will is included in Jack Reimer and Nathaniel Stampfer, eds., *So That Your Values Live On: Ethical Wills and How to Prepare Them* (Woodstock, Vt.: Jewish Lights, 1991).
   2. Coming of age ceremony.
   3. Day of Atonement

Introduction to Exodus

   1. On *continuity* between Genesis and Exodus: J. P. Fokkelman, "Exodus," in *The Literary Guide to the Bible*, eds. Robert Alter and Frank Kermode (Cambridge, Mass.: Harvard University Press, 1987), 56–65.
   2. Henrik Ibsen, *A Doll's House*, in *Eleven Plays by Henrik Ibsen* (New York: Modern Library, 1935), 3–92.
   3. Donald E. Gowan, *Theology in Exodus: Biblical Theology in the Form of a Commentary* (Louisville, Ky.: Westminster/John Knox, 1994), 169. Gowan divides Exodus into more than three parts, but he uses these terms.
   4. Horeb, where the bush burns, *is* Sinai. The revelations at Sinai and the bush are marked by fire (Ex. 3:2, 19:18). At the bush, God makes predictions and lays out what will remain as the enduring identities of the divine self, Moses, and the people Israel.
   5. Michael Walzer, *Exodus and Revolution* (New York: Basic Books, 1985).
   6. Arguably, women performed some limited sort of cultic service (Ex. 38:8), and held leadership roles earlier on. Drorah O'Donnell Setel, "Exodus," in *The Women's Bible Commentary*, eds. Carol A. Newsome and Sharon H. Ringe (Louisville, Ky: Westminster/John Knox Press, 1992), 34.

7. With subjugation came a degree of protection (Ex. 21:7f).

8. The listing in the Deuteronomic version is broken up differently, implying that wives constitute a category separate from property. Yet women remain unaddressed in Deuteronomy 5:18.

9. This is the "title text" of Judith Plaskow, *Standing Again at Sinai: Judaism From A Feminist Perspective* (New York: Harper and Row, 1990).

10. God's miraculous sensitivity to each listener at Sinai is demonstrated by divine modulation for pregnant women, who might not withstand a loud Voice (Ex. *Rabbah* 5:9). Cf. Ex. *Rabbah* 5:5. *Contra*, Ex. *Rabbah* 19:3, 46:3; BT *Shabbat* 87a. See also Rashi's comments on these verses. Women are *in*cluded in the Sinai revelation elsewhere in the Bible. See my introduction to Deuteronomy.

11. Thanks to Dr. Ed Greenstein for this formulation.

12. The ultimate message of Exodus is that God alone brought the Israelites out of Egypt. However, these women virtuously facilitate God's plan without orders to do so.

13. Placing blood on the doorposts to save sons evokes positive imagery of both birth and circumcision. Ex. 12:23; Ex. *Rabbah* 17:3; Setel, "Exodus," in Newsome and Ringe, *The Women's Bible Commentary*, 31.

14. God also apparently uses tools of dominance and oppression in relation to Pharaoh and the Egyptians. However, the *midrash* puts responsibility back on Pharaoh, who chose to harden his heart a few times before God began to harden it for him (Ex. *Rabbah* 13:3). God sent plagues by gradations (Ex. 9:19, Ex. *Rabbah* 12:2). Thus, it is traditionally understood that human stubbornness, not divine cruelty, necessitated and escalated suffering. At every stage, God offered chances for penitence (Ex. *Rabbah* 13:6). The punishment of an entire nation is traditionally justified because a) this will be a sign to all nations for all time of God's power and b) the entire Egyptian nation is held to blame. All Egyptians are understood to have complied with Pharaoh's command to "*all* his people" to kill every Israelite son (Ex. 1:22). Still, when the Israelites were saved and the Egyptians were drowning, God chastised the angels for singing (BT *Megillah* 10b; Ex. *Rabbah* 23:7).

15. Carolyn G. Heilbrun, *Writing a Woman's Life* (New York: Ballantine, 1988), 18. Cf. Letty Russell, *Household of Freedom: Authority in Feminist Theology* (Philadelphia: Westminster Press, 1987), 23ff.

16. Letty M. Russell, "Liberating the Word," in *Feminist Interpretation of the Bible*, ed. Letty M. Russell (Philadelphia: Westminster Press, 1985), 11–12. Cf. Mary Ann Tolbert, "Defining the Problem," in *The Bible and Feminist Hermeneutics*, ed. Mary Ann Tolbert (Atlanta, Ga.: Scholars Press, 1983), 120.

17. "Serving God as free people" is a key pun and ideological point in Exodus. The Israelites cannot be slaves (*avadim*—root '.b.d) to Pharoah because they must serve (*la'avod*—root '.b.d) God.

18. Click stories are tales of feminist epiphanies, realizations of why feminism is necessary and useful. *Lifecycles 1* included a selection of Jewish feminist click stories.

19. The example of *agunot* (women chained to dead marriages) was cited earlier. There is disagreement in the Conservative movement as to whether

women may serve as witnesses. Despite a few responsa to the contrary, Jewish law is still widely understood to prohibit homosexual acts.

20. Emma Goldman, "Woman Suffrage," in *Anarchism and Other Essays* (New York: Dover, 1969), 196f; Plaskow, *Standing Again At Sinai*, 65–74.

21. Rachel Adler, "Feminist Folktales of Justice: Robert Cover as a Resource for the Renewal of Halakhah," *Conservative Judaism* (spring 1993): 40–55.

22. Writing a *midrash* on that *midrash*, I would say that failure to choose a worthy covenant—despite witnessing theophany and revelation—is a kind of living death.

Fragments of an Old/New *Haggadah*

1. Many scholars attribute to Miriam the victory song that Moses leads. Frank Moore Cross, *Canaanite Myth and Hebrew Ethics* (Cambridge, Mass.: Harvard University Press, 1973), 125.

2. Anat and Ashera were dieties in the Canaanite pantheon, some of whose attributes were incorporated into ancient Israelite theology. Some of the oldest poems in the Bible are war songs associated with Miriam, Deborah (5:1–31), and Hannah (1 Samuel 2:1–10).

Critique and Transformation

1. Judith Plaskow, "The Jewish Feminist: Conflict in Identities," *The Jewish Woman: New Perspectives*, ed. Elizabeth Koltun (New York: Schocken, 1976), 3–10.

2. Judith Plaskow, "The Right Question is Theological," *On Being a Jewish Feminist: A Reader*, ed. Susannah Heschel (New York: Schocken, 1983), 223–33.

3. Elisabeth Schüssler Fiorenza, *In Memory of Her: A Feminist Theological Reconstruction of Christian Origins* (New York: Crossroad, 1983), 25.

Talmud Torah

1. Leonard Gordon has noted a correlation between Talmudic values and Carol Gilligan's characterization of women's moral decision-making. "Toward a Gender-Inclusive Account of *Halakhah*," in *Gender and Judaism: The Transformation of Tradition*, ed. T.M. Rudavsky (New York: New York University Press, 1995), 4f. Cf. Debra Orenstein, "Judaism and Feminism: Confluence and Marginality," in *Comment and Analysis* 3, no. 1 (May 1992), 1–4.

2. Shoshana Lepon, *No Greater Treasure: Stories of Extraordinary Women Drawn from the Talmud and Mishnah* (Southfield, Mich.: Targum Press, 1990); Devora Steinmetz, "A Portrait of Miriam in Rabbinic Midrash," *Prooftexts* 8 (1988): 35–65; Shumalit Valler, *Women and Womanhood in the Stories of the Babylonian Talmud* (in Hebrew) (Tel Aviv: Ha Kibuts ha me'uhad, 1993).

3. Rachel Adler, "The Virgin in the Brothel and Other Anomalies: Character and Context in the Legend of Beruriah," *Tikkun* 3, no. 6 (1992): 28–32, 115–121; Debra Orenstein's analysis of the Dinah and Samson stories in, respectively, Israel Mowshowitz and Debra Orenstein, *From Generation to Generation* (New York: New York Board of Rabbis, 1992), 32–38, and "Feminist Critique of the Rabbinical School Curriculum" (paper presented to the faculty of the University of Judaism, Los Angeles, Calif., March 1991).

4. One such "modern midrash" is "Applesource." Judith Plaskow, "The Jewish Feminist," in *The Jewish Woman*, ed. Elizabeth Koltun (New York: Schocken, 1976), 30–32.

5. A similar version of this story is found in Exodus *Rabbah* 23:8.

6. Other symbols of Passover also "cut both ways." *Maror* (bitter herbs) represents the bitterness of our experience in Egypt. But Rava explains that *ḥasa* (romaine lettuce) can be used for *maror*, since *maror* is a sign of God's compassion (*ḥas* in Aramaic) for Israel which led to our liberation (BT *Pesaḥim* 39a).

In God's Shadow

1. Ex. 20:9, 31:15, 34:21, 35:2; Deut. 5:13.

2. Studs Terkel, *Working* (New York: Pantheon Books, 1972), xxix.

3. Ex. 20:8–11, Deut. 5:12–15, Ex. 12:2, Mishnah *Shabbat* 7:2.

4. All biblical translations are taken from *Tanakh: The Holy Scriptures* (Philadelphia: The Jewish Publication Society, 1988).

5. For this and other commentaries on the verse: Nehama Leibowitz, *Studies in Bereshit (Genesis)*, trans. Aryeh Newman (Jerusalem: Hemed Press, 1976), 4–6.

6. *Mishnah Shabbat* 7:2 details 39 categories of labor used to build the tabernacle and forbidden on the Sabbath. It is unclear to what extent the Rabbis were creating or systematizing restrictions vs. justifying and authenticating them.

7. Ex. 35:22, 25, 26–29; 36:6; 38:8. In contrast, the *midrash* portrays women refusing to donate their rings to the building of the golden calf (*Pirkei Derabbi Eliezer* 45). Apparently, the women were able to discern the relative value of both projects.

8. A similar *midrash* (Mishnah *Sanhedrin* 4:5) specifies the creation of a single ancestor, so that no one may say to another, "My ancestors are superior to yours." Thus, in relation to equality as well as work, there is a midrashic link between creation and the *mishkan*.

9. Rashi on Ex. 33:11; *Tanḥuma Terumah* 8.

10. Phyllis Trible, "Eve and Adam: Genesis 2–3 Reread," in *Womanspirit Rising: A Feminist Reader in Religion*, ed. Carol P. Christ and Judith Plaskow (New York: Harper Collins, 1992), 80–81.

11. For finding meaning in paid work: Jeffrey K. Salkin, *Being God's Partner: How to Find the Hidden Link Between Spirituality and Your Work* (Woodstock, Vt.: Jewish Lights Publishing, 1994).

12. Martin Buber, *Tales of the Hasidim, the Early Masters.* (New York: Schocken Books, 1947), 68–69.

Creativity

1. Some sources define *taḥash* as "blue-processed skins...worked in such a manner as to come out dark and waterproof." Others identify it as a an animal—badger, wild ram, giraffe, seal, or narwal. Aryeh Kaplan, *The Living Torah: The Five Books of Moses and the Haftorot* (New York: Maznaim, 1981), 383. See Ezekiel 16:10.

Themes of Leviticus

1. Tillie Olsen, "I Stand Here Ironing," in *America and I: Short Stories by American Jewish Women Writers*, ed. Joyce Antler (Boston: Beacon Press, 1990), 156–164.

2. Harold Bloom, *The Book of J* (New York: Grove Weidenfeld, 1990).

3. Chava Weissler, "Prayers in Yiddish and the Religious World of Ashkenazic Women," in *Jewish Women in Historical Perspective*, ed. Judith Baskin (Detroit: Wayne State University Press, 1991).

4. Mary Douglas, *Purity and Danger: An Analysis of the Concepts of Pollution and Taboo* (London: Routledge and Kegan Paul, 1966); Mircea Eliade, *The Sacred and the Profane* (New York: Harcourt, Brace and Co., 1959).

5. Judith Romney Wegner, *Chattel or Person? The Status of Women in the Mishnah* (New York: Oxford University Press, 1988).

6. Carol Meyers, *Discovering Eve: Ancient Israelite Women in Context* (New York: Oxford University Press, 1988).

7. Obadiah Sforno's (c.1470–c.1550) commentary on Lev. 14.

8. Sherry Ortner, "Is Female to Male as Nature is to Culture?" in *Woman, Culture and Society*, ed. Michelle Rosaldo and Louise Lamphere (Stanford, Calif.: Stanford University Press, 1973).

Shelomit bat Divri

1. Adrienne Rich, *Of Woman Born: Motherhood as Experience and Institution* (New York: W.W. Norton and Company, 1986), 277.

2. Further information on Eve, Sarah, Miriam, Deborah, Jael, Beruriah, Sarah the Yemenite, Dahiyah Kahinah, and Esther Kiera can be found in Sondra Henry and Emily Taitz, *Written Out of History: A Hidden Legacy of Jewish Women Revealed Through Their Writings and Letters* (New York: Bloch Publishing House, 1978). Further information on Cecilia Bobrowskaya, Anna Kuliscioff, Felicia Sheftel, Sofya Ginsburg, Fanny Kaplan, Rosa Luxemburg, Esther Frumkin, Pessia Abramson, Rosa Manus, Emma Goldman, and Kadia Molodowsky can be found in Naomi Shepherd, *A Price Below Rubies: Jewish Women as Rebels and Radicals* (Cambridge, Mass.: Harvard University Press, 1993). —Eds.

The Power of Words

1. See pages 141–142.

2. *Kol Nidre* refers to vows not yet made. Some Jews believed it was not in keeping in the spirit of repentance to assume future error. Therefore, several prayer books translate instead: "May all vows taken in the *past* year be null and void."

3. Num. 6:1–21. Israelites attained sacredness through vows to abstain from liquor, haircuts, and contact with human remains.

The Altared Table

1. Thanks to the Jewish Feminist Research Network, Ruth Askren, Shoshanna Gershenzon, Judith Glass, Jane Litman, Debra Orenstein, Maeera Schreiber, Ruth Sohn, and Marvin Sweeney.

2. Two exceptions: Levitical laws stipulated a confession with the atonement sacrifice, and the presentation of first fruits (Deut. 26) required a recitation of Israel's history.

3. Prohibitions issued after the Flood (Gen. 9:1–4) applied to all; later restrictions applied to Israelites alone. Outside the domain of diet, a number of laws prohibit cruelty to animals (e.g., Ex. 23:12; Deut. 22:10, 25:4). Biblical resistance to vegetarianism as an ideal is clear in the time limit set on Nazarite vows of abstinence from wine and meat (Num. 6). These ascetic tendencies were further discouraged by the Rabbis. On vegetarianism in Judaism, see Louis A. Berman, *Vegetarianism and the Jewish Tradition* (New York: Ktav, 1982); Richard H. Schwartz, *Judaism and Vegetarianism* (Marblehead, Mass.: Micah Press, 1988).

4. Phyllis Trible, *Texts of Terror: Literary-Feminist Readings of Biblical Narratives* (Philadelphia: Fortress, 1984), 93–115.

5. This episode, commonly called the "binding of Isaac," is more aptly titled "the sacrifice of Sarah," for she is nowhere a participant in the episode, and like the substituted ram, she dies at the end.

6. Some prophets who criticized sacrifice anticipated a purified sacrificial system in the future (Jeremiah 33:18).

7. I have been rebuked for my vegetarianism by Jews who argue that it impinges on the joy of Sabbath (meat) meals or denies animal life the sanctification of ritualized slaughter.

8. On table and altar, see Reuven Kimmelman, "Judaism and Lay Ministry," in *National Institute of Campus Ministries* 2 (1980): 46–48.

9. Bernadette J. Brooten, *Women Leaders in the Ancient Synagogue* (Chico: Scholars Press, 1982). Shaye J.D. Cohen, "The Origins of the Matrilineal Principle in Rabbinic Law," *AJS Review* 10, no. 1 (spring 1985).

10. Illuminated manuscripts depict women in all areas of food preparation.

11. Chava Weissler, "The Traditional Piety of Ashkenazic Women," in *Jewish Spirituality: From the Sixteenth Century Revival to the Present*, ed. Arthur Green (New York: Crossroad Publishing Company, 1987), 245–275.

12. We cannot assume that women's power and responsibility in the domain of food always worked to their benefit or gave them power. Behavior promoted by women may be oppressive to themselves, harmful to others, and a distraction from more serious matters.

13. Kim Chernin, *The Hungry Self: Women, Eating, and Identity* (New York: Times Books, 1985). Leslea Newman, ed., *Eating Our Hearts Out: Personal Accounts of Women's Relationship to Food* (Freedom, Calif.: Crossing Press, 1993).

Shattered and Whole
1. A creative translation appears on page 173.

Afterbirth
1. Quoted in Peter Berger and Brigitte Berger, *Sociology: A Biographical Approach* (New York: Basic Books, 1972).

2. Mary Douglas, *Purity and Danger* (New York: Routledge, 1966), 50–52.

3. Catherine Keller, *From A Broken Web* (Boston: Beacon Press, 1986), passim.

4. Marcia Falk, *The Book of Blessings: New Jewish Prayers for Daily Life, The Sabbath, and the New Moon Festival* (San Francisco: HarperCollins, 1996).

5. Thanks to Debra Orenstein, Shoshanna Gershenson, and Jane Litman for their insights.

When the Siren Stops Singing
1. Thanks to Maeera Shreiber, Debra Orenstein, Jackie Ellenson, Sara Beck, and particularly S. E. Barnet.

2. Now called Brotherhood/Sisterhood Camp, run by the National Conference (formerly called the National Conference of Christians and Jews).

3. Judaism provided somewhat more information to men.

4. Although the "siren" is generally a Greek mythic creature, she is not alien to Jewish thought. See Rashi's commentary on BT *Bekorot* 8a.

5. Married women were entitled to sex for procreativity and security, rather than sexual fulfillment in itself. "What secures the woman's position in her home? Bearing children" (Gen. *Rabbah* 71:5).

6. Naomi Seidman, "Carnal Knowledge," *Jewish Social Studies* 1, no. 1 (fall 1994): 123.

7. Elliot Wolfson, "On Becoming Female: Crossing the Gender Boundaries in Kabbalistic Ritual and Myth," in *Gender and Judaism*, ed. T. M. Rudavsky (New York: New York University Press, 1995), 214–218.

8. Although the cultural understanding of sexuality was often *symbolic*, women were *in actuality* required to wear restrictive clothing.

9. Norman Lamm, *Hedge of Roses*, 4th ed. (New York: Philip Feldheim, 1972). Being the object of that level of symbolic and/or actual sexual desire might well be alienating. One formerly Orthodox woman told me, "Having sex after I returned from the *mikveh* was often a very lonely affair."

10. Many of these women suffered as a result of their sexual daring. See Isaac Metzker, ed., *A Bintel Brief: Sixty Years of Letters from the Lower East Side to the Jewish Daily Forward* (Garden City, N.Y.: Doubleday, 1971), 38–40, 45–47, 49–51, 103–105.

11. The Conservative Movement's current advocacy of early marriage and child-bearing in lieu of pre-marital sex is a case in point.

12. Arthur Green, "A Contemporary Approach to Jewish Sexuality," in *The Second Jewish Catalog* (Philadelphia: Jewish Publication Society, 1976), 96–99.

13. Riv-Ellen Prell, "Why Jewish Princesses Don't Sweat: Desire and Consumption in Postwar American Jewish Culture," in *People of the Body: Jews*

and Judaism from an Embodied Perspective, ed. Howard Eilberg-Schwartz (New York: State University of New York Press, 1992).

14. These include, but are not limited to, cross-dressers, transvestites, people taking hormones to change gender, and people who surgically alter their sexual organs.

15. Historically, sexuality has been categorized in terms of sexual relationships: E.g., a woman with a man was defined as heterosexual. Recently, sexual theorists have begun to speak of sexuality as a form of identity, a part of the individual, regardless of relationship status. I prefer to define sexuality in terms of personal, fluid, phenomenological feelings that change over the course of a lifetime.

16. These sexual activities involve the exchange of body fluids.

"In Your Blood, Live"

1. The other two are lighting Sabbath candles and "taking ḥallah" (setting aside dough for ritual purposes).

2. Rachel Adler, "Tum'ah and Taharah—Mikveh," in *The Jewish Catalogue*, eds. Michael Strassfeld, Sharon Strassfeld, and Richard Siegal (New York: Jewish Publication Society, 1972), 167–71; reprinted as "Tum'ah and Taharah: Ends and Beginnings" in *Response* 18 (summer 1973): 117–27, and in *The Jewish Woman*, ed. Elizabeth Koltun (New York: Schocken Press, 1976), 63–71.

3. Lev. 15:19–33; 18:19; 20:18. These prohibitions fall both inside and outside the confines of Lev. 17–26, which biblical critics designate "the Holiness Code" and regard as a separate law book.

4. For a thoughtful discussion of the pitfalls in this position, see Martha Minow, *Making All the Difference* (Ithaca, N.Y.: Cornell University Press, 1990).

5. Jacob Neusner, *The Idea of Purity in Ancient Judaism* (Leiden, Netherlands: E.J. Brill, 1973).

6. A traditional source for this view is BT *Niddah* 31b. Its most noted modern promulgator is Norman Lamm, *A Hedge of Roses*, 4th ed. (New York: Philip Feldheim, 1972).

7. I discuss this point more extensively in Rachel Adler, "I've Had Nothing Yet, So I Can't Take More," *Moment* 8 (September 1983): 22–26.

8. Mary Douglas, *Purity and Danger* (London: Routledge and Kegan Paul, 1966).

9. Mircea Eliade, *The Sacred and the Profane*, trans. Willard Trask (New York: Harcourt, Brace and World, 1959), 68–113, 129–35.

10. Maimonides, *Mishneh Torah, 'Isurei Bi'ah* 22:1–21.

11. Exclusion of menstruants from access to sancta is a matter of folk piety rather than law. See Shaye J. D. Cohen, "Purity and Piety: The Separation of Menstruants from the Sancta," in *Daughters of the King: Women and the Synagogue*, eds. Susan Grossman and Rivka Haut (Philadelphia: Jewish Publication Society, 1991).

12. Lamentations 1:8–9; Ezekiel 7:19, 36:17–18; Zachariah 13:1; 2 Chronicles 29:5.

13. Howard Eilberg-Schwartz, *The Savage in Judaism* (Bloomington: University of Indiana Press, 1990), 177–194.

14. See, for example: Elyse M. Goldstein, "Take Back the Waters," *Lilith* 15 (summer 1986/5746): 15–16; Susan Schnur, "Women Rabbis on Miscarriage," *Lilith* 16 (fall 1991): 3; Rebecca Alpert, "Our Lives Are the Text: Exploring Jewish Women's Rituals," *Bridges* 2 (spring 1991): 68–69.

15. Ezekiel 16:6.

Introduction to Numbers

1. Dennis T. Olson, *The Death of the Old and the Birth of the New* (Chico, Calif.: Scholars Press, 1985), cited in Everett Fox, ed. and trans., *The Five Books of Moses* (New York: Schocken, 1995), 648.

2. This deficit is the source of the title for a book of Jewish women's writings, Melanie Kaye/Kantrowitz and Irena Klepfisz, eds., *The Tribe of Dinah* (Boston: Beacon Press, 1989).

3. Mary Catherine Bateson, *Composing a Life* (New York: Atlantic Monthly Press, 1988), 13.

4. There is much debate about the practical and moral implications of this mysterious ritual. Debra maintains that *sotah* (ordeal of bitter waters to test a wife's fidelity), while clearly demeaning and reflective of women's inferior social status, was not entirely bad for women. As ritual "ordeals" go, it was certainly preferable to medieval witch tests in which a woman was bound and thrown into a body of water and, if she floated, considered guilty. The Bible frames the details of the ritual with the repeated statement that the accused woman may be innocent (Num. 5:14, 28–30). As *sotah* is described, an innocent woman would pass the test of the bitter water unscathed (5:19). The *midrash*, following the biblical text, emphasizes that a woman who was not guilty of adultery could weather the "bitter waters" without any ill effect. It is possible to imagine that the waters had no biological effect at all, but were a psychological test of the woman's own sense of guilt or innocence. In the case of innocence, the test was also a religiously sanctioned means of silencing her husband's unfounded accusation. He would not be punished (5:31), but he would also not be believed.

Jane considers this an apologetic and argues that the ritual of *sotah* represents a downturn in women's status and protection. In biblical society, women were generally protected by their clan—the fathers, brothers, sons, and cousins who would avenge their murder, and thus serve as a fairly strong deterrent against extreme domestic violence. (Witness the revenge for the rape of Dinah in Gen. 34.) The *sotah* ritual actually deprives kin of the right of revenge, and therefore makes women more subject to the violence of jealous husbands. It replaces a woman's personally invested protectors with a supposedly "objective" institutionalized bureaucracy similar to contemporary courts. These often fail to offer meaningful protection to women who are abused, stalked, or murdered by irrational husbands. The objectivity of the priest may well be called into question by the concluding statement about this ritual, "The man shall be clear of guilt, but the woman shall suffer for her guilt" (Num. 5:31).

5. Mary Daly has made the parallel argument: When God is male, men are deified. Mary Daly, *Beyond God the Father: Toward a Philosophy of Women's Liberation* (Boston: Beacon Press, 1985).

6. Dr. Alice Shalvi views Tzelofeḥad's daughters as role models, and takes up their story in her essay "Women, Leadership, *and Tikkun Olam*" in the Deuteronomy chapter. In this chapter, Dr. Ora Horn Prouser discusses the daughters in terms of transition and community.

Reclaiming the Fragments

1. Paloma Díaz-Mas, *Sephardim: The Jews from Spain,* trans. George K. Zucker (Chicago: The University of Chicago Press, 1992), 38, 52–3.

2. Sidney Goldstein, "Profile of American Jewry: Insights from the 1990 National Jewish Population Survey," *American Jewish Year Book: 1992*, David Singer, ed., Ruth R. Seldin, exec. ed. (New York/Philadelphia: American Jewish Committee and Jewish Publication Society, 1992), 138–9. Steven M. Cohen, *American Assimilation or Jewish Revival?* (Bloomington: Indiana University Press, 1988), Table 7-1, 100. Of the Jews Cohen terms "affiliated," only between 35 and 49 percent are members of synagogues or other Jewish organizations. Rates of non-affiliation are highest among those without children. Steven M. Cohen, "Alternative Families in the Jewish Community" (New York: American Jewish Committee, 1989), 10–11, 14-1.

3. Martha Ackelsberg, "Families and the Jewish Community," especially 16–18; "Redefining Family: Models for a Jewish Future," in *Twice Blessed*, eds. Christie Balka and Andy Rose (Boston: Beacon Press, 1989), 107–17; and "Jewish Family Ethics in a Post-Halakhic Age," in *Imagining the Jewish Future: Essays and Responses*, ed. David A. Teutsch (Albany: SUNY Press, 1992), 149–164.

Images of the Self in Moral Action and Community

1. Alfred Jules Ayer, *Language, Truth and Logic* (New York: Dover, 1952), cover.

2. Ayer, *Language, Truth, and Logic,* 118–119.

3. Lawrence Kohlberg and Thomas Lickuna, *The Stages of Ethical Development* (San Francisco: Harper, 1986).

4. E.g., Carol Gilligan, *In a Different Voice* (Cambridge: Harvard University Press, 1982); Jean Baker Miller, *Toward a New Psychology of Women* (Boston: Beacon, 1986); Catherine Keller, *From a Broken Web: Separation, Sexism, and Self* (Boston: Beacon, 1988). *Contra* Elizabeth Spelman, *Inessential Woman* (Boston: Beacon Press, 1988).

5. Nancy Chodorow, *The Reproduction of Mothering: Psychoanalysis and the Sociology of Gender* (Los Angeles: University of California Press, 1978), 110.

6. Sandra Bartky, *Femininity and Domination: Studies in the Phenomenology of Oppression* (New York: Routledge Press, 1990).

7. M. Brinton Lykes, "Gender and Individualistic Notions vs. Collectivist Notions About the Self," in *Gender and Personality*, eds. Abigail Stewart and M. Brinton Lykes (Durham, N.C.: Duke University Press, 1985).

8. K.J. Gergen, "The Social Constructivist Movement in Modern Psychology," in *American Psychologist* 40: 266–275.

9. *Mishneh Torah, Mattanot La'aniyyim*, 10:7–12.

10. According to Judah Goldin, *gemilut ḥasadim* was *any* fulfillment of a divine command, that is a *mitzvah*, until the time of Shimon Hatzaddik. Goldin believes the transformation of *gemilut ḥasadim* into acts of lovingkindness was Shimon's great religious innovation. Judah Goldin, *Studies in Midrash and Related Literature* (New York: Jewish Publication Society, 1988), 28.

11. L.I. Rabinowitz, "Gemilut Hasadim," in *Encyclopedia Judaica*, vol. 10 (Jerusalem: Keter, 1972), 376.

12. See Judith Plaskow, *Standing Again at Sinai* (San Francisco: Harper and Row, 1990), 156ff.

13. See Nancy Fuchs-Kreimer, "Holiness, Justice, and the Rabbinate," *Cross Currents* (summer 1992): 68–83.

14. Rachel Adler, "A Question of Boundaries: Toward a Jewish Feminist Theology of Self and Other," *Tikkun* 6, no. 3 (May/June 1991): 44.

15. Robert Jay Lifton, *The Future of Immortality and Other Essays for a Nuclear Age* (New York: Basic Books, 1987), 133–135. *Midrash* also teaches that the world was created through *ḥesed* (*Avot Derabbi Natan* 4:5).

16. Rabban Shimon ben Gamliel's set of three pillars that uphold the world includes *din* (strict justice), and not *gemilut ḥasadim* (Mishnah *Avot* 1:18).

Living in Transition
1. In the Bible, wars are not won by the stronger forces, but, rather, by God. Spying runs counter to that theological posture. In Numbers, the spies seem to do a good job of learning about the land, but their message is not at all in keeping with God's plan. In Joshua 2 the "spies" sent to Jericho engage in no actual espionage but return with the proper message. It is possible that the whole endeavor of spying reflects a lack of faith in God.

Introduction to Deuteronomy

1. See Deut. 17:18.

2. The root *sh.m.'* (hear, obey) is a *leitwort* throughout Deuteronomy, where hearing is believing (4:9–6:4). In Exodus, *r.'.h*—visual cues, signs, and wonders—predominate. Of course, as Moshe Greenberg has noted, Exodus can be a loud book—full of the groaning of slaves, the clatter of chariots, the singing of praises, and the sounding of horns.

3. See page 378, n. 18.

4. 3:12–20, 10:9, 15:3f, 17:15f.

5. According to conventional understanding, Deuteronomy was shaped into its (nearly) final form upon or shortly after the conquest of Jerusalem in 586

BCE. Stark predictions of disobedience leading to suffering, exile, and death are actually retrospective attempts to understand the people's misfortunes. Admonitions not to fear (1:29, 3:2, 22, 7:18f) were much needed, as were assurances of the persistence and distinction of the covenant. Times were unstable, and continuity was in question.

6. On love and awe: 10:12f; on gracious acts: 5:15, 7:19, 8:4; on holiness: 7:6, 28:9; on our own benefit: 6:2ff, 8:1, 32:47. On meaning and intent: R. E. Clements, *God's Chosen People: A Theological Interpretation of the Book of Deuteronomy* (Valley Forge, Pa.: Judson Press, 1968), 12f, 106f.

7. Moshe Weinfeld, *Deuteronomy and the Deuteronomic School* (Oxford: Clarendon Press, 1972), 282ff.

8. This image also fits subsequent developments in Jewish law, including the dialogical nature of the Talmud.

9. Clements, *God's Chosen People*, 15. Horeb is the Deuteronomic name for Sinai.

10. On translating from "male" to "female": Patrocinio P. Schweickart, "Reading Ourselves: Toward a Feminist Theory of Reading," in *Gender and Reading: Essays on Readers, Texts, and Contexts*, ed. Elizabeth A. Flynn and Patrocinio P. Schweickart (Baltimore: Johns Hopkins, 1986), 40ff.

11. 1:1–5; 2:20–23; 3:14; 4:41–5:1; 27:1f; 31:1, 7–10, 14f, 22; 32:44–45; 33:1f; 34.

12. Some say this prioritizes the narrator's generation. Robert Polzin, *Moses and the Deuteronomist: A Literary Study of the Deuteronomic History* (New York: Seabury Press, 1980).

13. See endnote 7.

14. Cf. *Sifrei Ekev* 49 on Ex. 34:6.

15. Carol Gilligan, *In a Different Voice* (Cambridge, Mass.: Harvard University Press, 1982); Nel Noddings, *Caring: A Feminist Approach to Ethics and Moral Education* (Berkeley: University of California Press, 1984); Rita C. Manning, *Speaking from the Heart: A Feminist Perspective on Ethics* (Lanham, Md.: Rowman and Littlefield, 1992).

16. On being special: Deut. 4:7–8, 19–20, 32f; 7:6–8; 10:15; 14:2. On being like others: Deut. 2:5, 9, 19; 8:20.

17. The question also arises: How does one interact with a contrary force one wishes to eliminate—be it idol worship or sexism? Deuteronomy takes an uncompromising and violent approach. In this chapter, Rabbis Shohama Wiener and Rabbi Emily Feigenson favor building up a new model, rather than tearing down an insufficient one.

18. See endnote 15.

19. Some have rejected the concept of chosen-ness altogether, arguing that distinction inevitably devolves into a hierarchy.

Another Mountain, Another Reading

1. After Ex. 32:7.

2. Aaron, Moses, and Miriam. See Num. 26:59, Micah 6:4, 1 Chronicles 5:29, BT *Ta'anit* 9a.

3. Ex. 32:19, Deut. 9:17.
4. Deut. 31:6, 7, 23; Joshua 1:6f; 1 Chronicles 22:13, 28:20.
5. Gen. 1:1

Women, Leadership, and *Tikkun Olam*

1. The sisters were the subject of a valedictory address by Rabbi Na'amah Kelman, the first woman ordained in Israel.

2. Theirs may be a hollow victory. At the close of Numbers, a revision of the judgement reiterates woman's legal subjugation to the male collective by ruling that she must marry—and her property must remain—within her father's tribe.

3. Moses may also be contrasted with Yitro and Betzalel, both of whom advocate a more decentralized and cooperative mode of leadership (Ex. 18:17–26, 36:1f).

4. *In a Different Voice* (Cambridge, Mass.: Harvard University Press, 1982). Similarly, Nel Noddings, Caring (Berkeley: University of California Press, 1984).

5. Elizabeth Spelman, *Inessential Woman* (Boston: Beacon Press, 1988).

6. Judy Chicago, *The Dinner Party* (New York: Anchor Books, 1979).

Women and Leadership

1. See Sherry Ortner, "Is Female to Male, as Nature Is to Culture?" in *Women, Culture, and Society*, eds. Michelle Rosaldo and Louise Lamphere (Stanford, Calif.: Stanford University Press, 1973).

2. See Carol Christ, "Why Women Need the Goddess: Phenomenological, Psychological, and Political Reflections," in *The Politics of Women's Spirituality*, ed. Charlene Spretnak (New York: Anchor Books, 1982).

3. Pauline Wengeroff (b. 1833) likewise wrote about "radical" men: "They preached freedom, equality, fraternity in public, but at home they were despots." "Memoirs of a Grandmother," in *The Golden Tradition: Jewish Life and Thought in Eastern Europe*, ed. Lucy S. Dawidowicz (New York: Holt, Rinehart and Winston, 1967), 164.

Practical Realities of Religious Leadership

1. See Carol Gilligan, *In a Different Voice* (Cambridge, Mass.: Harvard University Press, 1982).

2. Laura Geller, "From Equality to Transformation: The Challenge of Women's Rabbinic Leadership," in *Gender and Judaism: The Transformation of Tradition*, ed. T.M. Rudavsky (New York: New York University Press, 1995), 251.

Love Is the Answer

1. As far as I know, I am the first woman to head a seminary ordaining rabbis and cantors. However, there are historical precedents: Asenath Barazani was called *tanna'it* ([female] Rabbinic teacher) and headed a major *yeshivah* (academy of Jewish learning) in seventeenth-century Kurdistan. Yona Sabar, *The Folk Literature of Kurdistani Jews* (New Haven, Conn.: Yale University Press, 1982), 108–109.

2. See Rabbi Zalman Schachter-Shalomi, *Paradigm Shift* (Northvale, N.J.: Jason Aronson, 1993), especially 146, 195–197. However, many have argued that traditional *kabbalah* re-enforces sex-role stereotypes, and keeps the male in the dominant position. See E.R. Wolfson, "Woman—The Feminine as Other in Theosophic *Kabbalah*: Some Philosophical Observations on the Divine Androgyne," in *The Other in Jewish Thought and History*, ed. Robert L. Cohn and Lawrence J. Silberstein (New York: NYU Press, 1994).

3. For a traditional and fuller explanation of *kabbalah*, see the late Aryeh Kaplan's book, *Inner Space* (Jerusalem: Moznaim Publishing Corp., 1991).

4. The definitions offered are my interpretation of kabbalistic symbology, not translations. There are many other interpretations of the ten *sefirot*. E.g., Shoshana Devorah, "Praying the Amidah: Images and Reflections," in *Worlds of Jewish Prayer*, eds. Shohama Wiener and Jonathan Omer-man (Northvale, N J : Jason Aronson, 1993).

5. Many esteemed and learned rabbis had heavenly mentors, including Joseph Karo. See Louis Jacobs, *Jewish Mystical Testimonies* (New York: Schocken Books, 1977).

6. See Miriam Adahan, *Living with Difficult People (Including Yourself)* (Jerusalem: Feldheim Publishers, 1991).

Paradoxes of Authority

1. Hannah prayed to God by silently mouthing her words.

2. E.g., Deut. *Rabbah* 6:11. We need to ask what texts like these say about the men who wrote them, rather than interpreting them as instructive portrayals of women.

3. Moshe Weinfeld, "Deuteronomy," in *Encyclopedia Judaica*, vol. 5 (Jerusalem: Keter, 1972), 1580–1581.

4. David Roskies, "A Brief Position Paper on the Ordination of Women," in *The Ordination of Women as Rabbis: Studies and Responsa*, ed. Simon Greenberg (New York: The Jewish Theological Seminary, 1988), 124.

5. Judith Plaskow, "It is Not in Heaven: Feminism and Religious Authority," *Tikkun* 5, no. 2 (March/April 1990): 39.

Leynen

1. Though there is no law prohibiting women from leyning in a co-ed service, Orthodox and a few Conservative synagogues disallow it because: (a) a woman's voice distracts a man from his prayers and/or (b) such an act would detract from the honor of the community—people would think that women were chanting because there were no men up to the task! (Mishnah *Berurah* 75:17, *Shulḥan Arukh, Orekh Ḥayyim* 75:3, 282:3; BT *Megillah* 23a).

Justice

1. Herbert R. Lottman, *Albert Camus: A Biography*, (Garden City, N.Y.: Doubleday, 1979).

2. William Safire, "Bad Year for Women," *New York Times* 140 (Dec. 20, 1990): A23(N).

Re-visioning Jewish Education

1. *Banekha* can be translated as "your sons" or "your children." Some might argue on the basis of a few Talmudic texts that girls' education was valued. For both viewpoints, see Mishnah *Sotah* 3:4. The compromise was to teach girls Bible and laws directly relevant to them, but not the Mishnah and Talmud. The end result is clearly a message of exclusion, or, at best, vicarious inclusion through husbands and sons (BT *Berakhot* 17a).

2. In the Rabbinic era, the efficacy of study was measured not merely by one's ability to summarize, analyze, etc., but by the impact of study on one's actions (BT *Kiddushin* 40b).

3. E.g., BT *Berakhot* 62a. Talmud study was and is generally undertaken in pairs, though the primary goal of such partnerships was to facilitate mastery.

4. See Carol Gilligan, *In a Different Voice: Psychological Theory and Women's Development* (Cambridge, Mass.: Harvard University Press, 1982); Deborah Tannen, *You Just Don't Understand: Women and Men in Conversation* (New York: Ballantine Books, 1990). *Contra*, Elizabeth Spelman, *Inessential Woman* (Boston: Beacon Press, 1988).

5. See Myra Sadker and David Sadker, "Sexism in the Schoolroom of the '80s," *Psychology Today* (March 1985): 54–57. See also their "Sexism in the Classroom: From Grade School to Graduate School," *Phi Delta Kappan* (1986) 67:7.

Destiny

1. Forty is significant since there are commonly forty weeks in a human pregnancy, and the number is thus often associated with "birthing," e.g., the forty days of the Flood story.

2. Large cosmopolitan areas, such as Los Angeles, have already claimed this distinction.

3. Project Kesher, 1134 Judson Avenue, Evanston, IL 60202.

4. For example, Adina Levin's Web page at http://world.std.com/~alevin/Jewishfeminist.html

Afterword: Engaging with Torah

1. Mieke Bal, *Lethal Love: Feminist Literary Readings of Biblical Love Stories* (Bloomington: Indiana University Press, 1987), 37–67.

2. Debra Orenstein, "Jewish Lifecycle and Women's Perspectives" *Wilstein Institute Bulletin* (spring 1991): 4–5. Ahad Ha'am argues, e.g., that it doesn't matter if Moses was "real" or not. Asher Ginzberg, ed., *Selected Essays*, trans. Leon Simon (Philadelphia: Jewish Publication Society, 1912), 309.

3. A good general introduction is Richard Elliot Friedman, *Who Wrote the Bible?* (New York: Harper Collins, 1989).

4. Robert Alter, "Introduction," *The Literary Guide to the Bible*, ed. Robert Alter and Frank Kermonde (Cambridge, Mass.: Harvard University Press, 1987), 25.

5. Some go so far as to say that biblical studies gave rise to literary studies. Jason P. Rosenblatt and Joseph C. Sitterson, Jr., "Introduction," *"Not in Heaven"*:

Coherence and Complexity in Biblical Narrative (Bloomington: Indiana University Press, 1991), 1.

6. This was a major concern for the Rabbis.

7. Neil Gillman, *Sacred Fragments: Recovering Theology for the Modern Jew* (Philadelphia: Jewish Publication Society, 1990), 85. Emphasis his.

8. Hillel (end of first century BCE-beginning of first century CE) provided seven rules; Ishmael (first century CE) offered thirteen principles for textual interpretation; Eliezer Ben Yossi Hagelili (second century CE, but the list may be post-Talmudic) presented thirty-two rules, which focused on non-legal material; German pietists of the mid- to late-twelfth century named 73 methods of midrashic interpretation.

9. A book that covers these methods is: Michael Fishbane, ed., *The Midrashic Imagination: Jewish Exegesis, Thought, and History* (Albany, N.Y.: SUNY Press, 1993).

10. Elisabeth Schüssler Fiorenza, *Bread Not Stone: The Challenge of Feminist Biblical Interpretation* (Boston: Beacon Press, 1992).

11. Phyllis Trible, *Texts of Terror: Literary Feminist Readings of Biblical Narratives* (Philadelphia: Fortress, 1984).

12. J. Cheryl Exum, *Fragmented Women: Feminist (Sub)versions of Biblical Narratives* (Valley Forge, Pa.: Trinity Press, 1993); Ilana Pardes, *Countertraditions in the Bible* (Cambridge, Mass.: Harvard University Press, 1992).

13. There are feminists who disagree with this conclusion, but they are not among those writing about Bible.

14. Florence Howe, *Myths of Co-education* (New York: Feminist Press, 1988), 94f, 189, 217f.

15. See pages 63 and 79; Judith Plaskow, *Standing Again at Sinai* (San Francisco: Harper and Row, 1990).

16. We are never told What Dinah Thought—a subject Deena Metzger explores in her novel of that title. Debra Orenstein, "Finding Your Power: *Parashat Vayishlach*" in *From Generation to Generation*, Israel Mowshowitz and Debra Orenstein (New York: New York Board of Rabbis), 32–38.

17. See Peter Pitzele, *Our Fathers' Wells* (San Francisco: HarperCollins, 1995). James P. Carse, "Exploring Your Personal Myth," in *Sacred Stories: A Celebration of the Power of Stories to Heal and Transform the World* ed. Charles and Anne Simpkinson (San Francisco: Harper Collins, 1993), 223–232.

18. This is a far richer technique than one example can convey. See Esther Netter, "Synectics: Its Application to Jewish Education," Master's Thesis, Jewish Theological Seminary, 1982.

19. "Whether the poets knew it or not, and some of them did, they were writing *midrash*." David Curzon, *Modern Poems on the Bible: An Anthology* (Philadelphia: Jewish Publication Society, 1994), 3. As Curzon includes biblical texts side-by-side with modern poems, his anthology can be used for studying biblical and modern passages in relation to one another.

20. Barbara Holender, *The Ladies of Genesis* (New York: Jewish Women's Resource Center, 1991); Henny Wenkart, ed., *Sarah's Daughters Sing: A Sampler of Poems by Jewish Women* (Hoboken, N.J.: KTAV, 1990); Alicia Suskin Ostriker, *The*

Nakedness of the Fathers: Biblical Visions and Revisions (New Brunswick, N.J.: Rutgers University Press, 1994); Judith A. Kates and Gail Twersky Reimer, eds., *Reading Ruth* (New York: Ballantine, 1994).

21. Kenneth Koch, *I Never Told Anybody: Teaching Poetry Writing in a Nursing Home* (New York: Random House, 1977); *Wishes, Lies, and Dreams: Teaching Children to Write Poetry* (New York: Vintage, 1970). Groups or individuals might also write midrashic poems in response to the biblical texts and modern poems presented in Curzon, *Modern Poems*.

22. Jo Milgrom, *Handmade Midrash: Workshops in Visual Theology: A Guide for Teachers, Rabbis, and Lay Leaders* (Philadelphia: Jewish Publication Society, 1992).

23. Thanks to Andrea Hodos and Susan Freeman. See JoAnne Tucker and Susan Freeman, *Torah in Motion: Creating Dance Midrash* (Denver, Col.: A.R.E. Publishing, 1990).

24. Paul Ricoeur, *Interpretation Theory: Discourse and the Surplus of Meaning* (Fort Worth: Texas Christian University Press, 1976), 23.

25. This is only fitting, since the Rabbis teach that God used Torah as a blueprint when fashioning creation (Gen. *Rabbah* 1:1).

—⊲◉⊳—

Index

Index of Life Themes

Many of the life themes covered in this book are also treated in Volume 1 of the *Lifecycles* series.

On **Genesis** themes of beginnings, home, family, and parenting, see Chapters 1 (Beginnings), 3 (Welcoming Children into Name and Covenant), 8 (Marriage), 9 (Divorce), 12 (Parenting), and 14 (Aging).

On **Exodus** themes of freedom, holiness, and Torah, see Chapters 4 (Adolescence), 7 (Coming Out), 13 (Midlife), and 15 (Death and Mourning), as well as the Click Stories and Afterword.

On **Levitical** issues of body, sexuality, health, and speech, see Chapters 1 (Beginnings), 2 (Infertility and Early Losses), 4 (Adolescence), 5 (Being Single), 6 (Invisible Life Passages), 12 (Parenting, especially Kamin), 13 (Midlife), 14 (Aging), and 15 (Death and Mourning).

On **Numbers** themes of community and transition, see Chapters 4 (Adolescence), 5 (Being Single), 6 (Invisible Life Passages), 7 (Coming Out), 8 (Marriage), 9 (Divorce), 10 (Intermarriage), 11 (Choosing Judaism), 12 (Parenting), and 14 (Aging), along with the Afterword.

On the **Deuteronomic** theme of second law, new vision, see the Introduction to Volume 1, as well as Chapters 2 (Infertility and Early Losses), 3 (Welcoming Children into Name and Covenant), 6 (Invisible Life Passages), and 9 (Divorce).

Index of Biblical Figures

Index of Torah Verses

About JEWISH LIGHTS Publishing

People of all faiths and backgrounds yearn for books that attract, engage, educate and spiritually inspire.

Our principal goal is to stimulate thought and help all people learn about who the Jewish People are, where they come from, and what the future can be made to hold. While people of our diverse Jewish heritage are the primary audience, our books speak to people in the Christian world as well and will broaden their understanding of Judaism and the roots of their own faith.

We bring to you authors who are at the forefront of spiritual thought and experience. While each has something different to say, they all say it in a voice that you can hear.

Our books are designed to welcome you and then to engage, stimulate and inspire. We judge our success not only by whether or not our books are beautiful and commercially successful, but by whether or not they make a difference in your life.

We at Jewish Lights take great care to produce beautiful books that present meaningful spiritual content in a form that reflects the art of making high quality books. Therefore, we want to acknowledge those who contributed to the production of this book.

EDITORIAL & PROOFREADING
Sandra Korinchak

PRODUCTION
Maria O'Donnell

BOOK & JACKET DESIGN
Karen Savary, Deering, New Hampshire

TYPESETTING
Set in Palatino and Weiss
Doug Porter, San Antonio, Texas

HEBREW
Joel Hoffman, Excelsior Computer Services
Rye, New York

Joe and Peggy Davis
Colrain, Massachusetts

INDEXING
Anna Chapman, Arlington, Vermont

COVER PRINTING
Coral Graphics, Hicksville, New York

PRINTING AND BINDING
Royal Book, Norwich, Connecticut

Add Greater Meaning to Your Life

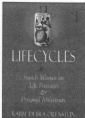

Spiritual Inspiration for Family Life

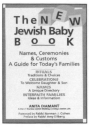

THE NEW JEWISH BABY BOOK
Names, Ceremonies, Customs—A Guide for Today's Families
by *Anita Diamant*

A complete guide to the customs and rituals for welcoming a new child to the world and into the Jewish community, and for commemorating this joyous event in family life—whatever your family constellation. Includes new ceremonies for girls, celebrations in interfaith families, and more.

"A book that all Jewish parents—no matter how religious—will find fascinating as well as useful. It is a perfect shower or new baby gift."
— *Pamela Abrams, Exec. Editor,* Parents Magazine

6" x 9", 328 pp. Quality Paperback Original, ISBN 1-879045-28-1 **$16.95**

PUTTING GOD ON THE GUEST LIST •AWARD WINNER•
How to Reclaim the Spiritual Meaning of Your Child's Bar or Bat Mitzvah
by *Rabbi Jeffrey K. Salkin*

Joining explanation, instruction and inspiration, helps parent and child truly *be there* when the moment of Sinai is recreated in their lives. Asks and answers such fundamental questions as how did Bar and Bat Mitzvah originate? What is the lasting significance of the event? How to make the event more spiritually meaningful? New 2nd Edition.

"I hope every family planning a Bar Mitzvah celebration reads Rabbi Salkin's book." — *Rabbi Harold S. Kushner, author of* When Bad Things Happen to Good People

New! 2nd Ed.

6" x 9", 224 pp. Quality Paperback, ISBN 1-879045-59-1 **$16.95** HC, ISBN -58-3 **$24.95**

BAR/BAT MITZVAH BASICS
A Practical Family Guide to Coming of Age Together
Edited by *Cantor Helen Leneman;* Foreword by *Rabbi Jeffrey K. Salkin, author of* Putting God on the Guest List; Intro. by *Rabbi Julie Gordon*

A practical guide that gives parents and teens the "how-to" information they need to navigate the bar/bat mitzvah process and grow as a family through this experience. For the first time in one book, everyone directly involved offers practical insights into how the process can be made easier and more enjoyable for all. Rabbis, cantors and Jewish educators from the Reform, Conservative and Reconstructionist movements, parents, and even teens speak from their own experience.

"Out of her vast experience as Cantor and educator, Leneman has written an important guide that strengthens and solidifies the family through the wisdom and warmth of Judaism."
—*Rabbi Harold Schulweis, Valley Beth Shalom, Encino, California*

6" x 9", 240 pp. Quality Paperback, ISBN 1-879045-54-0 **$16.95** HC, ISBN -51-6 **$24.95**

EMBRACING THE COVENANT
Converts to Judaism Talk About Why & How
Edited & with Introductions by *Rabbi Allan L. Berkowitz* and *Patti Moskovitz*

This book is a practical and inspirational companion to the conversion process for Jews-by-Choice and their families. Written primarily for the person considering the choice of Judaism, it provides highly personal insights from over 50 people who have made this life-changing decision. But it also will speak to their families—the non-Jewish family that provided his or her spiritual beginnings and the Jewish "family" which receives the convert—and help them understand why the decision was made.

"Passionate, thoughtful and deeply-felt personal stories....A wonderful resource, sure to light the way for many who choose to follow the same path."
—*Dru Greenwood, MSW, Director, UAHC-CCAR Commission on Reform Jewish Outreach*

6" x 9", 192 pp. Quality Paperback, ISBN 1-879045-50-8 **$15.95**

Spiritual Inspiration for Family Life

MOURNING & MITZVAH
• With over 60 guided exercises •
A Guided Journal for Walking the Mourner's Path Through Grief to Healing
by *Anne Brener, L.C. S.W.*; Foreword by *Rabbi Jack Riemer*; Introduction by *Rabbi William Cutter*

"Fully engaging in mourning means you will be a different person than before you began." For those who mourn a death, for those who would help them, for those who face a loss of any kind, Brener teaches us the power and strength available to us in the fully experienced mourning process. Guided writing exercises help stimulate the processes of both conscious and unconscious healing.

"A stunning book! It offers an exploration in depth of the place where psychology and religious ritual intersect, and the name of that place is Truth."
—*Rabbi Harold Kushner, author of* When Bad Things Happen to Good People

7 1/2" x 9", 288 pp. Quality Paperback Original, ISBN 1-879045-23-0 **$19.95**

WHEN A GRANDPARENT DIES
A Kid's Own Remembering Workbook for Dealing with Shiva and the Year Beyond
by *Nechama Liss-Levinson, Ph.D.*

Drawing insights from both psychology and Jewish tradition, this workbook helps children participate in the process of mourning, offering guided exercises, rituals, and places to write, draw, list, create and express their feelings.

"Will bring support, guidance, and understanding for countless children, teachers, and health professionals."
—*Rabbi Earl A. Grollman, D.D., author of* Talking about Death

8" x 10", 48 pp. Hardcover, illus., 2-color text, ISBN 1-879045-44-3 **$14.95**

HEALING OF SOUL, HEALING OF BODY
Spiritual Leaders Unfold the Strength and Solace in Psalms
Edited by *Rabbi Simkha Y. Weintraub, CSW, for The Jewish Healing Center*

A source of solace for those who are facing illness, as well as those who care for them. The ten Psalms which form the core of this healing resource were originally selected 200 years ago by Rabbi Nachman of Breslov as a "complete remedy." Today, for anyone coping with illness, they continue to provide a wellspring of strength. Each Psalm is newly translated, making it clear and accessible, and each one is introduced by an eminent rabbi, men and women reflecting different movements and backgrounds. To all who are living with the pain and uncertainty of illness, this spiritual resource offers an anchor of spiritual comfort.

"Will bring comfort to anyone fortunate enough to read it. This gentle book is a luminous gem of wisdom."
—*Larry Dossey, M.D., author of* Healing Words: The Power of Prayer & the Practice of Medicine

6" x 9", 128 pp. Quality Paperback Original, illus., 2-color text, ISBN 1-879045-31-1 **$14.95**

SO THAT YOUR VALUES LIVE ON
Ethical Wills & How To Prepare Them
Edited by *Rabbi Jack Riemer & Professor Nathaniel Stampfer*

A cherished Jewish tradition, ethical wills—parents writing to children or grandparents to grandchildren—sum up what people have learned and express what they want most for, and from, their loved ones. Includes an intensive guide, **"How to Write Your Own Ethical Will,"** and a topical index. A marvelous treasury of wills: Herzl, Sholom Aleichem, Israelis, Holocaust victims, contemporary American Jews.

"While the book is written from a Jewish viewpoint, its principles can easily be adapted by people of other faiths."
—*The Los Angeles Times*

6" x 9", 272 pp. Quality Paperback, ISBN 1-879045-34-6 **$17.95**

THE SHABBAT SEDER
by *Dr. Ron Wolfson*

The Shabbat Seder is a concise step-by-step guide designed to teach people the meaning and importance of this weekly celebration, as well as its practices. The activities of the Friday evening ritual are set out in a straightforward, simple way, along with instructions on how to perform them, and the information is presented through an exploration of the Shabbat ceremonies of real families representing a cross section of modern Jewish life.

Each chapter corresponds to one of ten steps which together comprise the Shabbat dinner ritual, and looks at the *concepts, objects,* and *meanings* behind the specific activity or ritual act. *The Shabbat Seder* is designed in a unique, easy-to-read format for people with varying degrees of Hebrew skills; the blessings that accompany the meal are written in both Hebrew and English, and accompanied by English transliteration. Also included are a question and answer section and a "Shabbat Gallery" offering craft projects, recipes, discussion ideas and other creative suggestions for enriching the Shabbat experience.

"A how-to book in the best sense...."
—*Dr. David Lieber, President, University of Judaism, Los Angeles*

7 x 9, 272 pp. Quality Paperback, ISBN 1-879045-90-7 **$16.95**

Also available are these helpful companions to *The Shabbat Seder*:
- Booklet of the Blessings and Songs   ISBN 1-879045-91-5 $5.00
- Audiocassette of the Blessings   DNO3 $6.00
- Teacher's Guide   ISBN 1-879045-92-3 $4.95

A TIME TO MOURN, A TIME TO COMFORT
A Guide to Jewish Bereavement and Comfort
by *Dr. Ron Wolfson*

A guide to meeting the needs of those who mourn and those who seek to provide comfort in times of sadness. While this book is written from a layperson's point of view, it also includes the specifics for funeral preparations and practical guidance for preparing the home and family to sit *shiva*.

Advice is given for attending a Jewish funeral, how to help during *shiva*, what to say to the mourners, and what to write in a condolence letter. Special sections deal with specific situations of modern life, including deaths from AIDS, helping young children grieve and understand *shiva*, and mourning the death of an infant or child.

"A sensitive and perceptive guide to Jewish tradition. Both those who mourn and those who comfort will find it a map to accompany them through the whirlwind."
—*Deborah E. Lipstadt, Emory University*

"Speaks in many voices: the voices of those who have endured grief, the voices of rabbis who deal daily with tragedy, the voices of those who are spiritually searching, and the voices of those who have found their own path through dark times."
—*Dr. David J. Wolpe, author of*
Healer of Shattered Hearts

7 x 9, 320 pp. Quality Paperback, ISBN 1-879045-96-6 **$16.95**

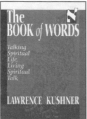

....The Kushner Series

GOD WAS IN THIS PLACE & I, i DID NOT KNOW
Finding Self, Spirituality & Ultimate Meaning

Who am I? Who is God? Kushner creates inspiring interpretations of Jacob's dream in Genesis, opening a window into Jewish spirituality for people of all faiths and backgrounds.

In this fascinating blend of scholarship, imagination, psychology and history, seven Jewish spiritual masters ask and answer fundamental questions of human experience.

"Rich and intriguing."
> —*M. Scott Peck, M.D., author of* The Road Less Traveled *and other books*

6" x 9", 192 pp. Quality Paperback, ISBN 1-879045-33-8 **$16.95** HC, ISBN -05-2 **$21.95**

HONEY FROM THE ROCK

"Quite simply the easiest introduction to Jewish mysticism you can read." An introduction to the ten gates of Jewish mysticism and how it applies to daily life.

"Captures the flavor and spark of Jewish mysticism. . . . Read it and be rewarded."
> —*Elie Wiesel*

"A work of love, lyrical beauty, and prophetic insight. "
> —*Father Malcolm Boyd*, The Christian Century

6" x 9", 168 pp. Quality Paperback, ISBN 1-879045-02-8 **$14.95**

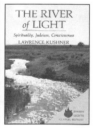

THE RIVER OF LIGHT
Spirituality, Judaism, Consciousness

A "manual" for all spiritual travelers who would attempt a spiritual journey in our times. Taking us step by step, Kushner allows us to discover the meaning of our own quest: "to allow the river of light—the deepest currents of consciousness—to rise to the surface and animate our lives."

"Philosophy and mystical fantasy exhilarating speculative flights launched from the Bible....Anybody—Jewish, Christian, or otherwise...will find this book an intriguing experience."
> —*The Kirkus Reviews*

6" x 9", 180 pp. Quality Paperback, ISBN 1-879045-03-6 **$14.95**

INVISIBLE LINES OF CONNECTION
Sacred Stories of the Ordinary

Through his everyday encounters with family, friends, colleagues and strangers, Kushner takes us deeply into our lives, finding flashes of spiritual insight in the process. This is a book where literature meets spirituality, where the sacred meets the ordinary, and, above all, where people of all faiths, all backgrounds can meet one another and themselves.

"Does something both more and different than instruct—it inspirits. Wonderful stories, from the best storyteller I know."
> — *David Mamet*

"A wonderful collection of stories charmingly told by a gifted storyteller."
> — *Booklist* (*American Library Association*)

5.5" x 8.5", 160 pp. Hardcover, ISBN 1-879045-52-4 **$21.95**

Add Greater Meaning to Your Life

THE SPIRIT OF RENEWAL
Finding Faith After the Holocaust
by *Edward Feld*

"Boldly redefines the landscape of Jewish religious thought after the Holocaust."
—*Rabbi Lawrence Kushner*

Trying to understand the Holocaust and addressing the question of faith after the Holocaust, Rabbi Feld explores three key cycles of destruction and recovery in Jewish history, each of which radically reshaped Jewish understanding of God, people, and the world.

• AWARD WINNER •   "A profound meditation on Jewish history [and the Holocaust]....Christians, as well as many others, need to share in this story."
—*The Rt. Rev. Frederick H. Borsch, Ph.D., Episcopal Bishop of L.A.*

6" x 9", 224 pp. Quality Paperback, ISBN 1-879045-40-0 **$16.95**   HC, ISBN-06-0 **$22.95**

SEEKING THE PATH TO LIFE
Theological Meditations On God
and the Nature of People, Love, Life and Death
by *Rabbi Ira F. Stone*

For people who never thought they would read a book of theology—let alone understand it, enjoy it, savor it and have it affect the way they think about their lives. In 45 intense meditations, each a page or two in length, Stone takes us on explorations of the most basic human struggles: Life and death, love and anger, peace and war, covenant and exile.

"A bold book....The reader of any faith will be inspired, challenged and led   •AWARD WINNER•
more deeply into their own encounter with God."
— *The Rev. Carla V. Berkedal, Episcopal Priest,
Executive Director of Earth Ministry*

6" x 9", 132 pp. Quality Paperback, ISBN 1-879045-47-8 **$14.95**
Hardcover, ISBN 1-879045-17-6 **$19.95**

THE EMPTY CHAIR: FINDING HOPE & JOY
Timeless Wisdom from a Hasidic Master,
Rebbe Nachman of Breslov
Adapted by *Moshe Mykoff* and *The Breslov Research Institute*

A "little treasure" of aphorisms and advice for living joyously and spiritually today, written 200 years ago, but startlingly fresh in meaning and use. Challenges and helps us to move from stress and sadness to hope and joy.

Teacher, guide and spiritual master—Rebbe Nachman provides vital words of inspiration and wisdom for life today for people of any faith, or of no faith.

"For anyone of any faith, this is a book of healing and wholeness, of being alive!"
—*Bookviews*

4" x 6", 128 pp. Deluxe Paperback, 2-color text, ISBN 1-879045-67-2 **$9.95**

FINDING JOY
A Practical Spiritual Guide to Happiness
by *Dannel I. Schwartz* with *Mark Hass*

Searching for happiness in our modern world of stress and struggle is common; *finding* it is more unusual. This guide explores and explains how to find joy through a time-honored, creative—and surprisingly practical—approach based on the teachings of Jewish mysticism.

6" x 9", 192 pp. Hardcover, ISBN 1-879045-53-2 **$19.95**

Motivation and Inspiration for Recovery

TWELVE JEWISH STEPS TO RECOVERY
A Personal Guide To Turning From Alcoholism & Other Addictions...Drugs, Food, Gambling, Sex
by *Rabbi Kerry M. Olitzky* & *Stuart A. Copans, M.D.*
Preface by *Abraham J. Twerski, M.D.*
Introduction by *Rabbi Sheldon Zimmerman*
Illustrations by *Maty Grünberg*
"Getting Help" by *JACS Foundation*

A Jewish perspective on the Twelve Steps of addiction recovery programs with consolation, inspiration and motivation for recovery. It draws from traditional sources, and quotes from what recovering Jewish people say about their experiences with addictions of all kinds. Inspiring illustrations of the twelve gates of the Old City of Jerusalem.

Experts Praise *Twelve Jewish Steps to Recovery*

"Recommended reading for people of all denominations."
— *Rabbi Abraham J. Twerski, M.D.*

"I read *Twelve Jewish Steps* with the eyes of a Christian and came away renewed in my heart. I felt like I had visited my Jewish roots. These authors have deep knowledge of recovery as viewed by Alcoholics Anonymous."
— *Rock J. Stack, M.A., L.L.D. Manager of Clinical/Pastoral Education, Hazelden Foundation*

"This book is the first aimed directly at helping the addicted person and family. Everyone affected or interested should read it."
— *Sheila B. Blume, M.D., C.A.C., Medical Director, Alcoholism, Chemical Dependency and Compulsive Gambling Programs, South Oaks Hospital, Amityville, NY*

Readers Praise *Twelve Jewish Steps to Recovery*

"A God-send. Literally. A book from the higher power." —New York, NY

"Looking forward to using it in my practice." —Michigan City, IN

"Made me feel as though Twelve Steps were for me, too." —Long Beach, CA

"Excellent—changed my life." —Elkhart Lake, WI

6" x 9", 136 pp. Quality Paperback, ISBN 1-879045-09-5 **$13.95**   HC, ISBN -08-7 **$19.95**

RECOVERY FROM CODEPENDENCE
A Jewish Twelve Steps Guide to Healing Your Soul
by *Rabbi Kerry M. Olitzky*
Foreword by *Marc Galanter, M.D., Director, Division of Alcoholism & Drug Abuse, NYU Medical Center*
Afterword by *Harriet Rossetto, Director, Gateways Beit T'shuvah*

For the estimated 90% of America struggling with the addiction of a family member or loved one, or involved in a dysfunctional family or relationship. A follow-up to the groundbreaking *Twelve Jewish Steps to Recovery*.

"The disease of chemical dependency is also a family illness. Rabbi Olitzky offers spiritual hope and support."
—*Jerry Spicer, President, Hazelden*

"Another major step forward in finding the sources and resources of healing, both physical and spiritual, in our tradition."
—*Rabbi Sheldon Zimmerman, President, Hebrew Union College-Jewish Institute of Religion*

6" x 9", 160 pp. Quality Paperback Original, ISBN 1-879045-32-X **$13.95**
HC, ISBN -27-3 **$21.95**

Motivation and Inspiration for Recovery

RENEWED EACH DAY
Daily Twelve Step Recovery Meditations
Based on the Bible
by *Rabbi Kerry M. Olitzky* & *Aaron Z.*
VOLUME I: Genesis & Exodus
Introduction by *Rabbi Michael A. Signer*
Afterword by *JACS Foundation*
VOLUME II: Leviticus, Numbers & Deuteronomy
Introduction by *Sharon M. Strassfeld*
Afterword by *Rabbi Harold M. Schulweis*

Using a seven day/weekly guide format, a recovering person and a spiritual leader who is reaching out to addicted people reflect on the traditional weekly Bible reading. They bring strong spiritual support for daily living and recovery from addictions of all kinds: Alcohol, drugs, eating, gambling and sex. A profound sense of the religious spirit soars through their words and brings all people in Twelve Step recovery programs home to a rich and spiritually enlightening tradition.

"Meets a vital need; it offers a chance for people turning from alcoholism and addiction to renew their spirits and draw upon the Jewish tradition to guide and enrich their lives."
—*Rabbi Irving (Yitz) Greenberg, President, CLAL,*
The National Jewish Center for Learning and Leadership

"Will benefit anyone familiar with a 'religion of the Book.' Jews, Christians, Muslims..."
—*Ernest Kurtz, author of* Not God: A History of Alcoholics
Anonymous & The Spirituality of Imperfection

"An enduring impact upon the faith community as it seeks to blend the wisdom of the ages represented in the tradition with the Twelve Steps to recovery and wholeness."
—*Robert H. Albers, Ph.D., Editor,* Journal of Ministry in
Addiction & Recovery

Beautiful Two-Volume Slipcased Set
6" x 9", V. I, 224 pp. / V. II, 280 pp. Quality Paperback Original,
ISBN 1-879045-21-4   **$27.90**

ONE HUNDRED BLESSINGS EVERY DAY
Daily Twelve Step Recovery Affirmations,
Exercises for Personal Growth & Renewal
Reflecting Seasons of the Jewish Year

by *Dr. Kerry M. Olitzky*
with selected meditations prepared by *Rabbi James Stone
Goodman, Danny Siegel,* and *Rabbi Gordon Tucker*
Foreword by *Rabbi Neil Gillman,*
The Jewish Theological Seminary of America
Afterword by *Dr. Jay Holder, Director, Exodus Treatment Center*

Recovery is a conscious choice from moment to moment, day in and day out. In this helpful and healing book of daily recovery meditations, Rabbi Olitzky gives us words to live by day after day, throughout the annual cycle of holiday observances and special Sabbaths of the Jewish calendar.

For those facing the struggles of daily living, *One Hundred Blessings Every Day* brings solace and hope to anyone who is open to healing and to the recovery-oriented teachings that can be gleaned from the Bible and Jewish tradition.

4.5" x 6.5", 432 pp. Quality Paperback Original, ISBN 1-879045-30-3   **$14.95**

Bring Spirituality into Your Daily Life

BEING GOD'S PARTNER
How to Find the Hidden Link Between Spirituality and Your Work
by *Jeffrey K. Salkin* Introduction by *Norman Lear*

A book that will challenge people of every denomination to reconcile the cares of work and soul. A groundbreaking book about spirituality and the work world, from a Jewish perspective. Helps the reader find God in the ethical striving and search for meaning in the professions and in business. Looks at our modern culture of workaholism and careerism, and offers practical suggestions for balancing your professional life and spiritual self.

"This engaging meditation on the spirituality of work is grounded in Judaism but is relevant well beyond the boundaries of that tradition."
—Booklist *(American Library Association)*

6" x 9", 192 pp. Hardcover, ISBN 1-879045-37-0 **$19.95**

SELF, STRUGGLE & CHANGE
Family Conflict Stories in Genesis and Their Healing Insights for Our Lives
by *Norman J. Cohen*

How do I find greater wholeness in my life and in my family's life?

The stress of late-20th-century living only brings new variations to timeless personal struggles. The people described by the biblical writers of Genesis were in situations and relationships very much like our own. We identify with them. Their stories still speak to us because they are about the same problems *we* deal with every day. A modern master of biblical interpretation brings us greater understanding of the ancient text and of ourselves in this intriguing re-telling of conflict between husband and wife, father and son, brothers, and sisters.

"A delightful and instructive book; recommended."
—*Library Journal*

6" x 9", 224 pp. Quality Paperback, ISBN 1-879045-66-4 **$16.95**
HC, ISBN -19-2 **$21.95**

Minding the Temple of the Soul

Balancing Body, Mind & Soul through Traditional Jewish Prayer, Movement & Meditation

MINDING THE TEMPLE OF THE SOUL
Balancing Body, Mind & Soul through Traditional Jewish Prayer, Movement & Meditation
by *Dr. Tamar Frankiel* and *Judy Greenfeld*

This new spiritual approach to physical health introduces readers to a spiritual tradition that affirms the body and enables them to reconceive their bodies in a more positive light. Relying on Kabbalistic teachings and other Jewish traditions, it shows us how to be more responsible for our own psychological and physical health. Focuses on the discipline of prayer, simple Tai Chi-like exercises and body positions, and guides the reader throughout, step by step, with diagrams, sketches and meditations.

7 x 10, 144 pp (est), Quality Paperback Original, illus., ISBN 1-879045-64-8 **$15.95**

GOD & THE BIG BANG
Discovering Harmony Between Science & Spirituality
by *Daniel C. Matt*

Mysticism and science: What do they have in common? How can one enlighten the other? By drawing on modern cosmology and ancient Kabbalah, Matt shows how science and religion can together enrich our spiritual awareness and help us recover a sense of wonder and find our place in the universe.

"This poetic new book...helps us to understand the human meaning of creation."
—*Joel Primack, leading cosmologist, Professor of Physics, University of California, Santa Cruz*

6" x 9", 216 pp. Hardcover, ISBN 1-879045-48-6 **$21.95**

Spiritual Inspiration for Children

BUT GOD REMEMBERED
Stories of Women from Creation to the Promised Land
by *Sandy Eisenberg Sasso*
Full color illustrations by *Bethanne Andersen*

NONSECTARIAN, NONDENOMINATIONAL.
A fascinating collection of four different stories of women only briefly mentioned in biblical tradition and religious texts, but never before explored. Award-winning author Sasso brings to life the intriguing stories of Lilith, Serach, Bityah, and the Daughters of Z, courageous and strong women from ancient tradition. All teach important values through their faith and actions.

For ages 8 and up

"Exquisite....a book of beauty, strength and spirituality."
—*Association of Bible Teachers*

9 x 12, 32 pp. Hardcover, Full color illus., ISBN 1-879045-43-5 **$16.95**

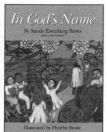

AWARD WINNER

IN GOD'S NAME
by *Sandy Eisenberg Sasso*
Full color illustrations by *Phoebe Stone*

For ages 4-8

MULTICULTURAL, NONSECTARIAN, NONDENOMINATIONAL.
Like an ancient myth in its poetic text and vibrant illustrations, this modern fable about the search for God's name celebrates the diversity and, at the same time, the unity of all the people of the world. Each seeker claims he or she alone knows the answer. Finally, they come together and learn what God's name really is, sharing the ultimate harmony of belief in one God by people of all faiths, all backgrounds.

"I got goose bumps when I read *In God's Name,* its language and illustrations are that moving. This is a book children will love and the whole family will cherish for its beauty and power."
—*Francine Klagsbrun, author of* Mixed Feelings:Love, Hate, Rivalry, and Reconciliation among Brothers and Sisters

"What a lovely, healing book!"
—*Madeleine L'Engle*

| Selected by |
| Parent Council Ltd.™ |

9 x 12, 32 pp. Hardcover, Full color illus., ISBN 1-879045-26-5 **$16.95**

For ages 4-8

GOD'S PAINTBRUSH
by *Sandy Eisenberg Sasso*
Full color illustrations by *Annette Compton*

MULTICULTURAL, NONSECTARIAN, NONDENOMINATIONAL.
Invites children of all faiths and backgrounds to encounter God openly in their own lives. Wonderfully interactive, provides questions adult and child can explore together at the end of each episode.

"An excellent way to honor the imaginative breadth and depth of the spiritual life of the young."
—*Dr. Robert Coles, Harvard University*

AWARD WINNER

11x 8½, 32 pp. Hardcover, Full color illustrations, ISBN 1-879045-22-2 **$16.95**

Spiritual Inspiration for Children

A PRAYER FOR THE EARTH
The Story of Naamah, Noah's Wife

For ages 4-8

by *Sandy Eisenberg Sasso*
Full color illustrations by *Bethanne Andersen*

NONSECTARIAN, NONDENOMINATIONAL.

This new story, based on an ancient text, opens readers' religious imaginations to new ideas about the well-known story of the Flood. When God tells Noah to bring the animals of the world onto the ark, God *also* calls on Naamah, Noah's wife, to save each plant on Earth. *A Prayer for the Earth* describes Naamah's wisdom and love for the natural harmony of the earth, and inspires readers to use their own courage, creativity and faith to carry out Naamah's work today.

> "A lovely tale....Children of all ages should be drawn to this parable for our times."
> —*Tomie dePaola, artist/author of books for children*

9 x 12, 32 pp. Hardcover, Full color illustrations, ISBN 1-879045-60-5 **$16.95**

THE 11TH COMMANDMENT
Wisdom from Our Children

For all ages

by The Children of America

MULTICULTURAL, NONSECTARIAN, NONDENOMINATIONAL.

"If there were an Eleventh Commandment, what would it be?"

Children of many religious denominations across America answer this question—in their own drawings and words—in *The 11th Commandment*. This full-color collection of "Eleventh Commandments" reveals kids' ideas about how people should respond to God.

> "Wonderful....This unusual book provides both food for thought and insight into the hopes and fears of today's young."
> —*American Library Association's* Booklist

8 x 10, 48 pp. Hardcover, Full color illustrations, ISBN 1-879045-46-X **$16.95**

of Copies   *Order Information* $ Amount

Aspects of Rabbinic Theology (pb), $18.95

Bar/Bat Mitzvah Basics (hc), $24.95; (pb), $16.95

Being God's Partner (hc), $19.95

But God Remembered (hc), $16.95

Earth is the Lord's (pb), $12.95

11th Commandment (hc), $16.95

Embracing the Covenant (pb), $15.95

Empty Chair (pb), $9.95

Finding Joy (hc), $19.95

God & the Big Bang (hc), $21.95

God's Paintbrush (hc), $16.95

Godwrestling—Round 2 (hc), $23.95

Hanukkah (pb), $16.95

Healing of Soul, Healing of Body (pb), $14.95

How to Be a Perfect Stranger Vol. 1 (hc), $24.95

How to Be a Perfect Stranger Vol. 2 (hc), $24.95

In God's Name (hc), $16.95

Israel: An Echo of Eternity (pb), $18.95

Last Trial (pb), $17.95

Lifecycles, V. 1 (hc), $24.95

Lifecycles, V. 2 (hc), $24.95

Minding the Temple of the Soul (pb), $15.95

Mourning & Mitzvah (pb), $19.95

NEW Jewish Baby Book (pb), $16.95

One Hundred Blessings Every Day (pb), $14.95

Passion for Truth (pb), $18.95

Passover Seder (pb), $16.95

Putting God on the Guest List (hc), $24.95; (pb), $16.95

Prayer for the Earth (hc), $16.95

Recovery from Codependence (hc), $21.95; (pb), $13.95

Renewed Each Day, 2-Volume Set (pb), $27.90

Seeking the Path to Life (hc), $19.95; (pb), $14.95

Self, Struggle & Change (hc), $21.95; (pb), $16.95

Shabbat Seder (pb), $16.95

So That Your Values Live On (hc), $23.95; (pb), $17.95

Spirit of Renewal (hc), $22.95; (pb), $16.95

Time to Mourn, Time to Comfort (pb), $16.95

Tormented Master (pb), $17.95

Twelve Jewish Steps to Recovery (hc), $19.95; (pb), $13.95

When a Grandparent Dies (hc), $14.95

Your Word is Fire (pb), $14.95

Other:_____

• The Kushner Series •

Book of Letters (hc), $24.95

Book of Words (hc), $21.95

God Was in This Place...(hc), $21.95; (pb), $16.95

Honey From the Rock (pb), $14.95

Invisible Lines of Connection (hc), $21.95

River of Light (pb), $14.95

Check enclosed for $_____ *payable to:* JEWISH LIGHTS Publishing

Charge my credit card: ☐ MasterCard ☐ Visa

Credit Card #_____ Expires _____

Name on card _____

Signature _____ Phone (_____)_____

Name _____

Street _____

City / State / Zip _____

Phone, fax, or mail to: JEWISH LIGHTS Publishing

P. O. Box 237, Sunset Farm Offices, Route 4, Woodstock, Vermont 05091

Tel (802) 457-4000   *Fax* (802) 457-4004   www.jewishlights.com

Credit card orders (800) 962-4544 (9AM–5PM ET Monday–Friday)

Generous discounts on quantity orders. SATISFACTION GUARANTEED. Prices subject to change.

AVAILABLE FROM BETTER BOOKSTORES. TRY YOUR BOOKSTORE FIRST.

# of Copies	Order Information	$ Amount
_____	Aspects of Rabbinic Theology (pb), $18.95	_____
_____	Bar/Bat Mitzvah Basics (hc), $24.95; (pb), $16.95	_____
_____	Being God's Partner (hc), $19.95	_____
_____	But God Remembered (hc), $16.95	_____
_____	Earth is the Lord's (pb), $12.95	_____
_____	11th Commandment (hc), $16.95	_____
_____	Embracing the Covenant (pb), $15.95	_____
_____	Empty Chair (pb), $9.95	_____
_____	Finding Joy (hc), $19.95	_____
_____	God & the Big Bang (hc), $21.95	_____
_____	God's Paintbrush (hc), $16.95	_____
_____	Godwrestling—Round 2 (hc), $23.95	_____
_____	Hanukkah (pb), $16.95	_____
_____	Healing of Soul, Healing of Body (pb), $14.95	_____
_____	How to Be a Perfect Stranger Vol. 1 (hc), $24.95	_____
_____	How to Be a Perfect Stranger Vol. 2 (hc), $24.95	_____
_____	In God's Name (hc), $16.95	_____
_____	Israel: An Echo of Eternity (pb), $18.95	_____
_____	Last Trial (pb), $17.95	_____
_____	Lifecycles, V. 1 (hc), $24.95	_____
_____	Lifecycles, V. 2 (hc), $24.95	_____
_____	Minding the Temple of the Soul (pb), $15.95	_____
_____	Mourning & Mitzvah (pb), $19.95	_____
_____	NEW Jewish Baby Book (pb), $16.95	_____
_____	One Hundred Blessings Every Day (pb), $14.95	_____
_____	Passion for Truth (pb), $18.95	_____
_____	Passover Seder (pb), $16.95	_____
_____	Putting God on the Guest List (hc), $24.95; (pb), $16.95	_____
_____	Prayer for the Earth (hc), $16.95	_____
_____	Recovery from Codependence (hc), $21.95; (pb), $13.95	_____
_____	Renewed Each Day, 2-Volume Set (pb), $27.90	_____
_____	Seeking the Path to Life (hc), $19.95; (pb), $14.95	_____
_____	Self, Struggle & Change (hc), $21.95; (pb), $16.95	_____
_____	Shabbat Seder (pb), $16.95	_____
_____	So That Your Values Live On (hc), $23.95; (pb), $17.95	_____
_____	Spirit of Renewal (hc), $22.95; (pb), $16.95	_____
_____	Time to Mourn, Time to Comfort (pb), $16.95	_____
_____	Tormented Master (pb), $17.95	_____
_____	Twelve Jewish Steps to Recovery (hc), $19.95; (pb), $13.95	_____
_____	When a Grandparent Dies (hc), $14.95	_____
_____	Your Word is Fire (pb), $14.95	_____
_____	Other:_____	

• The Kushner Series •

_____	Book of Letters (hc), $24.95	_____
_____	Book of Words (hc), $21.95	_____
_____	God Was in This Place...(hc), $21.95; (pb), $16.95	_____
_____	Honey From the Rock (pb), $14.95	_____
_____	Invisible Lines of Connection (hc), $21.95	_____
_____	River of Light (pb), $14.95	_____

Check enclosed for $_____ *payable to:* JEWISH LIGHTS Publishing

Charge my credit card: ❏ MasterCard   ❏ Visa

Credit Card #_____ Expires _____

Name on card _____

Signature _____ Phone (_____)_____

Name _____

Street _____

City / State / Zip _____

Phone, fax, or mail to: JEWISH LIGHTS Publishing
P. O. Box 237, Sunset Farm Offices, Route 4, Woodstock, Vermont 05091
Tel (802) 457-4000   *Fax* (802) 457-4004   www.jewishlights.com
Credit card orders (800) 962-4544 (9AM–5PM ET Monday–Friday)
Generous discounts on quantity orders. SATISFACTION GUARANTEED. Prices subject to change.

AVAILABLE FROM BETTER BOOKSTORES. TRY YOUR BOOKSTORE FIRST